The Collected Historic...
Sir Francis Palgrave, K.H.

In Ten Volumes

Volume Eight

TRUTHS AND FICTIONS OF THE MIDDLE AGES

I. THE MERCHANT AND THE FRIAR

II. THREE GENERATIONS OF AN IMAGINARY NORFOLK FAMILY

THE COLLECTED HISTORICAL WORKS
OF SIR FRANCIS PALGRAVE, K.H.

edited by his son

Sɪʀ R. H. INGLIS PALGRAVE, F.R.S.

TRUTHS AND FICTIONS OF THE MIDDLE AGES

I. THE MERCHANT AND THE FRIAR
II. THREE GENERATIONS OF AN IMAGINARY NORFOLK FAMILY

with Introduction by

A. HAMILTON THOMPSON, M.A., F.S.A.
READER IN MEDIEVAL HISTORY AND ARCHAEOLOGY,
ARMSTRONG COLLEGE, UNIVERSITY OF DURHAM

Cambridge:
at the University Press
1922

CAMBRIDGE
UNIVERSITY PRESS

University Printing House, Cambridge CB2 8BS, United Kingdom

Published in the United States of America by Cambridge University Press, New York

Cambridge University Press is part of the University of Cambridge.

It furthers the University's mission by disseminating knowledge in the pursuit of education, learning and research at the highest international levels of excellence.

www.cambridge.org
Information on this title: www.cambridge.org/9781107626379

First published 1922
First paperback edition 2013

A catalogue record for this publication is available from the British Library

ISBN 978-1-107-62637-9 Paperback

CONTENTS

NOTE

The Merchant and the Friar and the *Three Generations of a Norfolk Family* which form this volume were written by Sir Francis Palgrave in order further to illustrate the customs and conditions of life at the periods with which he was dealing in his other works. His letters show that he felt that a proper appreciation of history would be greatly assisted by the treatment of these subjects in a manner which would not naturally fall within the scope of a purely historical work.

Sir Inglis Palgrave therefore decided to include these stories in the present collection and on the advice of his friend Dr J. R. Tanner of St John's College, Cambridge, the work of editing was entrusted to Mr A. Hamilton Thompson of Armstrong College, Newcastle-upon-Tyne, to whom I wish to express my warm thanks for the comprehensive and sympathetic manner in which he has carried it out.

GEOFFREY PALGRAVE BARKER.

The Athenæum,
London,
January, 1922.

INTRODUCTION

THE first edition of *Truths and Fictions of the Middle Ages: The Merchant and the Friar* was published in 1837. In this narrative Sir Francis Palgrave gave a popular application to the fruits of his studies in legal and constitutional history. It is unnecessary to discuss the merits and defects of the method which he adopted; it is enough to say that, while, in the hands of a writer with a special genius for fiction, the historical setting of a tale is liable to distortion, the scholar, on the other hand, who embodies the results of research in narrative form seldom succeeds in making his story lively or interesting. Sir Francis had nothing of the creative power of the novelist; his merchant and friar, and the typical personages whom they encounter, are merely the mouthpieces of the information and ideas which it was his object to convey. His story is a succession of scenes without plot or central interest; it is discursive and interrupted by digressions; its allusiveness may well prove a stumbling-block in the path of the reader for whose benefit it was designed. At the same time, it was written with an obvious gusto and a vivacity of manner which distinguish it from the ordinary attempt to disguise the material of a historical manual under the cloak of fiction. Its author's phenomenal industry in the study and classification of the national archives stimulated his imagination, and the patient toil of which the great collection of *Parliamentary Writs* is the most remarkable monument was encouraged by his sense of the human element underlying the superficial dryness and formality of his records. If the thread which connects the scenes of his story is slight and perfunctory, there is abundance of life in the scenes themselves. His readers can share the enjoyment which he evidently felt in his account of the election of the knights of the shire[a] or of the *fracas* between the followers of the two archbishops[b]. Whatever may be the deficiencies of *The Merchant and the Friar* as a work of narrative art, there is compensation for them in the genial humour of its writer, his interest in all things human, his power of emphasising the salient features of his subject, and his frank expression of his own point of view.

[a] See below, pp. 18–39.   [b] See below, pp. 122 sqq.

The main object of the tale is to give a lively sketch of those English institutions with the history of which Sir Francis Palgrave was intimately acquainted, during the period in which they acquired a settled form. That period he indicates as the early part of the fourteenth century[a], at a somewhat indefinite date before the death of Edward I in 1307. Anyone who attempts to collate the various historical allusions will find that Sir Francis allowed himself considerable freedom in this matter, and mingled fact with fiction at will. Roger Bacon, the friar of the story, died in 1294. Marco Polo, the merchant, is in England, collecting the outstanding debts due to the executors of a bishop of Hereford who had died in 1268[b]. Antony Bek is waiting to step into the shoes of the dying bishop of Durham, which would fix the date in the early summer of 1283[c]. On the other hand, Sir William Ormesby, described as chief justice[d], was not appointed a justice of the king's bench until 1296. A careful study will reveal other discrepancies of which Sir Francis took as little heed as other writers of historical fiction. In this respect, however, he was wilfully negligent. The general setting of the story is purely imaginary. He warns us of his fabrications in the dedication written in 1844[e]. We may search *Parliamentary Writs* in vain for the certificate of the election of Sir Richard de Pogeys and Sir Thomas de Turberville as knights of the shire for Oxfordshire; and the *Rolls of Parliaments* will yield no original record of the petitions heard by the king in his council at Westminster in eight days from St Hilary in a year unspecified. Sir *Robert* Pogeys was actually returned for Oxfordshire in 1295 and 1302, and for Buckinghamshire in 1300[f]; but, so far as the purposes of this story are concerned, the names of Sir Giles Argentein and of the other knights are used merely as labels for figures typical of the age. Similarly, the abbot of Oseney who is the centre of an episode in the second chapter is, from the historical point of view, an indefinite personage. He has recently succeeded to the dignity vacated by the death of Abbot Richard of Dronebury[g]; but the name of Dronebury is not to be found in the list of abbots of Oseney, and, although the abbey was actually vacant at Easter 1297 by the death of its head, and although the election of his successor followed during Eastertide[h], Sir Francis, in making his

---

[a] See below, p. 4, etc.
[b] See below, pp. 18, 19.
[c] See below, p. 119.
[d] See below, p. 80.
[e] See below, p. ix.
[f] *Parl. Writs*, I, 23, etc.
[g] See below, p. 34.
[h] *Cal. Patent Rolls* 1292–1301, pp. 246, 247.

abbot state that he had been elected at Easter, probably hit upon a coincidence. At any rate, the abbot who died in 1297 was Roger of Coventry, and he had ruled the convent, not for twenty, but for only twelve years[a]. To point out these discrepancies is merely to show that the author had no intention of clothing the minor details of his story in an elaborate garb of verisimilitude. He was dealing with institutions, not with individuals, and his choice of types to illustrate his narrative was not made upon any fixed scheme. Any imaginary abbot or knight served his purpose of illustrating the main fact that persons summoned or elected by writ were eager to escape the burden of attendance in parliament. No essential anachronism is involved in this fluid treatment of dates and persons, for which Scott, the undisputed master of historical fiction, had furnished a conspicuous precedent. It may be remarked, however, that Sir Francis here and there permitted himself to anticipate history. A canon of St Stephen's was as yet impossible in the reign of Edward I[b], nor was the legal settlement of the dispute for precedence between Canterbury and York achieved until 1352[c].

Something of the same liberty, applied to essential facts of medieval life, may be noticed in the opening chapter of the story. Marco Polo and Roger Bacon meet as partakers of the hospitality of the abbot and convent of Abingdon. Sir Francis's profound acquaintance with the national records did not extend widely into ecclesiastical archives; and the study of monastic life, as distinct from the publication of charters and isolated documents by pains-taking antiquaries, was as yet in its infancy. Fosbroke's *British Monachism*, published in 1802, a work which showed remarkable diligence of research in an unexplored field, was, for its day, a valuable handbook of monastic polity, and must have been to many their first teacher of the lesson that a medieval monastery was something more than a picturesque ruin. Dugdale's *Monasticon*, however, the revised and enlarged edition of which appeared between 1817 and 1830[d], was primarily a collection of evidences bearing upon the landed property of religious houses; and its contribution to their internal history is surprisingly small. The inadequate condition of this form of research is largely responsible for the absurdities into which Scott fell in the second canto of *Marmion* and from which he was never free in his allusions to monasteries and their inmates. It is therefore not astonishing that

[a] *Cal. Patent Rolls* 1292–1301, pp. 154, 155, 246.   [b] See below, p. 120.
[c] See below, p. 124.   [d] See an allusion, below, p. 33.

an historian of political institutions should give a somewhat slight
and inaccurate picture of a department of medieval life which lay
outside his province. It was not until a few years later that
Carlyle's famous application of the chronicle of Jocelin of Brake-
lond to modern conditions in *Past and Present* gave to Englishmen
some true idea of the every-day life of a monastery. Sir Francis,
however, made use of Abingdon Abbey mainly as a convenient
meeting-place for two travellers who are about to see more important centres of life in company; and one need not lay too much
stress upon the fact that the official deputed to invite the merchant
and his retinue to the hospitality of the precincts would not have
been the sacristan, or, more correctly, the sacrist[a], whose duties
lay in the care of the church, but either the cellarer or the guest-
master, or upon the introduction of a miscellaneous company into
the refectory, from which strangers were excluded by rule and
custom. The division of hospitality in the larger monasteries followed
a general precedent which may be recognised in the remains of
the abbot's or prior's hall, the ordinary guest-houses and the
almonry, still existing upon many monastic sites[b]. While a distinguished foreigner like Marco Polo would have been admitted
to entertainment in the abbot's lodging, and might well have
found the vice-chancellor of Oxford a guest at the abbot's table,
some of the other guests would have been relegated to the hall of
the guest-house, and probably only the friar, as a man of religion,
would have had a seat in the refectory. There, too, to judge from
the constant infractions of the rule of silence to which records of
episcopal visitations bear witness, he might have found the reader's
part in the proceedings reduced to a mere formality in face of the
promiscuous conversation of the monks; but such conversation
would have been entirely contrary to discipline. The setting of the
scene is thus entirely conventional, and its reproduction of the
popular notion of a monastery as a place of good cheer, and of its
cellarer as entirely concerned with the provision of wine, need not
be taken too seriously. It may be added that the relaxation of
monastic discipline was already familiar in the age of which Sir
Francis wrote[c]. The tendency, however, to convert the common
meal in the refectory into a secular banquet was not noticeable.

[a] See below, p. 6.

[b] Willis, *Archit. Hist. of the Conventual Buildings of the Monastery of Christ
Church in Canterbury*, 1869, pp. 15, 93 sqq.

[c] See, e.g. injunctions issued by successive archbishops of York to monasteries
between 1279 and 1296 (Surtees Soc. vols. 114, 123, 128).

A far more usual symptom was the endeavour of the more unruly spirits to break up the common life and to desert the refectory for unlicensed meals elsewhere. For the refectory itself there was always a certain reverence observed, and, in the later days of some monasteries, as at Durham, it was abandoned, except upon special occasions, for a smaller dining-room where, doubtless, the monks found some relief from the constraint of silence enjoined by their rule, or, at any rate, felt themselves more fully at liberty to disregard it[a].

The refectory, however, is of secondary interest compared with the conversation which takes place there and has its origin in the merchant's tales of the marvels of the east. His descriptions of its fertility and perennial fruits and flowers remind the abbot of a legend related of Albertus Magnus, the great Dominican man of science, who had died in 1280, leaving behind him the reputation of a sorcerer. His name brings the friar into the dialogue, who, undeterred by the disapproval of the vice-chancellor, the sworn enemy of friars and their intrusion upon the prerogatives of university teachers, expresses the ideal of progress in knowledge which is his own aim and that of other supposed magicians, and hints gently at the popular exaggeration of their experiments and inventions into supernatural marvels. A further tale of the renown of Albertus Magnus as an alchemist is capped by the merchant with a greater marvel, the paper-money of the Tartar Khan, of which he produces a specimen. This awakens the interest of a sheriff's officer, to whom a system of paper currency is a mystery. In his words we have a rapid sketch of the well-known scene at the royal exchequer, the reckoning of the sheriff's account upon the squares of the green cloth. Here Sir Francis was upon thoroughly congenial ground, and, when the mayor of Abingdon rallies Master Griffe-de-Loup upon the procedure of the exchequer and its collusion with the county authorities, his rueful account of his losses embodies a lively allusion to the system of exchequer tallies and to the difficulty of extracting payment from a court which followed the king's movements and had no permanent place of session throughout the year. It is in such passages as this that the value of *The Merchant and the Friar* is most apparent. If its author did not aspire to be an artist in fiction, he had the imagination to discover the element of life in bygone institutions, and the power to stimulate the curiosity of readers to whom the *Dialogus de Scaccario* was a sealed book and Madox's

[a] *Rites of Durham*, ed. Fowler (Surtees Soc. vol. 107), pp. 86, 87.

History and Antiquities of the Exchequer would be a source of bewilderment.

It must be owned that, when the merchant and friar join forces and Roger Bacon becomes the *cicerone* of Marco Polo on his way to London, their exchange of opinions is given at too great length. The device of examining a period of history through the eyes of two famous men who saw, the one by his natural shrewdness and experience of many lands, the other by the force of his intellect, far in advance of their age, naturally suggested an attempt to reproduce their probable reflexions. These pioneers of commerce and science find common ground in their visions of the future, and Marco Polo is profoundly interested in Bacon's prophecies of an age of steam-power and machinery. The fortunate expedient of attributing the interruption of a conversation which promises to be endless to the illegibility of a supposed original manuscript brings about a welcome transition. The travellers arrive at a shire-oak, the time-honoured meeting-place of the county court. The friar, as learned in the past as he is prescient of the future, descants upon the remote antiquity of the tree and the early superstitions connected with it and the neighbouring spring, and the merchant brings his knowledge of foreign parallels to bear upon the friar's comments. It is not without design that the friar has brought him here, for the county court is about to be held and those who owe it suit are already gathering.

The details of the picture of the county court must be some-what modified in the light of more recent research[a]. Its place of assembly at the sacred tree upon the moot-hill need not be questioned. It is true that, in the days of Edward I, the *comitatus* usually met in the county town, but then and even later its place of meeting was not rigidly fixed, and some courts still met in the open air. But a court with as many as two thousand suitors would have been a rare spectacle at this date, or probably at any time after the Norman conquest. The origin of the shire-moot lies far in a past of which we know little, and it is not unlikely that at the period at which we have our first definite evidence of its organisa-tion, towards the close of the tenth century, the several townships of the shire may have been represented as fully as is described here. The burden of attendance, however, was great, especially when the meetings of the court were held once a month instead of twice a year, a change to which the second issue of the Great

---

[a] On the county court generally see Pollock and Maitland, *Hist. English Law*, 2nd ed. I, 532–556; Stubbs, *Const. Hist.* I, 128–130, 424–430.

Charter bears witness[a]; and freedom from counties and hundreds, i.e. from suit to the courts of the shire and hundred, was a privilege freely granted to lords of manors and their tenants[b]. Further, although the churl appears in early times to have been liable to suit of court as a freeholder, it is certain that, long before the close of the thirteenth century, churls had ceased to take any prominent part in the assembly. In the first place, their free status as a class had lapsed into villeinage; the peasant, generally speaking, was unfree[c]. Secondly, the presence of a full deputation from each township which owed suit would be found only upon extraordinary occasions, when the king's justices visited the county in the course of their eyre, i.e. their *iter* or judicial perambulation of the shires. The writ by which such meetings were called prescribed the summons of four *legales homines*, men approved by law, from each township, with their reeve[d]; and a villein, for such purposes, would be recognised as a *legalis homo*. On the other hand, the often quoted passage from the *Leges Henrici primi*, which seems to show that the duty of suit at the ordinary county court fell only upon land-owners, *domini terrarum*[e], implies that the township, for normal purposes, was sufficiently represented by its town-reeve, the *tungrevius* whose name occurs in the list of persons of rank and officials who were bound to attend. The *dominus terrarum* represented his tenants: it was only when he or his steward were unable to come that a full representation of a township was required[f]. Thus, at the beginning of the twelfth century, a churl who was a freeholder would be required to do suit in right of his holding; but the attendance of deputies from townships, apart from the town-reeves, was compelled only in special contingencies. Even the town-reeve seems to have been acquitted from attendance, if the lord's steward was present. It should also be remembered that the obligation of coming from places at a considerable distance was always irksome, and was hardly balanced by the consideration that the suitors were also the doomsmen or judges, upon whose decision rested the cases within the province of the court. When the churl had lost his privileges, it is hardly likely that his attendance would either have been insisted upon or readily given.

[a] Stubbs, *Select Charters*, 9th ed. p. 343 (art. 42).

[b] See Pollard, *Evolution of Parliament*, 1920, p. 109, for the effect of such privileges upon attendance at the county court.

[c] See general conclusions in Vinogradoff, *Villainage in England*, 1892, pp. 218–220.

[d] Pollock and Maitland, *op. cit.* I, 545, note 1.

[e] Stubbs, *Select Charters*, p. 123 (VII, 2).   [f] *Ibid.* p. 124 (VII, 7).

The fundamental view of the county court taken in the story is that it was a representative assembly to which members were contributed from three sources. There are the knights, present in virtue of their rank, the deputies from the hundreds, twelve from each, and four or five deputies from each township; and it is suggested that the last two correspond respectively to the yeoman and peasant classes. It has already been shown that no large attendance of peasants can be predicated. The attendance of the knights goes without question, and among the suitors there would, of course, be freeholders of a rank below that of the magnates of the county. Such freeholders, however, would attend as individuals; but their presence as "sworn centenary deputies"[a] is, to say the least of it, doubtful. The *centenarius* mentioned in the *Leges Henrici* is, with little doubt, the steward or bailiff of the hundred court; his title is formed in the same way as that of the *decennarius* or tithing-man of whom we read elsewhere; he represents his hundred as the *praepositus* or *tungrevius* represents his vill or township. But there seems to be no evidence that a full deputation from the hundred was required in the county. The hundred court owed no service to the county court; there was no appeal from it to the county[b], and the twelve freeholders who sat in it as jurors when the sheriff made his "turn" twice a year had no reason for appearing before him outside their hundred. The writ of summons to the eyre held in the county court mentions twelve leal, i.e. lawful, burgesses from each borough in the county, but it says nothing of the hundred or even of its officers[c].

The jurors of the hundreds may thus be eliminated from the court, and with them goes the triple class-distinction inferred from their presence. So far as anything may be said definitely of the principle upon which suit to the county court was founded, it depended, not upon the representation of knight, freeman and churl, but upon tenure of property. As long as the churl maintained his freehold, he had as much right there as anybody; as a representative of his township, whether free or unfree, his presence would be required only on rare occasions. The whole question takes us back to the much debated problem of the original status of the English villager, and those who advocate the servile theory would naturally exclude the churl or villein from a court of freeholders. The opposite theory, however, lends no support to the constitution of the court as described in these pages. For the large representa-

---

[a] See below, p. 29.   [b] Pollock and Maitland, *op. cit.* i, 557.

[c] *Ibid.* i. 545.

tive gathering we may substitute a small one, from which the hundred jurors will be absent, and in which the smock-clad villeins will play, if any, an inconspicuous part.

Its representative character, however, remains. The comparatively scanty body of freeholders represents those who owe suit and service to each of its members; his tenants do suit to the county in his person. The shire-court, as Dr Stubbs long ago pointed out, was quite distinct from the old English witanagemot, which had no representative basis[a]; and the friar too readily confirmed Marco Polo's conjecture that "this assembly had been the "legislature of an ancient commonwealth" with the statement that the suitors were successors of the sages who gave its name to the witan[b]. The witan was the king's council; its picked members were summoned rather upon their own merits than because they represented any subordinate bodies or areas of jurisdiction. The suitors of the county court, on the other hand, were summoned as responsible for the area of the county and the tenants under their protection; a complete county court should represent, in its composition, all the land and all the people of the shire. Its basis was thus democratic; the judgment given by the suitors was the judgment of the whole shire, and the sheriff, as president, was there not to judge, but to ratify the shire's decisions[c]. Indeed, the democratic character of the court was more thorough than Sir Francis shows. He seems to regard the knights as distinct from the commons of the shire; the yeoman John Trafford pleads before the sheriff that "we, poor commons," are not bound to proceed to the election of members of parliament[d]. But the county court knew no such distinctions; if its business came more and more under the control of a class, until its lesser members had no voice in its proceedings, it was still representative of the county as a whole, and its verdicts were the verdicts of the *communitas*, the common body of the county. The knights of the shire whom it sent to parliament were the spokesmen of the commons, elected, at any rate in theory, by a body in which all, for such purposes, were equal or, as the phrase ran, "peers of the county"; and the origin of the House of Commons is found in the county court[e].

Careful readers of the text will see that the knights present in the court included men or their attorneys who, individually, as barons, were liable to summons to parliament by special writ, and

[a] See Stubbs, *Const. Hist.* I, 133, 134. [b] See below, p. 29.
[c] See Pollock and Maitland, *op. cit.* I, 548 sqq. [d] See below, p. 35.
[e] See Pollard, *op. cit.* pp. 109–111.

sat there as peers of the realm. John Trafford was there in two capacities, as a freeholder and as steward and proxy of Sir Robert de Vere, the earl of Oxford[a]. The distinction between lords and commons in the county court is thus further disproved. The great tenants-in-chief in that assembly had no theoretical superiority to the lesser freeholders; in practice, it might be otherwise, but, from the county point of view, they were all members of the commons. When Trafford attempts to evade his electoral responsibilities, it is on the ground that the business of electing knights of the shire belonged primarily to the magnates of the county. His plea falls to the ground; the sheriff excuses him as a yeoman, because he inadvertently acknowledges that he stands in the place of a magnate. Incidentally the sheriff refers to the responsibility of stewards in the Yorkshire court[b]. With regard to parliamentary elections, this anticipates history by a good century; for it is not until 1411 that we have any definite record which shows that the court which elected the parliamentary representatives for Yorkshire was composed of the stewards of tenants-in-chief[c]; but it is clear that, from a county of so vast an area, the attendance of all freeholders was impracticable, and that representation would have a natural tendency to become reserved to the greater tenants. These appeared in the persons of their stewards, and were so appearing in the thirteenth and fourteenth centuries[d]; and from this to the recognition of the stewards as the customary suitors was only a short step.

The case of Yorkshire shows the way in which, through natural causes, the representation of the county in its court could become confined to a very small body. Those causes may be summarised under three heads. The loss of privilege by the villein class excluded the churl from any but occasional and passive participation. Difficulty and waste of time in reaching the court were an insurmountable hindrance to regular attendance. In itself, the duty of doing suit was a burden, excuse from which was gladly welcomed. Before the end of the reign of Edward I, a limit had been set to the obligation; the forty-shillings freeholder became the unit of the county court, and consequently of the parliamentary electorate[e].

As described, with considerable humour, by Sir Francis, the conduct of a parliamentary election was doubtless unsatisfactory, even when we have reduced the electorate to a minimum; and we

[a] See below, p. 35.   [b] See below, p. 35.
[c] Stubbs, *Const. Hist.* I, 424, 425.   [d] Pollock and Maitland, *op. cit.* I, 543.
[e] See the statute of 1293–4, *Rot. Parl.* I, 117.

can well credit the ignorance of their duties which made John Trafford and his friends unwilling to proceed and converted their actual proceedings into a farce. A sheriff of sufficient adroitness could unquestionably have imposed his will upon such an assembly. On the other hand, as has been pointed out, the sheriff was there merely as president of the court. Sir Francis seems to regard him as a judge, attended by the knights as his assessors. They, how-ever, in common with the whole court, were suitors and judges. The one plea which comes before the court is dismissed summarily by the sheriff[a]. The knights would probably have taken his view of the case, and, of the others, only a man of singular independence would have raised his voice against the infringement of justice; but the doom would have come from one of the suitors, and not from the sheriff himself. It was not by such autocratic methods that the county court could be managed, and more than one illustration exists of the powerlessness of the sheriff to over-ride the privileges of the suitors[b].

In our present state of society, when a representative position is regarded as an honour, it is difficult to imagine a time when it was avoided as a disagreeable tax. We have already shown that the suitor to the county court welcomed an excuse for absence. Sir Francis, with his knowledge of parliamentary documents, brings out clearly the unwillingness of the elected knights of the shire to serve in parliament, which is shown sufficiently by the fact that two sureties for their appearance, the *manucaptores* or mainperners, were required[c]. The story of the escape of Sir Richard de Pogeys to the Chiltern Hundreds possibly errs on the side of picturesqueness; the historical instance quoted in the dedicatory epistle, of a knight who "sought the protection of the four hundreds "and a half of Chiltern"[d] need not imply that he sought shelter in that district, famous as the haunt of robbers, but means rather that he obtained exemption by purchasing from the Crown the stewardship of the hundreds, a sinecure the fiction of which sur-vives to-day, but which might then be used as a source of profit. In the case of the abbot of Oseney, the reluctance of a tenant-in-chief to obey a parliamentary writ is well exemplified, with the mixture of fact with fiction which Sir Francis chose as the best method of illustrating his points. Incidentally we may remark that the removal of ecclesiastical cases from the county court would not necessarily have lessened the abbot's attendance, in

[a] See below, p. 30.   [b] See above, p. [xvii], reference in note *c*.
[c] See below, p. 39.   [d] See below, Ded. p. ix.

person or by his steward[a]. The fact that a certain number of cases came within the jurisdiction of the spiritual court affected the whole community, and had no exclusive bearing upon the clergy. As a land-owner, the abbot would have found abundant opportunities for temporal litigation; and, while his pleas in the "court Christian" of the bishop of Lincoln, with their possible sequels in appeals to the court of Arches and the papal Curia, might frequently engage his attention, it would still be to his advantage to put in a more than casual appearance as the suitor and doomsman of the civil court.

From the Oxfordshire county court we pass to London. The origin of the municipal institutions of London must always remain to some extent a debatable problem. There is no return for London in Domesday; and the brief charter granted by William I to the bishop, the port-reeve and all the burghers, merely confirms to them, with assurance of his protection, the privileges which they had enjoyed in King Edward's day and the transference of such privileges from father to son[b]. What these were is stated more definitely in the charter by which Henry I granted to the citizens the farm of Middlesex and gave them power to elect their own sheriff and justiciar[c]. The organisation thus sanctioned was that of a county, with the important difference that the county officers, instead of holding their authority from the crown as elsewhere, were elected by the citizens. London therefore acquired a singular independence; and when, in 1135, Stephen seized the crown, it was to the citizens of London that he first turned for recognition. The assembly which chose him was not a municipal corporation; it was the county court of London and Middlesex. This court, as in other counties, had its extraordinary and ordinary aspects; ordinarily, under the Danish name of husting, it was the court which met to do justice weekly[d], while, on special occasions, it took the form of the folk-moot or general assembly of the citizens. Each ward or local division of the city had its ward-moot, corresponding to the hundred court[e].

The hereditary succession of privileges confirmed by the Con-

---

[a] See below, pp. 29, 30.

[b] Stubbs, *Select Charters*, pp. 97, 98.   [c] *Ibid.* pp. 129, 130.

[d] See R. R. Sharpe, *Cal. of Wills proved and enrolled in the London Court of Husting*, 1889, pt. I, Introd.

[e] On the early constitution of London see Stubbs, *Const. Hist.* I, 439–442, and Round, *Geoffrey de Mandeville*, 1892, app. iv. Round, *The Commune of London and other essays*, 1889, pp. 221, 222, holds that the husting represents the "lawmen" found in the Danish boroughs of England.

queror, though its ultimate origin is unknown, probably began long before the days of Edward the Confessor. Whether, as Sir Francis was inclined to think, the privileged citizen was the descendant of a conquering race which reduced its predecessors to an inferior position, and the ordinary citizen represented the class thus dispossessed, is a point on which no certain opinion may be given[a]. It supplies a conjectural explanation, although the remoteness of the conquest so assumed may be doubted. At any rate, the government of the city was vested in an oligarchy with hereditary rights, whose members in the twelfth century were recognised as barons. The term *barones* is taken as a matter of course in Henry I's charter; the churches, the barons and the citizens may hold their sokes or special jurisdictions in peace with all their customs. There is no precise limitation to this baronial status; the bishop, the aldermen of the wards, and the lords of sokes, however, were barons. In process of time hereditary rights must have died out or been transferred, or new rights created, e.g. the lord of the soke of Baynard's castle owed his franchises to the establishment of a castle in the city after the Norman Conquest. There is an interesting allusion to the barons of London in a charter of William Longchamp, bishop of Ely, granted in 1190 and printed by Mr J. H. Round in his essay on *The Commune of London*, which states that he had bought the property which is the subject of the deed "by the verdict of the whole city of London," and that "this "was attested before him by the *majores barones* of the city at the "Tower of London."[b] This may imply the division of the barons into two classes, the *majores* who were tenants-in-chief in the city, and the *minores* who were not; but it is more probable that the phrase, not found in this context elsewhere, simply means "the "more barons," i.e. a majority of the whole number.

A revolution in the character of the government of London took place in October 1191, when, in Richard I's absence, his brother John and William Longchamp were contending for supremacy in the kingdom. As Mr Round points out, the liberties of the city which had chosen Stephen as king and repulsed the empress Maud had been repressed by Henry II, and Richard I had been faithful to his father's policy in this respect. The grant of a free municipal organisation, such as cities on the continent were rapidly acquiring, would not have been consented to by either king, says Richard of Devizes, for a million marks. John, however,

---

[a] See below, pp. 42, 43.

[b] Round, *The Commune of London, etc.* 1899, p. 253.

bought the support of the citizens by granting them the privilege of a "commune," to which he took oath in person. The county organisation ceased to control the affairs of London; its old courts remained, but under new conditions. The first record of the actual head of the commune, the mayor, does not appear until two years later; but it is probable that the grant of the commune was followed by the election of the first mayor[a].

Sir Francis, under the influence of the sinister meaning which the word "commune" had acquired at the time of the French revolution, implies that the commune of London was simply a form of government by mob-law which for a time overthrew the authority of the aldermen in the city. At the same time, he appears to regard the commune as a temporary phenomenon which arose during the disturbed state of London in the critical era of the barons' war. But, if the mob, while Thomas FitzThomas was mayor, got the upper hand, the fact that it styled itself the commune does not mean, as Sir Francis evidently thought, that it borrowed the foreign title for its own use[b]. It merely usurped the title and powers of the commune which had come into being seventy-three years before. The establishment of a commune in 1191, on the model, as Mr Round has shown, of communes, such as that of Breteuil, which had come into being abroad[c], was a symptom of a desire for civic independence and for a republican constitution; but the commune was not a collection of communists, in the modern sense of the term. *Communa, communia, communio,* the various Latin terms, was a common association of citizens under oath to assert and maintain municipal freedom[d]; and to this "sworn commune" John, as his brother's representative, solemnly assented. Mr Round's researches have brought to light the fact that the commune of London in 1191 was probably modelled upon the existing commune of Rouen; and his documents show that it was constituted of a mayor, two *échevins* and other *probi homines*[e]. Some years later, the *probi homines* come to

[a] Round, *The Commune of London, etc.* 1899, pp. 222–225.

[b] See below, p. 46. The passage in *De antiquis legibus liber,* ed. Stapleton (Camden Soc.), p. 55, says merely *populum civitatis, vocantes se communam civitatis.* But already in 1248, the same chronicle records an answer of the citizens to a royal demand *quod nichil inde facere potuerunt sine assensu totius commune* (*ibid.* p. 15).   [c] Round, *The Commune of London, passim.*

[d] Stubbs, *Select Charters,* 8th ed. p. 265, recognised the general meaning of *communa* as "a corporate identity of the municipality." Mr Round's discoveries have produced a more explicit definition.

[e] Round, u.s. pp. 235–237.

light as a council of twenty-four, who cannot be identified with the aldermen representing the wards, if only for the reason that their number does not correspond to that of the wards[a]. It would seem that for the time being the aldermen, though still elected by the wards as local officers, disappeared from or became a secondary element in the governing body of the city as a whole, which was elected by the whole body of citizens. In the two *échevins*, with their foreign title, we see the two municipal sheriffs, who have no connexion with the sheriffs of the period of county organisation; and in the twenty-four we have the germ of the common council of London. The commune of 1191 is the origin of the city corporation of to-day, and, if its name and authority could be usurped by turbulent demagogues, it was normally as representative and as respectable as the modern city fathers. How far the office of mayor was a revival of that of port-reeve is very questionable, for the port-reeve seems to have been magnified into the sheriff of Henry I's charter; and the mayor superseded the sheriff rather than succeeded to his office[b].

A version of the origin of the council of twenty-four is given as a gloss upon the story of the election of Walter Hervey to the mayoralty in 1272, which Sir Francis derived from the contemporary chronicle in *De antiquis legibus liber*[c]. It is represented as a committee, eventually rising to twenty-five, a number generally accepted until Mr Round showed that the true number was twenty-four[d], chosen by the mayor and aldermen upon extraordinary occasions. This theory appears to confound the special committee of ten, appointed jointly by Hervey and the aldermen, with the popularly chosen council which had long been in existence. It assumes the continuous predominance of a body of aldermen, magnates bent upon quashing, as they no doubt were, any popular attempt to control the city; and it imagines a subsequent amalgamation of the aldermen and a permanent committee, the *ordo* and the *plebs*, in the governing body[e]. This is contrary to the actual course of things. The power of the aldermen was reduced in 1191, and it is probable that the first commune tried to get on without them. The degree of influence which they subsequently recovered

[a] Round, u.s. pp. 237–239.

[b] Mr Round shows the connexion between the sheriff and the port-reeve, *Geoffrey de Mandeville*, pp. 354, 355.

[c] *De antiquis legibus liber*, u.s. pp. 148 sqq.

[d] Round, *The Commune of London*, p. 238. The authority for twenty-five is *De antiquis legibus liber*, p. 2, which mentions their election in 1200.

[e] See below, pp. 55, 56, 58.

was not enough to withstand the supporters of FitzThomas in 1264 and of Hervey in 1272; while the committee of 1272 was a committee appointed *ad hoc*, and was not identical with the council which was a result of the establishment of the commune. When Sir Francis wrote, however, little critical attention had been paid to this difficult subject; *De antiquis legibus liber* remained unprinted until Stapleton's edition in 1846, and it was not until long after that some of the documents which have shed more light upon the early constitutional history of London were discovered.

The conversation in which the merchant and the friar engage as they walk through the streets of London is a digression from the main subject of the chapter. Marco Polo, as usual, is the intelligent observer to whom the friar, by Socratic methods, suggests topics on which he himself enlarges. Only two points in his discussion of the relations between English and Norman law need be noticed. His comment upon the influence of Anglo-Saxon jurisprudence upon the *Grand Coustumier* of Normandy would hardly obtain credence nowadays[a]. The earliest law-books of the Norman duchy are long subsequent to the conquest of England; and it is true that the *Très-ancien Coustumier*, compiled about 1200, and *Grand Coustumier* of some decades later are founded upon the legislation of the first of the Plantagenets[b]. But they are French rather than English law; and it is now recognised that the most famous of Henry II's legal reforms, the inquest by jury, was an institution of French origin[c]. The developed system of the English law-courts under the second dynasty of foreign kings was a totally different thing from the conformity of the Conqueror to laws which he found in existence and which it was to his own advantage to maintain. A minor point is the friar's citation of the famous legend of the Traffords to illustrate the continuity of the English population after the Conquest. The story of the thresher, to which the friar added some details of his own, can be easily dismissed as a picturesque tradition; but Mr Round, with his usual trenchancy, has demolished the pedigree to which it is an appendage and has shown that the traditional founder of the family in the days of Canute was not born until after the Conquest, and that his Christian name affords the strongest presumption that he was not an Englishman[d].

---

[a] See below, p. 63.
[b] Pollock and Maitland, *op. cit.* I, 65.   [c] *Ibid.* I, 140–144.
[d] See below, p. 61; *The Ancestor*, no. 10 (July 1904), pp. 73–82, for Mr Round's criticism of the legend.

At the gates of the churchyard of St Martin's-le-Grand, into which the funeral procession of an alderman has passed, we are introduced to a personage learned in the customs of the city, Andrew Horn, the supposed compiler of *The Mirror of Justices*. Horn, a fishmonger of Bridge Street and chamberlain of the city from 1320 to his death in 1328, was a legal antiquary rather than a practising lawyer. His authorship of *The Mirror of Justices* has been doubted for some weighty reasons, but cannot wholly be disproved; the only MS of the work belonged to and was annotated by him. The book was long believed to be a trustworthy law treatise of a far more remote antiquity; and it was Sir Francis Palgrave who, in his *English Commonwealth*, was the first to reject its value as anything but "a very curious specimen of the apocrypha "of the law,"[a] a cross between a legal handbook and a political pamphlet. In more recent times, its analysis was undertaken by Professor Maitland, who dissected the various ingredients of the strange composition and gave a reasoned judgment upon it[b]. Horn was a patriotic citizen, and the authorship of the *Annales Londonienses*, a chronicle dealing in detail with political events through which he lived, was attributed to him by Dr Stubbs with great probability[c]; and, if he wrote *The Mirror of Justices*, the political opinions with which Sir Francis credits him were certainly his.

At the guildhall in Aldermanbury, where the seat of civic authority remained until its removal in 1411 to the present site, the statue of King Athelstan, engraved with the famous words in which his traditional grant to more than one borough of its franchises was embodied long after his day, arouses Horn's enthusiasm[d]. The court sitting in the guildhall is the court of husting, presided over by the mayor; and it will be noticed that Sir Francis employs the word "hustings" in its derived meaning to signify the platform or dais upon which the "court of aldermen," as he calls it, sat[e]. The husting itself, however, was actually the assembled court, retaining its old Danish title. In its proceedings

---

[a] *English Commonwealth*, II (vol. VII of this series), p. 159 n.

[b] Introd. to *The Mirror of Justices*, ed. Whittaker, 1895 (Selden Soc. vol. 7).

[c] Introd. to *Chronicles of the Reigns of Edw. I and Edw. II* (Rolls Ser.), vol. I. See below, pp. x, xi, for a mention of Horn's other work, the *Liber Horn*.

[d] See below, pp. 66, 67. See the text of the rhymed charter of Beverley in *Beverley Chapter Act-Book*, ed. Leach, II (Surtees Soc. vol. 108), pp. 280–287, and text and facsimile of that of Ripon in *Memorials of Ripon*, ed. Fowler, I (*ibid.* vol. 74), 90–93.

[e] See below, p. 71.

with the lord of Castle Baynard, whose privileges as banner-bearer of the city and within his own soke are confirmed, while his claim to sit as a member of the city council is rejected, Marco Polo recognises an analogy to the customs of the Florentine democracy, allusions to which have already been prompted by Horn's remarks. Such proceedings, in fact, were significant of the permanence of the communal government, the origin of which has been already summarised.

The episode which follows, the appearance of the members of a craft-gild before the tribunal to obtain confirmation of its privileges, is interesting as bringing before us a typical example of the bodies which played a large part in the town-life of the later middle ages. In his statement that "religion was the foundation of the "gild; divine worship the solid bond of the association," Sir Francis utters a doctrine which present-day research tends to confirm[a]; no hard-and-fast distinction can be laid down between craft-gilds and gilds which retained a purely religious character irrespective of any special craft. No direct descent of the craft-gilds from the Roman *collegia* can be proved[b]; such organisations are the natural outcome of the desire to protect individual trades and occupations. Sir Francis, however, has nothing to say of the gilds merchant which, before the rise of craft-gilds, had exercised some influence upon the civic government in many places. He has referred earlier to the Saxon *cnihten-gild* of London and to the transfer of its possessions to the prior and convent of Holy Trinity[c]. The origin of this is doubtful and its identity with a gild merchant improbable, and there was no continuity whatever between it and the commune of 1191. On the other hand, there were elements in the government resulting from that commune which closely resembled the constitution of the gild merchant. Two or more *échevins* and a council of twelve or twenty-four are found as integral parts of the early constitution of such gilds[d]; and the mayor represents its alderman—he was, as a matter of fact, customarily one of the aldermen of the city. Thus the municipal government of London was closely akin to the organisation of the gild merchant, and, speaking of England generally, we may say that municipal and gild corporations were so similar in constitution and membership that there has been a very natural

[a] See below, p. 73.
[b] See below, p. 74.
[c] See below, p. 44. See Round, *The Commune of London, etc.* pp. 102 sqq.
[d] Ashley, *Econ. History*, I (1), 72.

tendency to confound the gild merchant with the municipality whose members made up its constituents[a]. The craft-gilds, however, were apparently distinct in origin, although their relation to the gild merchant in England is obscure. Their opposition to its authority is a feature of continental rather than of English history[b]; but Andrew Horn's exposition of their attempts to enter and control the municipalities is true of Europe generally[c]. In the nature of things, no single craft could hope to get power into its own hands; but there are indications in some towns that the common council became an oligarchy composed of members of religious gilds which embraced the brethren of the several craft-gilds[d]. In general, as Sir Francis observes, "after various fluctuations, the gilds became "the only channels, through which the municipal freedom could "be acquired."[e]

The pretensions of the craft-gilds win little sympathy from Horn, whose ideals are of a more genuinely democratic character. Obsessed by his enthusiasm for the era of Alfred and Athelstan as the golden age of English freedom, he holds up the system of frankpledge, the enrolment of every man in his tithing or "tenne-mantale," the members of which are sureties for each other's good conduct, as the true basis of the franchise[f]. His patriotism affirms this to be a peculiarly English institution. All that need be said here is that its origin extends far beyond England, and that for his view there is no justification in the facts of history[g]. His remarks form a transition to the arrival of the chief justice with a commission of *oyer and terminer* and gaol delivery and the subsequent legal proceedings. Of these little need be said. They illustrate many points of judicial procedure with a lively humour; and, in Horn's defence of the prisoners and appeal to ancient custom against modern practice, we hear the voice of the author of *The Mirror of Justices*, the sworn castigator of abuses which he is ready to discover in every corner. Upon such points as

---

[a] Cunningham, *Growth of English Trade and Industry*, 5th ed. I, 344. He also suggests the alternative that the craft-gilds were "specialised branches of the "old gilds merchant." On the subject generally, see Gross, *The Gild Merchant*, 2 vols., 1890.

[b] Cunningham, *op. cit.* I, 343, says that "there is no evidence that they were "conflicting or rival authorities" in England. For a summary view of their probable relations see Ashley, *op. cit.* I (1), 78 sqq.

[c] See below, pp. 78, 80.

[d] The Corpus Christi gild of Leicester, whose gild house became the Town hall, is a case in point.   [e] See below, p. 80.

[f] See below, p. 79.   [g] See Stubbs, *Const. Hist.* I, 91–96.

benefit of clergy, compurgation, the nature and duties of a jury right of sanctuary and abjuration of the realm, the text is its own comment.

Of the original roll of the parliament of 1305 Professor Maitland said: "it was unknown in 1827 to Sir Francis Palgrave, and when "we have said it was unknown to Palgrave, we have said it was "unknown to any body."[a] The industry of the editor of *Parliamentary Writs* was exhaustive, and it is in his picture of parliament that we expect to find him at his best. We approach the main subject by somewhat tortuous by-paths: the reader could well dispense with the allusions to the Uzbeck constitution and Dyche's spelling-book on which Sir Francis' prolific fancy encouraged him to enlarge[b]. These tend to obscure the necessary features of the picture. There are two essential points which the reader needs to grasp, namely, the composition and the functions of parliament at this period.

The second is more simple than the first. Parliament is a council summoned by the sovereign for consultation upon national business. It will grant supplies to the crown and it will make statutes which will be binding upon the nation. But it is primarily the supreme court of justice in the realm, and at this epoch the *Rolls of Parliaments* will show that its judicial occupies far more of its time than its legislative business[c]. Petitions come before it from the whole realm; all classes are represented by its petitioners. It is the "high court" of parliament, the "court of the king in his "council in his parliaments," as the earliest definition puts it. The *curia regis* of the Plantagenets, for judicial purposes, has been split up into three divisions; above the court held theoretically "in the king's presence in his council" and "the king's court of "the bench," known later as the king's bench and the common bench stands this supreme court of appeal, in which the king himself sits to do the justice of which he is the source. In France, where the judicial functions of parliament became severed from its legislative duties, the term *parlement* was retained by the law-courts which sat in Paris and other principal towns and were totally different bodies from the *états* or representative assemblies

[a] *Memoranda de Parliamento* (Rolls Ser.), pp. xii, xiii.
[b] See below, pp. 99–101.
[c] See the 254 petitions etc. dealt with in the parliament of 1290 (*Rot. Parl.* I, 46–65). *Mem. de Parl.* u.s. records 487 cases which came before the parliament in 1305.

of the nation. While, in modern times, we regard parliament from its legislative side, which has overshadowed the other, the judicial tribunal of the House of Lords still reminds us that it has another character[a].

As regards the composition of parliament, its character, as it developed from an occasional meeting summoned by the king into the assembly of which the parliament of 1295 was the model, became representative of the whole nation. The bishops and abbots, the lay tenants-in-chief, who were summoned by writs addressed to themselves, represented those who held lands in their fees, just as the elected members, the knights and burgesses, represented the inhabitants of shires and boroughs. The bishops and abbots came, not as a special estate or class, but because they held land by the same tenure as the lay barons; they were all, clerical or lay, the king's *barones* or men, who owed their homage directly to him. Nor did these form a class distinct from the knights and burgesses; the knights, indeed, though they sat in parliament by popular election, belonged to the same social class as the barons. "The "commons," says Sir Francis, "only sent to parliament a few "more members of a class, which was already fully supplied."[b] Just as we have seen that too much may be made of the position of the knights in a county court, so we must beware of thinking of the parliaments of Edward I in the terms of a later age. The division of parliament into three estates of the realm, clergy, lords and commons, was due, in the first instance, to the occasional convenience of consultation between the elected members apart from those summoned by writ, and became an accomplished fact in the fourteenth century; yet, even then, while the representatives of the clergy, elected at first by writs issuing from the bishops, debated parliamentary measures in convocation together with their own affairs, the bishops and abbots retained their seats in the House of Lords among the great land-holders. The principle of the three estates was not the fundamental basis of parliamentary representation, but the practical outcome of a representative system which at first took no account of estates or classes; and it should be noted that, in the early deliberations of the commons, the knights and the burgesses debated apart from each other[c]. Two further details may be emphasised. Hereditary representation had no place in our early parliaments. A baron sat by virtue

[a] For a general discussion of the functions of the high court of parliament see Pollard, *op. cit.* ch. ii.   [b] See below, p. 104.

[c] See Pollard, *op. cit.* ch. iv, for a discussion of "the myth of the three estates."

of the king's summons, not because his father had a seat in parliament; nor did the House of Lords become a purely hereditary
assembly until much later in history. Secondly, as our experience
in the county court has shown us, a seat in parliament was not
regarded as an enviable right, but as a duty and a burden which
baron and knight of the shire alike were more likely to avoid than
to court.

Sir Francis accepted the doctrine of the essential character of
the three estates, in spite of the fact that he recognised the identity
of class between the knights and the barons and saw the insignificance of the influence of the commons in early parliaments[a]; and
from this view modern research has departed. On the other hand,
although in one place he speaks of the crown as the first estate of
the realm, his remarks elsewhere serve to remind us that the
estates actually were clergy, lords and commons[b], and that the
belief that they consist of king, lords and commons is a fiction of
comparatively modern growth, due to the decline of convocation
as a legislative assembly and as an element in the councils of the
realm. He also shows us the existence of an integral part of parliament which was not representative. Parliament, it should be remembered, was, in the view of thirteenth century lawyers, an assembly
in which the king sat in his council. In its widest sense, then,
parliament was the king's council, but it contained members who
were there as the king's council in a special sense. The constitution
of Edward I's council has been discussed by Professor Maitland
in his introduction to the *Memoranda* of the parliament of 1305[c].
If tenants-in-chief, who represented their own tenants, had their
place in it, its most active members were lawyers and crown
officials who appeared simply as members of council and had no
representative status. The privy council was as yet a body whose
presence was essential to a "full parliament." It is going too far
to call it, with Sir Francis, a committee of parliament[d]; the king
and his council might and did sit to receive petitions and hear
pleas in full parliament after the representative element had dispersed[e]. Modern historians impress upon us that a "full" parliament is not a complete assembly of members, but an assembly
which is open to do business; *plenum parliamentum* is the Latin
of men who thought in French, and the French *plein* has more

[a] See below, p. 107.   [b] See below, pp. 102–104, 128, 129.
[c] *Mem. de Parl.* u.s. pp. xxxvi–xlvii.
[d] See below, p. 110.
[e] *Mem. de Parl.* u.s. p. xxxvi.

than one meaning[a]. At any rate, if the presence of the representatives was required for the initial business of parliament, that business could be continued by the council without the help of the others.

The sitting of parliament which the merchant and the friar attend is actually a sitting of the House of Lords, of the prelates and magnates[b]; and, in view of what has already been said of the growth of the three estates, this is somewhat too premature. The elected representatives of the commons, of course, attended upon a different footing from the prelates and magnates. The element of representation was dual; but Sir Francis had previously pointed out the comparative unimportance of this distinction in early parliaments. The two elements might separate for discussion; but there was as yet no sharp distinction between them as estates, and the permanent division between lords and commons was as yet to come. Outside the actual parliament, where the king is present, there sit, in the room familiar by the name of the star chamber[c], the auditors or triers of petitions appointed by the house[d]. For the cases which come before them the *Rolls of Parliaments* offer plenty of parallels which occurred readily to Sir Francis[e]. Suitors who cannot find justice elsewhere appeal to the king in his supreme council for their remedy; others who cannot afford the delay and expense of bringing their pleas before the ordinary courts of common law attempt to obtain summary treatment of their cases at this tribunal.

When we have passed the serjeant-at-arms and entered the august presence, we have no clear idea of the subject or methods of discussion; for the business is thrown into confusion by the news of the street-brawl between the two archbishops. The description of the affray itself is not exaggerated, to judge from the existing records of these recurrent quarrels upon a question of privileges[f]. The behaviour, however, of the dean of the arches (the official principal of the court of Canterbury) and of the judge of the consistory court is a humorous touch for which historical warrant is certainly wanting[g]. It is also an anachronism to place the palace of the bishop of London in Aldersgate street[h]; for it

---

[a] Pollard, *op. cit.* p. 33.   [b] See below, p. 122.

[c] See below, p. 116.   [d] See below, pp. 110 sqq.

[e] See above, p. [xxviii,] references in note *c*.

[f] See, e.g. documents printed in *Letters from Northern Registers*, ed. Raine (Rolls Ser.), pp. 59–63.

[g] See below, p. 127.   [h] See below, p. 127.

was not until the great fire had destroyed the palace at the north-west corner of St Paul's churchyard that the bishops migrated for a time to the site here indicated. We have already noticed that the eventual composition which put an end to the disputes between Canterbury and York is considerably antedated.

At the conclusion of the chapter, some reference is made to the representation of the clergy in parliament. Sir Francis, we have said, still held to the theory that king, lords and commons were the three estates of the realm; and his statement that, by virtue of the *praemunientes* clause, which, in the writs addressed to the archbishops, empowered them to summon representatives of the inferior clergy, these last "became an unquestionable branch, or "house of parliament," shows the fallacy of placing the king among the estates[a]. While it is true that the house of clergy "became a "convocation," and that the writs issued by archbishops to bishops, and by bishops to their cathedral chapters and clergy were sum-monses to convocation, it should not be forgotten that convocation was an existing assembly with its own organisation when the clergy were first called to take part in parliament[b]. The change effected by the growth of the parliamentary principle was that convocation met upon the same day as parliament; and, had it not been for the insistence of the clergy upon their own privileges and for the rivalry between the two provinces which was the cause of a separate convocation of the northern clergy at York, the parliamentary house of clergy might have superseded a purely ecclesiastical assembly which was suspicious of participation in secular affairs.

With the chapter upon parliament the interest of the story as a picture of historical institutions ceases. The mysterious dis-appearance of Bacon from the London Greyfriars and the mer-chant's visit to him in his retreat at Oxford belong to fiction alone. We would not unwillingly exchange the detailed exhibition of Bacon's mechanical toys, the germs of the inventions of a more recent period, and his long concluding discourse, for a description of the university in which he resided and for a series of scenes, such as we have enjoyed in spite of digressions, illustrating its ceremonies and customs. This, however, was no part of Sir Francis' design. If his object was to instruct by means of narrative, his

---

[a] See below, p. 128.

[b] For the relations between convocation and parliament see Stubbs, *Const. Hist.* III, 330–332, and Makower, *Const. Hist. Ch. of Eng.* § 54.

method was not, like that of the author of *Charicles* and *Gallus*, severely utilitarian. Sokes, lyke-wakes and clerks of the pells enter his pages; but his object is to do something more than provide an attractive setting for the explanation of obsolete terms. His intention embraced the exposition of what the middle ages should mean to his own day; and, while his lesson is conveyed too diffusely to be clear or quite coherent, he at least shows us that that bygone age still has its answer for those who would read its secret rightly, and that its institutions and discoveries have their necessary place in the path of progress.

The story which follows *The Merchant and the Friar* is a series of fragments, some of which, in their present condition, are episodes entirely detached from the main theme of the tale. It seems that pieces of two separate stories, one dealing with the history of a family through successive generations, and the other founded upon the social and economic condition of the tenantry of the abbots of St Albans, have been brought together; while the concluding chapter is a fragment by itself. At any rate, after the second chapter, the fortunes of the imaginary family of Clare of West Walsham are interrupted and are abruptly resumed four chapters later. The history of a medieval family gives abundant opportunity for dilating upon feudal customs. Tenure by serjeanty, the right of a widower to enjoy his wife's estate for life by the "curtesy of England," the escheat of property upon the death of a tenant, the inquest held after his death to establish the extent and value of his holding, the proof of the age of the heir, the relief payable by the heir upon entering into possession of the property, the grant of wardship and custody of him and his lands, if he was a minor, to someone who thus made profit out of him, are all illustrated[a]. We may doubt the derivation of *feudum* or *feodum*, the fee held by grant of the over-lord, and of its adjective "feudal" from the Greek *emphyteusis*[b], and it is certainly a mistake to attribute to the court of exchequer a stable existence from the reign of William I, since our first evidence for its establishment belongs to that of Henry I[c]; but the practical working of the feudal system is set forth in a way that makes unfamiliar terms and obsolete methods of procedure clear to the ordinary student, whom a mere statement of facts is apt to puzzle.

Similarly, the four chapters which take us to St Albans present

[a] See below, chh. i, ii, pp. 189–217.   [b] See below, p. 206.
[c] See below, p. 203; see Stubbs, *Const. Hist.* I, 474.

to us vividly the relations of a great feudal land-owning corporation to its tenants. The era chosen is one of restlessness in the state: the opposition of Thomas of Lancaster, like that of Simon de Montfort in the previous century, to the crown has been construed by the common people into a popular movement, and Thomas, falling in a struggle which was due to his personal ambition, is worshipped as a saint and as the martyr of popular liberty. Against the abbot's bailiff and seneschal or, as English people more generally called him, steward on the one side, are ranged on the other typical members of the working class, the miller, the mason, the tiler[a]. We are introduced to the procedure of one form of manorial court, the court leet or view of frankpledge, in which the steward sits as judge[b]—a form of court distinct from the court baron, to which, just as the suitors to the county court, the tenants of the manor repair as suitors and as judges. The grievances of the subordinate element in the community are illustrated; and how they are encouraged to find expression is shown by the exhortations and comments of the friar, an anticipation of John Ball, the secular priest who was prominent in the peasant revolt towards the close of the century. Here, again, there are statements which call for criticism. The mason, John le Lathomere (the *lathomarius, lathomus* or stone-cutter), is represented, for instance, as a member of a fully organised craft[c]. It would be very difficult, however, to find any positive evidence at this date for the welding together of the English free-masons, the workers in freestone who were the architects and sculptors of the day, in one brotherhood. Masons working on special buildings were no doubt governed by local codes of rules; but, for any general attempt to give the craft as a whole a settled constitution, we must certainly look later. Nor, it may be added, is the evidence for the "comacine" theory complete or in any way satisfactory. Nevertheless, the introduction of the mason calls our attention to a fact which is still imperfectly realised, that the medieval architect was habitually a lay craftsman, trained in the practice of the work which he directed and surveyed, and that to him, and not to the bishops and abbots who employed him, or to the clerks and monks who were his paymasters, the design and execution of most of our great churches must be attributed[d].

The secret meeting in honour of Thomas of Lancaster adds a

[a] The tiler's name, Hellyer (*infra*, p. 226) = Hiller or coverer, i.e. roofer.
[b] See below, ch. iv, pp. 230 ff..   [c] See below, p. 225; cf. p. 247.
[d] For a general survey of medieval building conditions and documents bearing on them see *Proc. Somerset Archaeol. and Nat. Hist. Soc.* 4th ser. vol. VI, 1–25.

fantastic touch to the St Albans episodes which reminds us of the methods of Scott and of his prototypes, the inventors of subterranean conspiracies, mysterious friars and the stock-in-trade of Gothic romance. The religious service which forms part of it has also the indefinite character which the novelist of the day gave to medieval worship[a]. Of the intended sequel to this scene we have no trace; for the chapter which follows it is composed of isolated paragraphs, and in the seventh chapter we come back without comment to the family of Clare. Chronologically, the seventh and eighth chapters should change places; and the second of these, dealing with the economic consequences of the pestilence of 1349 and of the statute of labourers, is very incomplete. A generation of the family has been missed, and the great-grandson of the founder has come to London to raise money. His adventures, in the seventh and ninth chapters, bring him into contact with several financial magnates of the day and open the eyes of the provincial to the practices of contemporary usurers. It was certainly a bold anachronism to bring William Canynge or his brother into the company assembled in the tavern at Southwark; and Sir Francis probably forgot that even the Rowley MSS, to which he playfully refers, would have afforded no justification for putting the famous Bristol merchant, who died in 1474, into a company which met somewhere between 1377 and 1381[b]. William Walworth, John Philpot and Nicholas Brember are figures which belong to the chosen period[c]; but the cunning money-lender who is seen in these pages is a character somewhat at variance with that of the mayor who played a decisive part in repressing the insurrection of Wat Tyler, and William Lovekin the mercer[d], though bearing a surname well known in the Bridge ward of London at this epoch, appears to be purely fictitious. The scenes in St Paul's churchyard and in the "parvis" or open space in the front of the church— the proper application of a word which ecclesiologists are still in the habit of misusing—are well described; but the proceedings within St Paul's itself may anticipate rather too closely the purely secular use of the nave which was a public scandal in the sixteenth and seventeenth centuries. At the same time, this is not a point which need be insisted upon; the church must have

---

[a] See below, ch. v.   [b] See below, p. 254.

[c] See below, p. 282. Walworth's will is dated 20 Dec. 1385 (Sharpe, *op. cit.* II, 251); Philpot's 16 Nov. 1381 (*ibid.* II, 276); Brember, mayor in 1377 and 1383–1386, was hanged 1388 (*ibid.* II, 191, note 2).

[d] See below, p. 253.

been the resort of many idlers who strayed in from the adjacent churchyard, and the circumstances of the scene between Walworth and Rookesby are by no means unlikely[a].

The concluding chapter, in which Froissart appears in the library of the priory of the Holy Trinity, Aldgate, and witnesses from the window the punishment of a supporter of the house of Lancaster, has nothing to do with the Norfolk family, of whose ultimate history we are left in ignorance. There is a slight mistake in representing Robert Belknap as unpromoted to the bench in the reign of Richard II[b]; as a matter of fact, he became chief justice of the common pleas three years before Richard came to the throne[c]. Otherwise, the description of a medieval library, at a time when special rooms for this purpose were coming into more frequent use in monasteries and collegiate establishments, is accurate and valuable, and concludes a miscellaneous collection of scenes which are full of erudite information.

Despite the fragmentary condition of this second story and its conspicuous lack of unity, it brings us nearer the life of the middle ages than *The Merchant and the Friar*, which is concerned mainly with political institutions and their origin, and in which casual disquisition and prophecy have too large a share. Not that the second story is free from continual digression. The imaginary Cabezudo, whose name is merely the Spanish for "headstrong," had made his entry into *The Merchant and the Friar*[d]; and here he is the man of straw whose arguments are put up to be criticised by the author. He belongs to a type of literary convention of which Carlyle at this time was making abundant use; but it would be difficult to justify his pertinence to the special matter in hand. It may be said, on the other hand, that, if Sir Francis's allusions to comparatively recent politics and literature may sometimes perplex any but a singularly omnivorous reader, he seldom uses medieval allusions without giving a clue to their significance in the context. Sometimes terms are left unexplained. Anyone not familiar with the language of writs and of plea-rolls may be baffled by his mention of writs of distringas, alias and pluries[e], or by the meaning of the somewhat obscure word *trailbaston*[f]. To explain

---

[a] See the mention of Bishop Braybroke's monition on p. 270, which, however, is rather later than the date of the story.

[b] See below, p. 293.

[c] See Foss, *Biog. Dict. Judges of England*, 1870, p. 64.

[d] See below, p. 144.   [e] See below, p. 237.

[f] See below, p. 251; see note in *Mem. de Parl.* u.s. p. liii.

such passages and elucidate the text fully would require a fuller method of comment than has been thought advisable in the present edition. To the ordinary historical student who takes up these stories, they will offer no serious problems, in an age when books of reference are abundant and easily consulted.

In discussing the chief contents of the two narratives, we have devoted our attention principally to Sir Francis's view of the history of certain elements in English political life, of the growth of the representative system in county courts and in parliament and of the emergence of civic freedom as typified by the constitution of the municipality of London. We have seen that some of his details need considerable modification. His county court is too democratic in its actual appearance, while in theory it is too sharply divided by class distinctions. His conception of parliament relies too much upon the theory that the three estates were essential to its existence, and admits a recognised distinction between lords and commons before the two Houses were actually separate organisations, while his idea of the estates themselves is in conformity with the mistaken definition accepted in his age. His sketch of the history of London ignores the real meaning of the commune of the city and the change from county to civic government. Like Andrew Horn, he was somewhat too eager to uphold the continuity of the pre-Conquest element in English polity. Yet, while the theories set forth in these pages have been revised in no small part by later historians, the narratives themselves, in spite of their digressiveness and occasional irrelevance, may still be of use to stimulate interest in the life of a past, the importance of which to the present day Sir Francis saw more clearly than most of his contemporaries[a]. He bound himself to no minutely accurate method. His choice of a fictitious authority, the monk of Crowland, in *The Merchant and the Friar* was appropriately made by "the "illustrious scholar who delivered us from the Crowland forger"[b]: we need not expect from a member of the community which produced the so-called Ingulf absolute accuracy, but truth and fiction discreetly mingled. When the imperfections of Sir Francis as a writer of historical fiction have been admitted, the fact remains that in these stories we have the pastime of a great pioneer in historical scholarship, whose love of his chosen studies was so great

[a] See the estimate of the value of his historical work by Vinogradoff, *op. cit.* pp. 11–16.

[b] Maitland in introd. to *The Mirror of Justices*, u.s. p. x. See *Quarterly Review*, vol. xxxiv (1826), pp. 289–296.

that he thought it no waste of time to embody his thoughts upon them in popular form. Beneath the cloak of narrative is a body of solid learning, the fruit of an industry which may be compared with that of Prynne, Rymer and other historical antiquaries who, with few means to overcome difficulties now removed, ploughed their way with critical discrimination through masses of unpublished documents; and, if scholars of a later date have found some of Sir Francis's conclusions, as expressed here and elsewhere, open to correction, he himself, by his endless industry in sorting and classifying the records in his charge, did more than anyone else to put his successors in the right path of investigation and discovery[a].

A. HAMILTON THOMPSON.

[a] I am grateful to my friend Professor K. H. Vickers for his kindness in reading through the proof of this introduction and in making several useful suggestions.

TRUTHS AND FICTIONS OF THE MIDDLE AGES.

THE

MERCHANT AND THE FRIAR.

By SIR FRANCIS PALGRAVE, K.H.,

THE DEPUTY KEEPER, UNDER THE MASTER OF THE ROLLS,
OF HER MAJESTY'S PUBLIC RECORDS.

O voi ch' avete gl' intelletti sani,
Mirate la dottrina che s' asconde
Sotto 'l velame degli versi strani.

SECOND EDITION, REVISED AND CORRECTED.

LONDON:
JOHN W. PARKER, WEST STRAND.

M.DCCC.XLIV.

TABLE OF CONTENTS

TO

SIR ROBERT HARRY INGLIS, Bart. M.P.

&c. &c. &c.

My dear Sir Robert,

       It is with thankful satisfaction that I am again permitted to inscribe this work to you, as a very feeble testimony of respect and regard, and, I hope I may be permitted to add, of affection, sentiments which have been continually increasing throughout the long period, now exceeding a quarter of a century, during which I have been honoured by your steady and dependable friendship.

       Wearing, as you do, what has been termed the blue riband of literature, and so kindly interesting yourself in the fates and fortunes of its votaries, I do not doubt but that you sufficiently appreciate the reluctance with which the "trade" engage in any work purporting to consist of ancient documents, or relating to archæological inquiries, and, therefore, you will not be surprised at the difficulties I encountered, before I could persuade any bibliopolist, in or out of the Row, to undertake a production possessing such slender attractions. Cœlebs in search of a wife, had not nearly so much trouble as I have had, in search of a publisher; and no fair daughter of a Limehouse or Wapping millionaire ever experienced a greater number of rebuffs when trying to be introduced at Almack's, than Friar Bacon sustained in his attempts to be brought out into the reading world.

       In most cases the *declinals* were grounded upon reasons neither unkind nor uncomplimentary; for they were grounded upon the character acquired for me by my employments, of being a thorough-paced black-letter antiquary; and the sum of the objections was this. "We can only deal as men of business. Of all the "valuable publications included in the class of 'State Papers,' "Clarendon Papers, Sadler Papers, Marchmont Papers, Thurloe "Papers, Hardwick Papers, Losely Papers, Egerton Papers, Rutland

[v]

"Papers, did any, save the Pickwick Papers, ever enjoy the slightest
"share of public favour or popularity?—as to the rest, would any-
"body touch them with a pair of tongs, unless for the purpose of
"putting them behind the fire? Any work exhibiting much re-
"search and detail, extracted from obsolete chronicles and musty
"records, never will please the public. And in point of fact, the
"chance of success of any publication connected with history, is
"pretty nearly in an inverse proportion to the solid labour bestowed:
"the more flimsy the materials, the better the chance of sale.
"Certainly there are some splendid exceptions, so obvious that it
"is unnecessary to name them, yet, being only exceptions, proving
"the general rule, they are not sufficient to encourage further
"ventures in the same hazardous career."

It is obvious that the opinions enunciated in the preceding
paragraph, are not by any means applicable to the shape and
form assumed by the manuscripts of the monk of Croyland;
but I could not dispel these notions, and I had to encounter them
always as the motives of civil refusal, though occasionally modified by individual views, as the two following examples, taken
at hazard, will display.

But stop; how shall I designate my two selected personages
without a breach of professional confidence? Letters of the
alphabet are most exceptionable. *B.* or *C.*, or *L.* or *M.*, or any
others, may, by the cunning aid of the directory, be converted
into personalities; even *N.*, though standing for *Nobody*, would
hardly be safe in disclosures so delicate as these. Therefore
I will adopt the innocent nomenclature of the civil law, and
Titius and *Sempronius* shall serve my turn.

"I like some things which you have mentioned respecting the
"nature of the book," said Titius; "how big will it be?" "A small
"volume in duodecimo." "But with the ample matter which you
"have in your possession, could you not contrive to make three
"good-sized octavos?" "Quite impossible," quoth your humble servant, "the book, whether wise or foolish, has a definite plan and
"intention; it has a beginning, middle, and ending. The monk
"of Croyland, the original 'Toad in a Hole,' the author, whoever
"he may be, sketched the whole before he put in the details; and
"if it were to be extended, the merit (if any) which it may possess,
"would be quite destroyed by want of proportion. You might as
"well attempt to make a giant out of me, by interpolating a triple
"allowance of vertebræ in my neck and backbone." "Well then,"
replied Titius, taking out his pencil, "upon calculation, the thing

"won't pay. Everything is done by advertising in the newspapers:
"and it costs as much to advertise a book which sells for six shillings,
"as a book which will bear six-and-thirty, and therefore it will
"never suit me"; an honest declaration, by which I felt myself so
entirely put out of court, that all I could do was to retreat with
the utmost rapidity.

Sempronius was at first more gracious. He actually began
the work, when he took fright at some piece of antiquity exhibited therein; and he objected to proceed, unless I would add
explanatory notes, a proposition which, having fully made up
my mind upon the subject, I resolutely repudiated. "The work,"
said I, "is either a true history or a fiction. If it be a true
"history, notes will unnecessarily increase its bulk: for it really
"contains nothing but what is entirely intelligible to the ordinary
"reader, or which he can find explained in other books of common
"occurrence: and I think that the plan of making every thing
"'easy to the meanest capacity,' is as detrimental to the indi-
"vidual reader, as it is to the general cause of literature.

"On the other hand, if you were to consider the book as a
"work of fiction, then explanatory notes are ten times worse.
"Explanation at once extinguishes all illusion. Do you think it
"would be wise when the ecstasies, occasioned by the intellectual
"amusement of a *tableau vivant*, are at their height, to inform the
"welded mass of *haut ton*, or low *ton*—for whatever Belgrave
"Square does, instantly circulates to Finsbury—from whence Monna
"Lisa or the Chapeau de Paille borrowed each rag of their finery?
"What true admirer of the drama ever goes behind the scenes?
"Scott has exceedingly impaired the effect of his inimitable fictions,
"by the annotations appended to his last edition. Would that
"I could forget the unveiled 'Waverley,' in which every feature
"of Tully Veolan is, with such imprudent honesty, restored to its
"right owner, and the crude materials of a topographical dictionary
"forced upon me, for the purpose of compelling me to be convinced,
"against my will, that the Baron of Bradwardine and his manor-
"house are mere figments of the brain."

These and many similar arguments did I urge upon Sempronius, but without any success. Bookseller and author held dog-
gedly to their respective opinions; and as neither would yield,
several sheets of the work, which had been kept in type for nearly
a twelvemonth, were broken up, and the *Truths and Fictions of
the Middle Ages* returned to the repose of their portfolio.

Believe me, this abandonment of notes was a hard trial of

authorial principle. I have sacrificed both profit and pleasure. I should have liked much to have added my mite to the architectural antiquities of the middle ages, by informing my reader that such allegorical representations of the Law and the Gospel, the true Vine, and the Day of Judgment, as were seen in King Edward's council chamber, adorned the cathedral of Rochester, and the Liebfrauenkirche at Trèves, the cloisters of Norwich, the chapter house at York, and the stadthaus at Nimeguen. The rolls of parliament would have furnished me with a curious quotation, a peg whereupon to append the painting of Solomon and Marcolphus. The derivation of the German word "*Brillen*," or spectacles, from the ancient application of the lenses formed, or supposed to be formed, out of the beryl, suggested a dissertation upon the caprices of etymology, which it was painful to forgo. And the casual notice of the Chetham manuscript of Aquinas would, by levying due contributions from Aikin's *Manchester*, and Baines' *Lancashire*, and the charity commissioners' report, have given me good marketable stuff for half-a-dozen pages. Only think what I have lost by leaving out all the details how the Chetham Hospital was founded at Manchester by Humphrey Chetham, Esq., of Clayton Hall, near Manchester, and of Turton Tower, near Bolton, "whose memory is embalmed in "the grateful recollections of the people," and incorporated by Charles II. (by charter, in which the founder is styled, "our trusty "and well-beloved Humphrey Chetham"), for the maintenance of forty poor boys, out of the said town and parish of Manchester, to be taken in between six and ten years of age, and maintained with meat, drink, lodging, and clothes, till the age of fourteen, when they are to be bound apprentices to some honest trade or calling at the charge of the said Chetham Hospital; and how within the said hospital, and by the bounty of Mr. Chetham, is erected a very fine and spacious library (now containing upwards of nineteen thousand volumes); and how he settled one hundred and sixteen pounds a year on it for ever, to buy books, and support a librarian.

I can assure you that I shall be pounds out of pocket by my conscientious refusal, but so it is: and you have the work now before you as an *editio princeps*. Yet although note, explanation, and comment are rigidly excluded, you may, nevertheless, think it expedient I should briefly indicate the sources from which the *schedæ* of the monk of Croyland may be elucidated or confirmed.

May I venture to inform you that the portions of the monk's lucubrations relating to our parliamentary and legal constitution, receive ample illustrations from the several collections of original records and other ancient documents which I have edited. At least to this extent, that the narrations of the monk run on all fours, as lawyers say, with transactions of which we have more textual evidence; and, considering the losses which our historical records have sustained, that is surely as much as any reasonable archæologist could expect or desire.

Thus, for example, though when I collected the Parliamentary Writs, I did not discover the account of the escape of Sir Richard de Pogeys; I was, nevertheless, so fortunate as to find the return relating to the election of "Johannes de la Pole," who being elected to serve as knight of the shire for Oxford, 16 Ed. II., evaded the process by seeking the protection of the "four hundreds and a half "of Chiltern"; whilst his less fortunate colleague, Johannes de Harecourt, being within the grasp of the sheriff, was constrained to give good bail for his due appearance in parliament, in the persons of John Bokenore and John Bovetown.

In like manner an illegal return, exactly like that of Sir Marmaduke Vavasour, took place in Lancashire—for, as appears by the Rolls of the King's Bench, Michaelmas, 17 Edward II., the grand jury of West Derby wapentake indicted Willielmus le Gentil, the sheriff, "for that in the 14th Edward II., he had re-"turned Joseph de Haydock and Thomas de Thornton as knights "of the shire, without the assent of the county court, and had "levied twenty pounds for their expenses in attending the parlia-"ment at Westminster, going and returning; whereas the county "could, by their own election, have found two good and sufficient "men, who would have gone to parliament for ten marks or ten "pounds; and that the sheriff's bailiffs levied as much for their "own use as they had levied for the knights." A notable example of the ancient mode of parliamentary jobbery.

If the publication of my Parliamentary Writs had been continued, a work which would have afforded the materials for the whole history of the English constitution, the next volume would have contained the patent exempting the abbot of Oseney from parliamentary attendance. But you may, however, read the case of the abbot of Northampton, who with much trouble obtained an order from the chancery, that his name should be expunged from the register upon which the writs of summons issued: a proceeding which was carefully exemplified by his procurator, lest the malignant illwishers of the abbot or his successors, should ever procure him to be summoned again.

But were I to pursue this selection of parallel passages, I should probably try your patience, and certainly exhaust my own. Quoting one's own books is next worst to eating one's own words, and therefore, on this section, I shall say nothing more.

With respect to the chapter entitled "Guildhall," I must appeal to one of the blue books which are never read, as affording you a succinct, and, I believe, accurate view of the transactions noticed in the Croyland manuscripts. Perhaps you will not find the memorable judgments given by the court of aldermen, in the cases of Rex *v.* Romford, and Rex *v.* Lickpenny. I am, however, enabled to assure you, that in substance they are quite authentic: and if, when dining at Merchant Taylors' hall, you will take the trouble to tarry in your way at the town clerk's office, and request the truly learned serjeant who has the care of the archives, to produce the ancient register of the city, marked with the letter 𝕲, you may therein peruse the very records of two such trials. The names of the misdemeanants, however, are not the same as those given in my text, a variation which I am unwilling to attribute to any want of fidelity on the part of the monk of Croyland. I would rather ascribe it to a most praiseworthy forbearance. By disclosing the real names of the culprits, he might, without in any wise adding to the store of historical knowledge, have hurt the feelings of individuals connected with their families: an example worthy to be imitated in our times, in which a propensity to renovate ancient scandal for the purpose of gratifying malignant, or at least, idle curiosity, is but too frequently displayed.

When you pay such your visit to the civic muniment room, it will also be well worth your while to inspect the other volumes referred to by the monk of Croyland, or his editor. The volume entitled *Liber de Antiquis legibus*, contains an exceedingly valuable chronicle of the affairs of the city, with many notices of public transactions, and particularly relating to the civil or revolutionary wars between Henry III. and his barons. These annals appear to have been compiled contemporaneously with the events which they narrate. As far as my experience extends, this history is unique; for, whilst we have many monastic chronicles, we do not possess any similar *Fasti* of a lay community. The *Liber Horn*, compiled by Andrew Horn, the author of our ancient legal text-book, the *Mirror of Justices*, and also kept in the civic archives, is a collection of a miscellaneous nature. In addition to several exceedingly curious records relating to the history and privileges of the city, many authentic texts of ancient statutes are therein contained, constituting altogether a singular monument of the diligence and research of a mediæval antiquary.

In this same *Liber Horn* you will find the by-laws of the Painters' Gild, which, though bearing an earlier date than the ordinance made in the presence of Marco Polo, are interesting, as being exactly of the same import; and a portion thereof in the original Romance, but partially reduced into modern spelling, may be therefore compared with our text. "Sachent tous gens "qui cet écrit verront ou orront, que ceux sont les pourvoiances que "les prud'hommes peintres de la peinterie de Londres ont pourveu "l'an du Règne du Roi Edward que Dieu garde, fils du Roi Henri, "onzième, par assentement des bonnes gens du métier, et pour "amendement et relèvement du métier, et pour *fausives* (faussetés) "et toutes manières de guiles abattre * * *. Pourveu est, que "nul ne mette *fors* (hormis) bonnes et fines couleurs sur or ou "sur argent. C'est à savoir, bon azur, bon sinople, bon vert, "bon vermillon, ou des autres bonnes couleurs destemprés d'huile, "et niant de brasil, ne de inde de Baldas, ne de nul autre mauvaise "couleur." You will observe from this extract, that the metallic or body colours are to be tempered or mixed with oil, and not, as has been alleged, varnished with that fluid, and that they are put in opposition to the brasil-wood (the wood which gave its name to the Brazils in the New World) and the indigo probably used as water colours; and the last colour was called "*Indigo of Baldac,*" in consequence, as may be presumed, of its being exported from or manufactured at that Egyptian town. From other portions of those by-laws, it can be collected that the principal occupation of the guild consisted in painting heraldic bearings and ornaments. A bag of the Great Seal thus adorned is preserved in the ancient repository in the Chapter House: and a true and faithful lithographic representation thereof is prefixed to my publication of the Kalendar of Records[a], compiled in 1323 by my honoured predecessor, Walter Stapleton, Bishop of Exeter, late Lord High Treasurer of England, and who, as you well know, was the munificent founder of Exeter College in your University.

Should opportunity be given, I may hereafter enter into a full view of the study of physical science in the middle ages. On the present occasion it is sufficient to observe, that the general char-

---

[a] See *The Antient Kalendars and Inventories of the Treasury of his Majesty's Exchequer* (Record Comm.), I, p. cxlviii, plate v.

acter of the philosophy taught by Roger Bacon, has been given with singular felicity by our friend Foster, in his *Mahometanism Unveiled*. Bacon's printed works may also be consulted. They are neither high-priced, nor difficult of acquisition, and the references to the principal passages to which the Croyland manuscript alludes, will be easily found in the writers who have treated on Bacon's discoveries. Of these, the passages relating to the composition of gunpowder are very generally known; but it has, I believe, hitherto escaped observation, that there are two other very remarkable examples of the possession of the same recipe, towards the conclusion of the thirteenth, and the beginning of the fourteenth centuries, and as they only exist in manuscript, I shall place them textually before you.

Of Brother Ferrarius, "Frater Ferrarius," or "Efferarius," who flourished in the thirteenth century, we know little else except what appears by his designation, and that he is claimed as belonging to one of the northern provinces of the Spanish peninsula. He composed a treatise on alchemical science, in two sections, addressed to a pope whose name does not appear. It has been thrice published, first by Gratarolus, next by Lazarus Zetzner, and more completely by Combachius, all collectors of hermetical mysteries. This essay does not contain any matter worthy of particular notice; but another of the works of Ferrarius, an inedited epistle addressed to one Anselm, preserved or buried in the Bodleian, is of very great importance in the history of science. Purporting to be translated from the Arabic into Latin, it contains a selection of eighty-eight "experiments," detailed with great clearness. The manuscript appears to be of the age of Edward I. I think it is written by an English scribe; and it is possible that more exact or perfect copies may exist in continental libraries. Amongst these experiments are several recipes for making "Greek fire," and "flying fire," the second of which contains the mode of compounding the nitrate powder, composed of one part of sulphur, two of charcoal of the wood of the willow or lime-tree, and six of saltpetre, to be very finely ground upon marble or porphyry. And the writer then proceeds to describe minutely the pyrotechnic cases in which the powder is to be contained.

"Accipe partem unam, aut libram vel unciam sulphuris vivi,
"duas libras carbonum salicis sive tiliæ, et sex libras salis petrosi:
"tere subtilissime in lapide marmoreo vel porfirico. Postea pulvis
"ad libitum in tunicâ reponatur volatili vel tonitrum faciente.
"Notandum est quod tunica ad volandum longa debet esse et

"gracilis et prædicto pulvere optime conculcato repleta; tunica
"faciens tonitrum debet esse brevis et grossa, et prædicto pulvere
"semiplena et ab utraque extremitate filo fortissimo bene clausa.
"Et nota quod in qualibet tunica, foramen parvum faciendum est,
"ad hoc, quod *tenta* in illo reposita valeat illuminari; *tenta* vero in
"ambabus extremitatibus debet esse gracilis, in medio vero lata et
"prædicto pulvere bene repleta. Nota etiam quod duplex poteris
"facere tonitrum ac duplex volatile instrumentum, videlicet, tuni-
"cam subtiliter in tunica recludendo." It is hardly necessary to
observe, that the word "*tenta*," here used for the small roll containing the priming, is yet retained in our common chirurgical
nomenclature.

Another of these recipes for an explosive powder, in the proportions of eight parts of saltpetre, two of sulphur, and one of
charcoal, is found in a manuscript once forming part of the Spelman
Collection, and now possessed by Hudson Gurney, Esquire. "De
"mixtione pulveris ad faciendum le Crake. Primo accipe quanti-
"tatem quantum volueris de salpetro, et pondera eam per quatuor
"partes equales. Deinde accipe unam partem ex illis, et contra
"illam, pondera sulfurem vivum. Deinde divide ipsum sulfurem
"vivum in duas partes, et contra unam partem ex illis duobus,
"pondera carbones de salice. Omnibus istis aggregatis, fiat pulvis";
le *Crake* is evidently a *cracker*, nothing less nor more. The hand-
writing of the Spelman recipe is either of the close of the reign
of Edward I. or of the very beginning of that of his successor;
and it is not unimportant to remark, that instead of being inserted
in a regular treatise, it stands in a page of collectanea—traditional
rhymes and proverbial sayings—and, in all probability, is much
older than the era when it was thus jotted down.

The treatise of Ferrarius, as I have observed above, contains
many recipes for the Greek fire; but the compositions which he
gives, all designated by the same name, are much diversified in
nature and quality. Some of them, into which naphtha, resin,
and similar materials enter largely, appear to have been used as
projectiles; others are explosive, one of them being simply composed of twenty parts of saltpetre, eight of sulphur, and five of
charcoal.

Hindostan seems to have produced the invention of the
"nitrate powder," but it remains to be ascertained to which of the
races who have peopled her soil, the discovery belongs. Thence
it was acquired, either primarily or derivatively, by the Chinese,
the Tartar, the Arab, and the Greek, all distinguished, either by

mental acuteness or by warlike spirit, or by both these qualities. And if any one of these nations had been permitted by Providence to use the simple process of converting the powder into the grain, the people so acquiring the knowledge, would have obtained exactly the same predominance in the middle ages, which the modern European now exercises over the rest of mankind.

.   .   .   .   .

The preceding observations were in substance addressed to you when I first had the honour of placing the book under the patronage and recommendation of your name.   Some corrections have been introduced, and I have endeavoured that the monk of Croyland should preserve his identity.   Yet, if I were asked the question, I should have some difficulty in ascertaining the precise point where the Merchant and the Friar dissolve into air, and are succeeded by the individual, who, with the most sincere wishes for your happiness, bids you, for the present, farewell.

FRANCIS PALGRAVE.

April 4, 1844.

CHAPTER I.

THE REFECTORY.

IN the present age, when locomotion has been so wonderfully facilitated, and the means of communicating, not only between the various districts of the same country, but even to and from the most distant regions, are so greatly multiplied, we scarcely understand how we should feel or be circumstanced, were we to lose those connecting links of human society, the rail-road and the steam-boat, the chaise, the stage, the diligence, and the mail. Many of these arose but yesterday. The very oldest are of recent origin, hardly known to our grandsires. Yet, a considerable mental effort is required before we can fix our attention upon our ancient English policy, so as to obtain a definite idea of the scanty share of foreign intelligence, which, in the early part of the fourteenth century, and according to ordinary haps and chances, reached an inland town. Destitute of newspapers and post-offices, even bad news could not fly apace. Fame had no wings when she was compelled to limp with her dispatches through primitive ruts and patriarchal bridle-paths: or hobble, all bemired, upon the rugged ridges of Fosse, Watling Street, Ikenild Street, or Irmin Street, and the other renowned highways,

> That the old kyngs made, where thorough men may wend,
> From the one end of England until the other end,

and which continued, without much alteration, as the main lines of transit through our island.

With the exception of the concise and jejune letters, which passed amongst official functionaries upon matters of great importance, or were extorted, as it were, by urgent necessity, epistolary correspondence can hardly be said to have existed. Various causes concurred in producing this effect. So few persons among the laity, with the exception, perhaps, of the mercantile classes and the legists, were acquainted with the alphabet, that reading and writing itself acquired the name of "clergy." The term "clerk" became equivalent to "penman": our common nomenclature still bears testimony to the lack-learning of ancient times.

A singular prejudice prevailed against the use of our vernacular Teutonic dialect, in any composition which was to possess a character of gentility. Amongst the higher classes, the English, considered as a written language, was wholly banished from the business of common life. If a Northumbrian baron wished to inform his spouse in Yorkshire of his joys or his sorrows, his weal or his woe, the message, noted down from "Romance" into Latin by the chaplain of the knight, was read from Latin into "Romance" by the chaplain of the lady; both the principals being equally unable to indite the missive in which their anxieties and sentiments were clothed or concealed.

Latin and French were alone employed by those who had any claim to distinction. The language of the church had an inherent dignity. The dialect of the north of the Loire was the speech of the tale, the lay, and the satire of the trouveur. Introduced into England, not, as is usually supposed, by the power of the Conqueror, but by the gentle influence of Adeliza of Louvain, it was the language of fashion, the token of good breeding. As in the courts of Berlin or Petersburg, the native speech appeared far too rough for any well-educated tongue. That all the higher or wealthier, or learned or *pretending*, orders of society should avoid using the language of the *roturier*, the *rupturarius*, the churl who broke and tilled the soil, was a necessary consequence of this pride of station. Pride knows no pain: thus were they reconciled to the inconveniences, and even dangers, to which they were exposed by the intervention of a dragoman, who encumbered every transaction, and to whom every secret was necessarily revealed.

But our catalogue of the difficulties attending correspondence in the "early part of the fourteenth century" is by no means concluded. Tedious as the detail may be, you, reader, must listen with patience to the overture, before I raise the curtain, and allow the performance to begin.

Had the knowledge of letters been much more common, still, the want of any convenient and portable writing material would have imposed a very great check upon epistolary communication. The manufacture of papyrus had lingered long subsequently to the fall of the Roman empire: but after the use of the Egyptian reed was abandoned, a considerable interval elapsed before it was replaced, at least in the northern parts of Europe, by cotton or linen paper. Instead of taking an ample sheet from the quires contained in your well-stored desk, or portfolio, you would have

been enforced to compress your missive within the scanty bounds
of the strip of solid vellum, the fragment perhaps of some ancient
tome, from which the learning of Varro, the obscenities of Martial,
or the wit of Terence, had been effaced : or the shred or remnant,
carefully preserved, of the membrane previously used for the
engrossment of some charter.

Well, reader, do you expect that I am now going to begin
my story? By no means. *Soyez tranquil.* Have patience, more
patience : the personages are all ready upon the stage, but they
shall not yet be brought before you.

Suppose the letter completed, the parchment carefully folded,
encompassed with silken bands, and sealed with the mastic seal
which covered three-fourths of its surface : how was this same
letter to be dispatched? Instead of availing yourself of the
certain cycle of the post, regular in departure as the recurring eve,
and true in its arrival as the morning sun, you were compelled
either to transmit your letter by a special messenger, or to intrust
it to any individual who chanced to travel towards the place of
address, the abbot repairing to the general chapter or provincial
synod, the knight returning to his castle, the merchant prosecuting
his dealings, the priest soliciting his benefice; any person who,
for love or money, might be induced to take the letter in his charge.
Slow and tardy were the modes of communication so expensively
and irregularly obtained. Upon the best estafetted road, the
road to Rome, nearly three months necessarily elapsed, before
the pilgrim, quitting the shrine of Saint Thomas at Canterbury,
could reach the sepulchre of the apostle.

Thus much for ancient correspondence : but my story cannot
yet begin. Patience, reader, you must submit to another delay :
I cannot yet show you the scene, the "inland town" noticed, but
not named, in my first paragraph, until you are fully aware how
little cosmographical information was possessed by its residents.

Amongst the many remarkable facts teaching us the great
lesson, that there is no self-impelling power in human knowledge,
we may reckon the incapacity of the Greeks or Romans to produce
a neat or intelligible map or chart. Hands guiding the chisel
which could invest the marble with the most consummate beauty,
the taste and skill which planned and executed the most symme-
trical and sumptuous edifices, enabled them not to execute this
easy task. The deficiency was not the result of ignorance. Patient
observation supplied the place of those instruments which aid
the modern astronomer. In the tables constructed by Ptolemy,

we can, even now, distinguish the principal capes and bays in our British islands: and the lines and circles which connect and divide the earth and the heavens have been transmitted to us from the classical age. Yet the idea, apparently so obvious, of marking the points of latitude and longitude upon the *pinax*, with proportionate accuracy, and in their proper position within the degrees, and zones, and parallels of the globe, never occurred to the countrymen of Euclid and Archimedes. To speak more reverently and truly, such an idea was never permitted to occur to them; and their geographical delineations were as slovenly and rude as those of the Hindoos of the present day.

The geographical knowledge of the middle ages, so far as it could be collected from books, consisted in little else than scanty extracts from the meagre pages of Pliny and Solinus. But, had the inhabitants of our old English "inland town" possessed much more perfect descriptions of the world, there are some most important branches of information, concerning which no language, however clear and accurate, can convey a precise notion. Words never can impart a definite idea of shape, of form, of relative position, and relative size.

The terrestrial sphere, as portrayed in the "early part of the fourteenth century," consists of a circular projection, in the exact centre of which appears Jerusalem, the Temple being likewise represented in the exact centre of the Holy City, bearing about the same proportion to the ambient world, that the axle does to the felly of the cart-wheel. On the outermost verge is the flowing ocean, surrounding, with Homeric accuracy, the whole domicile of mankind. The regions more familiarly known, "Normannia," "Pictavia," "Gallicia," "Arragonia," "Lombardia," "Tuscia," "Apulia," and the like, are pointed out by towers and castles, bearing the emblazoned banners of their sovereigns. You will not, however, be enabled to discern the collective names, equally strange to the politics as to the geography of the middle ages, of a France, extending from the Channel to the Mediterranean, or Germany, Italy, or Spain. Beyond the countries on the verge of Christendom, nought is found but camels and ostriches, elephants and tigers, manticoras and hippocentaurs, whose representations, by covering the unknown regions in which they are placed, amuse the spectator, and excuse the ignorance of the artist.

The lucid idea which an accurate map pours at one view into the mind, through the medium of the eye, was thus wholly wanting; when the best instructed individual attempted to fix his thoughts upon foreign parts, they wandered in vagueness and uncertainty.

The form and position of the various portions of the globe, the shape of the continent, the outline of the gulf, the boundary of the kingdom, the locality of the city, the course of the river, the bearing of the mountain,—now familiar almost to the child in the nursery, were then all enveloped in mystery, darkness, and confusion.

The distant regions of Asia, the primeval seats of the human race, always objects of curiosity and interest, were, about the period to which our legend relates, the sources of great, and by no means ill-founded, anxiety. Europe had been repeatedly desolated, in earlier ages, by the barbaric tribes, the Alans, the Huns, the Vandals, who, pouring down from Caucasus, spread themselves like a devouring flood over its devastated realms. These hosts had passed away. Alans and Vandals are blotted out from the nations. The rocky sepulchre was pointed out by the Saxon peasant as the resting-place of the Hun; and the cottage-mother in Champagne scared or amused her babe by the tale of the devouring ogre. Such traditions are the only memorials of Attila's deeds in Germany and in Gaul: whilst in Hungary, the descendants of the fierce opponents of Charlemagne settled into a flourishing Christian kingdom, retaining somewhat of Asiatic splendour.

But now, all the earlier terrors were renewed. Wider in extent than any dominion which had yet existed on the face of the globe, the empire of the Monguls and their kindred, extended from the Danube to the Pacific Ocean, from the sunny banks of the Tigris to the icy cliffs of the Lena. The Tartar shaft appeared to sway the destinies of every race and country: the Arab yielded to a fiercer nomad: the proud czars of Muscovy ruled only as tributaries to the "Golden Horde": the Mahometan emir, the Palatine of Poland, and the Sclavonian boyard, all owned the supremacy of the khan: and the most ancient and most opulent empire then existing, Cathay, or China, had become the spoil of the haughty Kublai, the lord of lords, and king of kings. Vast as the territories were which the Tartars had subjugated, their acquisitions were, according to their own boast, only the basis of greater victories. Universal empire was claimed by them: they avowed their purpose of extinguishing all other dominions, which, as they asserted, continued only to exist by their forbearance and mercy.

Reading the lessons of experience, taking the past as affording the means of calculating the probabilities of the future, the least timorous and most reflecting might well anticipate, that the threats of these barbarians would be fulfilled.   There appeared to be scarcely a hope of averting the ruin of the European common-wealth.

The greater portion of the Tartar tribes professed a singular species of Pantheism, respecting all creeds, attached to none. Kublai not only tolerated, but supported and encouraged, the worship of the Jew, the Christian, the Mahometan, and the Hindoo.   Other of the Tartar khans and sultans were the children of Georgian or Armenian mothers; their liberality, their prepos-sessions, or their indifference, seemed to afford a hope that they might be induced to become converts to Christianity, and thus to sheathe the sword which they had drawn.   Hence, various missions of monks and friars had been dispatched across the Tanais, and beyond the Volga; some by the papal see, and others by Saint Louis.   If their accounts were to be credited, there was reason to hope that their endeavours would be successful.   This belief was further supported by the arrival from time to time of various Tartar legations: in particular, a brace of grim, shaggy, swarthy personages, calling themselves ambassadors from a khan, had even presented themselves at the council of the church at Lyons, and subsequently at the court of the French king.

It is true, that shrewd suspicions were entertained respecting the credentials of these well-furred and awful plenipotentiaries. But the same prudent reasons which induced the citizen-legis-lators of the National Convention to avoid any very rigid scrutiny into the birth and parentage of the "députés du genre humain," when Anacharsis Clootz conducted them to the bar of that august assembly, probably operated equally upon the ministry of Philip the Bold.   The mumming, as many supposed it to be, was allowed to produce its full effects upon the public mind.   At such a juncture, it may easily be understood how great a sensation, to use the modern term, would be excited in the abbey of Abingdon, when its inmates were informed by the sacristan, that a party of travellers from Cathay had just arrived at the town.

Kindness and liberality, no less than curiosity, instantly de-termined the abbot to request that the wayfarers would partake of the conventual hospitality; and the message was courteously conveyed by the sacristan to the Saracen's Head, where the strangers had alighted, though not to rest or repose.   He found them in the yard, where they were absolutely beset by townsmen, townswomen, and townschildren : some diligently comparing the countenance of the chief personage of the group with the sign, and conjecturing, from the strong resemblance between him and the bearded effigy, that he was a spy from Bagdad; others listening with eager anxiety to the discourse of the strangers amongst themselves; others touching their soft silken garments. Meanwhile, the junior population of Abingdon, found ample delight and amusement in scrambling for the dates, almonds, and pistachio-nuts, which the good-humoured foreigners dispersed with a ready hand.

Thus circumstanced, the abbot's invitation was readily accepted by the strangers, who were most happy to escape from the noise and throng of the hostelry. In half an hour, therefore, the whole party, masters and serving-men, valets and varlets, sumpter-mules and saddle-horses, reached their new quarters. And, neither last nor least in the sight and estimation of the bystanders, their sacks, manteaux, and valises, secured with many a bright steel lock, and tightly bound by many a whang and thong deeply indenting their bulging sides, were safely deposited within the precincts of the abbey.

"Welcome, sirs"; exclaimed the abbot, as he advanced to the pilgrims when they ascended the dais of the refectory; "and what is the last best news from Benamarin and Garbo? We are anxious to learn some fresh intelligence, for, as appears by our chronicle sheet which hangs in the refectory, we have had none since just about the battle of Evesham, when we heard how king Muley Almanzor had been discomfited by the Miramamolin. How stand matters at Constantine-noble? And how are the affairs of the Emperor Alexis and his Griffons going on?"

"We have one of their eggs, set in silver, in our garderobe"; exclaimed John Vinesaulf, the cellarer; "please your seignories, as soon as dinner is served up, it will be filled for each and every of you, with the best wine of Gascony."

"Hold your peace, you ignorant dolt," replied the abbot, zealous for the credit of the intellectual cultivation of his establishment; "ye ought to be soundly whipped at our grammar-school: the Griffons, of whom I speak, are not beasts, but human creatures—*Greeks*, you jackanapes, who are called *Griffons* wherever Romance is spoken. As for our griffon's egg, it is, in truth, a rare curiosity. We purchased it for twenty marks from Leo the Erminian merchant, a trusty and honest man, not a pestilent

schismatic like the Syrians, who took it out of the nest at the
peril of his life, for, had he not escaped before the return of the
griffoness—and he had just time to escape—she would have torn
him asunder.   When we first had it, Sirs, this griffon's egg was
covered with coarse brown hair, exactly of the colour of the parent
bird, as ye may see her portrayed from the life in the *Speculum
Naturale* of Master Vincent of Beauvais; but when we sawed
it asunder, different from all other eggs, it lacked a yolk.   Your
griffon's egg is hollow, the centre being partly filled with a milky
fluid, whilst the white of the egg, which adheres closely to the
shell, is sweeter than the almond."

The worthy abbot's dissertation upon the griffon's egg, was
interrupted by that pilgrim who was evidently the leader of the
party.   So much was his complexion darkened by the sun, that
observers, who, like those in the inn-yard, were little accustomed
to the varieties of the human species, might readily have supposed
him to be a Moor.   But to those of greater experience—and
the abbot was more conversant with outlandish strangers—his
regular features, and a few shades of auburn, still visible amongst
his grey hairs, betrayed his European origin.   This person had
been listening, with much smiling deference, to the account of
the griffon's egg.   And as the abbot, by displaying his own sound
information and correct knowledge of zoology, had nearly worked
off his anger and shame at the cellarer's ignorance, the pilgrim
completed the amnesty by complimenting the abbot upon his
learning, adding, "Your reverence need not be much surprised at
the error of good Master Vinesaulf, since in my own country
there are many, I believe, who might be apt to suppose that the
'Gran Cane' of the Tartars, from whose empire I have lately
returned, is really and truly a hound: not in his avowed and
acknowledged quality of a heathen, but as being actually the
animal designated by the word into which his title of 'Chagan'
—for this, please your worships, is the real term in the Mongul
language—is corrupted in our vulgar tongue."

The appearance of the reader in the pulpit, which jutted
forth from the wall of the refectory, gave notice to the company
that the meal was about to begin.   The servitors, lay-brethren
of the monastery, advanced, bearing the dishes, and chanting
an anthem: grace was followed by the recitation of an homily
repeated by the monk first mentioned, and to whom this task
was assigned.   In some of the persons present, such devotional
exercises may have become only an habitual form: but even at the

risk of degenerating into a ceremony, the practice of invoking the blessing of the Giver of all good before we partake of His bounty, is infinitely preferable to the usage of shrinking from the mention of His holy name.

The pilgrim's acknowledgment, that he had actually been received at the court of Kublai Khan, rendered him what in common parlance is termed the "lion" of the party, and innumerable were the questions, discreet and indiscreet, wise and foolish, with which he was assailed. Not only had he explored the continent of Asia, but he had also visited many of the islands of the Indian seas; and though the frank acknowledgment that he had never conversed with men whose heads grew beneath their shoulders, was evidently a balk, creating a certain degree of disappointment, still the circumstance of his having really been amongst the Anthropophagi in Sumatra, was considered almost as a full compensation by the greater part of the auditory. Few topics, however, excited more attention, than the pilgrim's description of the genial temperature and the luxuriant productions of "Ynde la Majeure." A country in which ginger, that high-prized, rare, and valued delicacy, seen only on the tables of the great, actually grew in the very fields, seemed as an earthly paradise. Still more delight was excited by the accounts of perpetual spring; trees constantly covered by foliage; gardens never destitute of fruit; the earth clad with perennial flowers.

"Your tale, sir pilgrim," said the abbot; "reminds me of a marvellous matter which occurred not long since at Cologne. I have it from the best authority, from Guillemart le Losengier, the minstrel of Lisle, one of the best trouveurs north of the Loire. Ye all have heard of Albert the Great, he to whom every secret of art and nature was unfolded."

"Well did I know him," answered a Grey friar, who had hitherto continued silent, having employed himself wholly in listening with steady attention to the discourse. "Albert wrote so many books, that it was said he might have been burnt on a pile composed solely of his own works."

"Would that he had been so consumed for a vile necromancer!" exclaimed a portly personage, whose scarlet hood denoted his Oxford degree, and who, in fact, was Master Nicholas de Marnham, the vice-chancellor of the university. "It is high time," continued he, addressing the friar with bitter asperity, "that my lord of Canterbury should take cognizance of those caitiffs, who, protecting themselves by the habit of St. Francis"; pronouncing these last words with much emphasis, and pointing at the friar's cowl; "act as traitors under this disguise; and with the specious excuse of pursuing the study of philosophy, practise the accursed arts of magic. Recreants, pretending to employ their knowledge for the benefit of the church, and proposing what they call a reformation; a reformation, forsooth, a deformation, in fact, which will lead to the destruction of the faith and the ruin of the hierarchy."

"Think not, that I flinch from the charge of professing myself a reformer," replied the friar, with great energy. "In my letter to the Holy Father, I have boldly shown, it is true, that a reformation is imperatively needed; but of what? why, of the calendar! By following the rules of computation now erroneously observed in the church of England, we place the equinox about eight days after the real time, in consequence of which mistake we frequently celebrate the Paschal festival, when the proper period has long since passed away. Why and how do I advocate the correction of this error, introduced by ignorance, and continued—shall I say venerated?—by obstinacy and sloth? Assuredly it is the spirit of the observance which sanctifies the commemoration of our Lord's resurrection, and not the astronomical precision of the hour. But, sirs, ye know that we profess to keep our Easter on the full moon next after the vernal equinox: we maintain that we are in the right, when we are absolutely in the wrong.

"I believe the point to be entirely indifferent; but we render it of vital importance by our pertinacity in attempting to advocate that which cannot be supported. Though the matter be not worth contention, we ruin our clerical character by fighting for the wrong side of the question. By our miscalculations, we, Christians, expose ourselves to the ridicule of the infidel philosophers: whilst it is our bounden duty to employ, in advancing the doctrine of the Gospel, all the talents which the Lord has bestowed upon us. Jew, Moor, Saracen, all scoff at our inveterate stolidity. Opening Albumasar, they convict us beyond the possibility of escape. We cannot, if we wished to do so, keep this knowledge from our flock; and when they become aware of our obstinacy, they will deride us, and extend that derision to the doctrines which we all, I trust and believe, equally and earnestly desire to defend. It is for the purpose of protecting the faith against scoffers, as I have fully explained in my letter to the pope, that I am so anxious to stop the cavils of our common enemies. Let us defeat them by their own weapons upon their own ground."

The vice-chancellor, whose naturally, or, to speak more correctly, not naturally rubicund countenance, had acquired a more intense glow from anger, now stood up, and, doubling his fist at his antagonist, was preparing to reply. But the pilgrim, who had exchanged a whisper with the friar, interposed, and stating that he was desirous of hearing more concerning Albertus Magnus, expressed a wish that the abbot would resume the tale which had been interrupted by this most unhappy controversy.

"Were I the mayor of Oxford, master vice-chancellor," quoth the abbot, making a sign at the same time to the cellarer, "despite of your privileges, your maces, and your charters, I would give you a syllogism in Bocardo, which should cool you in the gate-house, with bolts at your heels for a month. It is a shame thus to disturb good fellowship: but a truce to quarrels, you shall be excused if you empty the egg before it passes to his seignory"; (the vice-chancellor purchased his pardon by hardly leaving the stain of the wine in the cup). "And now for our minstrel's story.

"When the emperor came to Cologne, Albertus, with great humility, prayed the honour of his company, promising to entertain the whole imperial retinue to the best of his poor means. Much did they expect from Albert's lore, nor were they disappointed. Every chamber exhibited new marvels. The first contained a costly cabinet filled with precious stones of mystic virtue. Here was the hæmatite, which stanches the welling gore, the many-coloured cameo, which alleviates the pains of child-birth, the beryl, which restores sight to the blind. Though young, the vision of the emperor is most imperfect: were a choir-book, written in the largest text, open before him on the desk, he could scarcely read a word. He could not distinguish the features of his empress, were she sitting on the other side of this table.

"Albertus gave the beryl to the emperor, and desired him to apply it to his eye; how surprising was the effect produced by the occult power! The clouds which dimmed his sight were instantly dispelled; and, whilst he gazed through the wondrous gem, every object appeared distinct, clear, and bright as the day."

"Was the shape of the beryl described to you by the minstrel?" inquired the friar with some eagerness.

"Yes, and accurately, for he was allowed to take the gem in his hand. It was circular, and slightly hollowed on both sides—

so slightly, that the spherical concavity was scarcely perceptible to the touch. But of course, the shape was merely an accident, of no importance whatever. The assistance which the beryl affords to the sight, arises wholly from the occult power, the essential virtue of the stone; is it not so, friar?"

The friar did not answer the question, he gave no opinion upon the subject; he merely observed, "Brother Albert is an apt scholar, and I conjecture that the treatise *De Perspectiva*, written not long since by a certain brother of our order, who shall be nameless, has reached his study. On this occasion, your friend the minstrel hath refrained from poetic inventions; but pray proceed with your story."

"In the next chamber," continued the abbot, "were contrivances surpassing the skill of the fabled Dædalus. An eagle of brass flew down from the portal, and placed a crown on the head of the emperor. The imperial bird then soared again to the place whence it had descended. And a bee, formed wholly of steel, made three circles in the air round the company, buzzing all the while, and then alighted upon the emperor's hand."

"A story loses nothing in telling," said the friar with a slight smile, "especially if it pass through the mouth of a poet, a minstrel ballad-monger. I learned from one of our brethren, who afterwards visited the learned Albert, that the brazen eagle merely flapped its wings upon its perch, whilst the bee of steel, instead of describing three circles in the air, span three times round a silver salver."

The abbot, much as he evidently respected the friar, could not brook the contradiction. He was crossed and vexed by these corrections. Guillemart le Losengier, a good man and true, as he did not scruple to say, once affirmed that he had seen the flight of the eagle and of the bee with his own eyes.

In a lower voice, approaching to a whisper, the abbot made further remark, addressed to his immediate neighbours. Something might be heard about scientific envy and rivalry, and that the same spirit of detraction which induced the mere workman to carp at his rival in trade, was equally prevalent among philosophers, who, devoted to higher pursuits, should learn the practical lesson of restraining such ignoble feelings. Little as the friar really deserved such a reproof, he felt that, by endeavouring to put his host in the right, he had put himself in the wrong. The good folks who surrounded the table loved a marvel; in other words, they loved their own opinions, they were provoked at being undeceived. The friar made no reply, and the abbot continued his tale.

"At the end of the second chamber was a small door; opened slowly and cautiously by Albertus, it discovered a low passage of rather considerable length, into which he introduced the emperor and the imperial retinue. The door was then closed, and Albertus informed them that their entertainment would be heightened if they would submit to be blindfolded, with which request they willingly complied. The door was heard to open. Each, with his eyes covered by a kerchief, paced along, directed, gently and carefully, by the hand and voice of their host, the emperor taking the lead, and they felt that a very few footsteps had conducted them out of the gallery. But when, at the command of Albertus, they simultaneously removed the coverings from their eyes, they ascertained, to their inexpressible astonishment, that these few footsteps had conveyed them at once to such a climate as you, sir pilgrim, were only enabled to reach by a toilsome journey of months, perhaps of years.

"Without, the cold of the season was so intense, that the mighty Rhine was fettered by the frost, and laden wagons could cross from shore to shore. Yet, what did the spectators behold? Above and around them hung the grape in the most luxuriant clusters. Tuscany never produced such a vintage. The clear and translucent fruit of these enchanted vines, possessed a beauty which nature never could bestow. On either side of the path which led through the bower, grew the fairest flowers of the summer, the rose, the honeysuckle, the jasmine, in the brightest bloom, and diffusing the sweetest odours through an atmosphere pervaded by genial and dewy warmth, and reposing in undisturbed tranquillity."

"And what took place next?" quoth the pilgrim.

"A right merry jest. The magician—I beg pardon, brother Roger—the friar, now gave to the emperor, and to each of his nobles, a golden knife, and directed each man to choose himself a bunch of grapes, but to be very careful not to cut the bunch till he gave the signal. The emperor selected his bunch, so did the Duke of Brunswick, the Count Palatine of the Rhine, and all the rest; and then lifting up their hands, they only awaited the word of command before they should sever the clusters from the parent stems. Albertus struck the ground with his wand—the charm was dispelled—and the emperor and all the company perceived that, under the influence of the magical delusion, each, thinking that he held a bunch of grapes, had, in fact, seized his own nose, which he infallibly would have amputated without mercy, had not the glamour been dispelled."

At this conclusion of the tale, all the guests laughed aloud, and expressed equal credence and delight. The friar did not join in the merriment, though he was evidently amused; from the cast of his countenance, you might see that the words were on the tip of his tongue; but, warned by the rebuff which he had before experienced, he compressed his thin lips and held his peace.

"Albert did good service to the emperor by supplying his treasury," resumed the Abbot. "Frederick sent him the vesper-bell which hung in the chapel at the imperial palace of Geln-hausen, and Albert returned an equal weight in gold."

"I have seen a far greater marvel in Cathay," replied the pilgrim, "for my lord and master—I honour him still as such—Kublai Khan, with more than chemical skill, can turn paper into gold at his sovereign will and pleasure."

"Paper turned into gold!" was the universal exclamation of the company, the friar himself appearing to participate in the general surprise.

"Yea; paper turned into gold. Throughout the vast dominions of Kublai Khan, the currency consists, almost wholly, of paper-money. The paper, used in Cathay, is made from the bark of the mulberry-tree. This paper is cut into pieces of a convenient size. Each piece is in the shape of a parallelogram, rectangular, but longer than it is wide; and, on such paper, by means of small slabs of wood, upon which certain lines and characters are carved and covered with a pigment, they print an impression of the same characters, each expressing a word.

"The coinage, if I may so call the process by which the paper-money acquires its value, is performed with much precaution and ceremony. Certain officers, appointed for that purpose, subscribe their names and affix their signets; lastly, the principal functionary, who is especially deputed by the khan, adds a stamp, expressing his name and titles, and which, dipped into vermilion, leaves his mark. This process authenticates the document; and it passes throughout the whole empire. But I might have spared you this lengthened description, by bringing the object before your eyes, for I have a piece of paper-money about me.

"Here," continued the pilgrim, opening a splendid purse of yellow silk, upon which was expanded the five-clawed dragon, "is a specimen of Kublai's money. The piece of paper, which I hold

in my hand, will be received in any part or province of Cathay
for ten bezaunts. There are others of lower denominations, the
smallest being equal to a groat sterling."

"The characters printed or impressed upon the face of the
paper are numerous," said the friar. "The leaf might, in fact, be
a page of a book."

"Ay, and a very important page," replied the pilgrim, "for
these columns of characters contain a chapter extracted from the
criminal code of Cathay, an edict enacted by Kublai, declaring
that the offender who counterfeits the note is to be punished by
death."

"But the value of this paper-money is merely ideal. Can
such a rag be accepted even by those heathen infidels, those
ignorant votaries of Mahommed and Tarmagaunt, as readily as
gold or silver durable metals of intrinsic value? What use would
it be to my lord the king, if, upon my return to the treasury at
Westminster, I were, instead of emptying the bag of sterlings
on the chequered cloth before the chancellor, to present him with
a handful of paper leaves, saying, 'My lord, here are the proceeds of the tallage of the county of Berks for the service of his
royal excellency.' In good troth, the staff of the usher would
soon come in contact with my shoulders." Thus spake a lean-
visaged, crabbed-looking personage, who sat at the upper end of
the table, and who was treated by the abbot, as well as by the
mayor of the borough, in such a manner as to show that they were
equally anxious to display their deference and to conceal their
antipathy.

"You shall be satisfied, friend," answered the pilgrim. "The
note is virtually money, for it buys money's worth, as readily as
the purest coin. Every individual within the dominions of Kublai
receives the khan's paper-money without the slightest hesitation
or difficulty. Whatever merchandise you need, can be purchased
by Kublai's tokens, which on all occasions represent the sums
denoted by them. Nobody will ever turn them away. The
vendor never doubts their worth. You may, by this paper, obtain
the most valuable articles: pearls, rubies, gems of every sort, or
the precious metals themselves, gold and silver, if you require
them; but for the latter, it is more usual to apply at Kublai's
mint, where you may receive the value of your note in bullion.
The fact, however, is, that Kublai's paper-money is worth somewhat more than gold. If these notes become damaged by use,
and you will observe that the paper upon which the characters

are printed is very thin, the holder carries them to the mint, where, upon payment of what, in my own country, merchants call an agio, after the rate of three in the hundred, he receives new notes in exchange : and, on account of the greater convenience of the paper, this slight premium is willingly paid."

"Very different from your Exchequer tallies, Master Griffe-de-Loup," exclaimed John Goodchilde, the mayor of the borough. "In payment for five good bales of broadcloth, twenty quintals of wax, fifty fat hogs, and one hundred barrels of ale, supplied to our sovereign lord the king, for the use of his household, and amounting to fourscore marks, I received forty sticks prettily notched, which, as I was told, would be duly exchanged for the amount in sterling silver, next quarter. But pay-day at the Exchequer stands next in the calendar to Christmas-come-never. When I went to Westminster, I was informed that the exchequer had removed to York. After a troublesome journey to York, I found it had travelled to Carlisle. At last, after a desperate hunt, I caught my lord treasurer at Gloucester. But I made more haste than good speed."

"Was the Exchequer shut ? "

"No ; it was open, and so was the money-chest ; for just before I arrived, the last forty-shillings that remained had been extracted by my friend, Griffe-de-Loup, in payment of his quarter's salary. Woe is me !—I have been fain to sell my tallies to Haquin, the Jew, for one-half of the debt which they professed to secure. Would that King Edward's tallies could be converted into Kublai Khan's soft paper ! "

"Master John," retorted Griffe-de-Loup, somewhat nettled at this disclosure of secrets of state, "you have forgotten to say how wisely and discreetly you provided against any contingency of loss. A yard-wand reckoned as an ell, short weight, scanty measure, the delivery of an article which no chapman but the king's purveyor would have bought, and a higher price than any chapman except the king would have offered, will all leave a handsome profit out of the eight hundred clipped groats which Haquin has paid to you."

"I will not speak a word which may tend to the dishonour of his grace the king, or to the discredit of my brother merchant, for I am also a trader," said the pilgrim. "Yet, be it known, that honesty is always the best policy. If the king cheats the dealer, the dealer will cheat the king. It is not so in Cathay. Should Kublai detect the slightest fraud, a hundred strokes of the bamboo, at the very least, will leave a lasting impression upon the offender. My worthy and suffering friend, Hi-Ho, the richest Hong merchant of Nankin, was unable to sit on his chair, with any kind of comfort, during a whole twelvemonth, after the paternal chastisement bestowed upon him in consequence of the bad quality of a single pekul of pepper, which, as Poo-Puh, the master-cook, affirmed, did not make him cough more than six times when he opened the package: it ought to have made him cough seven. Kublai only demands from others that probity of which he sets the example. The fact is, that the value of Kublai's paper is based wholly upon good faith. Kublai's honour as well as his interest would prevent him from repudiating his debts. Kublai is fully convinced that the violation of any obligation contracted by or with any member of the state, rich or poor, is destructive of the first principles of human society. If he were, either directly or indirectly, to commit or countenance any trick or fraud, such as refusing to receive back his notes at the value for which they are issued, then their worth would be at once destroyed. It is the credit, the honesty, the truth of Kublai Khan, which is represented by this symbolical coin."

The hospitality of the church, like that of the east of the present day, forbade any of the modern niceties and punctilios respecting introductions. To be unknown, afforded at once a claim and a title to protection and kindness; and to have asked the travellers for their names would have been an act of rudeness and incivility. But curiosity might be discreetly expressed, and the abbot, who had formed a shrewd supposition concerning his guest, continued on the watch for some decent opportunity of verifying his conjecture. That the pilgrim was an Italian, he had already acknowledged: and the abbot hit upon the ingenious device of turning the winged lion, one of the emblems of the evangelists which adorned the silver beaker, towards the pilgrim, pledging him, at the same time, to the health of his Tartarian majesty.

The stranger, who had no wish to evade the question which was asked by the action of the abbot, replied, "Saint Mark is doubly my patron. He is the protector of our glorious and invincible republic; and in his patriarchal church, I, Marco, received his name."

It was not necessary that he should say more. Every person present felt himself at once as if he were the old and intimate acquaintance of the traveller, acknowledged by universal consent to be the citizen, not of Venice, but of the world.

CHAPTER II.

THE COUNTY ELECTION.

MESSER MARCO MILLIONE, the appellation which, as is generally known, our friend the pilgrim usually bore, was a commercial traveller in the strictest sense of the term. Gain sent him forth. However active his curiosity may have been, the mere wish of visiting strange countries, and then describing them after he had seen them, would no more have conducted him to England than to Cathay. It is, perhaps, to the circumstance that most of our early travellers were men of business,—and the missionary or the ambassador were, in their respective lines, as much men of business as the merchant,—that we owe the vivacity and interest of their narratives; and their great superiority over those writers whom authorship-prepense has conducted from their homes.

In the first case, the journey makes the book: but in the last, it is the book which makes the journey. The business-traveller, records those matters only which recreated him amidst his toils, or which were so remarkable as to command his attention, possessing a real and native interest. Whilst the author-traveller, turning his recreation into a toil, is perpetually on the stretch, striving to give a factitious, facetious, or fictitious interest to things which have none at all.

Indeed the same generic difference exists in every branch of literature, between the productions which spring from the fulness of the intellect, and those which are the results of compulsory labour. Let the writer be called to the work, let him willingly follow the employment for which his mind is prepared, and you quaff the Tokay. It is the juice expressed from the grape by its own richness and ripeness. If, on the contrary, he is forced or forces himself upon the task, you are not merely dosed with the crude and sour extract of the *marc*, but are compelled to swallow the very husks and stalks themselves.

As for Marco Polo, he was engaged upon a lucrative commission: the collection of the long outstanding arrears due to the representatives of Peter de Aquablanca, whilom bishop of Hereford. But although the merchant was looking after lucre and profit, he never neglected any opportunity of mental improvement. The reputation of Roger Bacon,—I name the philosopher without further introduction, for I presume that my readers have already recognized him in the friar,—might have induced even a less energetic observer than Marco to accept the invitation he received. Friar Bacon offered to conduct the Venetian to London, where he proposed attending a chapter-general of the order, virtually composed of deputies from all the Houses of that observance in England; a species of ecclesiastical parliament, not without influence, as I may, perhaps, explain elsewhere, upon the civil constitution of the realm.

Friar Bacon's conversation was very singular. Sometimes remarkably explicit and perspicuous; he would often again become silent, reserved, and obscure. He would pass from the most sound experimental observations, to a boundless expanse of theory and hypothesis: solid and correct reasoning would suddenly be faulted, as it were, by a vein of wild credulity: the full and clear display of a philosophical truth would suddenly be succeeded by an inscrutable enigma. At one moment, he appeared to put you in entire possession of his sentiments: at the next, you felt that he retired within himself, and laboured to deprive you of any indication by which you could ascertain his real thoughts. Marco Polo afterwards observed that the friar might be compared to the prospect of a mountain range, whose lofty summits are seen, now resplendent in floods of light, now shrouded in impenetrable mists; a ceaseless alternation of darkness and sunshine.

During a considerable portion of the road, the travellers continued skirting along the Thames, scantily dotted here and there with heavy barges and ballingers; some, drifting lazily down the shallow river; others, still more slowly punting their way upwards by dint of pole and oar.

"In Cathay," observed Marco Polo, "the people hold all other nations in such contempt, that, speaking of them according to their common proverb, they say, 'Cathay-man, two eye; Red-pate, one eye; Black-pate, no eye.' They found this complimentary scale upon their own imagined superiority over all other races, though they cannot help acknowledging the evident advantages which we European Red-pates possess over the Black-pates, the wild and nomade tribes in their vicinity. But if Kublai

Khan's subjects were to travel into our western parts, I am afraid
they would doubt whether Red-pate uses even the one barbarian
eye, which they are so kind as to allow him.   Water-carriage is
the life of trade.   And yet, with the exception of the Flemings,
who, as I hear, have formed a canal between Ghent and Bruges,
in some parts by cutting through the soil, but mostly by deepening
the beds of the sluggish streams, and a few other similar works in
Lombardy, there is not a nation or country in Christendom where
any attempt has been made to improve the advantages of inland
navigation.

"How differently they manage matters in Cathay!   There,
the broad expanses of the lakes are connected by excavations with
the ample floods which intersect the empire; forming communi-
cations denied by nature, enabling the most distant provinces
to exchange their productions, the abundance of the southern
regions helping the arid sterility of the north.

"Hence, the Cathaian commerce has been extended in a manner
of which you, in Europe, have no conception.   On the banks of
the Kiang, which unites itself with the largest of those artificial
channels, there are upwards of two hundred cities, each possessing
five thousand barks.   I verily believe that more vessels float upon
the Kiang than are to be found in all Asia besides."

"Much," replied Bacon, "hath certainly been effected by those
distant nations, who at once afford us an example and a warning—
an example in stimulating us to exert our industry, a warning
in teaching us to refrain from self-conceit: yet, how little has their
knowledge advanced, when compared to the wonders which will
be revealed by the combined powers of art and nature, exceeding
all the miracles ascribed to magical skill or necromantic art.

"Bridges, unsupported by arches, can be made to span the
foaming torrent.   Man shall descend to the bottom of the ocean
safely breathing; and treading with firm step on the golden sands
never brightened by the light of day.   No sail is spread, no
mariner is toiling at the oar; yet call but the secret powers of Sol
and Luna into action, and I behold a single steersman sitting at
the helm, and guiding the vessel, which glides like a spirit through
the waves.   And the loaded chariot, no longer the encumbrance
of the panting steed, darts on its course with fiery force and resistless rapidity.   Let the pure and simple elements do thy labour.
Bind the eternal enemies, yoke them to the same plough.   Make
the contraries unite, teach the discordant influences to conjoin
in harmony.   Aid the antagonists to conquer each other: and do

thou profit by their mutual victories.   True are my words, though
spoken in parables.   Open the treasury of nature, above, below,
around you, are the keys."

It might have been difficult for Marco Polo to annex any
definite idea to these sentences, so mysterious in the fourteenth
century, so intelligible in our own.   Circumstances had, however,
enabled him to form some reasonable conjectures respecting the
applications of the powers of nature indicated by the friar; and
the subject was not entirely new to him.   Friar Bacon had, some
time before, inscribed an epistle to Brother William of Paris,
bearing the title *De secretis Operibus Artis et Naturæ, et de Nullitate
Magiæ*, in the fourth chapter whereof all these discoveries are
enumerated.

This epistle, like many others upon similar subjects, which
the friar had addressed to Pope Clement, and to other distinguished personages, belonged to that extensive genus which, in
our times, has been designated as correspondence for the press,
and not for the post.   Neither press nor post then existed.   But,
nevertheless, the coy reserve which shrinks from the sight in
order to be more surely drawn forth into the universal gaze, obtained the degree of care and tenderness which such sensitive
shyness required.   Modesty is not always rendered indignant by
gentle violence: it was as well understood then, as it could possibly
be now, that the discreet friend who received the full answers
to questions which had never been asked—the satisfactory explanations of matters about which he had never inquired—the clear
solution of doubts which nobody ever raised—and the affectionate
explanations for the relief of non-existent anxiety—would ill
requite the kindness of his correspondent, unless he took effectual
means for preventing the world at large from being deprived of
the "private and confidential communication" with which he had
thus been favoured.

Brother William, therefore, did not scruple to show the epistle
of the English philosopher to all the curious who wished to inspect
it; and, as collectors are wont to do, even to many who did not.
Nor did he ever refuse the loan thereof to the transcribers by
trade, first exacting, it is true, a solemn promise that the document should be treated with as much precaution as it was imparted.
So that we need not wonder that a copy had very speedily—within
nine years from the day of its date—reached Venice, and that
Marco was therefore fully aware of the doctrines which the friar
held.

Indeed, even if Friar Bacon had practised more reserve with respect to the transmission of his opinions and discoveries, there was no breach of the social compact in promulgating his scientific views and schemes. He constantly made them the subject of his conversation; and many of the discourses which are here recorded, are found in substance in such of his works as are still extant. In some cases, I have really been quite surprised and astonished at the agreement between Friar Bacon's text, and the manuscript which I use. And this singular coincidence, by the way, is such a proof of the accuracy of the ancient chronicler from whose narrative this tale is rendered, that, if the reader chooses, he is at liberty to conjecture that all the other portions of the adventures of the merchant and the friar have been given with equal fidelity.

Marco, then, as one who was well prepared for the subject, began at once earnestly to interrogate the friar upon the means of realizing his predictions. "And why, then," continued he, "do you not place the keys of science in the hands of those who would use them for the purpose of opening the most valuable of all treasuries, the productive industry of the community? What an impulse would these occult powers impart to commerce, to every kind of handicraft! Let us suppose your inventions to be carried into practice, and since you make the assertion, I entertain no doubt of their practicability, I speak as if these wondrous engines were before us, and the very face of the world is changed.

"The rapid transit of commodities increasing the facility of supply, and the increased supply stimulating the demand, trade and traffic expand to the most gigantic scale. The merchant, instead of being compelled as now, to consume his time, to risk his health, his life, in long and toilsome journeys, is enabled, by his agents and factors, to conduct the most extensive concerns without departing from his dwelling."

"But these advantages," exclaimed the friar, not allowing Marco to proceed, for he had a bad habit of interrupting conversation, "display but partially the ministry of the elemental powers. The united antagonists, so irresistible in their strength, and yet so easily directed, may be compelled to perform any labour which their master may impose. Time was, when the hands of the captive crouching at the quern, afforded the sole source of motion to the only machine then known to man. Time is, and the rippling stream and the rushing wind are made to assist him by their impulse. Time shall be, and the virtues of nature will bestow upon him an energy of resistless activity.

"Whatever we now effect by human or animal strength, by nerve and muscle, or by the action of stream or gale, will be operated by a servant who will never tire, a slave who will never rebel, a vital force which will never slacken, never slumber, never rest, and susceptible of indefinite increase. Easily as the beldame twines the single thread, ten thousand thousand spindles may be made to revolve in ceaseless whirl through night and day. Self-moving, the loom will cover the mazy web. The hammer, which even the arm of Cyclops could not wield, vibrates like a reed through the yielding air.

"The objects ministering to the bodily pleasures, and ease, and comfort, and convenience of mankind will be so increased in quantity, as well as reduced in cost, that luxuries, which now the sovereign's wealth can scarce obtain, will be accessible to all who are but one grade removed from absolute poverty. Such will be the results of machinery!"

"And why," exclaimed Marco Polo, "do you jealously deprive your contemporaries of these benefits? Must the burning lamp be buried in your sepulchre, leaving to future ages the chance discovery of its flame?"

"I dread that all these worldly boons," said the friar, "will be purchasable only at too high a price. Recollect our old proverb, 'You may buy gold too dear.'"

"Surely," exclaimed Marco Polo; but Marco Polo's exclamation, which possibly elicited an explanation of these oracular declarations, as well as the remainder of the friar's argument upon the results of machinery, is nearly, perhaps, irrecoverably lost, the manuscript having become extremely blurred and unintelligible; partly by decay, but still more by the injudicious application of tincture of galls, a process which, though it affords a temporary aid to the reader in deciphering the faded writing, ultimately covers the whole surface with an impenetrable shade. From these and other similar injuries, I am apprehensive that the remainder of the narrative will offer rather a succession of fragments than a connected history.

I must also confess I have sometimes supposed, that the monk of Croyland, the author to whom I owe my original, has acted even as the ingenious painter, who enlivens the circle of his panorama with all the groups which might, could, would, or should have congregated in the locality of his scene during the whole revolving year. The caravan entering one gate, and the funeral going out at another. Here the celebration of a marriage, there the infliction of the bastinado. Storks on every cupola, and muezzins in every minaret. In short, whose pencil, true in each detail, but inventive in the composition, has decorated the canvas with a host of men and creatures, all natural to the place, all having a full right to be there at some one time, but who never assembled together at any one precise moment. Try what I can, I cannot find any given date under which Marco Polo and Friar Bacon could, according to the vulgarly received chronology of English history, have concurred in witnessing the transactions which my manuscripts disclose. And yet there is hardly any material fact here narrated, respecting which I have not read the same, or something nearly like it, either in authentic records, or in an extant chronicle. The main statements seem true, but I cannot make them synchronize : it is that which puzzles me.

I must now resume from the passage where the manuscript first becomes legible again. It tells us that the oak near which the travellers alighted was in the last stage of decay ; reduced to a mere shell, hoary with mosses and lichens. Yet the huge trunk still bore a few verdant branches, whose bright and tender freshness formed a striking contrast to the decrepitude of the parent stem from which they sprung. The landscape offered some remarkable features. The tree grew upon a small hillock, so regularly shaped, that the rising seemed to be a work, not of nature, but of art. A more attentive examination confirmed this supposition. Concentric ramparts and fosses environed the circular mound, whose form was distinctly seen, though their outline was rounded off at the summits and edges by the compact flowery turf, covering them as fully as the rest of the downs : thus affording full evidence of the many winters and summers which had rolled away since the soil had been disturbed.

Other tokens of past ages also appeared. A tall, rude obelisk, of unhewn rock, surrounded by smaller pillars of the same shape and material, stood at the foot of the knoll. A cool spring-head above welled out into a little stream, gliding through the rushes, steadily and rapidly, yet so tranquilly, that when you looked down upon it, the uniform direction of the blades, vibrating in the clear fluid, alone indicated the existence of the current. Indeed, the tiny rivulet would, perhaps, have been unnoticed by our travellers, had not their attention been drawn to it by a slight splashing

sound, like that of eight or nine pebbles successively cast into
the water: and by the appearance of a young girl, who tripped
away in a very great haste, as if she had been doing some deed of
which she was either ashamed or afraid.

"It is singular," said Marco Polo, "to observe how identical
these superstitious practices and opinions are in all parts of the
world. In the recesses of Hindostan, you find the same scheme
of planetary influences as our astrologers adopt, and the same
class of spells employed for obtaining a fallacious prospect of
futurity, as are in vogue, in spite of all the denunciations of our
prelates, in every country of western Christendom. Java's dark-
eyed daughters endeavour to reclaim an unfaithful lover by the
arts which have descended to the Apulian damsel from the Grecian
Amaryllis. And the tales repeated around the hearth of the
Italian peasant may be heard on the banks of the Ganges."

"Rather say, it is not singular," replied the friar, "that these
superstitious practices and opinions should be identical in all parts
of the world, since they all spring from the same common cause—
Man rebelling against the will of his creator, striving to obtain
that knowledge which has been withheld from us by mercy;
yielding to sinful lusts and wishes; and seeking aid and comfort
in any source rather than in submission to the divine will. The
spirit of this idolatry is universal. But the special form which
it takes in the case of the jealous, afflicted, or forsaken girl, who
has just taken flight, is derived from the heathenism of her Anglo-
Saxon ancestors. It cometh even within the letter of the fifth
chapter of the ordinance established by Canute the Dane, in the
council of the Witan, the wise men of England, and which wholly
prohibits the fantastic ceremonies performed in the worship of
the greenwood tree, the rock, the flood-water, or the spring.

"Here, we have the very idol before us. Race after race has
inherited these delusions. These circles denote the place of sacrifice, as well as the court of justice; it is more than possible that
this very oak hath whilom witnessed the rites of paganism. If
appearance and aspect can now be received as adequate evidence,
one might almost maintain that the British druids, of whom we
read in Pliny, had cropped the mistletoe from its boughs: though
I admit that we lack sufficient proof of the length to which vegetable life may be prolonged."

"In some cases," replied Marco, "it is afforded by tradition.
When Justinian yet reigned, the pilgrim in Arabia was shown the
oak of Mamre beneath which Abraham pitched his tent. And

this memorial of the patriarch was felled, not by the scythe of time, but by the axe of the destroyer."

"I should require some surer testimony, Master Marco, both of the antiquity and identity of the tree, than such unsupported Oriental traditions can afford."

"I will seek, then, to find examples for you in Europe, good friar. You know, without doubt, that the descendants of the ancient Cantabrians are to be found in the men of Biscay, who, defying alike the power of the Roman, the Goth, and the Moor, yet retain possession of their land and assert their pristine liberty, notwithstanding they have been compelled to acknowledge, from time to time, the supremacy of their more powerful neighbours. Certes, in all my peregrinations, I have never met with any Christian folk whose laws and institutions, manners, customs, and language, bear the impress of such unaltered eld. They possess a popular ballad, commemorating the resistance—that steady, patient, and determined resistance, grounded upon the love of all that makes our country dear to us, and which, humanly speaking, never fails, in the long run, to defeat an invader, opposed by the Cantabrians to the victorious Augustus, the emperor of Rome, or, as he is termed in the lay, the ruler of the world.

> Romaca arouac,
> Aleguin eta,
> Vizcaiac daróa,
> Cansoá.
> Octabiano
> Munduco jauna,
> Lecobidi
> Vizcaicoá."

"These verses may be very pathetic and interesting," quoth Friar Bacon; "but I really do not understand one word of what you are saying."

"Neither do I," replied Marco; "but that makes no difference at all in poetry. I liked the sound of them, that is quite enough for me, and so I learned the verses by heart."

"Messer Marco, Messer Marco," said the friar, looking somewhat stern; "in this vagary I cannot perceive your accustomed good sense: it seemeth to me wholly beside the purport and purpose of our conversation."

"Be not over hasty, friar," retorted Marco. "It is sufficient that a trusty interpreter has explained the general meaning of the lay to me, and assured me of its present currency, and its tokens of remote antiquity: and, now, friar, mark my reasoning.

I am about to allege a tradition, transmitted from father to son: and the only mode of appreciating the credibility of traditions, often the sole beacons which guide us through the night of history, is by considering them as a portion of the nationality of the people unto whom they belong.

"Take, for example, the Biscayans, dwelling in the land which possibly they reached during the earliest outwandering of mankind from the plain of Shinar, speaking a peculiar and unmixed language, cultivated in the highest degree by the affection which they bear to every token of their blood and race, and preserving the great outlines of their history by popular song. Amongst such a people, a fact, though resting only upon oral tradition, may be considered to be as well authenticated, as if it were recorded in the pages of the chronicler.

"You have asked me for some good evidence of vegetable longevity; therefore, I will tell you, that the Cantabrians point out the living oak of Guernica as the very identical tree beneath whose branches the lawgivers and magistrates of their commonwealth have assembled ever since the reign of Charlemagne, when it was already their ancient place of meeting.

"Around the oak of Guernica, the deputies from the different rural districts into which Biscay is divided, convene, and by their advice and assent the land is ruled. Ask the Biscayan for the *Fueros*, the charter guaranteeing the independence of this national legislature: in reply, he will draw the dagger, with which, pursuant to their immemorial usage, he may stab the messenger who bears any mandate from the Lord of Biscay, contrary to their rights and privileges. With all these collateral confirmations, with this accumulation of traditions repeated, and rights maintained, from generation to generation, you will, I am sure, readily admit that I have produced to you sufficient evidence of the oaktree's age. Travellers who have seen it, tell me that it is yet so green and vigorous, that there is scarcely any reason to doubt but that it may be flourishing and healthy five hundred years hence; a period which, if the world should last so long, will reach the nineteenth century of the Christian era."

"But can you find," said Bacon, "any other instance equally well authenticated?"

"Many," replied Marco; "all resting, however, upon the same class of proofs—usages conjoined to traditions, and continued from age to age. You know that in the old time it was the custom, still preserved in numerous parts of Europe, to hold the courts of judicature beneath the shadow of the tree. Coeval with the oak of Guernica, perhaps even of greater antiquity, are the oaks of Upstallsbaum, in the country of the free Frieslanders. Friar, they are the true brethren of your Anglo-Saxon ancestors, still speaking your own old English language almost without a change. Into Seven Sea-lands is the country divided. Governed by judges, elected in each Sea-land, the Frieslanders have, as yet, defended their laws and customs and liberties, against king and kaiser. And it is very possible, that the three oak-trees of Upstallsbaum, around whose stems the representatives of the Friesick Commonwealth hold their tribunal, may have been in full vigour before the keels of Hengist, whom the Frieslanders commemorate as their sovereign, had landed their crews on the shores of Britain.

"The trees of Upstallsbaum stand, like the oak before us, on the summit of a small hill or mound. And the spot where we now are, reminds me so strongly of the site where the Frieslanders are thus accustomed to assemble for the administration of their laws, that I might almost suppose——"

The friar, who had hitherto been quietly attending to this narration—though, by the way, as I have said before, he was not the most patient listener in the world—now suddenly silenced the speaker, and anticipated the conclusion of the sentence, by telling him that his supposition was a certainty. "For this," continued he, "is no other than Grimbald's oak, beneath whose boughs the Shire court, the earliest and most important of our national tribunals, is held at this present day."

Marco Polo and the friar had been so earnestly engaged in their discussions, that they had scarcely noticed the suitors, though the latter, during the last half hour, had been gathering around the Shire-oak, awaiting the arrival of the high officer whose duty it was to preside. Notwithstanding the size of the meeting—and Marco conjectures, if we read his numerals properly, that upwards of two thousand people were present—there was, nevertheless, an evident system in the crowd; for a considerable proportion of the throng consisted of little knots of husbandmen. The churls—by no means a term of reproach, but merely a designation of order—four or five of whom were generally standing together, each company seeming to compose a deputation, might be easily distinguished by their dress, a long frock, of coarse yet snow-white linen, hanging down to the same length before and behind, and ornamented round the neck with broidery rudely executed in blue thread. They wore, in fact, the attire of the carter and the ploughman, a garb yet lingering in some few parts of Cambridgeshire and Suffolk, common enough about five and twenty years ago, but which will probably soon be recollected only as an ancient costume, cast away with all the other obsolete characteristics of merry old England.

Every one of these groups of peasantry, who, it must be observed, were the representatives of their respective Townships, the rural communes into which the whole realm was divided, had a species of chieftain, in the person of an individual, who, though it was evident that he belonged to the same rank in society, gave directions to the rest.

Interspersed among the churls, though not confounded with them, were also very many well-clad persons, possessing an appearance of rustic respectability. These, also, were subjected to some kind of organization, being collected into sets of twelve men each, who were busily employed in confabulation among themselves. From circumstances which, at present, I shall for various prudent and cogent reasons refrain from detailing, Marco ascertained that they were the "sworn centenary deputies," a phrase by which I suppose he means the jurors who answered for and represented the several Hundreds.

A third class of members of the Shire court could be equally distinguished, proudly known by their gilt spurs and blazoned tabards, as the provincial knighthood, and who, though thus honoured, appeared to mix freely and affably in converse with the rest of the commons of the Shire.

"I see but few shaven crowns amidst the multitude," observed Marco Polo; "but for this deficiency, I might conclude that this assembly had been the legislature of an ancient commonwealth."

"Marco, in your last position, you are correct. Time was, when the predecessors of the suitors here convened, bore the name of the *Witan*, the sages of an Anglo-Saxon kingdom: and then the bishop might be seen as one of the chieftains of a people, taught, as all nations ought to be, that their civil policy was founded on their faith. But, one of the alterations in our government, effected by William the Norman, was the promulgation of an edict prohibiting the discussion in the County courts of certain matters, more specially appropriate, according to the new jurisprudence, to the ecclesiastical tribunals. Seldom, therefore, do the clergy now care to attend these assemblies, excepting when, like the abbot of Oseney,"—pointing to the abbot, who was just then ambling in upon his well-fed palfrey—"they are compelled to do so by reason of the business they have to transact in the County court, which offers a species of representation of the several ranks and orders composing the community."

A flourish of trumpets interrupted the discourse, and announced the approach of the high sheriff, Sir Giles de Argentein, surrounded by his escort of javelin men, tall yeomen, all arrayed in a uniform suit of livery, and accompanied, amongst others, by four knights, who, though they yielded precedence to the sheriff, were evidently considered to be almost of equal importance. No sooner had the sheriff and the four coroners—for these were the four knights who thus attended him—appeared in the court, than a girl, whom the travellers recognized as her who had cast the spell, the nine charmed pebbles, into the streamlet, rushed into the ring, exclaiming with a loud and agitated voice, "You sheriff, you coroners, you honest men of the shire, by the law and lore, which good King Alfred, all England's father, granted and taught, I appeal Sir Richard de Pogeys, for that——"

"My masters," said the sheriff, in a tone of great decision, and such as showed that he would brook no contradiction, "you must not listen to such idleness. You, John Catchpole, remove the silly wench from the court: if she continue her abuse of men of worship, silence her in the tumbrel, for we are bound to proceed to business concerning the whole commonwealth. Even now hath the porte-joye of the chancery delivered to me certain most important writs of our sovereign lord the king, containing his grace's high commands."

The said porte-joye of the chancery often acted as one of the messengers of the great seal: whatever may have been the original nature of the affairs wherewith he was charged in the time of Thomas à Becket, it is certain, that in the fourteenth century he was anything rather than a bearer of gladness. In our own times, our spirits are not particularly exhilarated by the approach of any process issued by the court of chancery: and, in good sooth, there was even then no particular reason to welcome the satellites of that awful tribunal. The chancellor, who might be designated as principal secretary of state for all departments, was the great medium of communication between king and subject: whatever the sovereign had to ask or to tell, was usually asked or told by or under the directions of this high functionary.

Now, although the gracious declarations which the chancellor was charged to deliver, were much diversified in their form, differing in their tone, and multifarious in their matter, yet, somehow or another, they all conveyed the same intent. Even as the several variations of a skilful composer, after conducting the hearer through every maze of harmony, round about and up and down, by flats and sharps, crotchets and quavers, sweetly slide and glide, at last, into the same identical thump, dump, thump, thump, thump, tweedle, tweedle-dee, of the *Tema*—even so, did the mandates of our ancient kings, whether kind or angry, whether tender or dignified, whether directing the preservation of the peace, or preparing for the prosecution of a war, whether announcing a royal birth, or a royal death, whether to declare that the royal son would wear his first spurs on his royal heels, or the royal daughter first receive the marriage ring on her royal finger, invariably conclude with a request or a demand for money's worth or money: either by express terms, or by implication; either by a plain peremptory demand, or by the enunciation of some potent cause, which would produce the salutary effect of pecuniary depletion, as surely as the blood is extracted by the application of the leech to the patient under the doctor's hands.

The present instance offered no exception to the general rule. King Edward, greeting his loving subjects, expatiated in most emphatic terms upon the miseries which the realm was likely to sustain by the invasion of the wicked, barbarous, and perfidious Scots. Church and state, he alleged, were in equal danger; and, "inasmuch as that which concerneth all, ought to be determined by the advice of all concerned, we have determined"—the writ continued—"to hold our parliament at Westminster, in eight days of St. Hilary."

Parliament! The effect of the announcement was magical. Parliament! Even before the second syllable of the word had been uttered, visions of aids and subsidies instantly rose before the appalled multitude:—grim shadows of assessors and collectors flitted in the ambient air. Whilst the sheriff and the other functionaries preserved a tranquil, but not a cheerful gravity, every one else present, high or low, earl or churl, as the Anglo-Saxon rhyme has it, seemed impressed with the common fear of the impending visitation, and occupied by the thoughts of averting or evading the blow. Sir Gilbert de Hastings instinctively plucked his purse out of his sleeve: drawing the strings together, he twirled, twisted and tied them, in the course of half a minute of nervous agitation, into a Gordian knot, apparently defying any attempt to undo it, except by the means practised by the son of Ammon:

but which, as the owner well knew by sad experience, would fail to defend the contents against the dexterous unravelment of the cunning emissaries of the treasury.

Hastings tarried in the field. Not so the abbot of Oseney. who forthwith guided his steed to the right-about, and rode away from the meeting as fast as he could trot, turning the deafest of all deaf ears to the monitions which he received. "My lord abbot, we want you!" shouted the Crier: My lord trotted on. "My lord abbot, I want you!" vociferated the sheriff in a voice of thunder. My lord heard nothing, but continued his progress until he was intercepted by the porte-joye, who, respectfully doffing his cap, and offering a salutation which the abbot seemed very unwilling to return, attempted to serve the prelate with the much-abominated process, the writ of summons, by which he was commanded, all other matters laid aside, to attend in person at the parliament, to treat with and give counsel to the king upon the affairs which should be then and there propounded.

Whether tenure or custom did or did not render the abbot of Oseney liable to the very disagreeable duty of taking a seat in parliament, by which he would be taxed amongst the possessors of lay fee or property, was a question long agitated, both in fact and in law. The name of the abbot of Oseney stood high on the roll of parliamentary prelates; yet, years had elapsed since such an abbot had been seen among the lords. Many attempts, it is true, had been made to enforce the attendance of the last abbot but one, Abbot Peter; who, according to the tradition current amongst the officers of the House of Lords, was what, in the technical language of Carey-Street and Bell-yard, would be called a very shy customer. It was almost as difficult to execute a parliamentary writ of summons at Oseney as it would now be to effect the execution of a writ of *capias* in county Galway. Every kind of device was resorted to for the purpose of obtaining a legal hold upon the abbot, and these attempts were resisted with singular energy.

On one very urgent occasion, the lord chancellor did not think it beneath the dignity of parliament to dispatch a Master, William de Eyreminne, afterwards advanced to the Rolls, and ultimately promoted to the bishopric of Norwich, who cunningly gained access to the abbot in the disguise of a penitent. So far he was successful, but as soon as his errand was disclosed, Master Eyreminne received such a salutary discipline from the knotted scourges provided by the monks for the benefit of the visitors to the shrine of Saint Brithwold, as induced him to decamp most speedily, adopting with entire sincerity the character which he had assumed.

On another occasion, it was reported that the messenger was agreeably surprised by the unexpected cordiality of his reception. No obstacle was offered; the abbot, receiving the parliamentary process with much respect, delivered it to his seneschal, telling him to take care that it should be properly returned. The summoning officer was then shown in a "parloir," and kindly requested to take a meal previous to the resumption of his journey. The dish was brought up and placed before him. Well did he augur from the amplitude of the cover, but, when the towering dome was removed, it displayed a mess far more novel than inviting—the parchment writ fried in the wax of the great seal. Before he could recover from his surprise, the attendants disappeared, the door closed, the key turned; and, amidst the loud shouts of laughter from without, he heard the voice of the pittanciary, declaring that he should never taste a second course until he had done justice to the first, the dainty dish set before him upon the table. Without the slightest mitigation the threat was carried into effect; of no other food did he partake, neither bite nor sup could he obtain, until after two endless days of solitude and abstinence, all-persuasive hunger compelled the unlucky representative of the chancery to swallow both the affront and the process.

Such were the reports, whether true or false—there were very many others of the same kind—concerning the ability shown by the abbots of Oseney in defeating the legal process intended to enforce their parliamentary duties: and during a long period, no further attempts had been made upon them. A learned member of the society of antiquaries, the principal contributor (*entre nous*) to that venerable periodical, the *Gentleman's Magazine*, and who collects materials for a supplement to the last splendid, new, and enlarged edition of Dugdale's *Monasticon*, to be published by subscription, in as many parts as the subscribers' resignation will bear, at one guinea per number, small paper, and two guineas the large, informs me, however, that there are certain entries in the abbatial accounts, now in the Augmentation office, entitled *Largesses and Donations*; in which all dates, names, and other particulars, have been carefully erased. But he surmises that they would, if legible, afford a more satisfactory explanation of the cessation of hostilities. Be this as it may, porte-joye acted

P. VIII.   3 like a man determined to do his duty, and seizing the horse's rein with the one hand, he attempted, with the other, to force the writ into the abbot's grasp.

"Gently, gently, gently, Master Porte-joye," quoth the abbot, "you may e'en put your scrap into your scrip again. My much-lamented predecessor, Richard de Dronebury, to whose station, after he had ruled us in peace and quietness during twenty years, I, all unworthy as I be, was called last Easter, hath set us quite at ease. A blessing be upon his memory! he obtained several most valuable privileges for our convent, and such as will for ever commemorate his name. A grant of twelve fat bucks yearly, and every year, from Woodstock Park. A thousand fagots of wood at each fall, to every stick whereof you shall be heartily welcome, Master Porte-joye. Lastly, a patent, declaring that the Reverend Abbot of Oseney, and all his successors for ever thereafter, shall be wholly exempted, exonerated, and discharged from attending parliament, or in any way resorting to the same, or from being held, bound, or obliged to give any advice or counsel to the king, his heirs or successors, upon any matter, cause, or thing whatever. Well do I know how anxious my lord chancellor is to fill the parliament house with the like of me; but with this patent I defy him. Let him do his worst, I won't come to parliament."

"You shall answer for this contempt before the chancellor, my lord, when the seals are next opened in Westminster Hall, on the table of marble stone. A commission of rebellion will bring you to your senses," exclaimed the porte-joye, scowling at the abbot. But all further discussion between these parties was prevented by the high sheriff, who commanded his clerk to read the whole of the writ, by which he was commanded "to cause two knights to be elected for the shire; and from every city within his bailiwick, two citizens; and from every borough two burgesses, all of the more discreet and wiser sort, and to cause them to come before the king in his parliament at the before-mentioned day and place, with full powers from their respective communities, to perform and consent to such matters as by common counsel shall be then and there ordained; and this you will in no wise omit, as you will answer at your peril."

A momentary pause ensued. The main body of the suitors retreated from the high sheriff, as though he had been a centre of repulsion. After a short but vehement conversation amongst themselves, one of the bettermost sort of yeomen, a gentleman farmer, if we may use the modern term, stepped forward and addressed Sir Giles: "Your worship well knows that we, poor commons, are not bound to proceed to the election. You have no right to call upon us to interfere. So many of the earls and barons of the shire, the great men, who ought to take the main trouble, burthen, and business of the choice of the knights upon themselves, are absent now in the king's service, that we neither can nor dare proceed to nominate those who are to represent the county. Such slender folk as we have no concern with these weighty matters. How can we tell who are best qualified to serve?"

"What of that, John Trafford," said the sheriff; "do you think that his grace will allow his affairs to be delayed by excuses such as these? You, suitors of the shire, are as much bound and obliged to concur in the choice of the county members as any baron of the realm. Do your duty; I command ye in the king's name."

"Prove your allegations, sir sheriff," replied the sturdy yeoman, who, as the reeve, headed the deputation of his township. "Quote the judgment, read the statute, cite the law, produce the roll, showing that our concurrence in the parliamentary elections is a part of our suit and service in the shire. If you succeed in finding that you have any coercive right over us in this respect, you shall harness me in the team; and know further, sir sheriff," continued John Trafford; "that I appear in this shire court as the attorney and steward of Sir Robert de Vere."

"So be it, Master John," retorted the sheriff, with all the delight of a disputant about to place his adversary between the horns of a dilemma. "Since I have you, as your master's representative in the Shire court, I will let you go as a suitor with all my heart. You have just alleged that the burthen and duty of the elections falls upon the earls and barons. This is your acknowledgment, in full and open court, which you cannot retract, and of which I and the coroners will all make a record by word of mouth before the exchequer. Deny, now, if you can, that, in all proceedings of this County court, you are fully empowered, by immemorial custom, to answer for Sir Robert, your master, in the same manner as if he were here present. Therefore, under peril of the king's high displeasure, as you tender life and limb, proceed at once to the election, as you, Sir Robert's attorney, are in duty bound. Has it not been ruled so, again and again, in Yorkshire!"

3—2

Fluctuating and uncertain as the elective franchise was, an-
terior to the creation of the forty-shilling suffrage, the only practice
almost, in which much uniformity can be discovered, or which is
defined with clearness and precision in coeval documents, is the
usage of the attorneys of the baronage concurring in the parliamentary nominations, and on some occasions electing, or rather
making, the members without the assent of any other parties
whatever—a professional arrangement which, as some folks say,
is by no means obsolete. John Trafford, therefore, had no help.
Like a wise debater, he yielded to the pinch of the argument,
without confessing that he felt it: and, having muttered a few
words to the sheriff, which might be considered as an assent, a
long conference took place between him and some of his brother
stewards, as well as with the other suitors. During this confabulation, several nods and winks of intelligence passed between
Trafford and a well-mounted knight: and whilst the former
appeared to be settling the business with the suitors, the latter,
who had been close to Sir Giles, continued gradually backing and
sidling away through the groups of shiresmen. And, just as
he had got clear out of the ring, John Trafford declared, in a most
sonorous voice, that the suitors had chosen Sir Richard de Pogeys
as one of their representatives.

The sheriff, who, keeping his eye fixed upon Sir Richard as he
receded, had evidently suspected some manœuvre, instantly ordered his bailiffs to secure the body of the member—this is rather
an Hibernian phrase, but, as I cannot depart from my authorities,
I do not know how it can be amended—"and," continued he with
much vehemence, "Sir Richard must be forthwith committed to
custody, unless he gives good bail—two substantial freeholders—
that he will duly attend in his place amongst the commons on the
first day of the session, according to the laws and usage of parliament."

All this, however, was more easily said than done. Before
the verbal precept had proceeded from the lips of the sheriff,
Sir Richard was galloping away at full speed across the fields.
Off dashed the bailiffs after the member, amidst the shouts of
the surrounding crowd, who forgot all their grievances in the
stimulus of the chase, which they contemplated with the perfect
certainty of receiving some satisfaction by its termination:
whether by the escape of the fugitive, in which case their common
enemy, the sheriff, would be liable to a heavy amercement; or
by the capture of the knight, a result which would give them

almost equal delight, by imposing a disagreeable and irksome
duty upon an individual who was universally disliked, in consequence of his overbearing harshness and domestic tyranny.

One of the two above-mentioned gratifications might be considered as certain. But besides these, there was a third contingent amusement, by no means to be overlooked; namely, the
chance, that, in the contest, those respectable and intelligent
functionaries, the sheriff's bailiffs, might, somehow or another,
come to some kind of harm. In this charitable expectation, the
good men of the shire were not entirely disappointed. Bounding
along the open fields, whilst the welkin resounded with the cheers
of the spectators, the fleet courser of Sir Richard sliddered on the
grass, then stumbled and fell down the sloping side of one of the
many ancient British entrenchments by which the plain was
crossed; and horse and rider rolling over, the latter was deposited
quite at the bottom of the foss, unhurt, but much discomposed.

Blaunc-estoyle had received as little damage as his master.
Horse and rider were immediately on their respective legs again:
Blaunc-estoyle shook himself, snorted, and was quite ready to
start; but Sir Richard had to regird his sword, and before he
could remount, the bailiffs were close at him; Dick-o'-the-Gyves
attempted to trip him up, John Catchpole seized him by the collar
of his pourpoint. A scuffle ensued, during which the nags of the
bailiffs slily took the opportunity of emancipating themselves
from control. Distinctly seen from the moot-hill, the strife
began and ended in a moment; in what manner it had ended, was
declared without any further explanation, when the officers rejoined the assembly, by Dick's limping gait and the closed eye
of his companion. In the meanwhile, Sir Richard had wholly
disappeared; and the special return made by the sheriff to the
writ, which I translate from the original in my custody, will best
elucidate the bearing of the transaction.

"Sir Richard de Pogeys, knight, duly elected by the shire,
refused to find bail for his appearance in parliament at the day
and place within mentioned, and having grievously assaulted my
bailiffs, in contempt of the king, his crown and dignity, and
absconded to the Chiltern Hundreds, into which liberty, not
being shire-land or guildable, I cannot enter, I am unable to
make any other execution of the writ, as far as he is concerned."

My readers are well aware that, at the present day, a nominal
stewardship connected with the Chiltern Hundreds, called an
office of profit under the crown, enables the member, by a species

of juggle—if such a term may be used without a breach of privilege—to resign his seat in violation of the principles of the constitution, and with some detriment to the purity of parliament and the political independence of the individual. But, it is not so generally known, that this ancient domain, which now affords the means of retreating out of the House of Commons, was, in the fourteenth century, employed as a sanctuary, in which the knight of the shire took refuge in order to avoid being dragged into parliament against his will. Being a distinct jurisdiction, in which the sheriff had no control, and where he could not capture the county member, it enabled the recusant to baffle the process, at least until the short session had closed.

As soon as the excitement occasioned by the chase had in some degree subsided, Sir Giles de Argentein commanded the suitors to proceed to the election of a second knight, as required by the writ. There was some doubt whether the sheriff might not be entitled to declare that the election of Sir Richard de Pogeys was void, and that they were therefore bound to choose another in his place; but after a tumultuous discussion, the question was waived. Indeed, several of the shiresmen maintained, that it was of no kind of consequence whether they returned one knight or a score, since, whatever the number might be, they believed that the knights of the shire, like the citizens appearing for London, had only a collective voice for the county—one joint vote amongst them—and not an individual suffrage. Yet, though this was asserted, nobody appeared to be certain as to the practice prevailing in parliament, upon a point which, one would think, was of great importance in all times, and most vitally so at a period like the present, when, as Marco Polo easily collected from the conversation of the bystanders, there was a strong feeling of opposition against the Crown.

A pause ensued, Sir Giles presented himself as if to receive the nomination of the court. No one came forward, and the high sheriff, with much more patience and forbearance than might have been expected from him, continued apparently waiting for the nomination. At this moment, a hawk which one of the followers of Sir Giles bore upon his fist, having broken her leash, soared upwards, and then descended in her flight, attracted by rather an ignoble object, a pigeon, after whom she winged her way. This spectacle, as might be supposed, drew off the attention of the crowd. Trafford, indeed, always maintained, to his dying day, that it was no accident, but that Matt'-o'-the-Mews had slipped the leash when nudged by Sir Giles, and during their diversion from the business, the sheriff, after a few minutes' conversation with the knights who were nearest to him, recalled the attention of the shiresmen, by declaring that Sir Thomas de Turberville was fairly elected by the county, as the other knight to serve for the same in parliament, and that John att Green and Richard att Wood were his manucaptors.

This declaration excited a universal outcry of discontent and indignation amongst the shiresmen. They whooped, scolded, groaned, and John Trafford, again acting as spokesman, loudly accused the sheriff with jobbing and collusion, employing the most uncourteous and unmeasured language. "It is a repetition of the fraud and deceit which you practised at the last Parliament, when you levied seven pounds sterling for the wages of your ally and cater-cousin Sir Marmaduke Vavasour, being at the enormous rate of four shillings and eight-pence a day—two groats above the settled allowance—whereas he was never duly elected by us, and we could have hired as good a member, aye, and a better one, who would have been glad to do all the work of the county for five pounds, yea, even five marks, and who would have agreed in the lump, to accept the said sum for all his expenses going and returning, and for all his keep at Westminster, let the parliament sit as long as it might—yea, even for a whole month." Voices were rising louder and louder, and there was every appearance of a new storm. But the banner of Sir Giles de Argentein, emblazoned with the bearing allusive to his name—the three cups of silver—was raised, trumpets sounded, horses were in motion, spearmen and knights, closing round the sheriff, pierced through the crowd, and the meeting was dissolved.

CHAPTER III.

GUILDHALL.

As I have before observed, my imperfect materials merely afford broken passages from a narrative of which the greater portion has perished. Yet I apprehend, that you, gentle reader— and I address you as gentle, according to old established usage, though it is very possible you are quite the contrary, looking on me and my production with aspect of verjuice and lips of scorn, nay, worse than all, preparing to discharge your long outstanding tailor's bill, by cutting me up in your next review—that you, gentle reader, may, in spite of these deficiencies, be able to form a very adequate idea of the objects here presented to your understanding.

There are on the outside of Lichfield Cathedral some singular monuments—Darwin, I think, has commented upon them—by which my meaning may be exemplified. Of each individual statue, nothing more is preserved, than head and shoulders, ankles and feet. These fragments, placed at proper distances from each other, are built up in the wall: and though the eye sees nothing but parts of a figure, yet the mind sees all the remainder, imagination supplies all that is wanting. You have the entire effigy before you. I hope that, in like manner, I have enough left of the several personages, to give you as good a notion of what they were, at least for all practical purposes, even as though the whole of the original history had been extant and printed at large.

Resuming, therefore, my tale, I must state, that I am utterly unable to trace the exact road by which our travellers reached London. All I do know is this, that Marco Polo arrived at a happy time, when there was a great deal of movement in the city, capable of exciting his curiosity. London did not claim the political attributes of sovereignty exercised by the Italian Republics, or the Teutonic Hanse towns; but *Troynovant*, as the city was named in old traditions, did nevertheless, in practice, possess such a degree of self-government as frequently to exhibit

[40]

the feelings of an independent community. Whatever liberties the burgesses of London had held in the Anglo-Saxon age—and I believe that the city was then in the nature of a republic, subjected rather to the supremacy than to the authority of the *Emperor* of Britain—they were, thanks to William the Norman bishop, secured to them by William the Norman king, and ratified, confirmed, and amplified by each succeeding monarch. To the fullest extent by which the forms and language of law could support their franchises, they were sustained by the most solemn compacts and assurances. The additional guarantees afforded by the good stone walls which encircled the city, and by the forty thousand fighting men who dwelt within these ramparts, were sufficient to cause their privileges to be respected, even by the most powerful sovereigns.

Not that the Londoners enjoyed these rights without disturbance. Repeatedly were tallages levied which they represented as enormous; but the closer the sheep were shorn, the faster the wool grew; the harder the sponge was squeezed, the more it absorbed. London's citizens throve in proportion to their pluckings; and all the contemporary writers who narrate the exactions which they suffered, equally bear witness to their increasing property.

Occasions more than once occurred, when their liberties were seized into the hands of the crown. These transient clouds were, however, simply the calamities of the free cities of Italy, in a mild and mitigated form: they were the result of the constant struggles between the crown and the communities of the people, which form the peculiar characteristics of Europe, from and during the middle ages, even down to our own times. The greater degree of authority possessed by the sovereigns of England, was, in truth, the safeguard of the people—even when they disputed the royal power—even when that power was most abused. It prevented the crown from proceeding to extremities. If Frederick Barbarossa could have summoned the citizens of Milan before his exchequer, a heavy mulct might have been imposed upon them, but their walls would not have been prostrated, nor their city given up to spoil and destruction.

Not less conducive to the real independence of London, was the safety-valve, which the king's courts of justice afforded for the escape of the angry passions and dissensions of the citizens. They frequently pursued and persecuted one another with great virulence and animosity; yet, the existence of regular tribunals,

by and through which vengeance could be enforced, even unjustly, averted the wholesale proscriptions of the Bianchi and
the Neri, of Guelfs and Ghibellines. And though it was by no
means agreeable to be outlawed without law, still there was a
wide difference between the most illegal legal proceeding of an
English special commission of *oyer* and *terminer*, and the sentence
of the democracy, who arrived at the *terminer* without the slight
preliminary of the *oyer*, pronouncing the doom, by which you were
banished, under the penalty of being burnt alive if you returned.

Nor amongst the causes of the well-being of London, must
we omit the kindly influence of civic hospitality—long may it
continue, and we be there to eat. Constantly in the habit of
assembling at the festive board, as well in the greater associations
of the city, as in the smaller bodies of the gilds, our citizens,
however much they might be at discord or variance, were always
in the way of being brought together by good fellowship. When
the rival parties at Florence would have been employed in razing
each other's towers to the ground, our London factions united
in demolishing the ramparts of a venison pasty. In fact, our
English municipalities were placed exactly in the middle term,
best calculated to insure the prosperity of the people at large.
The absence of a sufficient controlling power in the sovereign
of the Romano-Germanic empire, allowed the several members
of which it was composed to sever themselves into distinct communities, in which, after a painful and disturbed existence, every
trace of real liberty has now expired. In France, the absence
of sufficient consistency in the municipalities and provincial
governments, enabled the crown to overcome every obstacle, and
to leave the people no other franchises except those held by the
sovereign's will and pleasure. After every revolution which that
volcanic country sustains, its shaken elements gravitate again
towards a central despotism. Not so in England, where the
municipal communities were enabled to maintain their qualified
independence, until the development of a general legislature,
into which all the political powers of these minor orbs could merge
for the benefit of the community at large.

Were I in a mood to theorize upon the scanty vestiges of the
ancient state of society in London, I should be inclined to maintain, that the inhabitants, the Burhwara, or Burgesses, as they
are termed in the charter of William the Norman, were severed
into two distinct classes—the aldermen, magnates, or barons,
the representatives of some very ancient and remote victorious

race, in whom the powers of government principally rested—and the citizens at large, the descendants of a vanquished race, a mixed multitude, who were perhaps themselves subdivided into various plebeian castes.

In some respects, the city might be considered as a federal state: each of the districts or wards of which it was composed, subsisted under the local government of an alderman, the presiding magistrate of the little community. Several of these rulers held their authority in full property. The aldermanry descended from father to son, and might be sold by the son, if he chose to alienate his patrimonial inheritance. It may appear singular that such a species of authority in a great and populous city, should be susceptible of transfer by bargain and sale. But the inappropriateness will diminish when it is recollected, that the aldermanry bore a great resemblance to a baronial jurisdiction, a lordship, an honour, or a manor, to which analogous rights of jurisdiction were appurtenant, and equally susceptible of becoming the subject of dealings between party and party. Nor must it be forgotten that in this, as in many other apparent peculiarities of the middle ages, the strangeness is increased by the obsolete garb which they assume. Jurisdiction is at this present day lawfully bought and sold. When a commission in the dragoons is first purchased by a cornet, he acquires, by payment of the regulation price, the inchoate right of sitting as a judge in a court-martial, and inflicting the heaviest punishments known to the law. Other aldermen were elected by the "probi homines," the good men or inhabitants of the ward, holding office for life, but removeable for misconduct. Of deprivals, some remarkable instances occur.

There were also various *sokes*, as they were called, jurisdictions analogous to the aldermanries, also held in full property by their lords, with important powers. In these, the owner often possessed the then much-valued privilege of hanging the culprits belonging to his own demesne, or who had incautiously strayed into this legal preserve, a right known by the uncouth Teutonic terms of *out-fang-theof* and *in-fang-theof*. Such districts, which, as it may be remarked, existed in other towns, were often very minute. At Colchester, for example, we can distinguish one of these regalities on so small a scale, that if the unlucky *in-gefangene-theof*, or, *thief-caught-within*, had been placed in its centre, a hop, a step, and a jump, in schoolboy fashion, would have carried him beyond the awful boundary.

The lords of these sokes appear to have been originally included amongst the municipal magistracy or rulers, though not usually reckoned as aldermen. But amongst the functionaries, so denominated and called, there was nevertheless a prelate whose aldermanry had arisen out of a soke, by rather a singular combination of circumstances, which placed him in a situation little analogous to his ecclesiastical calling. Before the Norman Conquest, there existed a gild or body of knights, denominated, in Anglo-Saxon, the *cnihtena-gild*, and who possessed a plot of land just within the gate of the city, and thence called the *port-soken*. These knights retained their jurisdiction, as well as their land, in, and through, and after the great changes consequent upon the Norman invasion, until some time in the reign of Henry I., when they bestowed their territory upon the neighbouring convent of the Holy Trinity. By virtue of the transfer, the prior of the convent acquired the rank of an alderman of the city, and sat as such in common council till the dissolution. The demesne of the fraternity became, and still is, the well-known Portsoken Ward: whilst the name of Nightingale-lane, into which the denomination of the "*Cnihtena-gild land*" has passed by colloquial alteration, yet preserves a memorial of the ancient owners of the soil.

In this patrician order, these aldermen, magnates, or barons, as the lineage of the remote conquerors, the government of the city appears to have been originally vested. But upon all important affairs concerning the interest of the whole community, consultation was to be had with their subjects, the entire body of citizens, in folkmoot assembled. Of these occasions, none was more urgent, than when the king's justices itinerant appeared at the Tower of London.

The professed object of this periodical visitation, was the determination of "pleas of the crown," or of all offences of which the king could take cognizance, either as supreme conservator of the peace, or in vindication of his rights and dignity, constituting, indeed, a wide field of inquiry. The justices could punish the smallest and the greatest trespasses. From the encroachment of a footpath, up to high treason, manifold were indeed the defaults sure to be charged against not only the individuals, but the aggregate community. "As, in such case, it is impossible for us citizens to avoid being handled by the king and his justices, it is a great point to obtain their good will; nor should we grudge or spare a liberal compliment to them, not omitting their clerks and ministers in the distribution of the same. Thus did our wise ancestors act, who so strenuously defended our liberties; and it is no shame in us to do the like, and to follow the example which they have shown." These, are very nearly the words of an ancient volume treasured in the civic archives. In the margin of the latter clause an emphatic *"non bene"* marks the dissent of a sturdy town-clerk, who protests against such a mode of conciliating the ruling powers.

Practical prudence, however, prevailed over the theory of patriotism; pecuniary compromises were neither unfrequent nor ineffectual. Transactions of this nature would necessarily impose some additional burthen upon the citizens. It was expedient to conduct the business in such a manner as to obtain the confidence of the people, and at the same time to manage with due caution and discretion. Hence a practice was introduced, of appointing a small number, usually about twenty-four, out of the folkmoot, who were to assist the magistrates in dealing with the representative of royalty, or with royalty itself, on behalf of the community of citizens. A committee, in fact, by whom any proposition could be better discussed than in a large and tumultuous body: and who were dissolved when the business for which they had been appointed was concluded; though not, as we shall see hereafter, without exercising a permanent influence upon the municipal policy.

Internal disputes, as well as the various dissensions in the realm at large, frequently disturbed the tranquillity of the city. But no alteration appears to have taken place in the civic government, until the era of the famous parliament convened at Oxford, under the auspices of Simon de Montfort, Earl of Leicester, an assembly to which the contemporary chroniclers have given the name of the Mad Parliament. Hath it not most unfairly monopolized this title, to its own cruel disparagement? at least so far as any fair comparison with the actings and doings of some of its honoured successors may be concerned.

By the provisions made in this same Mad Parliament, the king was virtually deprived of the royal authority. Not indeed in style, he retained his crown upon his head, and all public enactments ran in his name; but all the powers by which a government could then be carried on were transferred to the barons, with whom the citizens of London entered into a close alliance and confederacy. Professing, at the same time, all due respect for the crown, they declared that they joined the parliamentary rulers, "saving their allegiance to our lord the king." But the spirit of their submission may be exemplified by the following passage. Thomas Fitz Thomas, when taking the oath of allegiance to the sovereign, whom it was found convenient to retain as a pageant of royalty, explained himself by saying, "My lord king, we Londoners will be your faithful and devoted subjects, so long as you will be good king to us"; or, in other words, "as long as you obey us, we, your humble servants, will obey you."

Concurrent with the great revolution in the state, was a corresponding revolution in the civic community. Thomas Fitz Thomas, completely excluding the "aldermen" or "magnates" from the dominion of the city, threw the whole power into the hands of the lower or lowest order of the people, "calling themselves the *communia*," a term borrowed from the opposite side of the Channel: and then denoting an alteration in the municipal policy, which, expounded in our modern political nomenclature, may be considered as designating an ultra-radical reform. A subversion, or rather inversion, of authority, which, though it shakes established institutions to the ground, never succeeds in obtaining for itself any permanent stability.

London now became a turbulent and disorganized republic, independent of the central government of the realm, and completely ruled by a democracy and its demagogue: for there really never was such a monster as an acephalous multitude. Base as the body of the reptile may be, a baser head is always its guide. "Our business"—the ancient civic chronicle relates—"was transacted as if no such thing as an alderman existed in the whole universal world. Whatever Fitz Thomas had to do, he proposed to the common people, advising with them, and them alone; and they cried out *Ya! ya!*"—literally thus in the manuscript— "or *Nay, nay!* just as he chose, and there was no way or means of making them either do justice, or suffer justice, except according to their will."

Simon de Montfort fell in the field of Evesham, earning a hero's honour and a martyr's name. He died like Saint Thomas of Canterbury, sang the minstrel, in defence of England's freedom. Popular predominance in the city, as it had risen and thriven concurrently with the prosperity of the barons, so did it sympathetically shrink and contract when De Montfort's party was subdued. In appearance, the aldermen resumed the preponderance and magisterial functions which they had previously enjoyed. Again were they seen upon the hustings in all their former pomp and pride, whilst Fitz Thomas, reviled and abandoned, was cast into a fetid dungeon.

I have said that this reinstatement of the city magnates to their ancient preponderance, was effected in appearance. Particular and local is the fact; the principle which it involves possesses a general and universal applicability.

Well would it be for the peace of the world, were it possible for political partisans, of all sides and parties, to understand how entirely they miscalculate the elements of the courses in which their tutelary planets move. As the luminary recedes, and diminishes, and fades away from the sight, they comfort themselves with the idea, that the star is revolving in a parabola. However protracted the period may be, they ween it will, at length, reappear with accelerated rapidity and increased splendour. But, alas! it has flown off in an hyperbola, never returning into the orbit from which it has once departed.

The orangeman, revelling in imagination in the renewed delights of "protestant ascendancy" and "Croppies lie down": and the inquisitor storing fagots for the future *auto da fé*. The *ancien noble*, tottering upon his crutch, in sure expectation that the fleur de lys will again unfold upon the scutcheon of Louis Quatorze, and the *de* regain its particular and monopolizing privileges: and the son of *la jeune France*, gaily chanting the hymns of Béranger, as he watches, with the red night-cap of liberty on his brow, until the Republic is awakened from her slumbers. The cavalier confiding in the revival of the High Commission Court: and the roundhead, calculating upon the profitable and pleasing spectacle of the sequestrators again hard at work in Haberdashers' Hall, all are to be ranked in the same category with the Britons awaiting the return of King Arthur from the fated fairy bower.

In such cases, there is much always to pardon, often to tolerate, sometimes to admire. Even undue veneration of the past is connected with the best feelings of our nature—even the selfishness of the friends of a fallen cause is closely allied to gratitude. But truth must be told—and it is the most egregious of follies to reject the lessons taught by the unvarying annals of mankind.

Never was there, never can there be, a restoration, by which, authority, once absolutely extinguished, can possibly regain its pristine power. When the statue is dragged from the pedestal, the very clamps which fixed the effigy so firmly to the support,

have acted as levers in rending and wrenching the marble asunder;
place the image upon the dislocated basis, and it stands but to
fall.   Titles may be resumed and proclaimed, the herald's voice
drowned amidst the clangour of the pealing bells, the shouts of
the multitude, the swelling notes of the clarion, and the blare of
the trumpet—again, upon the tower's battlements, the broad
emblazoned banner may be unfurled, and the bright regalia
brought forth from their concealment to deck the monarch returned from exile, and inaugurated upon his paternal throne—
bonfires blaze in the market-place—conduits run with claret
wine—healths are drunk by the kneeling carousers in the banquet
chamber—Charles Stuart is in his palace—but the Stuart king
is not restored.

The king never "gets his own again." The broken bone will
knit, and become even stronger than before the fracture—not so
the sceptre; if it be once snapped asunder, the soldered stem
never possesses the toughness of the original metal; its solidity
is destroyed.

But is there any reason to wonder, if the devices of mortal
man, the shadows of a shade, are seen to waste and wane away?
Should we sorrow, because the stability of the everlasting hills
is denied to the fabric raised upon dust and ashes?   Must we
not confess the truth, and submit, without repining, to the wisdom
of the dispensation which decrees that when human institutions
have once arrived at their fatal term, they never can be revived.
During the convulsions which alter the level of society, new
opinions have been adopted, new habits have been assumed.
Young spirits have arisen, confident in their own untaught conceit;
whilst ranks of contending champions have sunk in the grave.
Diversified as the human countenance is, by feature and expression, the human mind is still more varied by temper, education,
rank, position, and intellect.   Providence works by eliciting
modes of thought, not cyclical, but successive; and in which man
freely acts, though without the power of controlling their evolution.   No era which has once gone by, can ever be brought back.
Individuals are never reproduced: the creatures, not merely of
the last age, but of the last year, or even of the yesterday, will
never more be found together.   Never will the same combinations recur, so long as the world endures.

The fitness of the forms possessed by the extinguished policy
is utterly lost: and the same integrity which resisted the removal
of the old landmarks, will, as consistently, refuse to disturb the

new, within whose boundaries other rights of property have been acquired. Blessed is the protecting hand.

But I must continue my version of another passage of my manuscript, which, as far as I can judge, was originally extracted, and I hope without interpolation, from the year-book, or chronicle, still kept in Guildhall. And the transactions accompanying the election of Walter Hervey to the mayoralty, in the year 1272, will show how much the popular party, put down, but not put out, continued to act by means of the influence which recent events had bestowed.

The choice of the lord mayor, the chief magistrate, who succeeded unto the Port Gerefa of the Anglo-Saxons, had always been claimed as belonging of right to the aldermen, the men of worship of the municipality—a vestige, it may be supposed, of the ancient sovereignty of these magistrates, when they were a distinct and conquering race. Philip Taylor was by the aldermen duly called to the Chair. "Nay, nay, nay," vociferated the "small commons," assembled in the Guildhall, using the voices which they had so recently acquired, and which, according to the true and legitimate constitution, as *Liber Legum* informs us, they ought to have employed only for the purpose of cheering the nomination made by my masters, the aldermen. "Nobody shall be our mayor but Walter Hervey—Walter Hervey, he who hath already done good service to our cause"; and as such, upon the hustings was he installed.

Resistance on the part of the aldermen against the overwhelming force of the multitude, was quite impracticable. As the stout reforming common-councilman said to the spare conservative alderman, when they walked together out of the Egyptian Hall, after last Easter dinner—the common-councilman seizing the alderman by the top button, and poking him under the fifth rib—"I am free to confess you do us in the intellectual, my old boy: but we have all the physical on our side." Numbers prevailed; Hervey entered upon his office amidst thunders of applause. Some of the more thoughtful citizens, it is true, distrusted the earnestness with which Hervey had sought the mayoralty, for, as they whispered, "They had heard father and grandfather say, that when any man strives very hard to obtain the good place of mayor of our city—or any good place—he is labouring for his own good, and not for the good of those who are under him." A sage observation, neither the gloss of the old town-clerk, nor the result of the monk of Croyland's acuteness and wisdom, but taken, as I find by a careful examination, verbatim from the original civic chronicle.

Hervey, who had obtained a notion of the suspicions which were rising against him, forthwith addressed the crowd from the hustings, with the greatest spirit and energy. He declared, "That he most reluctantly came forward upon public grounds, to undertake so arduous and responsible an office. His inclinations and his interest tended entirely to the obscurity of private life; still it was his duty, his imperative duty, however irksome it might be, humbly to obey the call of his constituents. Their wishes were his commands. For them, he was willing to sacrifice his domestic pleasures. For them, he gave up the comforts of his home. For them, he quitted the cheerful fireside, the blessings of his family circle, the endearments of his smiling children." In this oration Hervey was interrupted by a shrill yell, proceeding from an open gallery, midheight in the Guildhall wall, where his wife and progeny had been stowed, and which was elicited by the forcible application of the maternal paw to the cheek of the most unruly of the urchins: but, though "evidently affected," as the newspapers have it, he proceeded. "For them, he would sacrifice the care of his extensive concerns, and most gladly bear all the labour; in order to uphold the rights of the people against the rich, who were ever seeking to throw all the load of taxes upon the poor. And, as to the calumny which had been so industriously circulated against him, he lifted up the adamantine shield of conscious integrity between his honest bosom and the envenomed shafts of his political antagonists; men who were willing to immolate every virtue upon the polluted altar of a bloated and factious minority. He fearlessly challenged the most searching inquiry into his public and private character; and, in particular, with respect to the base assertion that he had his own advancement or profit in view, he repelled the charge with ineffable scorn," &c. &c. &c. &c. &c. &c. In short, as appears by the notes faithfully taken by the town-clerk, and recorded in the *Liber de Antiquis Legibus*, (and to which for greater certainty I refer,) Hervey made a capital speech, which lasted until he was entirely out of breath.

Hervey said exactly the same kind of thing, which, under similar circumstances, is mouthed by every party-man, whatever that party may be—they are all alike, "the whole pedigree on 'em"—radical or conservative, whig or tory. He profusely showered down upon his adherents the clinking brass, which they professed to accept as sterling coin, fully knowing all the while, that the pieces were base metal: but satisfied that they would act as a useful circulating medium during the contest in which they were engaged.

Conceiving themselves deeply aggrieved by this usurpation, for, as I have said before, there was no possibility of withstanding Hervey's nomination by the folkmoot, the aldermen forthwith proceeded to lay their complaints and grievances before the king's council. This tribunal, in which the king actually sat and presided, then exercised the jurisdiction over corporate bodies, now vested in the court of king's bench, where, as is well known, the sovereign is present by fiction of law. That is to say, it was the court in which the king, as supreme magistrate, decided upon the legality of the elections of those, who, holding office under him, were, as the case might require, to dispense justice to the commonwealth in his name.

Hervey appeared before the court; and, from the minute account which has been preserved of these transactions, we can collect, that the council sat either in the venerable "White Hall" of Edward the Confessor, formerly the House of Lords, but from which their lordships have been so recently ousted by the Commons: or in the painted chamber, where the House of Lords are still accommodated in a temporary way,—buildings to be contemplated with the feeling that every stone in their time-worn, fire-scathed walls, which are crumbling down whilst we write, is a sentence in our constitutional history.

Hundreds and thousands of partisans supported the lord mayor intrusive: they escorted and accompanied him on foot and on horseback, and by them, Westminster Hall was entirely filled. The aldermen opened their case, but whilst they were pleading, the crowd in the hall took good care to be heard at the same time. In order to obtain an impartial adjudication, they shrieked, they shouted, they stamped, they stumped, they hissed, they hooted, they yelled, they groaned, they hallooed, they hulla'd, they bellowed, "We are the commons of the city— it is we who are the real electors of the city—we will choose our lord mayor—and we will not have any lord mayor excepting Walter Hervey."

During this wild tumult, the king, Henry the Third, was literally on his death-bed, in an apartment of the palace, close adjoining to the Hall. These conflicting claims greatly perplexed the members of the council. Some legal difficulties really attended

the most calm examination of the question.   Half intimidated by
the roars sounding in their ears, they felt a natural anxiety to
remove further disquietude from the expiring monarch; and,
actuated by these motives, they adjourned the discussion till the
morrow, when they required the parties to attend again.   At the
same time, the lord mayor intrusive was strictly charged that
his escort should not exceed ten in number.

Hervey received this command, and bowed assent: the citizens
returned back to the city, and forthwith dispersed to their mid-
day meal, for whatever political disputes are going on, folks will
dine, if they can:—if they can't, they foment the disputes to win
the dinner.

Early in the afternoon, Hervey called a full and free folkmoot
of the whole body of the citizens, with the slight exception of all
the aldermen, and of all those who adhered to the aristocratic
party; and the bats and clubs displayed in the vicinity of Guildhall, gave the minority constructive notice not to appear.

Hervey, addressing the multitude, strictly enjoined them, in
the king's name, and on the king's behalf, to follow him on the
subsequent day, for the purpose of assisting at the hearing of
the cause before the council: an injunction, which, whilst it
displays the consummate assurance of the popular leader, equally
shows the strong attachment of the people to the forms of a
monarchy.

The crowd most readily obeyed.   Congregating at the appointed time, they escorted Hervey to Westminster in as great
numbers as on the yesterday, and with equal fury and tempest.
Proceedings were resumed without any substantial variation.
Again the aldermen opened their case: again the good citizens
accompanied the pleadings of the aldermen, by a constant chorus
of "Hervey for ever!"   "It is we who are the real electors: we
will choose our own lord mayor: and we will not have any lord
mayor, unless he be Walter Hervey."   Various efforts were made
by the council to effect a compromise.   With other very interesting details, I must, however, reserve them for the new and
complete history of London now in preparation by me, and to
which I should like to add an ample appendix of illustrative
documents, taken from authentic records.   Sorry, however, am
I to state, that the materials will long continue laid up in my
portfolio, if, indeed, they ever appear; for my shrewd and active
publisher, to whom I proposed the work with the greatest possible
humility, put me down smiling, with his most civil but inflexible

decree, "I can't do the thing, except at your own risk. Quartos don't sell."

It is high time that some legislative measure should be adopted in relation to the distressed operatives in our line: and that in the pending bill, for "giving publicity to the prices of handloom labour," "literary labour" be also included. I do hope that the honourable member who has the charge of the bill will think of us, and move, at least, for a committee; the state of our branch of the trade being such as most urgently to require immediate relief. I belong to that ancient and highly respectable, but daily diminishing class of book-makers, who steal the materials for the brooms. That is all fair. But then we are quite beat out of the market, by those who steal the brooms ready-made. Honour there is amongst thieves, but none amongst authors. Crows will not pick out other crows' eyes, but authors do. Dog will not eat dog, but author does, though it makes him mangy. Taken altogether, we authors are certainly the most unkindly kind of beasts in existence.

Well, reader, it is more your loss than mine, if you refuse to encourage sound learning: for, since my publisher said that "Quartos don't sell," I infer that you won't buy. I wish you would; but I must revert to my brief and desultory tale.

During these proceedings, King Henry died, an event which was considered by the common people as suspending the royal authority, until fealty had been performed to his successor. Forthwith a patriotic plot was organized for diminishing the baneful influence of the aristocracy, by a general plunder of the aldermen and the richer citizens. The scheme was frustrated, in great measure, through the vigilance and activity of Humphry de Bohun, Earl of [Hereford], who, advancing into the city, caused the "king's peace" to be proclaimed. This ceremony was of great legal importance. Until the sovereign imparted his protection to his subjects by a formal act and compact, there was a species of interregnum: it seems to have been doubted whether any offences became cognizable before the royal tribunals. Bohun, an acute politician, and an old soldier, went to Guildhall: and, having with some little difficulty collected what, in newspaper language, is called "the sense of the city," a phrase, however, which a foreigner could not always interpret by a reference to Johnson's *Dictionary*, he advised the aldermen to alter their whole course, to desist from opposing the general feeling of the multitude, and to admit Hervey to the mayoralty.

Such advice is always more easily given than received. Indeed, Thomas Aquinas, in his celebrated treatise, *De Regimine*, addressed to the prime minister of the king of Cyprus, says that it is the case with all good advice given to people in power. This treatise has been often printed, from an imperfect copy, but the diligent antiquary, Charles Julius Bertram, professor of the English language at the Royal Military Academy, Copenhagen, discovered a more complete text upon the same shelf with his Richard of Cirencester. Both manuscripts were deposited by Dr. Stukeley, to whom they were transmitted by Professor Bertram, in the celebrated Chetham library at Manchester, where they now are: and it is this Chetham Aquinas which I use.

"No man in office, in the kingdom of Cyprus," quoth Aquinas, "likes good advice much, whatever he may pretend. If he tells you he does, don't believe him." Thomas Aquinas then devotes the sixteenth, seventeenth, and eighteenth chapters of his said work, to an elaborate and very instructive comparison between medicine and good advice.

Medicine is never nice to the taste, neither is the other article.

"Three modes there are," Aquinas continues, "of administering the medicine of good advice to prime ministers of the king of Cyprus, or other great men.

"The first is to pour it down their throats by a drench, as you do to mules. This," Thomas Aquinas says, "is thought by certain practitioners to be very effectual. Sometimes there is no other way. But then the patients do not fancy it: though it does good to them, it generally does harm to the physician. They recollect the disagreeableness of the operation, and forget the benefit which has resulted to them. They are cured of their sickness, but they are sick of the doctor: and he is not called in again." Indeed, I believe that Thomas Aquinas is in the right, for the patriotic rallying song of the brave Spanish constitutionalists, "*Tragala, perro, tragala,*" or "Gulp it, cur, gulp it," is not a tune which sounds harmoniously in any one's ears. It is not really admired by the hungriest dog that eats the dirtiest pudding; not even by the pledged representative of a radical constituency.

The second mode, according to Aquinas, of administering the medicine of good advice to prime ministers of the king of Cyprus, or other great men, is, as you do to little children—mix up the unpleasant stuff with some sweet thing. If they do not discover the trick, this may answer once or twice; but the chance is that they will. When the innocent device is detected, they ever after spit and sputter at the cup: and dangers may be incurred by the physician, which I dare not describe.

The third and last mode, according to Aquinas, of administering the medicine of good advice to prime ministers of the king of Cyprus, or other great men, is, neither to drench nor to coax: but, treating the patient as a creature of reason, to state, in plain terms, the nature of his complaint, and the ingredients of the prescription which you propose to employ. How to effect this result requires the combination of equal good sense and experience in both parties, patient and doctor; a combination rare indeed, and of which no mathematician can calculate the chance. Mankind may be defined as a species which does not grow wise by experience. Individuals may improve; the species, never.

The aldermen, who, in their own estimation at least, were far greater men than a whole cabinet of prime ministers, received Bohun's cathartic with great reluctance. Their worships coughed, and hemmed, and demurred. The minority looked confessedly silly. The majority tried to look wise. Had the proportions been inverted, the general look of the whole court would have continued unaltered. What was to be done? All stated that they wished to let the matter remain in the hands of a committee of ten persons, five named by the aldermen, and five by Hervey, who had been already appointed for the purpose of determining the validity of the election. But the earl having probably some good reason for supposing that the matter would not thus be brought to a satisfactory termination, persisted steadily in his opinion, and required that a folkmoot should be holden the following day in St. Paul's Churchyard.

In this accustomed spot, the whole body of citizens, possessing or claiming the elective franchise, assembled. The earl, assisted by [Walter] de Merton, the chancellor (well known to my Oxford readers as the munificent founder of the college which still bears his name), the Archbishop of Canterbury, and other lords of the council, held a private meeting with the aldermen in the chapter-house, advising them again, in a friendly way, to assent to Hervey's election. If this concession were refused, the earl hinted that something worse might happen; and the aldermen most unwillingly complied. In such cases our phrase is, that the assenting party makes a virtue of necessity: I should like to change the idiom, and say that necessity makes the virtue. Be that as it may, Hervey, by direction of the earl, engaged to abstain from any aggression against the members of the party who had opposed him. Lord Chancellor Merton, for the purpose of giving a solemn ratification to the transaction, came forward at St. Paul's Cross, and graciously declared to the crowd how the choice, made by the great body of the citizens, had been accepted and confirmed. In fact, the people substantially gained the victory.

To the increasing weight and influence of the civic commons, thus manifested, we may unquestionably attribute a most important alteration in the municipal constitution; and which united the two classes, hitherto separated as the ruling and the ruled classes, into one community. These transactions not having been hitherto explained by Strype or Stowe, a very brief notice of them may not be entirely unacceptable in this our age of reform.

During the earlier periods, the powers of government in London were exercised by the magnates, or patrician order. As far as we can collect, they disclaimed any legal responsibility towards the inferior citizens: but they were controlled in an irregular manner by the expediency of obtaining the cordial co-operation of the people on those important occasions, in which the interests of the whole body were concerned.

Aldermen, in those days, had occasionally a perception of the method which it was prudent to adopt as the means of conciliating the community. To have asked the assent of the "small commons," to have made them parties to a legislative act, would have been a degradation to these men of estate. But if the people could be coaxed into a belief that they were the advisers, those who gave the counsel would be mixed up in the business: and not only desirous to promote, but become responsible for its issue. Hence arose the practice of selecting the committees of twenty-five, for the purpose of treating with the king, or his justices, in the manner already described: and these committees gradually gave rise to a permanent branch of the civic legislature.

"I guess," said the philosophical supercargo, Jonathan Downing, when he wrote home from Canton to his uncle the major, "that there really be but two sorts of good government in the nature of things: bamboo, or the like, for every man jack of 'em, as in China; and bamboozle, or the like, for every man jack of 'em, as in the old country; but, we, in the States, use 'em both, and our's is the grandest government in the universe—bamboo for the niggers, bamboozle for ourselves."

A distinguished orator, whom I am proud to call "my friend," the grace and ornament of the Marylebone vestry, tells me, further, that man is an animal whom it is more easy to lead than to drive. If you can but tickle him up through his vanity, he is just like the Irishman's pig—you can make him believe he is going to Cork all the while you are taking him to Fermoy. Whatever collective body you may be dealing with—I must not be personal or particular—he, my authority, "my friend," says it is just the same. Make them—your mob, your members, your mob-members, or your mob of members—pleased with themselves, by teaching them to rely on their own wisdom, and you will do more with them than if you had done what no living creature has ever yet been able to do—than if you had read Bentham Dumont's *Tactique des Assemblées Législatives*, from end to end.

No one perceived the tendency of the alteration, introduced by the committees of citizens: no one felt the extent to which it would lead. New political institutions originate just as a path is made in a field. The first person who crosses the grass, treads it down. The mass of elastic verdure immediately rises up again: nevertheless some few of the more limber stalks and slender blades are bruised and crushed, and continue prostrate on the ground; yet so slight is the impression made upon the herbage, that the clearest eyesight can hardly discover the harm. After the first passenger, other people follow; and within a little while, marks of their footsteps begin to be perceivable. Nobody noticed the first footsteps. At what period they became visible, nobody can recollect. But now, there the footsteps are, the grass has changed its colour, the depressions are distinct, and they direct other wayfarers to follow the same line.

Not long afterwards, bits and patches of the soil, where very recently the grass was only flattened and trodden down, are now worn quite bare. You see the naked earth; the roots of the grass are dried, the grass is killed—it springs up no more; and then the bare places gradually and gradually extend, till the brown devours the intervening green: the bare-worn places join one another, all the grass between them is destroyed, the continuous path is formed.

But the path does not continue single. One passenger treads upon the bounding grass to suit his convenience: another, wantonly: a third for want of thought; more footsteps, more bare places. Tracks enlarge the path on either side; and these means of transit invite so many passengers that they break down the hedges for their further accommodation, without waiting to ask the owner's leave. The trespass has received the sanction of

usage : and the law, however unwillingly, is compelled to pronounce
the judgment that a public right of way has been acquired, which
can never more be denied or closed.

When this happens, how often does the proprietor regret that
he did not take due measures for preventing the invasion, by
decidedly stopping up the path at first, when he was possessed
both of the right and the power.   There is a moment when you
can warn off the trespassers and stop up the path; but if once
forborne, your power is gone for ever.   And then all that you can
do is to diminish the mischief, by making a stile so as to let the
folks go easily over.   Take matters quietly, when they have come
to this pass, for there is no help.   Grudge not what you have
lost; save what you can.

I must return, however, to the events which have extorted
this simile from the monk of Croyland—for you must not suppose
that a word of it is mine own.   The custom adopted by the
aldermen, of advising with the committees of citizens, a usage
appearing to have been in vogue in the earlier portion of the
reign of Henry the Third, and possibly at a more remote period,
expanded, in the following reign, into another practice; namely,
that upon most matters of internal legislature or business, a certain
number of good and discreet men were summoned, or called, from
the several wards, and sworn to consult with the aldermen.   They
were to help their superiors by their experience : to let them know
what the people thought, to intimate what would please the
people : and to aid them in feeling out how far they could venture
to go, in what would assuredly not please the people, but to which
all governments end and tend—to make the people pay—in short,
to carry on the whole effective administration of the civic community.   It is true that the city magistrates continued to hold
up their heads as high as they could.   But their position, though
they would hardly believe it, had been totally changed.

In theory, it was still unnecessary for the aldermen to solicit
the opinions of the territorial representatives; the aldermen
continued, as they still are, a distinct, and, in some respects, a
sovereign and conflicting court, making very large claims of
authority, according to the civic theory and the traditions of the
Hall.   But, in practice, no "common council" was ever held
without the presence of the delegates of the community.   The
Ordo and the *Plebs* were conjoined.

The mode, indeed, of nominating the members of the common
council sustained various revolutions and changes, all of which

my beforementioned quarto is intended fully to expound and declare. From the time when Marco Polo visted London down to the present day, the path has continued widening. The aldermen have let go the end of the rope. Often have they tried to catch at it, but in vain: and the good citizen commoners of London have not only kept the rope in their hands, but seem likely at no distant period to engross every yard of it to themselves.

Such was the state of London when the metropolis was visited by our Venetian traveller; and the city exhibited the full and vigorous activity of a rising commonwealth. Marco had obtained good information concerning the general aspect of English society; and, "I had expected," said he, as he was walking along Newgate Street, in company with the friar, "to have found amongst the common people in this country, more evident tokens of the Conquest—recent, I may call it—effected here by the Duke of Normandy. Though a stranger, I am sufficiently acquainted with your language to chaffer and cheapen with any gossip in your markets: but, I cannot discern much Romance, in the dialect of the English landsman. You, commons, are all *Tedeschi*, at the present day. The speech of the Flemings seems to me to differ from your English, scarcely so much as the *Volgare illustre* of Florence, from our Venetian language."

"But," replied the friar, "though the languages may not be much mixed, they flourish concurrently; what say you to the employment of the French, as some people call the Romance language, in court and camp, in all matters of business, even in this city?"

"I will admit," answered Marco, "that the first slight introduction of that tongue might have been rather connected with the conquest. Fully am I also aware that, it is considered as savouring of gentle birth, and betokening nobility, yet, we do not thereby obtain any proof or test of the point at issue. The French speech has become a language of general intercourse throughout Western Christendom. 'Son,' says the king of Norway, in his book of sage instruction, 'learn Welch, the Welch of France, for that is the language which goes widest in this universal world'; and I need not tell you, that by the Welch —that is to say, strange—he means the dialect derived from the Latin prevailing in modern Gaul. Messer Brunetto Latini tells me, that he intends first to compose his *Tesoro* in French, for the same reason. But, waiving this discussion, I ask for the more evident tokens of laws, and rights, and privileges, distinguishing the conquerors from the conquered, and retaining the Saxon race by positive institutions, in a condition of political inferiority. Is this the case in England?"

"Aye, Marco," replied the friar, with a good-tempered smile of encouragement, "you have discovered the clue, by which the inquirer will be most surely guided. Though I tried to put you on a wrong scent, you have found your way again. No, it is indeed a marvel, that so few chapters can be clearly traced in our jurisprudence to the Norman invasion as a cause.

"Popular opinion teaches otherwise. Visions of happiness, wholly inconsistent with the moral conditions of our earth, Landscapes tinged with ethereal colours, as if seen through the rainbow, are amongst the constantly recurring errors of the human mind, willing to delude and comfort itself with the belief that sin and misery can be subdued and eradicated by human policy and power.

"Ask those sturdy peasantry, whom you saw at the shiremoot the other day, they will tell you that all the 'servage,' and all the oppressions of the land, were occasioned by the Norman Conquest. To the era of the Anglo-Saxons, they now ascribe the perfection of good government, impartial justice, and universal prosperity.

"In the days of Alfred, the golden bracelets, which were hung by the roadside, continued untouched by the spoiler. Fondly is it supposed that the vigilance of the Anglo-Saxon monarch had repressed all violence; whilst the universal well-being and affluence of the people had withdrawn all temptation to crime: a picture, which, although avouched by many a grave chronicler, possesses about as much veracity as the description given by the rhyme of Cockney land, where, as they say,—

> Strewed with gold and silver sheen,
> In Cockneye streets no molde is seen;
> Pancakes be the shingles alle,
> Of churche and cloister, bower and halle;
> Running rivers, grete and fine,
> Of hypocras, and ale, and wine;

And which same Cockney land is localized, by popular humour, in the good city of London.

"With respect to the political condition of our country, I believe, however, that the main body of the English nation continued unscattered and unbroken, beneath the rule of the foreigners to whom the superiority of the soil was transferred.

"A large proportion of our earls and nobles certainly fell in the field of Hastings : most of the others were forcibly dispossessed. Still, I do not doubt, but that many of the lesser thanes retained their lands, under the obligation of rendering homage to Norman superiors, forming a race of middle-men, between the barons and the tillers of the soil.

"If time allowed, I could tell ye how Edwin of Sharnburne was confirmed in his domain by the Norman sovereign. Were not the thanes of Brougham and of Triermain, in the distant north, content to wear and bear a Norman name, veiling their old English ancestry? Recollect ye not John Trafford, the sturdy antagonist of the sheriff: he who took so prominent a part in the election, a scene by which you were so much amused?"

"I do."

"Well; if John Trafford were armed for the muster of the royal host, you would see upon his helmet a strange and uncouth crest: a man armed with a flail. And this, the bearing of the family, betokens their descent and history.

"Thurkill, whose name stands at the head of the Trafford genealogy—the Lancashire Traffords, the Cheshire Traffords, and the branch settled more recently in our county, are all one family—prudently refrained from continuing in arms after William had been consecrated at Westminster as sovereign of the realm. He continued at home, patiently, yet anxiously, awaiting the result; till at length the expected intelligence reached him, that a Norman marauder, who had recently ravaged the country, and lived at free quarters in that hundred, was now guerdoned by a mandate, a writ and seal, as it was termed, from the king, commanding Thurkill to surrender up his lands.

"Gislebert Mallore, when he arrived at Trafford, was neither welcomed, nor resisted. The gate of the curtilage was open, and the well-timbered house was tenanted merely by the maiden and the child. But when the foreigner stalked about the homestead, and examined with eager curiosity the possessions which he came to seize, the stables, the byre, the barn; he found in the latter, a sturdy thresher, intent upon his work, swinging his large, long, heavy flail, whose rhythmical bang raised clouds of chaff, ascending with each descending blow, and filling the air.

"Upon the entrance of Gislebert, the thresher intermitted his labour. Stern were his looks, but his language was cautious, almost courteous; and, producing a purse of decent magnitude, he made himself known as Thurkill, the Lord of Trafford. Strange and awkward was the greeting, as may be well supposed. But

Thurkill contrived to intimate, that possibly Sir Gislebert might prefer returning home with the value of the harvests during the last three years, rather than quit his castle of stone and lime in the smiling plains of Normandy. Would it be worth his while to migrate to this poor, cold, and rude domain? whilst, as Thurkill further hinted, the render of a pair of gilt spurs at Martinmas, and the accustomed suit and service due for the town of Trafford to the Hallmoot of Oldthorpe Mallory—a soke which Gislebert had acquired, and which he had designated by this Anglo-Norman compound—would preserve to him all the honours of the Seigniory. Thus saying, Thurkill began again swinging his large, long, heavy banging flail. The homestead in the meanwhile had been filled with a host of English churls, whose lines and ranks bristled with glittering scythes and sharp pitchforks. Gislebert, wholly unaccompanied as he was, did not feel entire comfort in his situation, and giving one glance at the gold, and another at the banging flail—the largest, longest and heaviest (as he afterwards told his wife) he ever set eyes upon; he did not feel very indignant when the purse dropped into his palm, which, in medical fashion, happened, by the merest chance imaginable, to be upturned, whilst he was looking the other way. And, wafted by a favourable wind from Southampton to St. Valery, Gislebert gladly permitted Thurkill to continue in the possession of the paternal acres, which his remote posterity yet enjoy."

"But if, as you say, the Anglo-Saxon population continued unbroken on the whole, do you think that there were many Saxons who managed with the adroitness of Thurkill, or that the Conqueror did not alter any of the laws and customs which he found?"

"In this crowded and noisy street I cannot well discuss a very complicated subject, which, perhaps, we may resume at a more fitting opportunity. At present, I will only give you one argumentative fact, or one fact in place of argument.

"You know better than I do, how, whilom the law, under which the individual lived, was the best part and portion of his inheritance. The law was literally his birthright; it regulated the price of his honour, his life, and his limbs, all of which were taxed and valued by an established tariff, so that, when two rival tribes or families settled their accounts, from the price which the heirs of Walter had to receive in compensation for the life of their slaughtered kinsman, was to be deducted the value of the arm, or the hand, or the finger, which Robert, his assailant, had lost in the affray. The noble, whose long-bearded ancestors had followed King Alboin to Milan, retained, even in the days of your grandsire, Marco, the right of being judged according to the edict of King Rothar; whilst one of the Roman Savelli or Frangipani, tracing their ancestry to the patricians of the capitol, though chancing to dwell in the same mansion on Lombard ground, reclaimed the privileges imparted by the awful shades of Theodosius and Justinian.

"Faint tokens of a difference of laws and privilege between the Norman and the Englishman may be discerned in the age of the Conqueror, but after the reign of our Rufus—whose by-name is identical with that of the Lombard *Rothar*—when we may suppose that the greater portion of the Normans in the first degree, had departed, we had not a trace of any such patrimonial law, which would have been assuredly insisted upon by them, had that law continued ruling and predominant. When the Anglo-Norman nobles have sought to obtain a rightful defence against any invasion of their rights or possessions, do you know whose protection they have invoked?"

"Not I," quoth Marco, with a jerk of impatience.

"Did they cry out 'Haro!' or claim the laws of Rollo?" continued Bacon, with the placid tranquillity of an experienced lecturer. "They would just as soon have claimed the tutelar patronage of Richard sans Peur, or Robert le Diable. No! These Anglo-Normans always asked and demanded, the laws of Edward the Confessor: whatever franchises they have, or had, they claim as the inheritance of England. Nay, what is even more remarkable, they have tried to bring England into Normandy:—they are willing to believe that their own country customs are transmitted to them from the wisdom and equity of the Confessor: and that the *grand Coustumier* of the Norman Duchy was grounded upon the jurisprudence of the Anglo-Saxon King."

Marco, unlike the friar, was a most obedient hearer, and anxious to obtain instruction: but his toleration was now almost worn out. Though the hand clapped before his mouth concealed what was going on behind it, yet, reader, the closing of his eyes, and the soughing of the inspiration, revealed the yawn, which doubtless, at this very moment, exercises its sympathetic influence upon you. If it does not, I shall be much surprised.

Marco, however, was compelled to hear a little more—far less fortunate in that respect than you are, reader; for you may close the book if you choose, and, as I presume you have paid for it, I shall not be the worse even if you throw it behind the fire.

Marco was pinioned to the stake, he might wince under the infliction, but he could not flee; will'ee, nill'ee, he was compelled to submit to the sequence of Bacon's colloquial essay.

"From these facts," continued Bacon, "we cannot fail to observe that the Anglo-Saxon laws were considered as wise and equitable. Affording a comparative degree of tranquillity, and a protection to all the inhabitants of the land, the conquerors adopted them as their own. I do not deny, that, in the ranks and orders of society, a curious inquirer may not suppose, that he traces the vestiges of the subjection of race to race. But I would rather refer these distinctions to a remote era. Perhaps to the subjugation of Albion by the Britons, by the Saxon tribes. Perhaps even, to still earlier conquests, effected by these tribes in their migrations, like your friends the Tartars, and which may have brought the Angles and the Saxons into this country as a mixed host of suzerains and vassals from the shores of the Northern Sea. One important point is not a matter of doubt and uncertainty. The most grievous characteristics of our predial servitude are found in the code of imperial Rome. Heavier was the thraldom which pressed upon the colonists when Britain was governed by the prætor, than the services demanded by the Norman Lord."

Whilst thus speaking, the solemn chant of the funeral psalm was heard, and the lyke-wake train was seen advancing towards them.

There was nothing new, or strange, or singular, about the burial procession particularly calculated to excite the attention of Marco Polo. A horseman bearing the crested helmet, the spurs, the gold-hilted sword, the emblazoned shield, announced, by conventional tokens known throughout the whole of Europe, that the deceased must be a baron, or one admitted into the aristocracy. The *De profundis* of the stoled priest spake the universal language adopted by the most sublime of human compositions, the Liturgy of Western Christendom. Yet, though no objects appeared which could awaken any lively curiosity in the traveller, there was much in their very familiarity to excite the sympathy of the wanderer in a foreign land. With an altered tone he said to the friar, "Saddened is the spirit of the pilgrim, by the fading twilight and the plaining vesper-bell. But he who braves every danger for himself, may feel his heart sink within him, when the pageant of triumphant death brings to his mind the thought, that those from whom, as he weened, he parted for a little while only, may have been already borne to the sepulchre.

Yet there is also a great and enduring comfort to the traveller in Christendom. However uncouth may be the speech of the races amongst whom the pilgrim sojourns, however diversified may be the customs of the regions which he visits, let him enter the portal of the church, or hear, as I do now, the voice of the minister of the Gospel, and he is present with his own dear ones, though Alps and oceans may sever them asunder. There is one spot where the pilgrim always finds his home. We are all one people when we come before the altar of the Lord."

During this discourse the procession had entered the cemetery of St. Martin-le-Grand, a secluded inclosure. Marco Polo, slightly desirous to know whose obsequies he had witnessed, yet hardly caring for the answer, carelessly asked the name of the deceased from a bystander, who, having lingered behind the other followers of the corpse, had fallen, as an acquaintance, into conversation with the friar.

"Simon de Frowyk, alderman of Langbourne ward," was the reply.

"An alderman, one of your city magistrates?" said Marco.

"Aye, and, therefore, according to the ancient custom of our city, we honoured him as a baron whilst he lived. Shield and banner hang over his tomb: and with the honours of a baron do we adorn his memory. My Lord Alan la Zouche himself has no greater dignity in his castle of Ashby than his bondsman possessed within our London franchise."

"His bondsman, say you?"

"Even so; Alderman Frowyk was a villein by birth and blood, and the churls his kinsmen, are now holding their lands by servile tenure. Lord Alan, it is true, made a bold attempt to detain the citizen, when he found him on his glebe, and claimed him as a fugitive. But the freedom of London, once obtained, clears off all stains of servitude. After a well-mooted plea before the king's justices at Westminster, which made master recorder, who was one of the counsel on our side, somewhat the richer, the emancipation of Simon de Frowyk was established beyond the possibility of further controversy. And the suffrages of his fellow-citizens then raised him to the rank which he so deservedly enjoyed."

"You could not, friend Marco," said the friar, "have possibly found a better instructor in our civic laws and antiquities than Master Andrew Horn, who, though young in years, is old in lore. He is one of the few who can read our old English Saxon character with readiness; and he has extracted the very quintessence of the doombook, which the citizens treasure in their municipal archives."

"Yea," exclaimed Andrew; "but the characters are fading, the leaves are crumbling into dust; the precious volume will never reach a future age, and the authenticity of Alfred's wise judgments, which I, Andrew Horn, have from thence transcribed in my *Mirror of Justices*, will perhaps be doubted by a sceptical and unthankful posterity."

The region of the city which they had now reached bore the appearance of the most venerable antiquity. Marco, gazing attentively at the nearest of the buildings, in which ranges of massy pillars, crowned with rude Corinthianesque capitals, supported many a deep-foliaged arch, said to his companions, "I could almost fancy the solid fabric to have been modelled from the palace of the Gothic Theodoric. Regal, this mansion seems to have been: and who was the monarch by whose refulgent effigy the arched portal is graced?"

The statue fully deserved the epithet thus bestowed upon it by the traveller. According to the ancient custom, which, with whimsical conceit, we call barbarous, since it was exuberantly practised by the Grecian artists, the image representing a royal personage, arrayed in purple, and crowned with an imperial diadem, was illuminated like a missal. Plaited with threads of gold, the long tresses of his yellow hair flowed even below his girdle: the sword was sheathed by his side. In the one hand, he held the wand of justice, surmounted by the dove of peace: with the other, he proffered to a group of kneeling burgesses, a scroll or charter, upon which the memorable verses—

As free
Make I thee,
As heart may think, or eye may see—

were deeply engraved.

"It was even he, who whilom dwelt here,"—replied Andrew, reading, from another inscription on the base of the statue— "The glorious Athelstane, King of the Saxons, King of the English, Dominator of the Scots, Ruler of the Nations, Sovereign of Albion and Emperor of Britaine, and all the circumadjacent lands and islands."

"Proud titles," said Marco Polo, "for the monarch of a remote barbarian realm, wholly severed from the rest of the world."

"The verse of the Roman poet," replied Bacon, "was contradicted by the polity of the state; the provinces of Great Britain became an integral portion of the great fourth monarchy, and at the period when the Anglo-Saxon ruler of this Island first assumed the imperial style, the supremacy of Western Europe, with exceptions too trifling to require notice, was shared between them and the Carlovingian Cæsar. Britain was as a twin empire."

"But now," said Master Andrew, "we citizens reverence our Athelstane, as the wise and gracious sovereign who laboured to establish the municipal liberties of England. Hence, such memorials as you now behold, grace the moot-halls of the chiefest burghs of his ancient dominions. Athelstane stands as the guardian of their rights. Behold the son of the shepherdess; listen to his words:

> As free
> Make I thee,
> As heart may think, or eye may see:

had his largesses obtained, or retained their full effect, no less would now have been the liberties of every community within these realms. These are the rights for which we strive. Though long delayed, the day will come when none shall rule over us, except at our pleasure, and according to our voice and will."

Marco, hearing these words, looked earnestly at the speaker, whose pale, hollow, and thoughtful countenance was instantly suffused with a deep but transient blush of emotion; he perceived that Marco was trying to read his inmost thoughts—perhaps had divined them.

This was, to a certain extent, true. But although Marco could well ascertain that Andrew would have been the first to raise the cry, *Popolo, Popolo*, in the London commonwealth: yet he could not discover the peculiar and national character of the visions in which the citizen indulged.

In the middle ages, history had the same practical influence upon men's actions, through the medium of the imagination, that the themes of political economy and government now produce through the calculating and reasoning powers. Barren as the mediæval chroniclers appear to the modern student, their facts, no less than their fables, operated with vital intensity upon the mind. Palled, surfeited, overwhelmed, in our era, with the empty nomenclature of pseudo-information, it is we who are unable to appreciate the effect produced by these compositions, when every idea was a belief, when words were realities.

To us, the events of past times are as the macerated specimens of ancient art in the dull solemn toyshop called a museum:

gewgaws without power, supplying a study to the artist, a lesson
to the giggling school-girl, an essay to the virtuoso, a phrase in
the guide-book, a number in the catalogue, a block to be entombed
in the chilling wall. To our forefathers, the events of past times
were living forms, voices which were heard, guides who directed,
leaders who commanded, teachers to be obeyed. In the same
manner as Rienzi received his call to the tribunate through the
perusal of the moss-grown inscription, speaking the language of
old Rome, and the contemplation of the hollow arch which had
echoed to the wheels of the chariot of the Cæsars, so did historical
traditions, embodied in the lay, the law, or the prophecy, vague,
and awful, constantly feed and nourish a mysterious spirit of
recovering a long-lost liberty.

Strange ideas were secretly cherished amongst us in England
of restoring some member of the true Saxon race, some descendant
of the ancient kings, under whom the commons alone should
exist, all intermediate distinctions being destroyed. Nor were
those wanting who brooded upon the visions of primitive equality,
and inculcated the duty of breaking down the distinctions in human
society, considered even then by large and increasing political
and religious sectaries, not in their true light, as essential portions
of the dispensations of Providence, but as the badges of servitude
and tyranny. Doctrines which, echoed and transmitted from
nation to nation, and age to age, became the inheritance of Wat
Tyler and Jack Cade, of Aske and Kett the Tanner, of William
Tell and Thomas Münzer, even until we arrive at the present day.

Andrew at once changed the tenor of his discourse, he felt
that he had spoken much too freely, and attempting to divert
the attention of Marco, he pointed to the grey castellated edifice
which spread its lengthened walls before them—"This," said he
to Marco, "is the Ealdormanna-Burgh, the fortress of the senators,
the spot which, from time whereof the memory of man runneth
not to the contrary, hath been the seat of the government of our
community."

"Such being the case," quoth Marco, "London is not wholly
unlike fair Florence, in which you may trace circuit within circuit,
town within town, denoting how the subjects had been separated
from their lords. Within the *Primo Cerchio*, dwelled the nobles
priding themselves upon their descent from the patricians of
the Roman state. A second circle included those who erewhile
fled from the neighbouring Fiesole, and also the Teutonic warriors,
who, when their strongholds were destroyed, were compelled to

shelter themselves beneath the seemly protection of the patrician race. Lastly, was erected the third and outer circuit of walls, whose ambit became the dwelling-place of the plebeians, the subjects of the combined aristocracy."

"Does this state of things still continue in Florence?" said Andrew.

"Long since have the walls of the interior. circles been destroyed. The authority of the nobles lasted much longer than their walls. But after many revolutions, of which it were sooth to tell, the patricians have become in effect the servants of those, who still, in theory, acknowledge them as their superiors.

"From any share in the rule and government of the Community, every individual who bears the name and arms of the noblest families of Florence is inexorably excluded by the plebeian authorities. The lesser nobles, if they seek to possess the rights of citizens, must be matriculated as members of the trade societies, the colleges of handicraftsmen, who have, not very long since, received a new incorporation and additional powers. Amongst the principal of these plebeian associations, the rulers governing the Florentine republic are chosen. The noble, doffing his helmet and his corslet, and blotting the bearing from his armorial shield, to replace it by the merchant's mark, may perhaps still contrive to steal into the signoria, disguised in the hood and gown of the artificer; but it is not difficult to foresee, that, even thus humbled, he will speedily be proscribed."

They were almost on the threshold of the building which towered above the rest of the Ealdormanna-Burgh—the site of which will be easily recognized by my readers, as being still known by the familiar name of "aldermanbury"—when a body of heavy-armed cavalry, led on by a knight in full armour, wheeled round through a narrow street, and compelled the three companions to stop till the troop should have filed away.

A standard of ample size was borne by the leader, displaying a red cross, and the figure of St. Paul. Amidst the authoritative cries of sergeants and beadles, "Make way for my Lord Fitzwalter, lord of Castle Baynard, banner-bearer of our good city of London," he swung down from his powerful steed, and entered the Guildhall. Marco Polo and his companions followed in the crowd.

Andrew continued scowling at the baron, with a glance of undisguised vexation, I may almost say, malignity; "And this," whispered he to Marco, "is the mailed ruffian who, violating the natural equality of mankind, still claims, as privilege and property, a pre-eminence, which, if granted at all, should result only from the voice and choice of the community, like those in whose assembly he now intrudes."

Friar Bacon felt these bold, and, as he truly considered them, culpable expressions, almost as a direct challenge. But he had acquired the true prudence of a philosopher and a man of science, and was quite content to be silent, instead of contending for the empty victory of confuting opinions, which the most complete refutation would neither influence nor control.

The mayor and aldermen rose to greet the Lord Fitzwalter, who advanced into the midst of the assembly, and preferred his claim to the franchises resulting from the tenure of his stronghold.

"In war, the lord of Castle Baynard is to lead forth the host of citizens."

The lord mayor nodded assent.

"The thief apprehended within the soke of the lord of Castle Baynard, is to be thrown into prison until due judgment."

"Even so, my lord, it is entered in *Liber Ordinationum*, at the hundred and sixty-third page," replied the town-clerk.

"If a traitor be convicted in the court of the soke of Castle Baynard, he is to be led, at low water, to the adjoining shore of the Thames. Strangled at the stake to which he is bound, his corpse is to be abandoned until it hath been thrice concealed by the rising tide."

"A true judgment," exclaimed the recorder, "such as your worships have always allowed my Lord Fitzwalter's progenitors to pronounce, and," continuing in a low tone to the common-sergeant, who stood at his side, "such as some of my Lord Fitzwalter's progenitors might have sustained; but one man may steal a horse, whilst"—"Hush, hush, brother," whispered the common sergeant, who was already more than half frightened at the boldness of his colleague.

As the Lord Fitzwalter was reciting his claims, the town-clerk carefully attested the accuracy of each demand by the authentic record, his finger travelling down the vellum page: and the said living index had now arrived at the concluding rubric, which, in manuscripts, was always in colour, what now it is in name. Lifting up his hand from the line of red letters, he opened his palm, and struck the book so loudly, that the vaulted roof echoed with the sound. The civic magistrate evidently expected this warning, and most of the bystanders seemed also to have a secret understanding that they were to prepare for some extraordinary occurrence.

"Lastly," continued the baron, in a clear and sonorous voice, "I, the Lord Fitzwalter, lord of the soke of Castle Baynard, within the city of London, demand, as of right, for myself, and my heirs, and appertaining to my franchise, that, whenever, by you, sir mayor, a full council of this city is assembled, the lord of Castle Baynard is to be summoned thereunto, duly taking his oath in form of city law."

Instead of the ready assent which had been given to the preceding claims, a pause ensued. Fitzwalter waited respectfully. No answer. Fitzwalter planted his standard firmly, and grasping the staff with both hands, leant forward. All was silence. The mayor rose, and with the aldermen, retired to the further part of the hustings, and, after a short discussion had amongst them, the recorder, as the mouth-piece of the city, came forward and replied, "My Lord Fitzwalter, it hath been considered by the good men of this community, that, in order to eschew divers inconveniences, it is no longer meet for your lordship to sit in council amongst them in this hall."

"What!" exclaimed the Lord Fitzwalter, "deny the right testified in the very page bearing witness to all the other franchises which have been so readily allowed!" "It may be so, my lord," answered the recorder, shutting the book, "but the citizens have advised upon it. And now, ye good men of the Painter's craft and mystery, come forward, and make your bidding and your prayer." Against such a determination to do injustice, no appeal could be made. Rudeness, nay insult, marked the conduct of the civic functionary. Fitzwalter deigned not to make any reply; he flung down the banner indignantly on the pavement, and forcing his way through the craftsmen, who were advancing to the bar, he disappeared in the crowd. Taken up by the lord mayor's henchman, the banner was brought in triumph to the hustings: the link which connected the community of London with the territorial aristocracy of the realm, was irretrievably destroyed.

"Citizens of London," said Marco to Andrew Horn, "ye have borrowed a lesson out of the books of Florence, in thus expelling from your councils the nobles of the land."

"In this country, it is hard to say who is noble and who is not, who may be the borrower, and who the lender," observed the friar. More he was about to add, when the business before the court was resumed.

About this era, the gilds or incorporations of craftsmen—containing within them elements destined to alter the whole condition of municipal society—were now rising simultaneously into importance throughout the commonwealth of Christendom. These bodies may, without difficulty, be traced to the colleges of workmen which subsisted in the Roman empire, and had, under that political dispensation, held an ambiguous place between servitude and freedom. Traditions ascribing their origin to Numa, only testify that these societies had existed at Rome from time immemorial. To say that such institutions are coeval with the first origin of the useful arts amongst mankind, would be an assertion unsusceptible of direct proof. All the Soodra castes in Hindostan are, however, founded upon the governing principle of these operative communities, namely, that the occupation is hereditary. The lot of the father descends upon the son: and inasmuch as we have every reason to suppose that this portion of Asia exhibits the faithful reflection of the usages of Mizraim, we can scarcely avoid admitting that this system was acknowledged in the earliest ages of civilization.

The castes in the east are strictly confined to blood and lineage; hence they tend to maintain society in a state of steady, and in many respects, most happy uniformity. But in Europe a new and expansive principle was introduced into these communities, that of aggregation, which modified the original principle of stability. It was this which ultimately rendered them equally powerful instruments of change, but change for good, by substituting moral influences for patriarchal inheritance.

According to the policy of the Roman law, it scarcely appeared as an innovation in these societies, if the disciple, the adopted child of the master, were allowed to obtain the privileges of the son by birth and blood. He was constituted heir, not merely to the common property of the college, but to the skill and knowledge of the teacher—his living, in the strictest sense of the term. This was the origin of our system of apprenticeship, now degraded by opinions and decried by philosophical reasoning, but which, in the middle ages, and, indeed, almost down to our own days, had a most beneficial influence upon the community.

So long as the engagement subsisted according to its pristine spirit, it rendered the master and the servant members of one household and family—the parties were united by the mutual obligation of protection and obedience. The mutual connexion recognized better elements than those of mere profit and gain.

He would be an unwise legislator for his fellow-men, who could omit to take self-interest into consideration as a most powerful impelling motive: but a sorry one is he, who relies upon self-interest as affording any kind of security for diligence or industry, or for any quality to which the name of virtue can be ascribed. Whatever the political economist may urge to the contrary, unless men begin by bettering themselves, all his assumed recipes for bettering their condition are in vain.

Motives infinitely more valuable than those of mere money and money's worth, were engrafted upon the system of apprenticeship, so long as its spirit was properly observed. The admission into the gild after the period of probation had concluded, was an attestation that, during the period of life when the human character is most susceptible of the influence of habit and example, the future citizen had conducted himself with a due attention to diligence and morality. Gratitude towards a kind master— emulation excited by an able one—the necessity of conciliating a harsh superior—affection towards an infirm or needy parent— the wish to be married—to form that union which the church so emphatically calls a "holy state," and upon which the happiness of the individual, and, through the individual, the happiness of the state, so mainly depends—all these rendered the guilds an unceasing source of moral renovation to the commonwealth.

The series of events so forcibly presented to us by the artist in the graphic scenes of his "industrious apprentice," were common in the last age, rare as they may be in ours. Every medal has its reverse. The same forcible pencil has delineated the "idle apprentice." Chains and fetters bound those who broke their indentures. Many a flat-cap was laid by the heels in the stocks, flogged in the hall, or awoke from his jovial carouse, in the dreary gloom of the "little ease," when, cramped in the chill solitude, he vainly attempted to stretch out his aching lubber limbs. But the system, though incompetent to amend human nature, professed to be founded upon those principles by which alone the human heart can be renewed.

Religion was the foundation of the gild; divine worship the solid bond of the association. The members were constantly reminded that it was not to the contrivances of the wit, or the strength of the labouring hand, that man owes his daily bread. Industry, they were taught, might be the appointed means, but God's providence was the only source, of our subsistence; its increase, the result of His blessing, not of our frugality; the alms, the testimony of our gratitude to Him from whom the bounty, unmerited and undeserved, is obtained. Imperfect as these institutions may have been, how much better calculated were they than our own, to ameliorate the condition of the lower and lowest orders of the community! The modern operative belongs to a degraded, and therefore to a hostile order. His feelings, views, interests, all are, or are sedulously represented to him as being, in dire opposition to the manufacturer, the cotton-lord, the capitalist, whom he considers as his tyrant and his enemy. But in the old time, the workman was the "brother," the "*compagnon*," the "*gesell*," of his employer, perhaps poorer in purse, inferior in station, younger in age, but all united by the most kind and sociable bonds. They repeated the same creed: met in the same church: lighted their lamp before the same altar: feasted at the same board. Thus they constituted the elements of that burgher aristocracy, which, as far as institutions can answer that end, reconciled poor and rich, equally protecting the rights and claims of capital and of labour.

After the scattering of the Roman empire, and until the thirteenth century, these societies, subsequently so influential, had subsisted, with very few exceptions, by usage and prescription: rarely deriving any protection from the state. Indeed, we find that attempts were occasionally made to suppress these trade societies, whose growing power excited the vigilance, possibly the jealousy, of the sovereign. These efforts did not succeed. In such cases, force is of no avail. The quicksilver divides beneath the pressure; but the globules run together again as soon as that pressure is removed. Voluntary combinations of all kinds are not unfrequently decomposed by their internal fermentations and discord; but no external and adverse force, short of the complete dispersion, or total extermination of the individuals, can kill the life that is in them. Not only did the gilds baffle all the adverse edicts and denunciations, but they continued steadily to advance, obtaining not merely the toleration but the favour of the state. Collectively they sought God's blessing, individually they obtained it. They prospered in their ways. From the thirteenth century, these associations, which had hitherto been governed by their private regulations, obtained full sanctions of their ordinances from those authorities who could render them coercive according to the law.

Such confirming authorities differed, of course, not only according to the constitution of the different states of Europe, but also according to the local policy of the different parts of the same state.   In London, the court of aldermen became the tribunal from which these minor communities acquired their legal existence, the crown not interfering until a later era: and it was upon such business that the body or gild of craftsmen, were now advancing to the Bar to prefer their humble requests.   Do you, reader, listen attentively to their words, for the monk of Croyland has extracted them from *Liber Ordinationum*, and I doubt if you have ever had an opportunity of hearing them before.

"Humbly, we good men of the Painter's Craft, of the Gild of St. Luke, beseech your worships to confirm the ordinances, by common assent made, for the advancement of our trade: and the prevention of fraud and falsehood, in our praiseworthy mystery.

"Imprimis.   That no craftsman shall use or employ other colours than such as be good and fine; good sinople, good azure, good verdigrease, good vermilion, or other good body colours, mixed and tempered with oil, and no brasil, indigo, or other of the last-mentioned sort and kind."

"It pleases their worships," said the recorder.

"Item.   That no good man of this Craft of the Painters shall entice away another man's apprentice or servant."

"It pleases their worships."

"Item.   That no stranger, not being a brother of this gild, shall work at his trade until he hath made gree to my lord the mayor for his entry into the liberty of the city: and hath caused himself to be put in frankpledge, and hath become buxom to our gild, and paid two shillings towards the sustenance of our poor."

Thus did the warden crave assent to the several constitutions of his gild, praying the approbation of his worthy masters, the aldermen, to each article.   The affirmative being given to the several propositions, or petitions, they acquired the force of law, and became the foundation of a code, which, having been from time to time increased, and altered as need required, still regulates the "Painter Stainers' company."   Without any disrespect to any other public body, I am bound to assert that this same city company is assuredly the real true and genuine and Royal Academy of England.

Queen Elizabeth, towards the conclusion of her reign, became extremely anxious to avert the rapid decay of the fine arts. Distressed by the "horrible counterfeits" of her countenance, which began to be current: and in order to ensure the transmission to her loving subjects of a likeness, which she might like them to

see, she granted to the said Company of Painters, otherwise
Painter Stainers, a most stringent monopoly. No one was to
paint any portraiture of the sovereign, or any member of the
royal family, save and except a freeman of the company,
under divers pains and penalties in said charter contained.
Despite of municipal reform, their privileges are not disregarded.
Albeit the main occupation of the freemen of the company at
the present day be that application of the art, which is usually
called into action in conjunction with the plasterer and the white-
washer: still the very distinguished and talented individual, who
now so deservedly fills the station of Serjeant Painter to the
king, followed the precedents of Kneller, and Reynolds, and duly
qualified himself for the appointment, by taking up his freedom
according to the charter.

Were the materials which still exist for the history of these
gilds, carefully investigated, we might perhaps be able to show
how the advancement of the so-called "fine arts," was connected
with the progress of mediæval "civility," a very different thing
from civilization. The outward form which they then assumed,
was the token of the institutions by which they were produced.
"Art" was then natural, it grew out of the condition and idiosyn-
crasy of mankind. Now, "Art" is factitious; it is extraneous,
superinduced upon our social relations, and not arising from them.
It has no real affinity to our mode of being. It is the forced and
sickly flower of the conservatory, not the vigorous product of the
soil. Except as an adjunct to our mammon, it has no hold upon
the multitude, no connexion with the *mind* of our utilitarian era.

A very curious proof of the intimate alliance between the arts
and national policy, is afforded by mediæval architecture. In the
north of Italy, where the municipal institutions were broken up
by the barbaric invasions, all Roman science suddenly ceases
and comes to an end. In the Roman "province" of Gaul, on the
contrary, where the succession of the municipal authorities was
uninterrupted, however uncouth and barbaric the union of the
several portions of the building may be, yet in each moulding and
capital, taken distinctly and severally, a Roman feeling is preserved. There is an evident transmission of doctrine from the
previous ages. In the first case, the untaught stone-hewer copied
the object which he saw; in the second, the instructed mason
practised what he was taught; and, imperfect as his attempts
may have been, the contrast between the productions is extreme:
and indicates, even to the eye, the difference between the legal

characters of the communities. In the first case, we discern a Teutonic population which had absorbed the Roman race; in the second, a Roman community humbled, yet retaining its integrity.

With respect to the practice of oil-painting, designated with such clearness in the ordinances of the Painters' Gild, as to leave no doubt as to the nature of the pigment, it must have been principally employed upon heraldic ornaments. The peculiar manipulations required, seem, however, to have been but little known out of the fraternity; and this circumstance may be in some measure explained by recollecting, that in these gilds, all the more important and essential processes were concealed as mysteries, in the strict sense of the term. Theory and practice were conjoined. During the earlier periods, the hereditary character of the handicraft must have greatly assisted in preventing the profane from withdrawing the veil. Other means were practised for the purpose of keeping the secrets of the trade, and defending the monopoly. Oaths, awe-inspiring ceremonies, initiations, sometimes terrific, sometimes painful or ludicrous. Here the candidate trembled beneath the arch of steel, the swords suspended over his head. There, unless his agility preserved him, the incipient workman enjoyed the full application of the lash of the cartwhip.

Even in this our age of triumphant publicity, some curious vestiges of this ancient system may be traced. "The gentleman who reports for our paper," at whose presence every other door stands open, has never been able to obtain the slightest insight into the proceedings of the Lodge of Cosmopolite Freedom, meeting at the Yorkshire Stingo, Gray's Inn Lane; the same being the true and legitimate scion, as my intended quarto will show, of the Masons' Company of London. The aspirant, admitted into the Worshipful Company of Cooks, binds himself under a heavy penalty, not to reveal to any stranger the secret of raising puff-paste. A fruitless precaution, since the arcanum is entirely in the possession of every publisher in town. And *Io Scrittore*, can further testify that having, in pure, unsuspecting, guileless innocence, put a question to the worthy Prime Warden of the Plumbers' Company respecting the proportions of the alloy of tin and bismuth employed in the process of "sealing solder," I found myself as completely baffled by the resolute silence which closed the mouth of the worthy beadle, the official superintendent of their metallurgic operations, as if I had sought to know the ingredients of the powder of projection, from the Grand Master of

the Rosicrucian fraternity.   But I am well nigh forgetting my
tagged and ragged manuscript, to which I must return.

Marco and his companions had, during the transactions with
the Painters' Gild, retired to a jutting oriel, in the new-fashioned
"Gothic" style, which had just been erected in the Hall.

"Our English gilds," said Andrew, "obtained great additions
to their powers in the mayoralty of one, who will long be remembered in this city, as the man of the people, Walter Hervey.
This happened much about the time, when, as I hear from Nicholas
Verkooper, the Fleming, the same bodies assisted the bishop of
Utrecht in the cares of government: and when, also, as you told
us, your Florentine craftsmen obtained the chief powers in their
commonwealth."   I am not sure whether Andrew knew the
probable issue of affairs in Germany, otherwise he might have
added, that the Zunfts or gilds of craftsmen at Nuremberg were
fast tending to a similar assumption of power.

These eras of contemporaneous movement throughout Christendom are amongst the most remarkable social phenomena of the
middle ages.   For the transmission and diffusion of opinions, we
now depend entirely upon the press.   As much, perhaps more,
was effected without its aid.   An ounce of mother wit, improved
by observation, is worth a stone of book-knowledge.   In all
things, in the present age, we depend far too much upon the pen.
The multiplicity of ideas imparted by means of printing obliterate
each other.   They destroy each other by interference.   In optics,
there may be "fits of easy transmission and reflection"; but "reflection" rarely follows "easy transmission" in matters of the mind.
When printing did not exist, the smaller quantity of mental
stimulants was fully compensated by their intensity.   In the tale
brought home by the one traveller, who, having witnessed the
revolution, came home after passing through the perils of fire
and slaughter, or the impassioned narrative of the one foreigner
recounting the deeds of his countrymen, there was a vivid vitality
producing the one leading idea, which pervaded whole masses of
population, displaying by conformity of results the uniformity of
the inducing cause.

"Have your craftsmen," said Marco, "like their compeers in
Tuscany, excluded all other classes from municipal authority?"

"They are trying, at least, to render themselves integral elements of our civic community.   According to our old English
customs, such as were whilom used and approved in the days of
King Alfred, when golden bracelets——"

"Tush, man," said the friar, "let alone the lies, and give us the law."

"They often go together," replied Andrew, half in laughter and half in anger; "but the notions which I am explaining to his seignory, are truth in very deed. According to the law, then, of King Alfred's reign, as confirmed by the Confessor, ratified by the Conqueror, and continued by constant usage, the enrolment in the frankpledge, and the possession of the tenement, ought to make the citizen, without any further or other qualifications being required."

"Frankpledge," quoth Marco, "what is that?"

"An institution which we owe to the profound wisdom of the immortal Alfred, the foundation of our civic and territorial policy, throughout all England."

"No, certainly not through England," said the friar.

Master Andrew, a true political antiquary—by the way, for that reason, I would not advise you to believe implicitly all that he says—plainly saw, that unless he rode, booted and spurred, through the friar's objections, he should never be able to establish his theory; so, without hesitation, explanation, modification, or alteration, he continued in the same tone: "The foundation of our civic and territorial policy throughout all England. Every layman is bound, by the laws of Alfred, to be enrolled in his tithing or dizeine."

"Dozen, not *dizeine*; twelve, sir, not ten," said the friar; supplying thereby, through Britton, who followed his opinion, a note to the future historian of the middle ages.

"*Dizeine*, not dozen," retorted Andrew, with imperturbable resolution. "Ten men they be, answerable for the deeds and misdeeds of each other, and placed under the superintendence of the chief pledge, the tithing-man, or the headborgh, their superior."

"It is a good law, and wise," observed Marco, "and contributeth much to the preservation of the peace in Cathay, where the same frankpledge is found. Every tenth householder is bound to look after the conduct of his neighbours; and with such a tithing-man did I lodge when I dwelt at Cambalu."

It is well known that Cambalu is the modern Pekin. And I, the editor, may perhaps here be permitted to add, by way of annotation, that, as I have been credibly informed, by one of the few Europeans who have entered its jealous precincts, this decennary police continues in full force in China at the present day.

"In similar, or nearly the same guise," continued Marco, "doth the law which you call your English law of frankpledge, subsist amongst the descendants of Trajan's legions in Wallachia. Fierce as they are, they have their 'loods,' thus call they these associations, their 'lots,' composed of ten men, formed exactly upon the same principle, mutually pledged for the security of the country. Indeed, I should think that any legislator, accustomed to military authority, would easily see the expediency and practicability of such an organized species of encampment upon the land."

"Thus, Master Andrew," said the friar, "whilst we admit the fact of this decennary arrangement in England, the originality of the invention must be denied."

Andrew heeded not the comment.

"Founded thus upon the institutions of the immortal Alfred, is the qualification of our burghs. But in addition to the rights thus derived from household residence, our craftsmen, like yours, Messer Marco Polo, seek to render the matriculation in their gilds, an essential element in the qualification for the municipal franchise. They reckon upon being able to introduce a law, that no one shall be admitted into our freedom, unless he be of some certain gild or mystery. Instead of calling our councillors from the wards, they talk of a scheme for electing from these mysteries alone, the members of our civic community."

In this, and in many other matters, Master Andrew was singularly gifted. The innovations which he foresaw or foretold, did actually take place. After various fluctuations, the gilds became the only channels, through which the municipal freedom could be acquired.

Meanwhile, a great bustle had arisen in the hall. It continued to increase. Marco and his companions looked round towards the hustings, and found, that whilst they were talking, not only had Sir William de Ormesby, the chief justice of the king's bench, arrived; but the king's commission had actually been read, without their hearing one word of it. Mayor and aldermen, with the king's justices, were sitting as a court of oyer and terminer, and gaol-delivery.

Andrew Horn, who was quite at home in the Guildhall, conducted his companions upon the hustings, just as the sergeants were compelling by main force a manacled criminal to stand at the bar.

The malefactor had been apprehended in Cheap, in the very act of cutting a purse from the girdle of Sir John de Stapleford, vicar-general of the bishop of Winchester. Cases of flagrant delict, according to our ancient common law, or, to speak more accurately, according to the law of all nations in the simpler stages of society, required no other trial than the publicity or incontrovertibleness of the fact, no further proof of the offence was needed, and no defence allowed. They proceeded by law in the same manner as the mob now do by impulse, when the pickpocket is dragged through a horsepond; or like the gardener thrashing the school-boy, whom he has caught in his apple-tree. Trivial and almost ludicrous as these comparisons may appear, they are apposite and pertinent examples of our ancient law as laid down by Bracton, and displayed in our ancient records. Open guilt was instantly followed by vengeance. The murderer grasping the deadly weapon: the "bloody hand" of the violator of the royal forest: the robber bearing his spoil, received at once the punishment of their misdeeds. According to these principles, Sir William de Ormesby therefore intimated to the officers, that as they might, and, indeed, ought, to have struck off the head of the prisoner before the Conduit, it was unnecessary thus to have given the court the trouble of passing judgment.

"Let him be hanged upon the elms at Tyburn," was forthwith pronounced as his doom. Pale, trembling, suing for mercy, the wretch was taken from the bar, not indeed without exciting some suppressed feelings of compassion in the court. Evidently was the punishment disproportioned to the crime; but the maxim of considering that the sentence once denounced by the law was immutable, had practically the effect of stifling the natural sentiments of humanity.

Louder and louder became the cries of the miserable culprit as he receded from the judges; and just when the sergeants were dragging him across the threshold, he clung to the pillar which divided the portal, shrieking in a voice of agony which pierced through the hall, "I demand of Holy Church the benefit of my clergy!" Perhaps, in strictness, the time for claiming this privilege had gone by, but the officers halted with their prey: and one of the prothonotaries having hurried to them with a message from Chief Justice Ormesby, the thief was replaced at the bar. During the earlier portion of the proceedings, the kind-hearted vicar-general had evidently been much grieved and troubled by his enforced participation in the condemnation of the criminal. Stepping forward, he now addressed the court, and entreated permission, in the absence of the proper Ordinary, to try the validity of the claim.

Producing his breviary, he held the page close to the eyes of the kneeling prisoner; he inclined his ear. The bloodless lips of the ghastly caitiff were seen to quiver. *"Legit ut Clericus,"* instantly exclaimed the vicar-general; and this declaration at once delivered the felon from death, though not from captivity. "Take him home to the pit," said the vicar-general, "where, shut out from the light of day, and the air of heaven, he will be bound in iron, fed with the bread of tribulation, and drinking the water of sorrow, until he shall have sought atonement for his misdeeds and expiated his shame."

Whatever abuses may have arisen from this privilege, the "benefit of clergy," which by the well-known merciful connivance of the law was (as in this case) extended to all who could read, or could be supposed to read their neck verse, we should reject the common, though most erroneous idea, that it was intended to afford an indemnity to crime.

The imprisonment, as you have just heard it truly described, was most severe, and though, in some cases, the ecclesiastical immunities mitigated the common law, by saving the life of the offender: yet there were others in which signal chastisement was bestowed upon those who would otherwise have escaped all retribution.

But a higher principle was developed. In the theory of her criminal jurisprudence, the mediæval church had fully and unhesitatingly adopted the wise and truly beneficent doctrine, that punishment is to be inflicted by fallible man upon his fellow creatures, not merely in terror but in love. The imprisonment, with its accompaniments of hardships and privations, was considered as an ecclesiastical penance. Not thundered in vengeance for the satisfaction of the state, but imposed for the good of the offender: in order to afford the means of amendment, and to lead the transgressor to repentance, and to mercy. From the doors of the dungeon he was to come forth, not as a degraded criminal, but as a contrite sinner. This was the doctrine of the legislation of the mediæval clergy, now the butt and mark for commonplace contempt, and shallow contumely. The "penitentiary system" was not the invention of a Bentham or a Dumont, but of those who were utilitarians in the highest sense, who sought to render all the laws, and studies, and pursuits of men subservient to the salvation of the soul.

As matters are arranged in our age of civilization, we take good care not to be deficient in keeping up a stock of sin to supply stuff for repentance. "I, for my part," said a most active and exemplary magistrate, "always support the renewal of the licenses of the minor theatres, Vauxhall, and all those kind of places, in order to give full effect to his majesty's proclamation against vice and immorality, which our clerk always reads to us while we read the newspapers, when our session begins.

"I was once," continued he, "rather doubtful upon the subject, I could not quite reconcile it to my conscience, until I talked with the worthy governor of Newgate; when he told me, that to these and similar sources of rational amusement and innocent recreation, and the various establishments and accommodations which arise and flourish around them, he could trace the largest proportion of metropolitan crime. Now, sir, if vice and immorality were to be put down, how could we possibly pay due obedience to his majesty's commands? If there was no vice and immorality, what use, sir, would there be in the proclamation? The proclamation would become a dead letter. Sir, the proclamation would be a mockery. We magistrates, sir, standing as we do as public men, with the eyes of the whole civilized world always upon us, accountable to the country, and subject to the strictest scrutiny from the vigilance of the press, are bound to do something also, to show that we are efficient in our stations. Let us be consistent, and if we can keep Madam Vestris and the Olympic a-going, we shall always be sure to create a greater supply of 'vice and immorality,' by which we may be able to give full effect to the proclamation, than all the missions and model prisons will ever be able to prevent, punish, amend, or cure."

Marco and the friar beckon me back again to Guildhall, where we shall behold another criminal placed at the bar. "William of the Palace, thou art indicted as a felon, for that thou hast broken open, and robbed the treasury of our lord the king at Westminster. How wilt thou be tried?" The culprit was about to speak: when Andrew Horn, who had suddenly determined to retain himself for the prisoner, loudly took up the word, and silencing William of the Palace by the wave of his hand, he exclaimed, "The culprit wages his law as a freeman of the city of London, as one of the burgesses, to whom it is granted by the Conqueror, that they should be *worth* the same law as in the days of good Saint Edward. Therefore is he entitled to refute the accusation by the declaration of his friends. Seven shall be the compurgators chosen and named by the prisoner himself according to our old Anglo-Saxon law. If they all concur in testifying his innocence, if their oath declares him guiltless, he is quitted for ever of the transgression which the king has laid to his charge. This franchise of our city bars the plea of the crown."

Even as the candidate who now promises to advocate the abolition of imprisonment for debt, excites the warmest response from the shirtless multitude: the same being received by them as an "instalment of justice," a part payment on account of their just demand not to pay any debts at all, so did a shout of applause from the crowd testify the satisfaction with which the bystanders heard this declaration of their city privileges. This Anglo-Saxon law was a matter in which a great many of them took an interest by no means theoretical, since it afforded, could it be established, a comparatively easy mode of escaping the legal noose.

An observation of Marco Polo, that possibly Master Andrew might be anticipating the fruition of some good thing in the gift of the good citizens, was answered by a knowing nod of unwilling assent from the alderman whom he had addressed. There is a peculiar state of the atmosphere producing a mirage, by which he who, long practised in the management of public bodies, "doth bend his eye on vacancy," is enabled to discern the approach of such vacancy of place or office, when the same is still far below the political horizon. Andrew Horn was a seer of this class: thus, within a short period afterwards, the sturdy and patriotic champion of popular rights was rewarded by the consciousness of his deserts, and the honourable and lucrative employment of town-clerk of the city. I would wish, however, to speak of Andrew Horn with great respect. He compiled a most valuable and authentic collection of documents relating to the liberties and franchises of the community, entitled *Liber Horn*, still kept with great care amongst the archives in Guildhall, which I have perused with extreme delight: and the emphatic "*non bene*" quoted at the beginning of this chapter proceeds from his own hand.

Andrew Horn's city law, however, was not allowed to pass unquestioned by the court. "The right of compurgation, which you claim for the prisoner, is taken away by the implication arising from the tenor of the Assizes of Clarendon, re-enacted at Northampton," sternly exclaimed the chief justice.

"Cry you mercy, my lord," replied Andrew, with firm humility; "your objection, most humbly do I submit, is wholly nought. London is not specifically noticed in the Assize. The enactment is in general terms: and it is the franchise of the London citizens, that no statute affects their privileges, unless they be therein specially named."

"But the culprit, good Master Andrew," observed the recorder, trying to trim his course accurately between the chief justice, to whom he looked up for promotion, and the common-council, to whom he looked down for his salary, "must be a full citizen, and not merely a nominal member of our community: unless he is actually resident, paying scot and bearing lot with the rest of the ward, he cannot claim these rights. I sincerely hope that the poor fellow at the bar is duly qualified: I should regret exceedingly if master chamberlain were compelled, in the exercise of his duty, to inform the court that the name of William of the Palace doth not appear upon the tallage roll."

This hint was not lost upon the chief justice. Search was made upon the roll, and, as may be anticipated, the name of William of the Palace was absent, he had not been rated or assessed to the charge. The want of participation in the civic contribution deprived the culprit of the franchise of the civic community, and he was left to the common law.

"Culprit, how wilt thou defend thyself?" was the question now put by the town-clerk.

William of the Palace was about to answer, he was small and debilitated, and sickly, yet hot and angry: so he began to pull at his glove, preparing for the battle ordeal. But, before it was half drawn off, Master Andrew again stepped forward, and, speaking for the client upon whose business he had employed himself, said, "He puts himself upon the country."

"Sheriff! is your inquest in court?" said the mayor.

"Yes, my lord," replied the sheriff, "and I am proud to say it will be an excellent jury for the crown. I, myself, have picked and chosen every man on the panel. I have spoken to them all, and there is not one whom I have not examined carefully, not only as to his knowledge of the offence wherewith the prisoner stands charged: but of all the circumstances from which his guilt can be collected, suspected, or inferred. All the jurors are acquainted with him, eight out of the twelve have often been known to declare, upon their troth, years ago when he was a naughty orchard-robbing boy, that they were sure one day he would come to the gallows. The foreman always used to say he hoped he should live to see Willikin hanged, and the remainder are fully of opinion that he deserves the halter. My lord, I should ill have performed my duty, if I had allowed my bailiffs to summon the jury at hap-hazard, and without previously ascertaining the extent of their testimony. Some, perhaps, know more, and some less, but the least-informed of the jury have taken great pains to go up and down in every hole and corner of Westminster: they and their wives: and to learn all they could hear, concerning his past and present life and conversation. Never had any culprit a better chance of having a fair trial."

I don't doubt but that my readers are horror-struck at the iniquity of our ancient legal administration. But, "trial by jury," has most singularly retained its original form, wholly changing its original nature. Until the reign of the Tudors, the jury, instead of being the peers of the accused, by whom his guilt was to be tried, a court before whom the validity of the evidence given by the witnesses was to be investigated, were the sworn witnesses themselves, and their true saying, the *veredictum*, or verdict, was the summing-up of their own testimony. Hence it was the duty of the Sheriff to learn their previous knowledge of the facts, and to summon those by whom, in the words of the process yet in use, "the truth could be better known." Thus, for example, if the authenticity of a deed was contested, the parties named as witnesses in the charge of attestation were not subpœnaed to give evidence that they had seen it duly sealed, but were themselves associated to the jury.

So consistent was the ancient law, that if the crime was of such a secret nature that "the neighbourhood," the *visne*, or *vicinetum*, the name technically given to the jury, could not reasonably be supposed to have a knowledge of it,—murder by the administration of poison, may be instanced,—then the accused party could not be tried by a jury at all. The jurors were brought before the judge by the sheriff upon the same principle that the attorney now collects his witnesses in order to obtain a conviction. He got together those who, in his opinion, could best make out the case. It is to be feared that the sheriff—of the modern limb of the law we will say nothing—was not always over scrupulous as to the means by which that end was to be attained.

"William of the Palace," the prisoner, not having challenged any of the panel, the good men were duly sworn to say the truth, and after retiring for a few minutes, delivered their *veredictum* by their foreman in the following form.

"As soon as the robbery was bruited about, and even before the sergeants-at-arms were empowered to make inquiry for the offenders, William of the Palace quitted Westminster, and repaired into this city of London. Furthermore, when his house was searched by the sergeants-at-arms, there was found hid in the dovecote a golden mazer, and a broken reliquary in the shape of a cross, both of which, as we have been told, by the usher of the deputy chamberlain of the exchequer, came, as his master the deputy believed, he having been so informed by the chamberlain, out of the king's treasury, in the cloister of the abbey of Westminster, hard by the chapter-house of the said abbey." And I may here remark that this broken reliquary was no other than the cross of St. Neot, upon which the Scottish nobles swore the oaths of allegiance, and which oaths were then in the same condition.

"Furthermore," continued the foreman of the jury, "the culprit is idle: he is a glutton: he is a drunkard: he borroweth and payeth not: he keepeth company with suspicious persons: he diceth: he sweareth: he haunteth taverns: he rioteth: he liveth much above his means: he hath deserted his lawful wife, and now consorteth with his leman Eleanor, the daughter of Richard the Barber, dwelling in the lane of Guthrun the Dane, otherwise Gutter-lane, in the ward of Cheap: therefore we say with one accord, partly knowing these matters of our knowledge respectively, partly as we have heard from our companions, and partly from other persons of good credit, that the prisoner at the bar is guilty of the robbery of the king's treasury."

Illogical as the conclusions of the jury may appear to us, and such as might even bring many a member, even of the Alfred, the most virtuous of all clubs, into trouble, it will be seen that the verdict was grounded upon circumstantial evidence of the fact, united to a knowledge of the character of the party: thus raising a sufficient presumption, according to the jurisprudence of the age, to warrant his conviction of the crime with which he was charged.

"Culprit," said Sir William de Ormesby, "what hast thou to allege, that judgment be not passed upon thee?"

"That the indictment is wholly void," said Andrew, "inasmuch as the prisoner hath been forced, by artifice and deception, from the Sanctuary of the Blackfriars,"—a franchise then wholly, and still partially, exempted from the jurisdiction of the city.

The assertion thus made was substantially proved by the sacristan. A message brought in the name of John of St. Alban's, a master mason, strongly suspected of being the prisoner's accomplice, and about whom very strange stories were told, had inveigled the criminal out of that ancient precinct, in which he could laugh the Marshalmen to scorn, and placed him within the grasp of his captors.   After some discussion, Sir William de Ormesby re-luctantly admitted that, as a Sanctuary-man, the prisoner was to be permitted to purchase his exemption from capital punishment, by submitting to perpetual banishment.

The last defence raised by Andrew Horn was therefore so far effectual, that, like the plea of Clergy, it saved the life of his client. Bareheaded, barefooted, ungirt, and a white cross placed in his hand, he was sent forth on his painful pilgrimage.   Neither turning to the right or to the left, he proceeded to Dover, as the nearest sea-port, and there embarking, he abjured the realm for ever.

Other felonies were then tried : and this portion of the calendar being cleared, the chief justice arose and left the mayor and aldermen to dispose of the minor delinquents.   An individual was now, however, brought to the bar, who scarcely appeared to belong to this last-mentioned class, for, as soon as he "caught the eye" of the mayor, the worthy magistrate rose up from his seat, and greeted him with the loud execration, "Here he is, here is the wretch who hath sought to poison the whole city!"   This fearful accusation, however, was reduced into a smaller compass by the indictment.   Divesting the crime of the attributes which it had received from the glowing fancy and poetical imagery of the lord mayor, Stephen Lickpenny was simply charged with having sold rabbits in a state "abominable to man, and unfit for human food."

"Bring them before the court," exclaimed the town-clerk.

Placed upon the bar, an odour spread around, which indis-putably notified the presence of the rabbits to the assembled olfactory.

"Is it your worship's pleasure, that Lickpenny be allowed to put himself upon the country?" said the Crier.

"Hand up the rabbits to the court," spake the lord mayor.

No sooner said than done.   Almost before the command was completely given, the Crier, with dutiful alacrity, had brought the long-since murdered animals in contact with the nose of the junior alderman, who started back, with a loud "Paah!"   The rabbits continuing their gyration, the next alderman in seniority, who had already huddled up his gown, before his mouth and nostrils, signed to the trusty functionary .to pass on : when the lord mayor, who, if he had been as blind as love or justice, would have been fully aware of the distant approach of the savoury

cates, rose, apparently in a state of much excitement, and exclaimed, "What need have we of inquest or jury, or of further
testimony, beyond that which our senses thus supply? Let Lickpenny stand in the pillory, with the rabbits hung around his
neck." Ruthful Lickpenny was removed from the bar, where his
place was immediately supplied by a brother in the trade.

Substitute pigeons for the fourfooted stock of the poulterer,
and you have the accusation as before: and, as before, the birds
made the circuit of the bench of aldermen. This case, however,
was not so clear, and, for the credit of the court, it was requisite
to use a sound discretion.

Some of the aldermen snorted and shook their heads, others
appeared impassive, whilst one actually snuffed and snuffed again.
The aldermen retired to a small adjoining chamber, with the
pigeons. They closed the door: and after one hour and three
quarters' deliberation, they returned into the Guildhall.

Addressing Peter Romford, the lord mayor told him, that as
one of the most experienced aldermen could not satisfy himself
that the birds came within the compass of the indictment, as being
abominable and unfit for human food, the great majority of the
court, though they were of a very different opinion, considering
the great difficulty and importance of the case, would allow him
the benefit of a jury of cooks. And they were forthwith summoned from Eastcheap by the town-crier.

Shortly afterwards the twelve cooks entered the hall, with
much decorum and gravity; the boards creaked beneath their
tread. Being duly charged, they retired with the dubious victual:
and, after some discussion, the foreman, Stephen Towzle, pronounced, on behalf of himself and his fellow-jurors, "That the
pigeons were not abominable, nor unfit for human food: provided
they were duly seasoned and baked in a pie."

The delivery of this special verdict was immediately a signal
for a battle between the town-clerk and Master Andrew, who, as
usual, had retained himself for the prisoner. Andrew contended
that a "negative qualified" was equivalent to an acquittal: the
town-clerk, with equal vehemence, maintained it to be a declaration of the guilt of the party. But the Mayor, with much sound
sense, ended the matter, by rising and breaking up the court,
leaving the poulterer to go where he pleased, and the pigeons to
go wherever it should please the jury to convey them. Bearing
off the spoil, the cooks accordingly departed. Operated upon by
the skill of these predecessors of Ude and Jarrin, the birds quickly

found a gastronomic purchaser in the person of the very alderman who had most sniffed their previous flavour. With respect to the sentences in the cases of Rex *v.* Lickpenny, and Rex *v.* Romford, I must finally add, that they are left upon record in the city books, where I have consulted them, having carefully verified my manuscript thereby, and corrected the reports of the trials, for the instruction of the profession, in this branch of criminal law.

CHAPTER IV.

PARLIAMENT.

My intention is not to write a treatise upon the abstract principles of government. If it were, I am not quite sure whether I should not arrange my ideas in the inoffensive shape of a vocabulary or dictionary: expounding each term, not exactly by its verbal import, but according to the actual application of the word in the country to which the same belongs. Should we not thus obtain a cosmographical nomenclature of the civil institutions of mankind? We should then see—perhaps more clearly than would be quite agreeable—how exceedingly fluctuating is the value of the symbols by which political institutions are represented: and how they vary in every degree of latitude and longitude on the face of the globe.

Liberty in Constantinople consists in being entitled to have four wives at once, and to sew up all your four wives in four sacks, and throw them all four in the Bosphorus, either in four several plumps, or in such proportions and numbers as you choose. If this privilege be not infringed, your true Osmanli puffs away his unutterable contempt of the Giaour, who can submit to the degradation of beholding his denuded spouse quadrilling with unveiled face in a full-dress fancy ball.

Liberty at Benares consists in leaving your widow in full possession of the right of suttee, and in having your own bones crushed under Juggernaut's car. Take these rights of conscience away, as we have done, or are about to do; abolish the cruel doctrines of the Acharuburmitroduya and the Shoodee Kowmoodee; substitute our whole constitutional code from Magna Charta down to the Poor Laws' Amendment Bill, with the agreeable collateral embellishments of a Brahmin, starving himself on the treadmill, where the first step inflicted the exquisite mental torture of loss of caste, and a rajah beneath the gallows, agonized, not by the approach of death, but by the polluted touch of the pariah executioner; and our consistently humane endeavours to promote the happiness of the Hindoo, will, strange to say, be received with sullen ingratitude, as the most humiliating tyranny.

[91]

Liberty in "the States" consists in the full prerogative of "extinguishing" the red man by the progress of civilization; cuffing and kicking the free coloured man away from the ballotting box, burning your black man alive in a slow fire, having run him down with your blood-hounds, and slicking and cropping the white man under suspicion of being suspected of teaching the nigger to read his Bible: all these invaluable privileges being secured to the people who, in their glorious declaration of independence, claimed their emancipation from unhallowed and absolute tyranny as resulting from "the self-evident truths, that all men are created equal, that they are endowed by their Creator with certain inherent and unalienable rights, and that amongst these are life, liberty, and the pursuit of happiness."

Thus might we make the circuit of the globe, examining the internal principles of every extinct or subsisting community. Intelligently and honestly pursued, can we doubt but that such an inquiry would be an investigation of great curiosity? And so would it be of great instruction. After all, we should find no government, ancient or modern, founded upon a basis equally firm with our own. If there ever was a sentence which could be considered as so excellent as to be incapable of amendment, it is the old phrase, the good old whig phrase—the liberty of the subject —in which all the theory, all the doctrines of our mixed government are comprised.

Our English liberty, let the truth never be forgotten, is not the liberty of the country; nor is it the liberty of the nation; nor is it the liberty of the people: but a liberty which, as it belongs only to the subject, cannot be severed in idea or imagination from the person of the sovereign. Not a liberty, founded on theoretical reasonings; not a liberty in the abstract; but a liberty springing from the monarch. A liberty depending upon supremacy. A liberty to be earned by obedience. A liberty held with reference to peculiar duties and obligations. A liberty to be enjoyed only in conjunction with the rights and prerogatives of the crown, and in entire subservience to the law.

A tourist living in those happy days, when a monkey who had seen the world was a rarer animal than any of the present tenants of the rival Zoological Gardens—and then enjoying much unmerited reputation, the author of *Zeluco*, exemplifies the ignorance of the continental noblesse by telling an anecdote of a Neapolitan lady of high rank, who, hearing an Englishman discourse with much animation respecting "parliament," exclaimed in reply, "parliament! what is it, a *corso*? a horse-race?" She was not able, as our doctor says, to suppose that any other matter could excite so much interest, and be remembered with so much pleasure.

I will not characterize this anecdote as a traveller's story in the disagreeable sense of the term, though it seems to be in the highest degree improbable, that even a Neapolitan contessa should have been ignorant of the existence of the parliament, which, composed as nearly as possible upon our ancient Anglo-Norman model, continued to meet and sit in Sicily until the conclusion of the late war. Be this as it may, it is certain that our learned doctor had not any more notion than his supposed contessa of the existence of such an assembly. Indeed, even now, when historical information is generally diffused, we perhaps do not sufficiently recollect, or recollecting, do not attend to the inferences to be drawn from the fact, that in the age of Marco Polo, great councils of this nature, all grounded upon the ancient ecclesiastical assemblies of the church, were formed, in the various realms and states of Christendom. Why did they become effete, and either wholly die away, or become shadows and forms, destitute of all practical utility? Such considerations, interesting to the philosopher at all periods, possess a singular pertinence at the present era, when the struggle for the establishment of constitutional modes of government, all more or less borrowed from our own, desolates the fairest realms of Europe, and keeps up a feverish and unhealthy degree of excitement in most of those which are ruled by absolute power.

When the curate and the barber visited the hero of La Mancha, previous to his third sally, he gave an account of himself with much judgment and many elegant words. In the course of their confabulations, as we are told by the immortal Miguel de Cervantes Saavedra, they fell into a discussion about state affairs and modes of government; correcting this abuse; condemning that one; reforming this custom; abolishing another: and in such manner, saith Cervantes, did they deal with the Commonwealth, that it seemed as though they had put it upon an anvil, and hammered it quite into a new shape and form.

Now what curate, barber, and knight did figuratively, modern continental constitution makers, menders, and marrers, well represented, perhaps, by the shaver and by Don Quixote—but much too liberal to take the curate into their cabinet—have been doing literally. They might have learned better modes of workmanship, if they had looked into our English smithy, and asked how our own pattern-piece was manufactured out of the rough material. Our constitutional form of government has been produced by evolution. As the organs were needed, so did they arise. Not so amongst our contemporaries on the firm land. They are striving to produce theirs by revolution; they begin by hacking and hewing the body politic into pieces, and expect that, by the magic of republican palingenesis, it will be resuscitated in a new and perfect form.

More wisely have we been hitherto guided. In the worst of our convulsions, we have always respected some rights and principles. In the best aspect of their phases and mutations, they acknowledge none. The truest and most profitable history of the rise and progress of our commonwealth is to be found in the documents which evidence the development of our legal constitution. Comparatively an invention of recent date, our political constitution has not resulted from abstract speculations, but from the growing wants and desires of a progressive state of society. Parliament, according to its present form, derives its modern functions from the period when it proceeded, step by step, out of the ancient administration of remedial and coercive justice: and the real springs of movement of our government "in the early part of the fourteenth century," are found in the dispensation of the law.

If the committee of Queen Isabel's cortes would take my advice—and I will give it in spite of the unsavoury proverb respecting proffered counsel—they would forthwith begin to study our Rolls of Parliament and Statutes at Large; if they can't understand them, it is not for me to say where a good commentator can be found. In the meanwhile, let us accompany Marco Polo, when, entangled amongst the crowd in West Cheap, he heard the proclamation that "on the octave of St. Hilary now next ensuing, our lord the king will hold his high court of parliament at Westminster."

To this effect, did a grave, handsome-looking personage read from a long parchment scroll containing the "crye," which, in manner before-mentioned, announced the appointed meeting of the great council of the realm.

After a short pause, the master in chancery continued his promulgation by proceeding to another paragraph, more particularly addressed to the people at large. All who had any grace to demand of the king in parliament: or any complaint to make

to the king in parliament of matters which could not be redressed
or determined by ordinary course of the common law: or who
had been in any way aggrieved by any of the king's ministers
or the king's justices, the king's sheriffs, or their bailiffs, or
any other officer: or who had been unduly assessed, rated, charged
or surcharged to aids, subsidies, or taxes, "are to deliver their
petitions to the receivers, whom for that purpose our lord the
king hath appointed, and who will sit openly, from day to day,
ready to listen to you, ready to attend to ye, in the great hall of
the king's palace of Westminster, at the foot of the staircase on
the left hand side, just as ye enter the same."

Murmurs of applause were heard amongst the crowd, when
the king thus proffered his readiness to hear any complaint which
might be brought against any of his ministers—what promise
could possibly be more grateful to a true-born Englishman?—
and a loud and joyful shout rent the air when the proclamation
was concluded.

The whole proceeding, indeed, appeared so pleasing and welcome, as to present a singular contrast to the species of apprehension excited in the county court when the announcement was
first made of the impending parliamentary election. Yet a short
consideration brought the traveller to a perception of the truth.

"If your sovereign, in his parliament," said Marco to the
friar, "threatens to demand money from those who are able to
pay, he promises at the same time to dispense justice to those who
are not. Exactions made upon the rich are compensated by relief
afforded to the poor. Those who have neither voice in parliament,
nor suffrage in the election of its members, who defy the tax-
gatherer and the assessor, may all have good and valid reasons
for invoking the jurisdiction of the legislature. This mixed
character of your parliament may, I think, give it ultimately a
more permanent character than is possessed by the councils,
which, similar to yours in many respects, do not in this manner
fix their roots, if I may so express myself, in practical benefits
afforded to the people."

"Correctly judged," said the friar, "but you must not suppose
that the remedial authority of our king is restricted to his presence
in the assembled parliament. His aid is certainly afforded in
parliament with more readiness, and with greater solemnity.
Many a demand, urgently required for the service of the state,
may then be opportunely united to tokens of grace and benignity.
But the king is the stem of our constitution: and from him, the

other branches spring and derive their vitality. All the relief
which the king affords to his subjects, when he holds his parliament, might, if he choose, be dispensed just as well without that
assembly."

"As how?" quoth Marco.

"Because our constitution is essentially monarchical in its
principles as well as its forms, all of which will be better understood
by you, if you will walk with me to-morrow to the Palace of
Westminster, where the parliament is held."

"So be it," said Marco. "But we are acting differently in Italy.
Professing, with all due humility, to be members of the empire,
we take good care to keep more and more out of the reach of the
beak and claws of the imperial eagle. Our own republic is
ruled by its nobles. The citizens of fair Florence have granted,
and they hope irrevocably, to the *priori*, in whom, as ye know,
the whole executive power of the state is vested, the power of
filling up each vacancy as it arises. The whole body is thus
renewed six times each year: and this system is followed in every
commonwealth, which takes Florence for its model, as the best
which could be devised."

"Destitute, as they would appear to me, of unity and stability.
But have you, men of Lombardy, of the Riviera, of Venice, of
Tuscany, thriven under these authorities?" said the friar.

"Ask the tributary shores of the Hellespont and the Black Sea.
View our arsenals, filled with our triumphant galleys; enter our
vaulted fondachi, where the daylight is intercepted by piled bales
of sendal and cloth of gold. Interrogate our merchants, our
Frescobaldi, our Buoncompagni, our Peruzzi—who have the
revenues of this kingdom in farm—who make the potentates of
the earth their tributaries."

"And," quoth Andrew, who had fallen into the conversation,
"well will it be for us, when we can do the like, or more, binding
those three fierce leopards, the blatant beasts of Poitou and Normandy," pointing to the royal pennon, "in the same chain which
you have cast round the rapacious bird of the Cæsars."

"I love my own republican city," replied Marco, "but as to
birds, there is none so bad as that which befouls its own nest.
Had you travelled far and wide, as I have done, you would not
have thought yourself compelled to draw the conclusion at which
you have arrived. Institutions, wise on the banks of the Arno,
may be sheer folly here, upon the borders of the Thames."

"You must have seen," said the friar, interrupting the

conversation, as he was wont to do, "a great variety of head-dresses in your travels, Messer Marco?"

"Sure have I," replied Marco, gesticulating and counting, according to Italian fashion, upon the thumb and fingers of his left hand as he spoke:—thumb, "turbans at Damascus," fore finger, "sheepskin kalpacks at Balkh," middle finger, "red berrets at Fez," ring finger, "scarlet hats at Rome," little finger, "buttoned caps at Cambalu," thumb again, "broad-brimmed chapeaux at Paris," fore finger again, "hoods here in London," middle finger again, "coifs for the court," ring finger again, "cowls for the cloister," little finger again, "helmets for the field, and many, many more, every possible variety."

"But, inasmuch," resumed Bacon, "as all men's heads are round on the outside, even so are all coverings, which fit the same heads, round within, however different they may be in external shape, stuff, or colour. If you are sufficiently protected against sleet and snow in the mountains, and defended from the sun in the plains, I do not suppose that you, as an experienced traveller, would censure the fashion which that portion of your attire assumes."

"Certainly not," replied Marco: "I neglect the guise, if comfort and protection be attained."

"So it is," said the friar, "with the real and essential main-springs of human policy. Alike are they all the world over. Let these be answered: and the sages of all nations are secretly persuaded that the wisdom of the machinery through which political principles are worked, is merely a matter of locality. Your true philosopher estimates the various plans of policy adopted by mankind, simply as the means of insuring the greatest average of happiness to the greatest numbers of society. Therefore I am quite willing to believe, that those who most loudly, aye, and most uncompromisingly, advocate the most opposite institutions, are not unfrequently acting with equal sincerity. The despotic rule of Kublai, and the popular authority of the Florentine *priori*, may each be regarded by their respective advocates as being the mode of government best adapted for that end."

"With no difference of opinion upon such matters," continued the friar, speaking slowly and emphatically, "do I quarrel. But though I wrangle not, I warn. The greatest and most mischievous error which can be committed, is to suppose, that because any given political institution has been productive of certain good effects in one country, it will continue equally beneficial when adopted in another. Foolish, indeed, would be the husbandman, who should attempt to crop an English farm after the precepts of Columella: or who, because rice flourishes with artificial irrigation, would endeavour to raise his wheat or his barley, by the same mode which produces a plentiful supply of nutritious food in the plains of Hindostan.

"You may remove the grape-stem from Montepulciano to Orvieto: but you cannot transfer the fruit, the flavour will not quit its original vineyard. The minute particularities of air, of soil, of aspect, and position, concur in no other habitat. Discrepancies of habits and customs, modifications prevailing in the nature and rights of property, so numerous and so minute, as utterly to baffle the researches of the desk and closet legislator, will equally qualify and affect the results of any borrowed scheme of authority and rule."

"Add," said Marco, "to your catalogue of the causes of diversity, one not the least important, though frequently the most disregarded, I mean the great incentives of prejudice, taste, and fancy, as influential upon nations, as upon individuals—

> Varii son degli uomini i capricci,
> A chi piace la torta, a chi, pasticci."

"True," said the friar, "and the misery of the thing is, that each man endeavours to force his own favourite mess down the throats of other folks, without at all stopping to consider whether the zest which he finds in the dish, may not be in the highest degree disagreeable to his neighbour. Nay, forgetting that, in our homely English phrase, what is one man's meat is another man's poison."

Marco Polo, in his age of darkness, was more consistently philosophical than we are, in this our era of epidemic innovation, the age in which judges shed their wigs, and Turks shave their beards. Let us compare the opinion of Marco Polo with the amusing work of a recent traveller. "No people," says he, "can be more thoroughly enslaved than the Uzbecks, there is no shadow of popular government: but still," continues our observer, with honest surprise, "there is no evidence of popular discontent," a phenomenon which appears to him thoroughly unaccountable. Popular contentment without popular government! Happiness without brawlers in the town-hall, and bawlers in the senate. Is not this as strange as nourishment without food, or light without the sun? How do they manage matters amongst the Uzbecks? What recipe keeps this singular people in a state of tranquil contentment? Is it to be attributed to the bang which they smoke, or the bangs which they receive?

Both these sedatives may help: both are capital in their way; but how is Bokhara governed—let us read the traveller's own words. "The Koran is the base of the government. The khan, who is unremitting in business, attends daily at the court-house, with the cadi and the mollahs, to decide every cause, according to law. The Koran, their guide, may not be the best standard of legislative excellence, but this sort of decision is exceedingly popular, and relieves them from the 'jus vagum aut incognitum' of a despot. They are protected by the strict enforcement of its law, and it leads the people to consider their clergy as their best defenders against the abuse of the ruling powers." Thus does a man of no ordinary intelligence, entirely confound form and substance: and actually lose all perception of the truths which he so lucidly unfolds. Because he cannot find the precise form which we in Great Britain consider as the machinery of a popular government, he denies the name to institutions founded upon the supremacy of faith, and therefore cherished and supported by the people, deriving their whole strength from the consent and approbation of the people, and effectually protecting the people against every abuse of power, and against every act, which, according to their notions and views, would be oppression or tyranny.

Not that it is desirable to adopt the Uzbeck constitution in the United Kingdom. I delight in the excellence of the Uzbeck policy, I bend before the mollahs and honour the cadi, yet, dear countrymen, do not catch any enthusiasm for the Uzbecks, do not try to imitate them, do not attempt to purchase tranquillity by such superstition, do not reform too much, let us let well alone. As inexpedient would be the introduction of such a Moslem government amongst us, as it would be to ask you and me to sit cross-legged on the carpet, scoop out our pudding in our palms, and tear our roast beef with our fingers.

Neither would I advise the dear Uzbecks to copy from us. Let them let well alone. Place Ibrahim in an English attitude at a dinner-table, he sits upon thorns, and, when he attempts to feed himself, his fingers instinctively ascend to his mouth, whilst the morsel at the end of the fork travels upwards to his eye. Whilst the Koran is the rule of faith and government in Bokhara, the khan, the mollahs, and the cadi, the fear of hell, and the hope of heaven, will do quite as well for the barbarous Uzbecks, as

Parliament, and the union workhouse, and the model prison, for our enlightened and civilized society.

Have I ventured upon dangerous ground? Sincerely and earnestly do I hope that no observation which I have made will, in the slightest degree, impede the march of improvement in the Ottoman empire. Crowned heads I flatter not; but I am bound to render my humble tribute of respect unto Sultan Mahmoud, in acknowledging the efforts which he makes for the purpose of enlightening his subjects, though some people think he goes rather too fast. It may be doubted whether he will derive much advantage from the seizure of the *wakoofs* appropriated to the support of the dancing dervishes, for the purpose of endowing a *corps de ballet* in their stead. Should the Turks become infidels, his highness will have gained little by exchanging the bullets of Fieschi and Meunier for the bowstring of the janissaries. A good pacha with three tails, is a cheap and effectual substitute for the most systematic system of codification which the jurists of the new school can supply.

But the truth is, and I hope the sultan will know it, that I introduced the Uzbeck quotation, for the purpose of giving a collateral explanation of the working of the ancient constitution of this realm, when we and the Uzbecks were perhaps upon a par.

Every writer who attempts to develope the history of our English liberties, takes his stand upon the first appearance of the House of Commons, which is generally treated as the first and potential cause of our national prosperity.

Whenever I am in a gloomy and desponding mood, and think that all the world is out of joint, and everything going wrong, it often occurs to me, that if society is disorganizing itself at present, and rapidly progressing towards its dissolution, for so I am convinced when I am hipped, that, without repudiating the influence of other causes, all of which may have co-operated, it is very much owing to the disuse of Dyche's Spelling Book.

What a book of books it was! There stood the portrait of Mr. Dyche, with his rod, at the beginning. I think I see him now. No *Journals of Education*, no Normals, no Norwoods, no Pestalozzis, no Hofwyls, no Fellenbergs, were known in his wise days. No societies of national instruction, forbidding us to weep for the loss of birch: and founding their systems for the expansion of intellectual cultivation upon returns of pigs, prints, and pianofortes, and statistical tables showing incontestably, that in those districts where knowledge is most diffused, parricide becomes a rare crime at the age of seventy, and at eighty is almost null. Nobody cared about discipline in the prison, everybody agreed upon its expediency in the school. Then the spelling lessons, ascending with such beautiful regularity from *a-b, ab*, to *ab-om-in-a-ti-on*. But, above all, the invaluable treasure of political wisdom, contained in the *Easy Fables*. The last check upon our morbid appetite for ceaseless change was destroyed, when King Log was wholly forgotten. The last means of repressing self-interested empiricism vanished, when the rising generation had ceased to dog's-ear the page containing the moral deduced from; "Depend upon it, sir, there is nothing like leather." However, what I have more particularly in view is the wide-extended application of the philosophy of "the belly and the members." Its general moral, as given in the old book, may, perhaps, be faintly recollected by some of my octogenarian readers, but it has another, not less profitable. We may consider it as reminding us that constitutional historians generally forget the truth, that the relative uses and respective strengths of the members of the commonwealth, vary exceedingly in its different periods: hence they often apply to the infancy of political institutions the characteristics which only belong to their maturest age.

In the early part of the fourteenth century, the representatives, whom we now consider the popular branch of the legislature, had become permanently engrafted upon the old stock of the constitution. Yet we greatly err, if we assume that the feelings of the present generation have descended to us from our ancestors. Direct and textual evidence perhaps cannot be adduced, to show that, in their opinion, the knights, citizens, and burgesses, were not much more than a chip in the porridge, a virtual nullity, neither doing good nor harm, except as to the benefit derived to themselves, and the damage to the constituents, measured by the amount of that great and standing subject of contest, the amount of their wages. Such a position, I admit, cannot be proved: but we cannot fail to discover many cogent inferences that the knights, citizens, and burgesses, then appeared to be of small importance. All we can say is, that it was generally, though not constantly, thought necessary, that the sheriff should be commanded to return them, whenever the "full parliament" was assembled. Beyond this fact we do not advance.

Amongst the many indications of the comparative inefficiency of this branch of the legislature, a prominent token may be selected. It is well known that the date of the first assemblage of the commons, is involved in impenetrable obscurity. What practical value, therefore, could there be assigned to an innovation then considered to be of so little importance, that it never excited the attention of a single chronicler? By what standard shall we measure the consequence attached to a right of suffrage which the people were at this period never anxious to exercise: and which was on many occasions, so neglected, that it might almost have fallen into desuetude?

But the nation, thus indifferent to popular suffrage, manfully defended the laws of England from the old time "used and approved." All prerogatives, however important to the sovereign, however calculated to increase his authority, however congenial to his pride and feelings; had, whenever they really became a grievance, been restricted, restrained, abolished. Every attempt to exact any tax or tribute beyond the legal rights of the community, was ultimately defeated. The present exertion of arbitrary power always suggested the creation of a barrier against the future abuse. As soon as any weak point in the fortress was discovered, the garrison erected a bulwark to defend it. There was no lack of protectors of popular rights. Where, then, were they to be found?

Divesting ourselves of modern opinions and prepossessions, an answer can readily be given by consulting the chronicle and the charter. Amongst the "prelates, magnates and proceres," are we to seek for all the real and potential materials of the now popular branch of the legislature. Examine the origin, the position, the influence of the dignified ecclesiastics, and the hierarchy will rise before us as the most democratic element of our old English commonwealth.

Consider the ancient clergy, in their relation to what may be termed the individuality of the country. Much of the value of a popular government consists, not as the demagogue employs it, for the purpose of opposition to authority, but as the means of imparting the benefits and rewards of a well-governed society, in due gradation, to the several ranks and orders of the community. Whatever inequality might subsist in other respects amongst the people, they met on equal terms on sacred ground. An easy path for the civil or political ennoblement of talent, was always opened through the Christian hierarchy. The mitre, the cardinal's cap, the tiara itself, fell oftenest on the humblest brow. An established church is the surest possession of the people. When the people pillage the altar, they despoil their own property; they waste their own means; they desolate their own children's inheritance; they rob themselves.

Such an institution made honour and station accessible to the lowest of the low: and amongst the prelates, who sometimes constituted the most numerous, and always the most influential portion of the great council, the majority had risen from the humblest rank in society. Were they all truly deserving of their honours? Certainly not. Some obtained their advancement by flattery, by simony, by casting aside the real duties of their station, or by making the business of the world their primary object. But this was the sin of the man, and not the vice of the hierarchy. The most favourite sophism, employed by those who seek to attack or vilify existing establishments, whether ecclesiastical or temporal, is to ascribe to institutions the faults of the human individuals who compose the institutions and to maintain that by reconstructing the State you can eradicate the abuse. But the stones with which you raise the structure are infected in the quarry. Pull down and rebuild the dwelling as often as you list, change or alter its plan or elevation as much as you please, and the old moral leprosy will streak and fret the new walls as foully and deeply as before. Princes and rulers, magistrates and judges of the earth, are only men; the visible church is composed of men; collectively, man's nature is unsusceptible of reform. The main source of evil is inexhaustible. It is an atmosphere which constantly follows us, surrounds us. Plant the *mal seme d'Adamo* where you choose, the same bitter fruits will always rise above the ground.

Shall we add to the political integrity of the clergy, by rendering them the paid agents of a national treasury? Seize the lands, rend the mitre, place the priest as the expectant upon the contributions of his congregation: what has the cause of religion gained? He who flattered the king, becomes the baser sycophant of the greasy multitude. The permanent endowment of a clergy, trains them into moral courage, whilst their dependence upon the voluntary donations of their flock, as surely sinks them in moral slavery.

England, under Charles the Second, has seen two thousand clergy, in one St. Bartholomew's day, abandon their preferment, rather than their doctrines. Venerate their conscientious adherence to the tenets which they professed and held.

England, under James the Second, equally saw seven bishops conducted as captives to the Tower, testifying against the tyranny of the sovereign, whom they honoured and obeyed.

England, under William the Third, again saw seven fathers of the church submit to the deprivation of their princely domains and high estate, rather than violate the dictates of their conscience.

These are the disciples of an endowed church; whilst among the endless varieties of sects, sectaries, and persuasions, which fill the eleemosynary pulpits of the American Union, not one single minister has dared to breathe a syllable in reprobation of that inhuman system of slavery, which contaminates their commonwealth. Amongst those great and flourishing transatlantic republics, who ground their policy upon the equal rights of man, not one Christian minister dares to risk the loss of a cent in defence of the most sacred rights of humanity: whilst in England, the members of the different hierarchies have, each in their turn, surrendered every worldly possession, ungrudgingly, unhesitatingly, rather than purchase them by the compromise of their principles.

The Anglican church is not an extraneous or oppressive order, possessing a character adverse to the state; it is not a caste estranged from the community. It is formed out of the people: it exists for the people. The church is the democratic leaven of our balanced monarchy. The dignified ecclesiastics of the Church of England were, during the middle ages, always the best, and not unfrequently the only advocates of the poorest, and, therefore, the most defenceless classes. So have they also been the means by which the gifts of intellect and intelligence raise the possessor to the highest station in the community, the connecting link between the cottage and the throne.

Whilst the prelates thus acted on behalf of the people, the functions of popular representation were also shared by the great landholders, summoned to parliament by special writ, on whom so large a portion of the strength of parliament depended. However they may have come into that assembly, and, by whatever custom or usage, for no law or principle can be discovered, by which the so-called baronies of those who owned domains designated by this name, could be distinguished from other analogous tenures: they were, in every respect, as truly the representatives of their shires, as if they had been nominated by the reluctant suffrages of the suitors of the county court, anxious only to lighten or evade the trouble and charge which the return imposed.

The plain state of the case, is this: that the commons only sent to parliament a few more members of a class, which was already fully supplied. As for the cities and boroughs, they rather lost in power, by the introduction of parliamentary representation. Before London sent members to parliament, the king treated as with a dependent state; but afterwards they took their chance as an integral portion of his kingdom. Knights of the shire attended parliament upon compulsion, if they were elected, whilst the life-holders of parliamentary baronies sustained the same obligation without the preliminary of an election. In the early part of the fourteenth century, the *personnel* of the baronage consisted simply of the great proprietors, who, summoned to parliament, because they had large territorial possessions, were exactly of the same genus as their virtual successors, who, in the last age, were called "squires." The only specific differences that I can find, are, that they wore greaves instead of leathern breeches: bore a real shield on their arms, in place of a painted one on the panels of their carriages, and crests upon their heads instead of their spoons. They were entirely identified with the representatives of the shires; both kept the key of the money chest; their interests were the same; their feelings were the same. So tardily was the idea of nobility attached to the parliamentary baronage, that in legal pleadings the addition of baron was not treated as a title of dignity: nor was the baron permitted to decorate his brow with the coronet, until a few years before the expulsion of the Stuart dynasty.

Strange is it, that the assailants, as well as the defenders of our aristocracy, equally forget the great truth, that the body now called the House of Lords, is of much more recent origin than the House of Commons. Neither is there, in fact, any legal nobility of blood in England. Nobility of blood, where it exists by law, implies a right, imparted by birth, to every scion of the patrician stock. It infers privileges peculiar to the race: it is a caste among the people, not an order and rank in society; and these conditions are not in any degree satisfied by the English peerage.

Hereditary dignities in England, if considered as personal honours, passed and pass, to an eldest son alone. In the dark and dubious era, when we conjecture that they were territorial, they resulted from the possession of land. The honour was not partible, one member of the lineage only could claim the privilege and no more than that one. If the possessions were alienated or lost, the dignity departed. With the exception of the earldoms, which were always transmitted by descent, no proofs or arguments can be adduced to show that any distinct notion of an hereditary

House of Lords subsisted in this country, until after the period when our connexion with France had familiarized us with the nature of a body of hereditary nobility.

View them under any aspect which you will, our English dignities, failing to impart any legal privileges to the cadets of the family, do not possess any resemblance to the inherent, indelible dignity of a gentilitial aristocracy. But the absence of any legal nobility of blood in England, never has diminished the value attached to noble birth by the natural and universal feelings of mankind: perhaps, most of all by those, who attempt to cry down that value. The respect rendered to ancestry, the influence which it bestows, is a dispensation of Providence in the moral government of the world; not a conventional institution resulting from human authority. It is a talent cast upon the owner, for which he is awfully responsible. Shame fall upon him if he misuse the gift; but the disgrace is his, and the gift itself is unstained. Birth is a possession which cannot be acquired by those to whom it has not been granted by the Father of mankind. It is a pre-eminence which may be rendered more useful, or more illustrious, by wealth, or intellect, or station; but which neither wealth, nor intellect, nor station can impart. It is a power not conceded either by king or by people, and which, neither the arbitrary will of the despot, nor the still more arbitrary tyranny of the multitude, can obliterate. Man cannot bestow dignity of birth, man cannot take it away. Whatever results from time is incommunicable, and cannot be supplied by any other element. Hence, nobility of birth is an authority before which man's natural rebellion humbles itself most unwillingly, and which, "the age of great cities and civilization" seeks most anxiously to destroy.

If there is any one part of the world in which this "spirit of the age" is most unjustifiable, it is amongst ourselves. Leaving to this nobility, based upon sentiment, its full weight, we, in England, have been enabled to discard the mischievous policy which, in so many other countries, gave to the one order the monopoly, so unenviable and so envied, of civil rank and power. Under the Tudors, attempts may have been made to restrain to "gentle birth" the honours unknown in an earlier age; and the herald declared that he who was "no gentleman of blood" was unworthy of the decorations, the collar or the mantle, which rendered him the companion of his sovereign. Had this doctrine, borrowed from the continent, been accepted, it would have spread like a canker through the state in all its departments: the birth-

right of the English freeman would have been taken away. But
our English feeling annulled these attempts. They vanished away
without notice: thus have we preserved the institutions which
give us all the advantages of aristocracy without any of its defects.
Our constitution, yielding to the nobility of birth its due ascendancy, has always allowed the full claims of the aristocracy of
wealth, and encouraged the accession of the aristocracy of intellect
and knowledge. There has been no jealousy, no grudging. The
merchant's mark has been admitted to be as honourable a bearing
as the baronial shield: the robe of estate, exchanged but yesterday
for the forensic gown, commands as much respect as though the
pedigree of the chancellor could be traced from the Norman
Domesday. Our *Libro d' Oro* has never been closed.

But another most important branch of our ancient constitution
remains to be considered, namely, the prerogative of granting aid
or relief to the aggrieved, in those cases not susceptible of decision
by any settled rule: and for which, therefore, no tribunal can be
appointed, and no law provided. If, in the early part of the
fourteenth century, redress was to be sought against oppression,
if the error of the judge was to be corrected, if his corruption was
to be punished, if the rigour of the law was to be mitigated, if
grace was to be craved—where was the application to be made?

It would have been a "bootless bene" to have referred the
suppliant to the third estate, the commons in parliament, whilst
they themselves scarcely ventured to appear as humble petitioners
on their own behalf. Had the suitor presented himself to the
prelates and magnates, the second estate of parliament, they
would have denied their own competency to entertain his prayer.
It was, therefore, to the first estate, the king in parliament, that
the prayer was to be addressed, and the suit made. The other
branches might solicit, but they could not grant, an alteration in
the mode of administrating the law. They might advise the king
to interfere, they might assent to his propositions, but all plenitude
of power resided in the crown. From the crown proceeded all
grace, all mercy, all favour. Whatever remedial jurisdiction the
high court of parliament ever possessed, can be distinctly traced
to the crown as its source and origin. Our king was the popular
member.

Such, then, was the character of our parliament in the "early
part of the fourteenth century." And let us now repair to the
locality, where, at this particular juncture, it happened to be held.
Westminster was a wide and straggling village, rather than a

town; whose inhabitants were principally supported by their dealings with the suitors of the courts of justice, and the expenditure of the royal household: but the castellated palace, extending along the bank of the river, surrounded by pleasant groves and cheerful gardens, and the sumptuous abbey, imparted a character of mingled amenity and importance to the residence of the English sovereign.

To the north, however, the aspect of the country was bleak, wild, and uncultivated, marshy and flooded swamps indicated the site of the Isle of Thorns, so solitary and secluded in the days of the Anglo-Saxon kings.

"That campanile," said the friar, as they passed beneath a lofty buttressed tower, "is a recent monument of the unyielding principles of our common law. Equity, as distinguished from law, belongs only to the crown. One of our judges having, out of pity, altered the record by which a fine was imposed upon a poor suitor, was himself amerced to the extent of ten thousand marks, a sum which our lord the king employed in building this clock-house. Look up, and you will see the great clock, the bell some people call it, swinging in the belfry, upon which the watchman tolls the hours." "A task," said Marco, "which at Venice, thanks to the skill of Jacopo Dondi, is performed by the weights and wheels of the horologe adjoining the ducal palace."

"Do your citizens of Venice," replied the friar, "regulate themselves by this, the horologe of the signoria?" "Yea, do they," quoth Marco, "as in duty bound."

"Then if so, I trust that due care will always be taken to make your government horologe go right, since otherwise, one of two unpleasant things will take place in your republic. Either the people will be constantly misled in their transactions by a time-teller, whose inaccuracy they do not perceive: or, discerning its errors, they will try to take the regulation of it into their own hands, and destroy the wheels by their rude and untempered violence."

"May be so," quoth Marco, "but still on the whole, there is less chance of confusion than if every man had an horologe of his own. In my opinion, the main object in a state is to go altogether; and a diversity of reckoning in the community is an evil by no means compensated by the accuracy which any individual may acquire." Marco here was not quite so sensible as usual. But as I feel myself bound to edit all I find, I could not venture to abridge my original, and fortunately his discourse received a new direction before he could commit himself further to posterity. "What is this, friar?" said he, touching with his foot a small packet, neatly folded and closed with green wax, which was lying on the pavement of the walk leading to the door of the hall.

"Oh! I can guess," said the friar, eagerly snatching up the parchment, and tearing it asunder, "but," added he, "the kingdom will profit little by my diligence in suppressing treason or sedition. All will come out fast enough, for that worthy canon of St. Stephen's chapel, pacing before us in his amice, who hath lighted on a similar dispatch of evil, is, I see, carefully treasuring the same for the use of parliament." We shall soon ascertain in what manner the friar's observation was verified; perhaps we may even obtain an insight into the secrets which this mysterious packet contained.

It will be recollected that the people were invited, nay, urged to prefer their complaints to the king in parliament. Marco now witnessed the course of proceedings by which the sovereign redeemed his pledge, and displayed the noblest of his prerogatives, acting as the protector and guardian of the people over whom he extended his authority.

The receivers of the parliamentary petitions, in which such relief was solicited, were stationed at the foot of the Hall stairs: and, when the visitors entered, they were in the full bustle of their employment. Applicant after applicant crowded up to them, no suitor was turned away.

"The king," said Marco, "is virtually sitting at the gates of his palace, listening to the prayers of his subjects."

"He is, in truth," replied the friar, "thus performing the most essential portion of his duties. Did our rulers, as of old, and according to the custom which, as you well know, prevails in the east, attend in person to the claims of the suitor, justice would, perhaps, wear a more impressive garb, but the substance would be sacrificed to the form. Of the complaints thus preferred, many are trivial, many unfounded: and, if the sovereign in a realm like this, were to attempt to hear the cause and case of every demandant, none of the other functions of royalty could be properly performed. Not that our king absents himself from this, his high court of justice: but he divides the labour with those selected councillors who, chosen at his pleasure, assist him by their sagacity and wisdom. He deputes his functions to them. He is not above their advice, although he is above the law. But follow me, and you will know how, by the ordinance and appointment of King Edward, the proceedings before him or those who in parliament act by his delegated authority, are methodized and reduced to order. Thus is justice administered with due dispatch and fitting equity."

In the chamber which they had entered, sat the Triers of petitions, officers who seem to have been first instituted by the monarch, upon whom the title of the English Justinian has been bestowed. Taken with reference to the mere form and guise of the statutes and ordinances of his reign, this epithet may, perhaps, appear as conveying more praise than the first Edward deserves. But throughout his conduct we may trace a consistent principle of legislation : and, at all events, he may be considered as having imparted order and stability to the system of our common law, and to the jurisdiction of parliament, as the king's remedial or equitable court, when the common law should fail. Liberty was insured, not so much by the permanent addition of a popular branch to the legislature, as by rendering that legislature more efficiently and permanently a court for the people. For the king's council became virtually a committee of parliament; and, as I have before observed, the idea of the relief of private grievances became an essential character annexed to the legislature of the realm.

Parliament, in the early part of the fourteenth century, cannot be exhibited as the perfect model of a remedial court. But it was far more efficient as a remedial court than any that has been created in subsequent ages. Parliament was the poor man's court. Nothing but a complete examination of the petitions presented to the king in parliament, can convey an idea of the facility with which the humblest suitor obtained at least a hearing, or the promise of a remedy. Legislators should consider that the speedy redress of minor complaints is the great secret by which the tranquillity and well-being of state and commonwealth is sustained. Every man knows where his own shoe pinches; and if you give him ease, he will forthwith thank you, and fall to his own work again. Individual hardships are the stings which irritate the common people. They refer them as a matter of course to "government," and to those institutions by which government is upheld. The mechanic who is unfairly cast in the courts, miscalled of conscience, or racked by the broker, hies to the political union, and looks for a remedy, in vote by ballot and universal suffrage, for all the misfortunes which he sustains.

My readers may, perhaps, not be aware that at the opening of every new parliament, Triers or Auditors of petitions are still appointed in the ancient form by the House of Lords. Now, of course, they do nothing. It was not so in the "early part of the fourteenth century"; they were busily and usefully employed in giving answers to the petitioners, a motley crowd, anxiously awaiting at the door until called in to receive the interlocutory judgment of the tribunal.

A lively discussion was going on amongst the auditors when Marco and the friar entered the chamber. "There is no doubt whatever," said a stately personage, who was already well known to the visitors as Sir William de Ormesby, "of the general principle by which we ought to be guided when we sit as the depositories of the transcendent prerogative of the crown, namely, that no remedy is demandable from the king in parliament, when the relief can possibly be obtained elsewhere: but the difficulty is in the application of the principle. It is quite clear that, in itself, the case of William de Walton requires nothing but a writ at common law. It is not a case for parliament. Walton sustains no duress, he makes no allegation that the assize cannot be fairly had, or that he is in any wise in fear or danger from the power of his adversary. The petition ought to be forthwith dismissed, for it showeth nought to which the king's equitable jurisdiction can be applied."

"True," observed Sir Richard le Scrope, "yet, if driven to the common law, the utter poverty of the petitioner will entirely prevent his suit. He hath a right to demand his land, but my lord chancellor hath an equal right to demand his due. The Great Seal will not open until it is touched with silver. Then, since we must send him to the common bench, let us at least smooth the road by ordering that he shall have his writ without payment of fees to the chancery, or fine to the king"; a proposal against which no dissentient voice was raised.

"Your poor bedesman," said John of Boothby, a very simple and quiet-looking countryman, who now addressed the court, "bears a wolf's head upon his shoulders, which said head he will assuredly lose if he returns into Lincolnshire: inasmuch as the coroners, if they can catch him, will chop it off without further delay." Please, reader, to recollect, that, as I have before shown and remarked, decapitation, in the fourteenth century, did not constitute an indulgence reserved for a privileged class, but was the ordinary mode of inflicting the summary punishment of the law.

"How universally," said Marco, "this unaccountable delusion

of Lycanthropy still extends. Even in Bengalá I have heard exactly such tales of transformations as those by which the peasant of Artois and Ponthieu is scared. The beast, indeed, is different. In Hindostan, the hated sorcerer assumes the shape of the tiger, and thus assuages the fatal thirst of blood, which ultimately consigns him to destruction."

"We have no lack of loups-garous in England," replied the friar, "but you must not suppose that, as yet, they claim privilege of parliament, though there is no knowing how we may improve in after times. You are, in this instance, excusably misled by the figurative imagery employed by our Anglo-Saxon ancestors. Law spake in verse, the decree was set forth in rhythm, the legal transaction was clothed in a metrical form. Hence, the language of the ancient Teutonic jurisprudence abounds in allegories.

"The outlaw is compared to a wolf. He who flees from the tribunal, breaks the bond which unites him with the community. Refusing obedience to the law, he deservedly loses the protection of the law, his property is forfeited: and our customs teach that he is to be hounded and slain like the wolf, the ravenous beast whose head he is said to bear. Rebelling against the obligations of civil society, he is justly deemed unworthy of its safeguard."

"And for what trespass, Boothby," said Sir William to the petitioner, "were you by the coroner in county court duly exigented and proclaimed?"

"A little misfortune about a sheep:—a matter of which I am as guiltless as a lamb: and I humbly crave of your lordship's mercy that I may be made a man again."

"You mean, I suppose, to solicit that your misfortune, which some folks unkindly designate by the appellation of a theft, should be pardoned. Know, then, that the power of forgiveness belongeth not to us, it is a prerogative appertaining alone unto our lord the king. Yet parliament is adorned by grace. Parliament is a season of kindness and mercy, as well as of justice. It is a time when the suppliant may more easily approach the throne; ye shall have the benefit which the king in parliament can afford ye." So Sir William took up the petition, and endorsing the recommendation of the auditors, that the pardon should be issued, "*S'il plait au Roy*," the clerk forthwith placed the petition in the *liasse* or bundle which was to be presented to the sovereign: and the wolf departed, not as he came, but in cheerful expectation of resuming his station in human society.

"Thrice have I been denied the right which I have craved,"

exclaimed a young woman, who now approached the table, "and from our lord the king, he who wears the English Saxon crown, he who hath sworn to observe the good laws of the Confessor, do I now demand that even justice which hath been refused to me at home."

Marco and the friar immediately recollected the damsel. She had lost the freshness which brightened her nice cheeks when they first saw her on the brink of the clear Okeburne; yet, though harassed and worn by fatigue, she still looked extremely pretty. A handsome face is usually supposed to win favour: but, paradoxical as it may appear, this circumstance, instead of conciliating magistrates and magisterial personages, not unfrequently elicits an extra degree of harshness from them. I cannot exactly tell why this effect is produced, unless from the apprehension, on the part of these excellent functionaries, that the consciousness of personal attraction emboldens the owner to make undue inroads on the patience or forbearance of the tribunal: or that they wish to earn the character of the most untemptable and rigid justice. And so it was on this occasion, for Sir William angrily checked the girl. "Silence," said he, "Mauther, or state your grievance, if you have any: prate not about the days of yore."

"The observations of this wench are more out of season than out of place," quietly replied Sir John le Breton to his colleague, "for the supreme remedial power which the king enjoyeth in parliament is, as I ween, deduced from the laws of the Anglo-Saxons which whilom prevailed in this realm."

Ormesby relaxed; and the maiden, possibly under the influence, not entirely unsalutary, of the awe inspired by the gravity of the court, set forth her case with more brevity and clearness than could have been anticipated. If her story was true, she had indeed sustained a fearful wrong.

Of free birth and blood, the lord of the manor, Sir Richard de Pogeys, where the parents of the orphan dwelt, had claimed her as his nief or native, the name by which the female villein was designated in England: with extreme difficulty she escaped from his violence. And more than this, "A tenant of the manor"— the damsel blushed as she mentioned him—"who duly performed his services, and acquitted himself towards his lord, had been cruelly assaulted by the bailiff of Sir Richard, ejected from his holding, and cast into prison. Such was the power and influence of the knight, supported as he was by his friends, and by the patronage of Sir Robert de Vere, that unless a speedy remedy was provided, they would be utterly undone by his malice and fury."

Facts thus detailed, left no doubt, even in the cautious mind of Sir William de Ormesby, that the aid and interference of the king in parliament was fully justified; but the case required a two-fold remedy. The freedom of the parties was to be claimed by civil process, and the writ *de libertate probanda* was forthwith ordered to be issued out of the chancery: but the wrongs perpetrated by Sir Richard de Pogeys were to be redressed by a special commission; and as it was very important that the commission should be worked by judges equally above temptation and above fear, Sir William himself allowed his name to be inserted in the patent, which was forthwith made out and duly docqueted *per petitionem de parliamento*: and pretty Alice withdrew from the chamber, with many a benison for the king and the lords of his council in the high court of parliament assembled.

Let me request the reader to pause and consider the symmetry and consistency of our ancient legal constitution. In the crown, the first estate of parliament, resided the power of originating relief. Extraordinary jurisdiction was exerted on behalf of the otherwise helpless suitor; but when the process was launched, the remedy fell again into rule, and was to be received from the ordinary tribunal. A prerogative above the law was exercised in consequence of the exigency of the case; but the proceeding was entirely within the compass of the law; and whilst the plaintiff was supported by the special aid of the legislature, the defendant yet retained all the protection which he was entitled to claim from the forms and maxims of the jurisprudence of the realm. Whether, at the present day, the extraordinary jurisprudence of the third branch of parliament possesses the same harmonious consistency, will be a question which future Seldens may discuss: as for me, it is above my station and beyond my powers.

Like every other portion of the palace of Westminster which had been renovated by "Henry, the son of John," the council chamber was richly decorated with sculpture, and also with paintings: some few similar specimens survived until the late conflagration: several others might also have existed until that period, had they not been rudely destroyed for the purpose of raising the very buildings which principally contributed to feed the devouring flames.

Of these representations many were symbolical or allegorical, belonging to a class which sometimes strangely perplexes the antiquary, until he learns to read the mystic lore displayed to every observer, and yet concealed. Here might be seen the law under the semblance of a queen, her crown falling from her tresses. A thick veil covers her downcast eyes, the broken tables drop from her grasp. Opposite is the emblem of the Gospel, a maiden, brightly looking heavenwards, her head endiademed, the budding lily in her hand. These occur in the deep recesses of the windows; the wall between them displays the legendary tale of Solomon and Marcolphus, a fiction, possibly rabbinical in its origin, and recounting the trials which the wisdom of the monarch sustained from the rude mother-wit of a Syrian husbandman. Over the Throne reserved for the king, was a representation of the day of judgment. But the door opening into the chapel had no other ornament excepting a vine, which, springing from the impost, spread around, richly filling and most gracefully entwining every moulding and columnette with flowing branches, tendrils, fruit, and leaves.

Each of these embellishments thus recalled a text of scripture to the mind, or taught a lesson connected with the purposes to which the building was applied. It was the custom of the mediæval architects thus to appeal to the imagination, sometimes to the conscience, in the decoration of their edifices, by which they gave a degree of sentiment to their structures which the moderns cannot attain. Allegory constitutes the intellectuality of the æsthetic arts; but it is wholly alien to the multitude in our own age. We have no means whereby it can be vernacular. None of the forms, none of the graphic symbols which we can beg or borrow, ever became naturalized. We may be clever mocking-birds, but we have no song of our own.

"Would it not be possible," said Marco, "to give greater durability to the works of the pencil which adorn our buildings, by employing oil as the vehicle of the pigment, according to the regulations of the painter's craft? I do not see why the art used in decorating the gay and variegated war-saddle, might not be adopted for the effigy of the knight mounted on the steed; nor why the material which fixes the tinctures of the armorial shield, represented on the satchel which contains the Great Seal, appended to that charter, should not equally be used by the cunning workman, in portraying the figures before us; nor why the azure of this starry roof"—the roof, in fact, was thickly sown with golden stars—"should not be mixed according to the directions of the ordinance affirmed in Guildhall."

Unusual sounds interrupted the speaker, chains were heard clanking without, as the wearers of the bonds paced slowly and painfully along. Marco looked with eager curiosity towards the door, and a numerous body of culprits, in the custody of the marshal of the household, stood trembling before the council-table.

"Perjured jurors these, may it please your lordships," said the marshal, "who, as it hath been proved before you, have preferred a false and malicious indictment."

"Take them hence," was the sentence of the council, pronounced by the mouth of Sir William de Ormesby, "lead them at mid-day, through the highways and streets of the city unto the Tower of London. Be their guilt known, their infamy proclaimed, that the country may be warned by their punishment and shame."

"The stars of this chamber," observed Marco, "do not present a benign aspect."

"Say not so," replied the friar. "Were it not for the rigid and searching jurisdiction exercised by the council, our mode of trial by inquest or jury, would be the destruction of the commonwealth. On ordinary occasions, when no angry passions are excited, and no conflicting interests are at stake, there is no reason to apprehend that the jurors will falsify the truth, or wantonly pervert the righteousness of judgment. But it is far otherwise, when a powerful individual possesses the means of intimidation or corruption: or when the hot and angry feelings of those dissensions which have too often divided our state, rage in the community. Trial by jury then places the sword of justice in polluted hands, who wield the weapon merely for the purpose of satisfying their avarice or glutting their vengeance. And it is only by the power which the sovereign possesses, and which is very often exercised in this starred chamber, of affording redress when the common law fails to reach the evil: and of inflicting signal chastisement upon offenders, by whom the common law is abused, that any reasonable degree of good order is maintained."

Marco Polo, during the sitting of the board, had frequently looked at one member of the council with much earnestness and curiosity, and with that kind of puzzle which we feel, when we think we see an acquaintance whom we cannot exactly make out. This individual sat at the lower end of the table amongst the civilians, but the other councillors seemed to be frequently asking his advice: all treated him with much respect and courtesy. "I cannot exactly recollect," said Marco, "where I first saw that

Doctor, or some one bearing the strongest likeness to him : I think either at Padua or Pavia."

"Most probably at Bologna la Grassa," replied the friar.

"Bologna," said Marco, doubtingly, "he cannot be one of the Accursii ? "

"Even so," replied the friar, "and an old acquaintance of mine. He is Principal of Beaumont Hall at Oxford. Much also is he honoured at court and in parliament, being the king's private secretary. King Edward has great views, he labours always to be enabled to defend himself by the pen, before he draws the sword. What a case hath he not thus made out against the Scottish rebels? He wishes to found his empire upon public opinion, to appeal to reason as the basis of his authority."

"Written reason," said Marco.

"Yea," said the friar, "the written reason of the civil and canon law, which, known to all the nations of Christendom, might, if obeyed by common assent, furnish the means of deciding all questions of international policy, without the necessity of the last 'grand assize' of war."

The council was now breaking up, and its members preparing to join the peers; when the friar, beckoning to Accursius, introduced him to the Venetian traveller.

"King Edward is gracious and wise," said the civilian, in reply to the inquiry made by Marco, "he hath guerdoned my services by a grant of the manor of Martello."

"Martleigh, we call it in English," said Bacon.

"Martello or Martelli, it is all one, provided I receive the rents and profits thereof," replied Accursius; "and, from time to time, the king remembers me most kindly. The annual salary of forty marks of silver, and the robe, the livery which I wear, retain me in his service, and it was but the other day, that the sum of two hundred pounds in sterling money, testified the estimation in which he was pleased to hold my poor endeavours."

"Assuredly," said Marco, "not a higher price than they deserve; but I rejoice to find on this side the Alps, one whom I will make bold to call my compatriot, holding so distinguished a station in this flourishing kingdom."

"Would that we of Italy could really call ourselves compatriots, would that we really had a country," replied Accursius, "and that, instead of beholding each city raising its banner against its own kindred, we were united under a protecting monarch, who, like the king of these realms, could exercise the high offices of chief conservator of the peace, and dispenser of remedial justice, when all other authorities fail. We, on the contrary, acknowledging in our books and laws the supremacy of the emperor, discover in his sovereignty nought but the means of mutual vengeance."

"Are the people happy and contented under this English government?" said Marco.

"Judge by the policy of the realm," replied Accursius. "Every man in England, whatever may be his degree, is not only allowed but compelled, to bear arms in the defence and safeguard of the country. I believe that such was always the law, but King Edward hath enforced it by his statute, enacted or promulgated at Winchester; the very poorest churl, who tills the field, must display his sword and his dagger, or at least his arrows and his bow."

"Praise to your courtly caution," said Marco, "in thus evading my question. The fact, at least, is interesting to the traveller; but if this trust and confidence, placed in the people, be a proof of their loyalty, how came it that the weapons have been so often turned against the sovereign? At this very moment, as I know full well, a most determined opposition will be offered against the subsidy required by the crown."

"In truth," remarked the friar, "the temper of the English affords problems which it is difficult to solve. All I can say is, that concurrent with extreme fits of turbulence, and not unfrequently of violent and unsparing hostility towards the person of the sovereign, there is yet a strong attachment towards the royal authority. They feel it is good for them, but neither this attachment, nor the duty which they owe to their country, has ever been sufficient to dissuade them from the most envenomed discord."

"Know ye Dino Compagni, the Gonfaloniere of Florence?" said Marco.

"He," replied Accursius, "who, as it is bruited, intends to write the history of the Republic?"

"The same," said Marco; "and the story which I shall tell you as succinctly as possible, will perhaps be inserted by the Gonfaloniere in the pages of his chronicle. Look for it there, should he complete the useful work upon which he is engaged.

"But a little while ago, when the fury of the Bianchi and the Neri ran so high upon the expected intervention of Charles of Valois, there came, as Dino said, into his mind, "a good and holy thought." Summoning, by virtue of his office, a general assembly of the citizens in the baptistery of Saint John, where every Florentine is christened; he there urged the people to peace and concord. How could they, he asked them, all brethren of one state, joint owners of one noble city, and who had all beneath that dome received the seal of baptism, thus live in perpetual hostility. Upon that holy font which stood before them, and in which they had all been adopted as the children of one common Father, he besought them to swear that they would fulfil the pledge of love and charity. Melting into tears, they unanimously gave the promise which he required, and promised to put aside their enmity for ever.

"Florence will, I fear, soon forget her vows. But the argument employed by the Gonfaloniere contains the only principles upon which government can be securely founded. Without neglecting, as collateral inducements, to insist upon the temporal blessings which Providence always confers upon those who faithfully seek the paths of peace: still the only mode of insuring our continuance in them, is by looking to the example, and following the precepts, of the Shepherd of mankind."

"What news?" exclaimed Friar Bacon, to Master William de Bremesgrave, one of the clerks of the Pells, who approached in great apparent dismay.

"News which has no novelty—the old story: refusal to grant the subsidy, unless the king complies with the demand of again confirming the Great Charter. All seemed going on well. Master Anthony Beck, the king's secretary, who manages well for his highness, and better for himself, since they say he is to have Durham—the poor old bishop is given over—had required the tenth penny as an aid. It was more, the secretary was well aware, than would be granted: but he knew that, in parliament, nothing is lost by asking. On the part of the king, we of the treasury were quite prepared and ready to accept the fifteenth, for which the way was opening finely before us. The chancellor of the exchequer was in high glee, and sent word to the king that all was safe: but albeit he is my superior, I am his senior; so I ventured to give a word of advice, I told him not to halloo till he was out of the wood. Scarcely had I said the word, when the barons, joined by the knights of the shires, rose in a body, and demanded a new perambulation of the forests, and full pardon for all offences against the king's deer.

"We had no authority to concede this point. And, as we were considering how to act, in came Sir Ralph Chaworth, one of our great barons, who, as you know, always takes the lead on the discontented side, being moreover exceedingly out of humour in consequence of some judgment which has just been passed against his nephew, Sir Richard de Pogeys, in the council, and accompanied by Whethamstede, the factious canon of St. Stephen's, who appeared with much mock solemnity as the bearer of a letter from Merlinus the Wild, the mad prophet of the Western Britons, and which had been found in an old wall."

"From Merlin, the prophet," said Marco.

"Please you," said the clerk of the Pells, "such are the devices which malignants are wont to use, when they disperse their sad prose and sadder rhymes, for the detriment and confusion of the commonwealth."

Entirely correct was this description of the epistle. Merlin is made to rejoice therein, that a heavier servitude has now fallen upon the English, than ever they inflicted upon the sons of Cambria. Forgetting, however, his character, as a Briton, Merlin deploreth the loss of the good old Saxon liberties, when in the days of Alfred, and in one single year, forty-four justices suffered the righteous penalties of the law. Equal vengeance is imprecated upon the cankered council of the king, and the quibbling lawyers who entertain every complaint which shameless quean and unbuxom churl prefer against their superiors: and when the lord is deprived of his lawful franchise of taxing his tenants without their consent: and of not being taxed without his own. "Barons," Merlin saith, "you lose in your parliament what you have conquered in the field." "Certain other matters," continued the clerk of the Pells, "were mentioned, but were not read aloud; some say that a privy message was brought from Guildhall, declaring how the good men of London would stand by the knights, citizens, and burgesses of the realm, in opposing all iniquitous demands. Merlin's exhortations instantly commanded disobedience, and no command could be more readily obeyed. In fact, it seemed as if the message from him had been expected. As I have told you, the upshot of the business is this, barons and commons are in one and the same ungracious mind, the subsidy is lost."

This adventure requires some little explanation to render it intelligible. You must be informed that, in the middle ages, nay, at a later period, it was a very usual practice to disseminate opinions literally. Not by presenting them to you upon a broad sheet at your breakfast-table, but by sowing or casting the writings in the highways and byways, dropping them in the cloister, or thrusting them under the door, leaving the productions to take their chance, as to the small fraction of the "reading public," into whose hands they might fall.

It may be recollected that Lord Coke, in his reports, gives special directions how a good subject should demean himself in the case of *finding* a libel in the street, an event which we should scarcely contemplate as a probable occurrence, however rife these effusions may be in the land. The usage of thus practising actual dissemination continued even after the Elizabethan era, when the printing-press, under the active guidance of Martin Marprelate, Timothy Trouncepriest, and Christopher Clawclergy, had begun to supply a readier mode of pouring forth malice and sedition. Were this the place, I could add some remarkable historical examples of the efficiency of these means of fomenting discontent, and exciting resistance against lawful authority.

The nomenclature, as well as the style of these exhortations, was sometimes borrowed from romance: more frequently from the apocryphal prophecies so current in the middle ages. The rebel chief assumed the name of the fabled Arthur. He, the pigmy fomenter of agitation, who now struts like a giant in the columns of the newspaper as Civis or Scrutator, or Vindex or Publicola, then sought to enshroud himself in the character of Sybilla, or Waldhave, John of Bridlington, or Malachi of Armagh, the sedition acting more powerfully upon the imagination from the mystery in which it was enshrined.

Treason, in all its varieties, owes a considerable portion of its attractions to the same cause. The mind receives a strange pleasurable stimulus from concealment, hazard, danger: and the same feelings which give attraction to the dramatic tragedy, tempt us, when but a little heightened, into all the excitement of crime.

With respect to the effect here recounted to have been produced by such a flat and pointless composition as Merlin's prophecy, it is an event of which we see the like every day. If it be true that a word to the wise is enough, we may affirm that half a word is more than enough, when addressed to any bad principle implanted in the human heart. The effects produced by these and analogous appeals frequently appear singularly disproportioned to their cause. Efforts the most energetic to rouse the feelings of a people or a popular assembly, often end as they began, in empty sound: whilst, on other occasions, comparatively feeble means of excitement are responded to by the whole community.

In all such cases, the voice gives the last concussion to the air, which was required to bring down the impending avalanche. But the snow which composes the avalanche itself, brought forth from the treasury of the clouds, has been long accumulating on the edge of the mountain precipice, heaped up by the winds of heaven in preparation for the fall. It is neither the activity nor the ability of the demagogue which gives him might. Rage as much as he may, he does nothing by his own power. He appears to the crowd as an active and actuating cause; but he is only employed or suffered as an instrument, receiving all his energy from the influences around him. He fancies he guides the storm; but he is merely the conductor through which the electricity of the atmosphere is discharged.

Return we now to our voyager and his companions. "The prelates and magnates are still sitting," said Marco. "Yes, though in great turmoil," replied the clerk of the Pells; "but as yet, we have not seen either metropolitan, and all men marvel much at the delay; but follow me into the parliament chamber," continued he; an invitation which both Marco and the friar gladly obeyed.

The door was guarded by the king's sergeant-at-arms, who, at the present day, still attends the House of Commons by the special permission of the sovereign, and not by any authority properly belonging to the house: in token of which, the mace is surrendered by the Speaker at the close of the session, and deposited in the royal treasury, now called the Jewel house, in the Tower. It was a strange concatenation of events, that the apprehensions excited by the ataghan of the old man of the mountain should have been the primary cause of the placing the ensign of the Speaker's authority upon the table of the House of Commons. An officer, first created as the special guard and attendant of royalty, now does duty before the popular branch of the legislature. It might be as well if our commons would sometimes bear such historical facts in mind, in order that they might recollect that it is as the king's high court of parliament they assemble, and that if they are the representatives of the community, they are also the council of the crown.

At the beck of the clerk, the door unclosed, and the strangers had scarcely entered the chamber when Bardolph du Tyl, the Gascon, the king's pursuivant, rushed into the hall, exclaiming in tones of horror, "Murder, Murder! My lord the archbishop of York is murdered by the lord archbishop of Canterbury in his way to the parliament house." The whole assembly was astounded. "The road by the side of the river along the Strand, as your majesty well knoweth, is but a perilous slough ; my lord of York's mule, sure-footed as she is, could scarcely pick her way amidst the ruts and mire. Just as my lord of York was in that solitary spot, not far from the pound, over against the church of St. Martin, my lord of Canterbury, who had stationed himself in the adjacent fields with a large body of forces, suddenly rushed upon the flank of the procession. At the same moment, my lord of York was furiously attacked in front by the prior of St. Bartholomew's, who had been warily lying in ambush behind Charing-Cross. My lord attempted to retreat to York-House : but my lord of Canterbury furiously pursued his brother prelate, and with one fell stroke brought him to the ground, the prior then drawing his——"

"Master chancellor," exclaimed the king, rising hastily and anxiously from the throne, "you shall answer for your negligence in permitting this most dreadful affray."

"Gracious sovereign," replied the chancellor, dropping off the woolsack upon his bended knees, "every precaution was taken to prevent hostilities between the two primates, which could be suggested by the sad and woeful experience of their long-continued and inveterate feuds. In order to furnish a sufficient defence, the whole *posse comitatus* was raised for my lord of York's protection in every county on the great North Road, from the borders of Nottinghamshire, where, crossing the frontier of my lord's province, he entered the hostile country. All the constables of the hundreds marshalled their forces in every town in which his Grace was expected, for the preservation of the peace, and for guarding him against the attacks of his enemies. Furthermore, the lord mayor and the sheriffs of London were most strictly charged, to prevent any battles or affrays between the dignitaries——"

The chancellor was proceeding with these details, relating to his own vigilance ; even at this distance of time, they appear so satisfactory, that we cannot doubt but that he would have fully exculpated himself from the charge of want of true regard to the safety of the prelates, had not his explanation been interrupted by the appearance of both archbishops, both alive, though not merry, both round and sound, both unhurt and unwounded, but each looking as fiercely at his adversary as the gargoyles of a Gothic building, and keeping at a distance from each other, which distance, though in ordinary language it might be termed respectful, clearly indicated anything rather than the mutual respect of the respective parties.

The subordinate personages, however, who followed in the train of their principals, were not in equally good plight, and their appearance clearly showed that there had been, what the energetical letter of the archbishop of Canterbury afterwards styled "*ung moult horrible debat,*" between the prelates or their partisans, though its consequences had been much exaggerated by the reporter. But to do justice to Bardolph's veracity, he had told his tale, as he had heard it from the usher, who had heard it from the doorward, who had heard it from Gerard Vantbrace, the porter of the palace-gate. As for Vantbrace, he wisely supposed that, during parliament time, the most constitutional course which he could pursue would be, to leave the gates open to all petitioners. Therefore, after carefully fastening them back, and leaving little Margery, his daughter, to supply his place, he retired for a while to the Rose—an inviting hostelry at the east end of the adjoining abbey, upon the site of which, in aftertimes, was erected the gorgeous mausoleum of the first of the Tudors.

Gerard himself, when refreshing himself at the Rose, had obtained the intelligence from Walter the Bowman, who, during the skirmish, had scrambled up to the top of one of the great elms which surrounded Charing common. And the narrative having been transmitted through so many tale-bearers, we need not wonder at the enlargements which it had received.

The two chief combatants, the prior of St. Bartholomew's and the abbot of Fountains, who officiated as crosier-bearer to the northern metropolitan, had been pretty evenly matched. St. Bartholomew's, however, received the worst punishment, for, though he was the more powerful man of the two, yet Fountains was his superior in agility. The abbot's cope all tattered and torn, and his bleeding nose, bore testimony to the prowess of the prior: whilst the prior's shaven crown equally displayed the dexterity with which the abbot had wielded his weapon, the crosier, the dire cause of the present most indecorous contest.

Resulting from a rivalry, which dated its commencement from the era of the Saxon Bretwaldas, the conflicting pretensions preferred by the two archbishops of the English Church, had been legally settled by the celebrated decision from which parliament never departed, that York should be primate of England, and Canterbury of all England. Canterbury always sat as the premier peer of the realm. All the doctors of the Sorbonne, excepting perhaps the learned professor who wrote the treatise *De omnibus rebus et quibusdam aliis,* might have been dumbfounded by being called upon to explain in what manner a whole can be less or greater than itself: or how the primate of England could find a spot from which the jurisdiction of him of all England was excluded.

Whilst the prelates continued in their respective provinces, each could, nevertheless, comfort himself with the undisturbed exercise of his primatial dignity. The convocation or synod of York might follow the example of Canterbury, in assenting to the same identical canons as had been adopted in the south, and yet without directly quoting the precedent, or acknowledging the authority of the concurrent assembly. But the case altered most materially when either archbishop was required to pass out of his own province into the country of his rival, for the purpose of attending a council or a parliament: and which contingency happened, of course, whenever such a meeting was called. On these occasions, the bearing of the crosier before the archbishop of York, as an ensign of his dignity, was grievously resented by the archbishop of Canterbury, or his officers and retainers: York did the like whenever occasion offered: and, without in anywise neglecting their canonical appeals to Rome, they equally proceeded by the old English mode of assault and battery.

Thus, when, in the reign of Henry II., the archbishop of York took the post of honour, the numerous suffragans of Canterbury, against whom the few prelates owing obedience to York were most unequally matched, rushed pell mell upon him, and, after knocking him off his seat, fairly or unfairly beat him out of the council. So little was this indecorous rancour diminished in subsequent reigns, that, whenever a parliament was held, the writ of summons to the archbishop was accompanied by urgent instructions to the sheriffs and magistrates for the preservation of the peace. They were required to use their utmost endeavours to protect the northern metropolitan during his progress through the province of the southern primate, exactly in the manner stated by the lord chancellor in his exculpation, and almost in the words employed by him: and of which the repeated examples found upon the rolls, are familiar to every one who has investigated our ancient parliamentary history.

In the present instance, until the archbishop's arrival in the immediate neighbourhood of London, the journey had been

effected with singular tranquillity and comfort.   At Barnet, however, the first exception occurred.   In that comfortable town,
a brace of wicked urchins contrived to tack a fox's brush to the
robe of the archbishop's apparitor, but which was immediately
removed by John Boulter, the miller.   Though the man of meal
had no sympathy with the clergy, he was rather afraid of the joke.
He recollected that an indignity, thus offered to the followers of
Thomas à Becket, had occasioned the permanent addition of
similar rear-appendages to the inhabitants of Folkstone and their
descendants : occasioning a caudate variety of the human species,
as yet undescribed by physiologists.   John Boulter, though he
said he did not quite believe the whole of the story, was yet under
some apprehension lest the ornament should be in like manner
entailed upon the men of Barnet in perpetuity.

When the archbishop arrived at the High-gate, more decided
symptoms of opposition appeared.   The bar was closed.   A very
numerous body of the tenants of the bishop of London were
drawn up in battle array for the purpose of defending the pass.
They were headed by the steward of the manor, who loudly
exclaimed that the road passed through the land of the bishop :
it was a private way : it had been opened by the bishop's licence,
and the permission thus granted to the public could be resumed at
his will.   All honest folk were welcome to its use, but my lord
bishop would never suffer his ground to be trodden by an intruder
to the prejudice of his revered metropolitan.

Vainly the Yorkers urged that it was not a private way, but
the king's highway, and that such an obstruction was in direct
contravention of common and statute law from the days of King
Mulmutius.   The seneschal traversed the fact, while the battalions
of armed villeins continued at the same time stationed athwart
the road.   York and his train had no choice but to retire, and
proceed as they best might, by tramping over the fields, taking
a route which conducted them through Harringay or Hornsey
Park.   Here they were so undoubtedly trespassers upon the soil
of the bishop of London, to whom the estate yet belongs, that it
would have been an unpardonable act of treason on the part of
the faithful subjects of Canterbury, had they neglected displaying
their zeal and attachment by giving every possible annoyance to
his enemy.   The news of the invasion quickly spread through
every part of the domain.   Horns sounded, dogs barked, stones
and clods were hurled at the archbishop from every thicket.
The slow and steady pace of the Yorkist train rapidly changed

from amble to trot, and from trot to gallop. Their persecutors, the host of Canterbury, now burst forth with hue and cry, and fairly chased the primate of England through the episcopal park. Yet little injury was sustained; for the huntsmen, perceiving the lord mayor and the sheriffs advancing at the head of the city forces, immediately turned back, leaving the northern archbishop under the kind protection of the municipal magistrates.

Once in the city liberties, the partisans of Canterbury, though all at their posts, were prevented by fear of the law, from any act of bodily violence, but the feelings displayed by them were such as to render the parliamentary duties of the much persecuted prelate of York, no very agreeable task. Loud groans saluted him as he passed beneath the windows of London House, in Aldersgate Street. In the steeples of all the "thirteen peculiars"—the parishes which belong to the diocese of Canterbury—the bells rang a muffled peal; and, when the archbishop passed by the portal of Bow Church, who should stand there in full robes but the judge of the consistory court, and the dean of the arches—*Arcades ambo*—sonorously trolling, in alternate verses, a ribald roundelay against him: all the little choristers joining in the burden of the song. Kept in check by the municipal authorities, the partisans of Canterbury, who could not do more within the city, employed their musical staves as a demonstration; but they had fully determined to use stick, stock, and staff, as soon as the Yorkers could be hit without the walls. Canterbury, therefore, held a full council of war at the house of Everard Pleynchaunt, the minor canon: where it was finally determined to intercept York on his way to parliament on the following morning; and, the plan being adopted, such consequences ensued as have been detailed.

The king and the temporal lords, after earnest entreaty, induced the archbishops to take their seats. Parliamentary business had, however, been entirely interrupted by these commotions. The chancellor, wiping his hot face, found it impossible to restore order: and the unusual lateness of the hour, it being near ten in the forenoon: the increasing appetite of the members: the distinct view of the fires in the kitchen in the adjoining quadrangle; before whose blaze, joints and animals of all sorts and sizes, pigs and sheep, chines and shoulders, legs and sirloins, hens, ducks, geese, mallards, maids, and turnspits, could be seen equally roasting :—scullions busily employed in basting the meat—cooks busily employed in basting the scullions—all suggested the propriety of an adjournment till the following day. Not a voice was raised against this motion. The quarrel between the two archbishops, however, had excited great anxiety; their mutual friends were very seriously alarmed; and therefore, before they left the parliament chamber, the chancellor, acting in the capacity of Speaker, compelled the prelates, after considerable hesitation on both sides, to promise, that "the matter should not be carried any further," a prohibition, which, in those *bonâ fide* fighting days, was obeyed as unwillingly, as leave on the part of the House, that "the matter should be carried further," would be accepted in ours.

The principle, however, out of which the dispute arose, gradually assisted in effecting a great change in the parliamentary constitution. The theory of parliament, as established in the fourteenth century, required a full representation of the clergy, upon a scheme similar to that which had been adopted for the laity. Each cathedral chapter was required to send one procurator; and the clergy of each diocese two, empowered to consent on their behalf, nearly upon the plan of the members returned for the boroughs and the shires.

The inferior clergy thus became an unquestionable branch, or house of parliament: and the "Premunientes clause," as it is termed, by virtue of which they sat, is continued in the parliamentary writs to this very day. But the attendance of the clergy in parliament, unwillingly given, never was established for the entire kingdom. The king might call, but the clergy, excepting such as held in barony, held that they were not bound to come out of their own province. Insisting more and more upon their rights, they kept away from the laity, became a convocation, and ceased to be a branch of the legislature. Acting thus, they severed themselves from parliament, and were left without any spokesmen or advocates in that assembly, excepting the bishops, who sit also by reason of the baronies which they still hold of the crown; and for which, when consecrated, they perform homage in the closet of the sovereign.

Whether the presence of so many ecclesiastical members would, on the whole, have been advantageous to the clerical character of particular individuals, may be a question requiring consideration; but it is clear that, by the loss of their ancient privilege, their power has been exceedingly diminished, to the incalculable detriment of the church in its corporate capacity. Those who declaim the loudest against ecclesiastical authority, ought to recollect that, in all ages, the clergy have never by their own strength been able to defend their civil rights, when the laity have been determined to pillage or despoil them. Preserved as an order, and they will be preserved in despite of their individual negligences, errors, and sins, their continued existence is a tribute which the powers of this world are compelled, however unwillingly, to render to an authority beyond the world's control.

CHAPTER V.

THE FRIAR'S STUDY.

"I AM a toad in a hole," quoth the monk of Croyland. There
are two species of toads in a hole, toads so designated in figurative,
allegorical, or poetical language; toads who are really what the
term implies.

The figurative, the allegorical, the poetical "toad in a hole,"
a dish well known to my East-Anglian readers, is the most savoury
of the

> . . . . . . messes,
> Which neat-handed Phyllis dresses.

It consisteth of a baked viand, surrounded by alliaceous roots,
concealed beneath an adipofarinaceous covering, representing, not
unaptly, the batrachian reptile, from whence it derives its name.
I am using very fine language, which I do not quite know how
to apply or spell, but that is not my fault, for—, I won't say who,
objects to the whole of this passage as vulgar; I am therefore
trying to make it elegant by the help of hard words. But, at
all events, I think that you, reader, will be able to make out the
nature of the allegorical "toad in a hole," which affords so many a
comfortable dinner to the Norfolk and Suffolk yeomen, and occasionally to those in a higher degree.

So much for the allegorical "toad in a hole"; the real toad in
a hole is such a one as the monk of Croyland, the original author
of this book, or his humble editor, I.

Throughout the mediæval period, the abuses prevailing amongst
the members of the hierarchy call forth severe and unsparing
remarks from the chroniclers. Incidents like those detailed in
the last chapter, might suggest some salutary reprehensions: the
monk of Croyland declares that they were by no means absent
from his mind; but he was greatly restrained by a strong and
honest feeling of his own insignificance. Actuated, therefore, by
all the blushing modesty of the member who opens his maiden
speech, with the corrected slips of the report of said speech, duly
colophonized, "The honourable member sat down amidst loud and

repeated cheers," in his pocket all the while; he begins, "I am a toad in a hole"; and, confessing his entire incompetence for the task, he proceeds to unravel all the contemporary delinquencies of the episcopal bench. If people's faces burn when they are written of, in the same manner as they do when they are spoken of, I am sure poor Cardinal Beaufort's cheeks must have been in a perfect blaze.

I, who am also a real toad in a hole, and not an allegorical one, have no right to express any opinions upon such a momentous question as that of ecclesiastical reform. Were I merely to translate literally what the monk of Croyland has said concerning Cardinal Beaufort, I am morally certain that my text would be wrested and perverted into an open expression of opinion respecting similar subjects at the present day. Or, what would be more dangerous to me, as containing cleverly concealed allusions to reverends, and right reverends, just as my good friend Whistlecrafts' inimitable narrative of the adventures of Queen Genevra's maids of honour in the Castle of Giants, was construed into a very awkward disclosure respecting Carlton House and the Royal Pavilion. I will therefore expunge the monk's commentary, which might thus expose me to suspicion, and rejoin our friends, Roger Bacon and Marco, though I know not how they were employed during the remainder of the day. The monk of Croyland only informs us that, quitting the hall towards the evening, they entered the great quadrangle, and found Gerard Vantbrace, the porter, in a state of extreme plague and perplexity. Engaged in active warfare, perpetually recurring, always beginning, never ending, offensive and defensive, against the host of urchins, who, in busy idleness, were disporting in New Palace Yard, the worthy janitor seemed almost at his wits' end, a point which the best of us may reach with wonderful expedition. But in what state and condition was our friend Vantbrace? How shall I describe it? We are indeed a happy, elegant, moral, and transcendent people. We have no masters; they are all principals: no shopmen; they are all assistants: no shops; they are all establishments: no jailors; they are all governors. Nobody is flogged in Bridewell; he merely receives the correction of the house: nobody is ever unable to pay his debts; he is only unable to meet his engagements: nobody is angry; he is only excited: nobody is cross; he is only nervous: lastly, nobody is drunk; the very utmost you can assert is, that, as was the case with Gerard Vantbrace, "he has taken his wine."

It is impossible to anticipate what improvement may ultimately be effected, in the manners and morals of the people, by
the diffusion of political economy.   But hitherto, amongst
English folks, Malthusian prudence has never produced sufficient
effects in preventing production.   Abstract speculations don't
suit us.   People do not take practically to such metaphysical
studies, nor can they readily ascend from the abolition of the
rights of primogeniture, to the abolition of primogeniture itself.
Assuredly, in spite of small-pox, chicken-pox, measles, chin-cough,
whooping-cough, we have always, in England, had too many
children.   When John Baliol burnt two hundred poor little school-
boys in one bonfire, this useful, though unfortunately temporary,
check to redundant population is a sufficient proof of the mischievous extent to which their numbers had attained at Corbridge,
though even at present, that town, according to the last return,
only contains about two thousand inhabitants; and I have not
any doubt, from what I find in my story, that, due consideration
being had to its proportionate extent, Westminster, in the early
part of the fourteenth century, swarmed with the minor unwashed,
in every lane and alley, just as it does at the present day.

New Palace Yard, the structure of William Rufus, which,
being new in his time, by comparison with the structure erected
by the Confessor, has acquired a most enduring juvenility, was
the spot which this portion of King Edward's subjects considered
as their most favourite resort.   Here they were playing at pitch
and toss: there they employed themselves in throwing the bar:
others were kicking the football, and eke their shins.   Grievously
did these games interfere with the tranquillity of the passers-by,
who, in addition to all contingent mischances, were, if their
appearance betokened a sufficient expectation of non-resistance,
or, resisting, of non-effectual resentment, frequently despoiled of
hoods, coifs, caps, and kerchiefs.   Miniver and satin inspired as
little respect as serge and ray; the favourite practical joke among
the noisy cohort was to twitch off these useful coverings, and to
deposit them in the nearest puddles; of which there were generally
abundance, even in the driest weather.

Such gambols, it is true, stood strictly forbidden by a royal
proclamation.   A reminiscence of this ancient inhibition appears
at the beginning of the sessions in a vote of the lords, commanding the high constable to prevent all disorders in the neighbourhood tending to the annoyance of the members, as well as all
gaming in the passages leading to the house; and which most of

my readers may have seen affixed in various parts of Westminster. Gerard Vantbrace was held particularly responsible for the due execution of this regulation: but, to preserve decorum out of the walls of Parliament was then as difficult as it is at present to compel the observance of the rules enjoined by decency and good-breeding within. Consequently, the porter had almost as hard work, and nearly as ungrateful a task, in enforcing due order, as the speaker has now.

Quite beyond the mental or physical powers of sturdy Gerard Vantbrace, conditioned as before described, was the preservation of tranquillity. Had Gerard's broad shoulders been hung with as many arms as a Hindoo idol, they would scarce have sufficed to bestow an adequate thrashing, even upon a selection of the most deserving amongst the urchin crowd: yet Gerard did his best, to give them the benefits resulting from this essential, though now neglected, element of national education. Dire and exemplary castigation by fist and foot had been just inflicted with so much impartiality upon the zenith and nadir of an impish offender, that neither extremity had any reason to envy the other: both received equal justice; and the sufferer fled howling and blubbering from the grasp of his assailant. But this summary punishment had not, in the slightest degree, deterred the rest of the cohort; who, it being twilight grey, adopted the entertainment of tossing about burning wisps of straw, in addition to such other recreations as could yet be pursued.

Gerard Vantbrace, though marvellously irate and very unsteady on his legs, was nevertheless in a mellow state of conversability. When Bacon had drawn near, the porter made up to the friar, and plucking him by the sleeve, began to detail all the persecutions which he sustained. "In parliament time," said Gerard, "no honest man can enjoy a mouthful in quiet. Parliament brings all the *rascaille* of the country to the king's very doors"; and let it be here annotated, that this same term of rascality is real authentic mediæval parliament language; the number and membrane of the roll can be quoted in which it occurs. "I would that good Judge Hengham, whose money made that bell-tower arise, could be called upon to do such duty upon them as is suggested by his name."

During this discourse, the fugitive before-mentioned, who had ensconced himself in the dark angle of a projecting buttress, stole slily out of his hiding-place: and, creeping gently behind Vantbrace, affixed a string composed of a dozen or more small cases or packets to the skirts of the porter's doublet. Bacon, who saw the operation, was about to give warning, but before he could speak a word, the squibs and crackers, for such they really were, went off in full fizz, whizz, flash, pitter, patter, bounce. Away darted Vantbrace himself, as if he had been launched from a catapult, in vain attempt to capture his ruthless enemy. Bacon and Marco Polo, thus released from their detainer, pursued their homeward path.

The display of pyrotechny was, however, still continued, a rocket rushing upwards before them in a quivering stream of sparks, burst: and illuminated the atmosphere on high by the transient gleams of its explosion. "A Saracen device," quoth Marco, "but in which they themselves are only imitators of my friends in Cathay. Exceedingly well known to them, is the art of fireworks. Upwards of a thousand artificers in the army of the Tartar khan, were employed upon such weapons, tending much to the alarm, though little to the hurt, of the enemies against whom he was opposed. Children now outrun philosophers: the sage meditating in his cell, imparts to us as a precious and recondite experiment, the sport of the boy. Doth Friar Ferrarius belong to your order?" continued Marco, "he, who like yourself, hath addressed the pope on the secrets of chemical science. With great pains, Ferrarius hath rendered into Latin, the proportions of the composition; how the salt, the live sulphur, and the coal, must be finely triturated upon the hard porphyry stone; how the match is to be applied; and with what subtlety the parchment cases are to be folded, containing the powder which propels these flying thunders or flying dragons, as by some they are called."

Bacon stopt, took out his tablets, and Marco Polo, who looked over his shoulder, saw him writing down a note, possibly the origin of the purposely obscure paragraphs upon this subject, now found in his folio, though Ferrarius is therein unnamed. Bacon is far less explicit in his details than the Spaniard: and upon a careful comparison of their two works, it becomes evident that they wrote upon totally different principles, the Spaniard as a mere collector of recipes, the Englishman in the spirit of a philosophical inquirer, strangely affected by the peculiar mysticism of his age; but who had obtained the knowledge of the process of granulation, so simple, and yet so concealed from his contemporaries, and by which the commixture of ingredients alone obtained its mischievous perfection. Bacon concealed the dangerous secret. Yet the pyrotechnic recipe must have continued generally known; and the mode of compounding the "pulvis ad faciendum *le Crake*," as it was uncouthly and barbarously termed, was transmitted innocuously from generation to generation, until it reached the one inventor through whom it was destined that the manipulation should be again discovered, and gunpowder applied to the destructive art of modern war.

Bacon made his memorandum, closed his book, pressed his thin lips together, knitted his brows, and the companions continued their walk in silence. Marco, merely for the purpose of rousing the friar from this not unusual fit of taciturnity, said, "Astronomers calculate the diameter of the seventh heaven at one hundred and thirty million, seven hundred and fifteen thousand miles; think ye they are correct in their reckoning?" Not a word did Bacon reply. Merchant and friar walked on in silence.

Marco got his figures, as I suppose, from the Almagest. We who have checked them, know that they are wrong, *nous avons changé tout cela*. All the civilized world is now on our side. Pope Pius VII. certainly showed great kindness to us heretics, he acted much like a man of the world, and a gentleman, and behaved very handsomely, when he came into the consistory, and repealed the edicts against Galileo and the Copernican system. Before that surrender of ancient dogmas, though the Heliocentric system was taught in all popish universities, excepting Salamanca, it was always required of the professors, in deference to the decrees of the church, to use the term Hypothesis, instead of Theory. Salamanca, however, stood out, and the professor of astronomy would have resigned his chair rather than agree to the change.

Professor Cabezudo was lately here, and as I thought it was a sad thing that any member of "the great European family" should exhibit such woeful ignorance, I did all I could, it is not much to be sure, to enlighten him. But all my efforts were in vain. I attended a whole course of lectures, and went to the expense of buying a complete set of the little red pocket encyclopedia, and tried to confute Cabezudo out of it; yet I always got the worst of the argument. Often was I so puzzled, that I began to think that the examiners treated the undergraduate of St. John's very unfairly when they plucked him, for having answered the question, "whether the earth moved round the sun, or the sun round the earth," by saying, "Sometimes the one and sometimes the other."

The way in which Padre Eusebio Cabezudo argues is this:— You are a heretic, and as a heretic you must admit that the pope is not infallible, and unless he can convince me by reason, that his creed is true, I am not bound to adopt it at all. Your modern heretical philosophy is completely grounded upon observation and experiment. You ultimately resolve all exact science into the perceptions of sense, so much so, that if your physical evidence appears to contradict what you philosophers term the "preconceived notions of theology," the latter are without any hesitation to be abandoned as the slavery-brand of the human mind. Yet, how are you philosophers treating me. You tyrannically demand my unqualified assent to propositions entirely opposed to observation and experiment. All the evidence which I obtain from my senses entirely contradicts this new philosophical belief. All my perceptions are opposed to it. I feel the earth to be immovable. I see the sun and stars in motion: and the ball dropt from the summit of the tower, falls straight to the base instead of being left behind. Yet more. You teach me that the philosopher "can always be satisfied that he has discovered a real law of nature when we can show by strict argument or mathematical reasoning," that "the facts must follow from it as necessary logical consequences, and this, not vaguely and generally, but with all possible precision in time, place, weight, and measure." Now how stand these facts? Ptolemy places the earth in the centre, and refers all the motions of the planets to the earth alone, altogether independent of the sun. Upon this assumption, allowing only for the inaccuracies and deficiencies occasioned by the imperfections of his instruments—for Ptolemy would have extended his theory to the satellites of Uranus, could he have seen them—he was able to account for all the features of the motions of the planets, as logically and as precisely as you do who cause them to revolve round the sun. In the theory of Ptolemy, the testimony of our senses, and the hypothetical law, a true law according to your own logical standard, agree. The most staunch and most able of your Copernican heretics candidly admits, that, considered in its true import as a system of calculation for explaining the apparent motions of the planets, our Ptolemaic system, now so glibly derided on account of its complexity of cycles and epicycles, "is not only good, but that in many cases no better has been discovered"; and that "an unquestionable evidence of its merit and value is to be found in the circumstance, that it was able to take in and preserve all the exact knowledge of the world, until a new theory arose."

"Therefore," said Padre Eusebio, "what certainty have we that a further advance in 'exact knowledge' may not even bring you heretics back again to Ptolemy and the Almagest. Shall I surrender my creed? What do I gain in real knowledge by the exchange? If you philosophers will compel belief in defiance to our senses, and upon postulates which, according to your own showing, afford no test of truth, why do you accuse us of intolerant bigotry? If you submit cheerfully to this yoke yourselves, why do you tax us with servility of intellect in obeying implicitly that which the church has taught? As for me, I will not sell my dear-bought liberty to such hard task-masters. Science makes infinitely heavier demands upon faith than religion ever does, and without promising the same reward."

Yet, in spite of all Padre Eusebio Cabezudo can say, inestimable are the obligations which we owe to the investigations of modern astronomers. We learn, for example, that "the greatest eccentricity of Jupiter" is confined within definite limits. Now, nobody could have ever guessed this fact from that admirable record of Jupiter's acts and deeds, Lemprière's *Dictionary*. Were we to reason upon Jupiter's character, therein so profitably illustrated *in usum studiosæ juventutis*, we might suppose that he was capable of indulging in any possible or impossible eccentricity, excepting, perhaps, that of becoming a decent and respectable husband. But amongst all these discoveries, I value the proof which scientific astronomy affords, that there are no men in the moon, or at all events, that they are not locomotive. For, if men in the moon had such a venous and arterial circulation, adapted to the lunar and terrestrial gravitation beneath their feet, as would enable them to live on the off-side of the satellite, the increased attraction above them, if they travelled to their antipodes on our side, would occasion so great a pressure of blood on their brains that they would die of apoplexy.

So much for men in the moon. But Marco thought, that, perhaps, the man in the moon might engage Bacon to open his mouth, and pointing to the orb, he said to Bacon, "How strange are the freaks which fancy plays to us: the varieties of light and shade which our vulgar configurate into the churl with the bunch of thorns on his back, are considered in Cathay as being very like a rabbit pounding rice in a mortar." This observation might have been a tempting challenge for discussion at other times, but it utterly failed to produce any effect: Bacon, absorbed in thought, continued silent as before.

They were now in sight of the new Temple. Red and misty

rays, shed by the lamps within, streamed through the upper windows of the round church, whose structure still remains to excite, rather than to satisfy, the curiosity of the architectural antiquary.

"I apprehend," resumed Marco, "that the knights are holding their nocturnal chapter; I had almost said their orgies. Strange things are told of them in Palestine. It is commonly supposed that the Templars are devoted to the foul fiend, and that when they break up after their meeting, one of the masters of the bench is always, some how or another, missed out of the number."

"H'm," replied Friar Bacon, in a manner which indicated that he did not care to hear a word of what Marco had said. And, with that same semi-vocal "H'm," although Marco Polo kept continually, but fruitlessly, provoking him to conversation, their discourse for the evening was inexorably concluded.

During the following day, Marco Polo could not get any talk with Bacon, though, as I have told you before (at least if I did not I ought to have done so; you must hold me excused for my negligence, Homer himself nods sometimes, and so do I) they were lodged at the great Franciscan monastery in Newgate Street, now the Blue Coat School, or Christ's Hospital. Bacon occupied a cell in the cloister, while Marco was accommodated with a comfortable apartment in the *hospitium*, the portion of the building reserved for those secular visitors whom the Friars most kindly and readily received.

Bacon kept himself in utter seclusion, neither coming into church nor refectory. But, towards evening, a lay brother, who seemed less than his companion, and more than his servant, a hybrid between a chum and a scout, one John Bungay, asked the pitanciary of the house to tell him the nearest way to Lothbury.

"Lothbury—that is where the braziers carry on their noisy trade; ran dan, randaridan: tink of a kettle, tank of a pan: ran, dan, randaridan," quoth he, "what doth your master wish to handsel?" "Can you keep a secret, brother pitanciary?" said Bungay. "Aye, marry," replied the pitanciary. "So can I," quoth Bungay; and thus he departed on his master's errand, without giving hint or inkling of his purpose, or intentions, or any token of his master's employments.

Bacon's cell continued hermetically sealed during the remainder of the week, except that he was once seen at an upper window. What he was doing, has never been precisely ascertained. One of the friars said that Bacon was taking the altitude of the steeple by means of a Jacob's staff. Another maintained that the instrument looked rather like a pillar of metal directed at the summit of the building. A third affirmed that a huge mortar had been previously brought into the convent from Lothbury at night, upon a truck; but it must be acknowledged, that no real account of his proceedings could be obtained.

Marco Polo generally supped in his own room. He had much to do in keeping his accounts, and he speedily dispatched his sober and solitary meal: but, on the evening of the day when Bacon's instrument had been seen through the window, he was over-persuaded, contrary to his usual custom, to take his refection with the prior. This worthy principal was urgent in his recommendations of some malt liquor, sent to him out of the cellar of his own Hall at Cambridge, so that Marco was induced to partake more freely of the blood of Sir John Barleycorn than ever he had done before. "Other guess stuff this than your Tartar koumis, Signor Marco," said the prior, as the stoup was in its fifteenth gyration. "We have a proverb in England, that good ale is meat, drink and clothing." "And heaviness in the head, and lightness in the heels," added Marco, who, unaccustomed to such potations, found his way, with some difficulty, to his chamber, anticipating an unquiet couch and disturbed slumbers. These expectations were fully realized: and he submitted to all the usual penalties incurred by the misdeed of a good supper, and protracted jovial cheer. Horror succeeds to horror. He falls down, down, down, down an unfathomable depth, and then he suddenly hitches into his bed again. Then he feels as if all his limbs had swollen to the size of woolsacks. Then he is engaged in a dreadful struggle. Wandering in the tropical forest, he strives with all his might to escape from a Batta: the hungry epicure pursues his prey with a sharp knife in one hand, and half a lemon and a pepper-pod, for seasoning, in the other, the gaping mouth of the visionary savage being garnished with a double row of white and black teeth, opening beyond the lobe of either ear; but in the vain attempt which the groaner makes to flee, his feet adhere immoveably to the ground. Then he is transported to Stromboli. Huge invisible paws keep the feverish sleeper prostrate upon the burning ashes; the mountain grumbles and roars again and again. An awful explosion takes place, and Marco awakes with a start.

Marco, thoroughly roused, stared about his room with amaze. The impression of the noise was so strong, so lively, so much like reality, that he could hardly convince himself that it was only a dream. He was unable to compose himself to rest again, and he continued turning and tossing till the matin-bell began to ring.

When the merchant came down, there was an unusual bustle in the cloister: and, approaching nearer to the spot, Marco found a bevy of friars and other inmates of the convent, gathered opposite to Bacon's cell. Truly awful was the scene which here presented itself to the beholders; door, wide open; casement, shattered all to pieces; not a pane whole; the apartment filled with smoke, and smelling so strongly of brimstone, that no one would venture to enter. Friar Bacon himself had disappeared.

"It must have been," cried Friar Giles, who practised as a physician, and who, from an ugly professional jealousy, had always borne a peculiar grudge against Bacon, "during the last fearful clap of thunder, which seemed as if it would bring down the roof of the dormitory."

"Aye," said the prior, screeching at the top of his voice, "this is what comes of your Oxford learning. Such a thing never happened to a Cambridge man. We never dabble with the accursed studies of mathematics, forbidden, as they have been, as the clergy's scandal and shame." In the most bitter strain did the prior thus proceed, quoting every passage which his memory could furnish (and to do him justice, it was very tenacious) against the unfortunate science of mathematics, under which term, the delusions of astrology and even magic were signified.

When the cause of the event became first known, and it was fully ascertained that Bacon was carried off by the fiend, the hot and bitter rivalry prevailing between the two universities had thus betrayed the prior into exquisite delight at the catastrophe which ended the career of the great ornament of Oxford. But after the hubbub began to subside, the prior felt the truth of the adage, "Near is my shirt, but nearer is my skin," to his affection for Cambridge he was sacrificing the repute of his own order; therefore he gave strict directions that nothing whatever should be said about the abduction. "It should be confined to ourselves," said the prior, "and for our own credit, we must do our best to keep our own counsel, and hush up the matter." Every body promised to observe the strictest secrecy, and the sacristan forthwith made an entry in the obituary of the house, to the following effect: Brother Roger Bacon died suddenly on the eve of St. John, having been struck with an apoplexy, in the fifty-ninth year of his age, and the thirty-second of his profession; he was buried on the right side of the choir, just by the high altar.

These precautions, however, were fruitless. Somewhat according to the compendious practice of the celebrated Dr. Last, "Bleed the north ward and blister the south ward to-day: blister the north ward and bleed the south ward to-morrow," it was the custom in all well-regulated communities to have a general phlebotomization at stated and regular periods of the year, when, according to the ancient almanacks, in many of which we find the several *tempora minutionis* still noted, the due and fortunate time for this operation had arrived. It just happened to be the appointed time, and they had secured the services of one Richard le Pyot, the best barber in Addle Street, to bleed the community.

Unfortunately, Richard was already in the house. Before the prior could issue his injunctions, the barber, abandoning pole and basin, had started at full speed, happy to impart the news far and wide, and what the conjectures, or rather the convictions, of "the public" were, I shall not repeat. I have much too much good sense to rake up the forgotten calumnies against the Franciscans, for whom, indeed, I entertain a certain degree of family feeling, especially as they have been long since collected and refuted, as well by honest Anthony à Wood as by Lucas Waddingius in his popular *Annals of the Minor Friars*. All I can repeat with propriety is contained in the following particulars.

About noon, there were crowds in Newgate Street looking at the corner pinnacle of the tower which the sorcerer had broken off by trying to seize at it in his flight. However strange the fact may appear, the pyramid was truncated and the fracture fresh. It was impossible to doubt but this portion of the building had been struck down since the preceding evening.

About vespers, it was well ascertained that one of the wretched friar's sandals had been picked up on Hounslow Heath, and that his cowl had been caught by the cross on the top of Salisbury steeple.

And, before compline, the well-known Nicholas Trivet, the Dominican or black friar, and whose colour, therefore, rendered him the inveterate foe of the greys, had inserted a detailed account of the dreadful catastrophe in his well-known *Chronicle of England*. Every particular of the bargain was given, together with a bitter invective against the Franciscans for their futile attempts at concealment. A mere narrative, however, was not thought sufficient by Trivet, and he illustrated his tale by an illumination, which he had manufactured with equal ingenuity and expedition. The theory of this process is not entirely unknown to artists at the present day. He made a clever copy from the miniature of the witch of Berkeley carried off by the fiend, which illustrated the history of William of Malmesbury, adapting the original composition to his new design, by substituting Friar Bacon *en croupe*, instead of the old lady.

I must now revert to the convent where the adventure occurred. Marco well recollected the conversation which had ensued, when the sight of the children's sport had induced him to expatiate upon the warlike pyrotechny of the east. Putting the circumstances together, he had little doubt as to the real state of the case. Therefore, waiting till the commotion had in some degree been calmed, he suggested, in the course of the evening, that it might be as well to see whether the departed had left any memorials behind him in the cell which he had so recently inhabited. Some demur ensued upon this proposition. Without disgracing their cloth by owning to any distinct cause of apprehension, it was sufficiently evident that every friar dreaded entering this scene of horror: and the offer made by Marco, that he would be the first to encounter the danger, scarcely allayed the general consternation. Holy water was sprinkled with such unsparing profusion that the floor looked like a swamp. At length, the prior ventured to follow, though not without considerable hesitation, when the sudden appearance of a figure, sable as a Mandingo, caused him to retreat in the greatest dismay.

The well-known voice of the apparition, however, soon restored confidence. It was no other than Friar Bungay, who, as it should seem, had descended from the small upper chamber over Bacon's cell, making his way, as Marco well perceived, like a reasonable man, down the steep ladder communicating with the loft in which he had been concealed. But the prior was entirely convinced that it was no such thing: whenever he felt himself at liberty to speak confidentially on the subject, he always stated, that he was placed in a most painful situation when compelled to bear testimony against his own order; yet he had a conscience, and he was under the necessity, disagreeable as it was, of confessing he had, but too clearly, seen how Bungay came down the chimney riding on a black goat, with a fiery beard. Indeed, Bungay was such an object, that his appearance really afforded some support to the prior's version of the story.

Bungay's hands, his face, his attire, his everything, looked as if, to use the household phrase, he had been rolled in the coal-hole. Dirt, however, discomposed him not, he was used to it: and he retained all his usual calmness and tranquillity. The message which he gave to Marco, that the friar expected to receive him at Oxford, was accompanied with no explanation whatever as to the time or manner of Bacon's departure. The great credit of the Franciscans coinciding with their interest, so far prevailed, that no further investigation was instituted. Yet the matter, taken altogether, was always considered by a small though respectable party, even in the Order, as having a very suspicious aspect. Soap and towels duly employed in the lavatory, removed, after no little labour, the smut and grime from Friar Bungay's physiognomy: but I cannot say that Bacon's reputation for orthodoxy was ever entirely restored.

No adventure, requiring any particular notice, occurred to Marco Polo and Bungay, during the journey to Oxford, which the former willingly undertook for the purpose of taking leave of his friend, until they reached Headington Hill. It was one of the wise police regulations of Edward the First, that all woods and underwoods should be felled to the extent of two hundred feet on either side of the highway, in order to deprive the robber of his place of concealment. But in this part of the country (whether the fault was to be imputed to the conservators of the peace or to the sheriff, I cannot tell) the statute had been imperfectly observed. In one place, indeed, the ground was cleared: and the descent was there so precipitately rapid, that you quite looked over the thick underwood which surrounded you and apparently closed up the way below. Marco, at this point, reined in his steady steed; he dismounted, stationed himself upon a crag and enjoyed the full bright prospect of the steeples and spires of Oxford spreading before him. In the remote distance, though entirely commanded by the elevation on which they stood, a small tower, whose summit could be seen rising through a grove beyond the massy fabric of St. Frideswide, was pointed out to him by Bungay as the favourite retirement, the study of the friar.

"Ah," exclaimed Marco stooping, "surely some pilgrim from San Jago de Compostella, hath just preceded us; he hath dropped these cockle-shells from his garment. But no," continued the Venetian, more closely examining the fossil which had attracted his attention, and which he carefully deposited in his gibeciere, "it is one of those strange configurations, a form of life imbedded in the rock, attesting the plastic power of the stars, or perhaps, as some think, bearing record to the great catastrophe of the globe: and I have elsewhere...."

Professor Cabezudo lags so terribly behind the age, and is so swayed by his "preconceived theological opinions," that he holds the geologists even cheaper than the astronomers. He says, they "pursue the slow and toilsome path which leads to physical truth," just as one of their own "erratic blocks" would do: they crush all difficulties instead of removing them; not piercing their way by acuteness, but lumping through by ponderosity. In particular, the professor likes to repeat the Irish story which he heard from Father O'Toole, formerly a student in his class at Salamanca, and now parish priest at Clonagoose, in the County of Carlow; and who well deserves the name of O'Toole by metonymy. "Paddy, how far is it from Mullingar to Michaelmas?" "Plase your honour, as far as from Christmas to the ace of spades." Cabezudo, as I have heard, applies this story to the geologists, being of opinion that the deductions by which they calculate the length of the "periods of creative operations," exhibit the same pertinency: inasmuch as they measure by the laws of mechanical dynamics the intervals of appearances, which, upon their own showing, are the results of vital forces and chemical action, whose intensities are wholly inappreciable by such mechanical laws. "Geology, moreover," said Cabezudo, "usurps the name of science without definitions and without data; and I never found a geologian who did not shirk the questions upon the answers to which all his theories depend. They have been put, why does he not reply? What is the creation of a new species? How long does the process require of creation? Where do you find the measure of time required for creation? Was the first ichthyosaurus gradually evolved from some embryo substance, or did myriads suddenly start up from the ground in full perfection? Is more time required for the production of myriads than of one? Under pain of excommunication, the geologist insists that I should accept deductions without premises; assumptions without proof from sense or experience. No pontiff insisting upon transubstantiation ever expected such implicit obedience from his hearers, or required so unbounded a confidence in his assertions, as the geologist, compelling me to believe in the 'centres of creation' upon the earth's surface, which produced organic beings without a creator, each a *punctum saliens* starting from nothing. The miracles of the Golden Legend are more agreeable to human reason than the wonders of geology, for the hagiologist assigns an adequate cause, the geologist none. The doctrines of the geologist cannot be received without the utter prostration of the human intellect.

Those who tremble before all that the nurse and all the priest have taught, do not believe so much as the geologist requires."

I wonder whether Marco was about to blow a new geological theory. Their average duration is ten years and three quarters, so that the Uniformitarians must prepare to go as Catastrophists have done before them. What delightful things theories would be, if they did but endure. As the geologist spends his precious vital breath upon them, they grow larger, and larger, and larger: and the iridescent tints and colours play and float brighter, and brighter, and brighter upon the swelling film, as it becomes thinner, and thinner, and thinner; but when they are at the brightest, they are rapidly succeeded by dark spots, these dark spots increase, the bubble bursts, the geologist is quite out of breath, perhaps for ever, and some other geologist forthwith begins to blow another theory in his turn.

Marco certainly intended to say more: when he was startled by a feeble groan of distress proceeding from an adjoining dell. He and Bungay followed the faint sound, and after a strict search, they were able to ascertain the cause. The poor man, whom they raised up, told them, that being purblind, and just able by the guidance of his dog to go along the well-known path to market, he had been robbed by a ruffian, who suddenly attacked him without the least warning. "Not a living creature was nigh," said old Herbert of the Bower, for that was his name, "and I have been lying here, unable to move, many long hours. It happened just as I heard the bell afar off, beginning to ring for matins in Saint Mary's the great church of our town."

Herbert added, he had sat down to rest himself at the foot of the stone cross, joining in heart with those whose voices were resounding beneath the roof of the distant choir, when a murderous blow felled him to the ground. Lying close by, was the staff used by the ruffian who had done the deed, extremely massy, and evidently having more the appearance of the weapon of a marauder than the support of a peaceable wayfarer. Marco therefore rightly conjectured that the bandit had parted with his bludgeon in order to avoid suspicion, and had supplied himself instead with a sapling, riven from a beech tree hard by, as appeared by the fresh stripped wood and juicy riband of pendent bark.

"Could you recognize the villain again?" said Marco.

"I fear not," said the old man, "I could not see him: and he took good care not to let me hear his voice. I turned and caught at him as I dropped. I think my weight brought him down on one knee into the road; and I felt that he was clad in a leathern coat. But how can such tokens serve?"

"And thus," said Marco, "the act concealed from every mortal eye, will escape all temporal retribution due to the crime, for, in this closely-sheltered spot, unless the human sight could pierce from some one of those distant structures, no observer could witness the assault. Without doubt, the robber was encouraged by the certainty that he could not be perceived in this solitude."

Such reflections did not exonerate the travellers from the care of attending to the wounded man. They were considering how they could best assist him in his state of suffering, and convey him to Oxford, when they were relieved from their anxiety by the arrival of some country people, who at once recognized old Herbert as their neighbour, and who promised to convey him to Shotover, where he dwelt.

Marco and Bungay consigned him to their care, and resumed their journey to Oxford, which they completed just before the setting of the sun. It was fortunate that they hastened their march as the day declined, otherwise they would not have been able to enter the town. Pursuant to "the Statute of Winchester," the origin of our present system of the conservancy of the peace, the vigilant wardens were preparing to shut the gates, and the travellers just escaped the unpleasant necessity of passing the night in the suburbs. As they entered, the horn sounded, and the heavy valves swinging round, as they creaked upon their hinges, closed behind them. Further precautions, however, had been taken by the municipal authorities; and the travellers proceeded but a few paces, when they were stopped by the chain drawn across the street. Only a small passage was left on one side of this barricade, near which stood stationed one of the nightly watch,—the others were patrolling the street a little further on,— who instantly crossed his gisarme over the aperture, and challenged the strangers before he allowed them to pass.

"Cry you mercy, your reverence," said William le Parmentier, or the Parchment Maker, a substantial burgess, and eke a matriculated member of the university, then on guard, who had thus arrested the progress of Bungay and his companion; "and, to think that I should have stopped you; but your reverence knows that the cowl does not make the friar."

"I know that," quoth Bungay, rather angrily, as if he suspected that the phrase had a special application to himself.

It is an awkward thing to blunder upon any speech which

may appear personal. But there is one thing still more awkward: and that is, to try to explain it away. Do you suppose that William le Parmentier endeavoured to hint an inferential apology? Oh no, it was not without improvement in tact, that he had dealt with the dons of his age, so he simply proceeded, "Our country just now is full of robbers and rievers: ye have reason to rejoice that ye 'scaped any bushment on the road, and that ye did not pay tribute to such freebooters as the caitiff, who was committed to prison early this morning as the man who rifled blind old Herbert on Headington Hill."

"Early this morning," said Marco, with much surprise.

"Yes, your worship," continued the burgess, "early this morning. Just as St. Mary's bell had begun to ring for matins, the mayor received a most unexpected visit from Friar Bacon,— the friar hardly ever comes out of his study,—who told him that when old Herbert was making his way on Headington Hill, and had sat him down to rest at the foot of the stone cross, one Richard Maufee, an ugly, ill-doing varlet, whilom a scholar, but who hath long been suspected of taking to evil courses, and who had been lying in wait for the old man, rushed upon him, and with one blow of his massy staff, felled him to the ground. Maufee thus having despoiled the old peasant, he forthwith cast away his weapon, and was coming towards the town; 'and according to the rate,' said Friar Bacon, 'at which he is now walking, he will assuredly have reached the gate before the last psalm is sung. Send forth your sergeants, master mayor, see that he evade not, your trusty men will know him by his attire. He weareth a leather jerkin; instead of his staff he carries a slender beechen sapling, just riven from the tree, and his leg, up to the right knee, is clotted with soil.'

"Master mayor did not venture to ask the friar," continued the Parmentier, turning with a significant look to Bungay, "how he had obtained this intelligence. Indeed he did not know what might come to him next in his turn"; here some whispering took place, which Marco Polo could not make out, the matter, whatever it was, excited laughter; "but the sergeants were forthwith dispatched, and the iron grasp of Dick Saunzentrailles was upon Maufee's shoulder as he passed under the arch. Words cannot describe his dismay, when he suddenly found himself discovered. At once, and without hesitation, Maufee confessed the robbery, which, as he said, could not, in that closely sheltered spot, have been seen by mortal eye. So that we shall pass judgment upon

10—2

him even without any prosecution on the part of Herbert, who as yet hath not entered the town. Indeed, it is quite impossible for him to be aware that the robber hath been apprehended."

Friar Bungay interrupted the discourse, by requesting the Parmentier, whose party was on the point of being relieved by the second Watch, which was seen coming up, to conduct the stranger to Friar Bacon's domicile; he, Bungay, having certain errands to execute in the town by the way. They would occupy but little time, perhaps he might meet Marco before he reached the study.

Three muffled figures now seemed to emerge, as it were, from a door-way in one of the collateral streets, and a shrill thrilling whistle was heard. Bungay hastily turned down and joined these mysterious apparitions; and speedily they were lost in the darkness. Forthwith the Parmentier, abruptly halting under a lamp which was burning before a statue of the Virgin, said to Marco, clutching him with nervous anxiety by the arm, "Here it is, here it is," producing at the same time a small twig, carefully wrapped in scarlet silk, and bound by seven azure threads. "I don't mind them, I defy them, I defy the three serpents: it is witch-elm, as long as I carry it about me, Bacon can't get a glimpse of me, though he can see through stone walls."

"I have heard of such things in Cathay," replied Marco; "as for me, I am content if, on ordinary occasions, I can peep through a boulting sieve, as your Spaniard has it in his proverb; though when need requires, I can look as deeply into a millstone as the rest of the world."

"But," continued the Parmentier, in a lower and somewhat altered voice, as if he was not quite sure that the rowan would act as a thorough phylactery, "the friar hath a mirror, a magic mirror, which bringeth the form of any creature whom he listeth into his very chamber. Past becomes present. Distance impedes not. By the help of his glass he could show you every pebble on the most distant hills which bound the view from his tower; nay, the very stars come down at his behest."

Marco was not pleased with these apparently wild and idle tales of Bacon's skill. He had a great respect for Bacon, he truly appreciated the character of the philosopher, and he began to fear that his friend condescended to practise the tricks of a vulgar trejetour or jougleur, seeking to amuse idleness instead of bestowing the means of labour to the mind. Philosophy in sport is folly in earnest. So he replied with some little *dispetto*, "Figures described to you, I suppose, by some cozening urchin, who alone beholds the vision, and to whose well-tutored response, you must trust for the truth of the magician. A gross imposition, as I have oft witnessed at Cairo."

"Nay, nay," replied the Parmentier, "seen by yourself, if the friar favoureth you; and," continued he, with a shudder of horror, "he uses the glass of Abraxas, made out of dead men's eyes. Aye, you may be as unbelieving as you choose; the glass of Abraxas made out of dead men's eyes. He concealeth not his dreadful art: nay, so bold is he, that he hath written a letter to the Pope, describing the incantations by which it is prepared. Corpse after corpse hath been disinterred by him, thus to supply the material for his necromantic mirror. Shame that such enormities should be practised in this Christian land. They would be forbidden by the very Saracens, from whom he learns his wicked lore."

They were now fronting the tower upon the bridge, Bacon's celebrated study, in which, secluded from the throng, he held communion with the intellectual universe. Impregnated by the exhalations from the slow-spreading Isis, the air was damp and heavy, but sweet. The odours of the flowers clung in the humid atmosphere. And the plash produced by the fish rising to the surface, brought the dark unseen water and its circling ripples before the eye; marking also the repose of the hour more forcibly than a total absence of animated sound. Jupiter and Venus, sending forth the solid splendour which so peculiarly distinguishes the wandering fires of heaven from the fixed gems of the astral firmament, bore company to the moon, within whose lucid crescent the residue of her orb, evanescent yet not obscure, could faintly be discerned.

Strange machines could be traced behind the battlements of the tower, which were unusually lofty: and just when the visitors were covered by the overhanging machicolations, the "welcome" of Friar Bacon was heard from above. A light rapidly gleaming and disappearing, gleaming and disappearing, as it sunk downwards through the narrow loopholes in the angle of the tower, indicated that some one was descending the winding staircase within: and now, Miles, "Mad Miles," as he is called by the Oxford students, opens the door.

Marco Polo entered alone, for the Parmentier, losing all confidence in his counter-spells, had retreated with the utmost rapidity: and, following Miles, he found himself within that chamber in which so few had trod, the object of so much mystic awe.

Wide open upon the table was a volume, which, even to the most erudite in those days, might have seemed, from its uncouth characters, to justify the suspicions entertained concerning the friar's magical science. Marco, always delighting in the reminiscences of his eastern peregrinations, was much pleased by having an Arabic book again in his hand, although he could not read the Mughrebin character, used by the Spanish Moors, and in which it was written, quite so currently as the flowing Nesjid, the new fashion, which in Asia had then recently superseded the more ancient semi-cuphic form. However, upon turning to the beginning of the book, which, as Miles told him, his master always read backwards, he had no great difficulty in spelling out the name of Jacob Alkindi, in what Miles resolutely affirmed was the last page at the end.

"Welcome again, Marco," exclaimed Bacon, as he walked into the room, giving him a hearty English shake of the hand. "Let me greet thee with the *Salam* of Bagdad, and the *Chære* of Byzantium."

"Cary, Polly Cary," quoth Miles, "thus our popinjays are taught, when the birds are hither brought."

"Peace, lozel," said Bacon to his busy valet, and turning to Marco, he proceeded, "A good treatise that of Alkindi on Optics, but somewhat too condensed to be entirely instructive. Alhazen, more deeply versed in the science of vision, errs on the side of unnecessary length and diffusion; yet I reverence these Hagarenes as my masters," continued he smiling, "nor will I criticize them. If perfect numbers are rare; you know there are but four between one and ten thousand; even the remotest approach to intellectual perfection is rarer still. The further we advance in knowledge, the less are we disappointed by the inherent and incurable weaknesses and failings of mankind."

A sudden flourish from the pipe and tabor of Miles interrupted the friar, who silenced the minstrel by an angry look: and a momentary pause ensued. Marco, resolute as he was, started back with amazement on hearing a voice, which, though only a whisper, was piercing, distinct, and intelligible, proceed from the gaping mouth of a grim brazen head, standing upon a truncated column, and so placed as to be nearly in a line with his ear. The words, however, thus spoken, were neither mysterious nor oracular: the magical figure said nothing but what was very simple, and might have proceeded from the head of a house, or any other *caput* of flesh and blood. On this occasion, the whole speech of the brazen head was confined to the phrase, "Miles, Miles, please let me in."

Miles, running down the staircase, obeyed the call. Some-while afterwards, a noise was heard, as if the bearers of a cumbrous dead weight had much difficulty in slowly pitching and dragging their heavy burden up the steep stone stairs. There was silence, as if they rested: and shortly afterwards Friar Bungay, accompanied by three muffled figures, entered the apartment. The four were laboriously supporting a long chest, covered with a black cloth, which, Friar Bacon pointing, they deposited near the window. Two of these mysterious personages bowed and quitted the room: the third remained, casting off his veil, he appeared as the renowned Friar Vandermast, and Bacon introduced him to Marco as one from whose co-operation he had derived important aid. A small mattock and pickaxe slung over his shoulders, and a dark lantern suspended from the cord which girt Friar Vandermast, excited the notice of the traveller. "Doth the Brother," said he, "come from any house of observance at Goslar, or Elbingerode, or elsewhere, near the Saxon mines? a help, I trow, in your metallurgic experiments, though I could not have divined that ore was to be found beneath the soil of this part of the country."

"He delves deeply," replied Bacon, hastily, in a tone which did not invite further inquiry, and Marco, knowing well the peculiarities of his friend, said no more.

Round the hearth the settles were placed, whilst Miles appeared bustling about with singular activity. "A pretty toy," exclaimed Marco, pointing to the head. "A useful one also," replied Bacon; "the tubes conveying the sound extend both upwards and downwards: the contrivance saves time to myself and to those of my visitors who are initiated in the secret, and spares trouble to Miles. But the Oxford folks are good enough to suppose that the constellated image will teach me to surround England with a wall of brass. Such knowledge has perhaps been given to me, though it is not from this empty sconce that I learn the lore. Could man now profit by the lessons of my rede, our island coasts would be guarded round and round by floating castles armed as with thunder. You recollect, Marco, our last meeting at the palace gate."

"Yes," replied Marco, "and when it seemed as if your reverence were entranced like a Tartarian Schaman."

"That childish sport which we there beheld, displayed the

means of constructing engines of war, capable of bearing death and destruction through the air: not in vain terror, as is now practised by the Tartar and the Arab, but so as to mow down the armies in their panoply, raze the strongest bulwarks, beat the loftiest citadel to the ground.   Form, measure, and resistance only were to be known.   Form, measure, and resistance were to be found.   Form, measure, and resistance have been found.   I rested not, until from experiment, the great teacher of truth, I learned how to concentrate and guide the sulphurous flame."

"There is a curious tale current in Tartary," quoth Marco, "concerning Prester John.   This mighty sovereign, it is said, once gained a great victory by bringing into the field a host of men of metal, each placed upon a brazier: and as the fire below was kindled, each blew such a blast above, as utterly routed his enemies."

"Miles is now introducing you to one of Prester John's warriors," quoth Bacon.

A rushing sound was heard, and Marco beheld a chafing-dish, surmounted by a most uncouth effigy, with enormous distended cheeks, puffing through an extremely small pursed-up mouth a furious blast, directed against a small furnace, in which the coals glowed with intense combustion.

"I claim not the honour of the invention," said Bacon; "the antick idol which you see, whilom bore the name of Puster. On the shores of the Baltic, the hollow image was the object of the fear and veneration of the fierce Vendic tribes.   Simple as the means employed for producing the blast may appear, the secret was confined to the juggling priesthood.   The same trick was practised in the temples of our Saxon ancestors.   Jack of Hilton, as he is called in Staffordshire, and who now performs his merry part in the Christmas festivities of the hall, had, without doubt, originally his station in a heathen fane."

"It is passing strange," said Marco, "that any nation, however savage, who had the knowledge of fire and water, could be deluded by a trickery grounded upon such a familiar cause."

"Not perhaps so strange," replied the friar, "as awful: their ignorance indicating how entirely man's knowledge of the properties concealed within the most familiar objects of sense, is overruled and controlled."

This great truth is so very obvious and familiar, that it therefore passes unnoticed.   We are constantly expressing our astonishment at the recurrence of such deficiency of knowledge amongst those whom we term uncivilized nations, or in what we consider as a dark or ignorant age: quite forgetting that exactly the same absence of human perception, until the arrival of the appointed time is equally exemplified amongst ourselves.

How unaccountable, we say, is it that the Tahiteans should never, until visited by the English circumnavigator, have discovered that water could be made to boil; and that such its property should have appeared to them as contrary to nature as if it had been made to burn. Be it so, but seat yourself in the theatre of science, listen to Davy, whilst he comments upon the operations,—so important in the deductions to be drawn from them, and up to this moment so neglected,—converting the limestone into marble by the contrivance which prevents the escape of the subtle element. Explain why, with those palpable tokens of the wonderful effects produced by the coarsest of all processes, mechanical pressure, the chemist gifted with the most extraordinary rapidity and resource in experimenting, fails to perceive that the glass tube held by his assistant, Faraday, will exhibit and contain the "permanently elastic carbonic gas" visible and tangible as the ocean wave.

Whilst Bacon and Marco were speaking, other machines were disclosed to view by the ready service of Miles. A shrine-like temple appeared, the pediment supported by miniature Doric columns, before which was placed an altar in antique form, covered by tiny fagots of cedar, heaped as for the sacrifice, and kindling into a flame. Shortly afterwards, when the fire was in full blaze, the door of the temple opened, hissing dragons protruded forth: and sparkling jets ascended from the vases on either side, shooting higher and higher as the temperature increased. Hard by, was seen a brazen ball, rising and falling in a cylindrical tube, its gravity counteracting the forcible gusts of aqueous vapour which issued by fits from the receptacle below. On the same range a whirling sphere revolved with extreme rapidity, enveloped in the white clouds of steam by whose generation the motion was produced.

"All these automata, which to future ages will afford the fullest proofs of my doctrine," said the friar, "thus derive their vitality, for I can scarcely avoid employing this term, from the same elementary cause. Applied simply in the next immediate term of progression, and these devices, which the mathematician, Hiero of Alexandria, presents as the sportive accompaniments of the banquet, will become the mighty engines destined to alter the whole frame of human society, nay, almost to change the physical aspect of the globe.   Thus far could the Greeks advance, but no farther.   The march of intellect was stayed by an Almighty hand.   They could not make one step beyond the boundary destined for them.   Seeing, they saw not; and, at distant periods, these antagonist powers of fire and water will continue to be employed, the knowledge of their physical energies now advancing, now receding, now revived, now forgotten.   Nevertheless, seeing, men will see not; until the appointed hour arrive, and the use of that knowledge shall, whether in wrath or in love, be imparted to mankind.   But more of this hereafter.   The hour of observation is approaching, he who watches the silent motion of the spheres, must not slumber in weariness.   Farewell, Farewell, Farewell, until the morn."

Miles had for some time past evidently been watching for his master's departure, and for the arrival of some visitant.   According to the regulations of the "Cofradia de los Tontos," or "Brotherhood of Boobies," as preserved by the celebrated Don Mateo Aleman, one of the acts and deeds which entitle you to admission into that ancient and honourable fraternity is, when you expect any body, looking in and out of the window, as if by so doing you could make the said body come.   Since it was now pitch dark, Miles, in giving the same tokens of expectancy, might be considered as doubly making good his claim.

Worthy Miles, gentle reader, was more knave than fool. Bacon, like many other wise men, was as unknowing in his own domestic concerns as he was surpassing in general knowledge. Whilst Bacon steadily repudiated all pretensions to magical science, of which he had forcibly demonstrated the nullity, the little knot of dependents who surrounded him, managed him, and lived upon him, were just as anxious to assert their claims to occult lore.

Such pretenders were common enough in the middle ages. By the doctrines of the church, magic and necromancy were severely condemned, and the fagot was denounced against their votaries: but in England, at least, the superstition was neither rigidly inquired after by the ecclesiastical courts, nor, during a very long period, punished by the secular tribunals.   In parliamentary documents, we find "nigromauncer" attached to a man's name as an addition of lawful calling, not so frequently, indeed, as "smith" or "baker," yet evidently without any idea of concealment or absurdity.   And the details preserved concerning these respectable practitioners, all tend to show that their vocation was tolerably lucrative and successful: provided the individual who tried the profession possessed the proper qualifications.

But these were not so common as might be supposed. It requires a peculiar knack, approaching to diplomatic talent, to be an assistant-conjurer, a sub-necromancer, a pocket-wizard, an under-managing magician to a professor of the black art. Not quite so much as is required for a private secretary to an ambassador, but entirely of the same description. Giovanni Alessio, who officiated in that capacity to the celebrated Cagliostro, was particularly suited for his office. The great adept, when he honoured London with a visit, had caused it to be well understood that he was in possession of the elixir of life, with its usual accompaniment, the philosopher's stone, he having been initiated in the lodge of Sesostris held in the Great Pyramid, some time, I believe, during the first crusade.

Giovanni Alessio had been heard to say that he did not think his master's account of himself was entirely the truth: and various expressions which he had dropped, induced two, then young members of White's, to suppose that by a clever examination of the attendant, they might unmask the charlatan. The "Most Noble Grand" was not at home, when they called at his lodgings up three pair of stairs in Round Court, Saint Martin's Lane. But Giovanni came out, and a guinea having been duly administered, they soon led him into confidential communication. Giovanni made no scruple of intimating his doubts about the count's entire veracity, yet, without coming to the point, till at length one of them pressed him closely as to his master's age.

"I cannot quite believe him," said Giovanni. "I don't wish to act the traitor, and to betray him. I don't go the length of saying that he is a mere impostor: but I more than suspect that he exaggerates. As an honest man, and as one who has a character to lose (my character, gentlemen, is all I have to depend upon) the very utmost that with regard to truth I can possibly say in support of master's story amounts to nothing more than this: when I came into his service, he did look quite as old as he looks now. He is not altered in the least. I can't see any change in him, neither for the better nor for the worse."

"But when did you come into his service?" quickly retorted his interrogator.

"Why," said Giovanni slowly and considerately, evidently reckoning carefully by head, "let me see, it was in December that he hired me: so that, next Christmas, it will be four hundred and

ninety-seven years and some odd days since I came into his
service; beyond this, Eccellenza, he can have no help from my
testimony."

The numerous details which have been preserved in the
Bodleian respecting Mad Miles, and the clever *défaites* which he
gave to those who attempted to steal information respecting the
extent of the friar's necromantic powers would, if I had been
allowed to insert them here, have shown that he was at least
equal to Cagliostro's valet. In my opinion, they would furnish
some very curious particulars of the manners and customs of
Oxford, besides some interesting private anecdotes, highly valuable
to all Grangerians and other interleavers. But my inexorable
censor, my publisher, who inspects the sheets before they are
worked off, has compelled me to expunge them all, because he
maintains they are digressions, and make the book too large.
Besides which, he is a careful man, seeking to give further extension to his increasing business, and as he looks for some sale
at Oxford, he is not quite sure, whether he may not offend the
proctors and bull-dogs on the one part, or the sheriff and the
town-council on the other. It is impossible to be too cautious
in these sad controversial times, especially at Oxford; I dare not
repeat, for whom, as I have heard, they are scouring that great
gridiron which they show you in the kitchen at Christ Church,
nor why they are smoothing the ground and sticking in a stake
in front of the Martyrs' memorial. So I must content myself
with saying, that it was the practice of Bungay and Vandermast,
aided by Miles, to turn an honest penny when occasion served,
by availing themselves not only of Bacon's reputation, but also
of his science. And the faint knock at the door, announced the
arrival of the client who had been appointed by the two friars to
meet them, when, as they were aware, Bacon would have retired
into his observatory. Bungay quickly covered his head with a
huge furred cap, which came down almost to his eyes: and a big
black cat which had been slowly patting its creeping paws about
the room, was forthwith installed upon the table. Gib, however,
did not contribute much to the efficacy of the charm. After once
or twice arching up its back a great deal higher than the tip of
its ears, it stretched itself out at length, and fairly fell asleep
during the remainder of the ceremony.

"What seek ye?" growled out Bungay to the pale and trembling
youngster who now entered the study, ushered in by untrusty Miles.

"A sight of her who is to be my best beloved."

In a solemn voice Bungay replied, repeating the verses not only preserved in my manuscript, but also in the printed black-letter history.

> " Now we hear the croaking toad,
> Now the owl is roused abroad,
> Flittermice, that flee the day,
> Through the gloaming make their way.
> In Friar Bacon's name I charm ye,
> Nought shall scare, and none shall harm ye."

And thus speaking, or rather chanting, the solitary cresset, by which the chamber was scantily illuminated, suddenly expired. More than compensated, however, was the loss, by a bright circle of light, which immediately expanded itself on the opposite wall, wherein appeared, slowly traversing the disk, Dame Venus, in her dove-drawn car.

Bungay informed the aspirant, that this apparition was an indispensable element in the spell. The mystic rites, he said, were attended with great difficulty. Unless the patroness of "ladies' love and druery" condescended to appear, it would fail. "And now," said Bungay, "let us next evoke Helen of Greece, her most favoured daughter, in whom the features of your paramour will be displayed."

Venus had departed, and was replaced in the circle by a richly-attired damsel, owing her splendour to garments which, as might be supposed, had but little affinity to the costume of classical antiquity, being, in fact, the fashionable dress of the day.

The enamoured student was intently endeavouring to make out the countenance of the figure (which seemed familiar to him) when a flourish from the pipe and tabor of Miles momentarily distracted his attention; but, looking eagerly again, he beheld all the gay adornments of the visionary fair, sliding, as it were, away. Sendal and samyt, gold and pearls, had vanished. Helen of Greece was metamorphosed into a sturdy, comely kitchen-maid, with a ladle in her hand.

Had there been sufficient light in the chamber, the countenance of the inquirer would have revealed a most uncomfortable consciousness of the vision's verity. As it was, he felt thankful for the obscurity which ensued when the illuminated circle faded into darkness. Miles, shortly after re-entering with a lamp, conducted him down the winding stair: and Marco, much amused, retired to his chamber.

CHAPTER VI.

KNOWLEDGE.

BACON was already busy at work, when, on the following morning, Marco, without waiting for any previous announcement, entered unhesitatingly into the secluded retreat of experimental science. In the deep recesses of the window, the friar was standing, absorbed by meditation. Earnestly wrapped in thought, he neither heeded nor heard the footsteps of his visitor. The mysterious coffer, brought by the veiled attendants, was placed open beside the Friar on the stone floor, half covered by the mournful drapery of the sable pall, which dropt into the empty sides.

Marco came up to his friend in full confidence, but he was stayed with surprise, nay, almost with alarm, when, upon the table, he beheld a blue and livid carcass recumbent in hideous length, the object by which the mind of the anatomist was completely engaged. Fore-shortened to his view the body was stretched out, the clayey muscles of the rigid arm were seen divested of their integument. More than usually skull-like and ghastly, did the poor disfigured countenance appear. The organs of sight had been extracted from their orbits: indeed, one of the visual balls had just been lifted out of the socket by the scalpel of the operator.

Marco shrunk from the fearful display of mortality, yielding to the natural, and, in many persons, unconquerable, disgust, excited by the presence of a mangled corpse. Argue as we may, such a spectacle is, in the first instance, abhorrent to our feelings. He sickened at the loathsome display: yet his attention was strangely fascinated. Turn away he could not. As he gazed, his horror rapidly subsided; and soon was it entirely conquered by the expression of lofty intelligence, beaming in the countenance of the operator.

Bacon was contemplating his subject with that tranquil and intelligent solemnity, which, until the dissection of the dead body became, as it now is, a familiar and daily portion of medical study, characterized the tone of thought brought by the investigator to his pursuits.   Deep and considerate reflection, heightened by devotional respect, were the sentiments which physiology inspired.   In some degree, the grave feelings of the ancient anatomist may be attributed to the character of mystery then enveloping the posthumous examination of the human remains.   Conducted, not unfrequently with danger, the opportunity for such investigations was rare.   These incidents gave more value to the study. They imparted a solemn preparatory tone to the inquiry, and the same sobriety followed it onwards.   Instead of being attended merely by a crowd of unthinking youth, of rude and untutored students, even old grey-headed men came eagerly to learn: all presented themselves prepared as for an important event.   They encountered the task with minds predetermined to their studies by religious reverence.

Thus were they preserved—well was it for them that they should be so—from the assumed defiance of death, the scurril treatment of the placid corpse, the ribald jest, the impure gibe, the hardened jeer: all no less baleful to the individual, than to the dignity of the noble science imparted for the relief of suffering mortality.

"You have heard, without doubt, how I plunder the yawning grave," said Bacon. "Qualified, as it has pleased Providence to render me for these studies, I still follow, in cultivating them, my own vocation. I trust I may be enabled to impart some useful lessons to the physician of the body, without deserting the service of the Physician of the soul. Approaching with awe that substance of dust, which, though polluted with sin, was nevertheless the living temple of the Holy Spirit, we dimly read the sentences of the book wherein all our members were written, before the creation of one atom of the material world, before time itself was called into existence.

"The belief in God's perfect Providence has no foundation except in the evidence of things unseen. Yet, guided by His word, he permits us in some degree to understand the adaptation of this wonderful structure, not merely to the general term of human life, but to the particular length of days assigned to each of the children of man. God's all-wielding power determines in each of us the special and peculiar application of the universal law.

"Coeval with the first thrill of the embryo, when the fibres quiver, and the organs quicken into vitality, is the germ of death. Before our members are fashioned, is the narrow grave dug, in which they are to be entombed.   Before the heart begins to beat, yea from all eternity, has every pulsation been told and numbered.

"Imperfect as these our glimpses of knowledge may be, they all convince us that no more oil could have been poured into the lamp, than would nourish the flame until the pre-ordained hour of its extinction.   The youth expires apparently in his prime. Are his weeping kindred tempted and agonized by the thought, that mental exertion or bodily fatigue brought on the catastrophe, or that care might have averted the danger?   Develope the frail vessels, and it is proved that their coherence could not have possibly sustained the pressure of the purple tide beyond the age when the vigour of adolescence was attained.

"Do we term the departure premature?   Premature! the word belongs not to the vocabulary of faith.   It has no presence in the thoughts of the believer.   Ask not why the pale colourless babe, mysteriously brought to the confines of this vale of tears, heir to our transgressions, and yet spared from participating in their bitterness, who never looked upon the light of day, who never felt the warmth of the mother's bosom, and whose voice never sounded in the mother's ear, is carried away as in a sleep, parent and child separated, until they shall both awaken at the same trumpet blast and stand before the Throne.   Ask not why the span of fourscore years is given to him who is gathered to his fathers, after passing through the full length of his weary pilgrimage.   But, be thankfully assured, that under every individual dispensation, comprehended from and through all eternity in the unity of the Divine design, the tares are not rooted up, until they can no longer be rescued from the fiery furnace, nor the good corn gathered, until it is ripe for the garners of the sky."

"You are now," replied Marco, "more particularly employed upon the visual organ."

"I am," said Bacon.   "From the examination of this dull and glazed orb, we may collect the import of those laws, which it now pleases the Lord of nature to impress upon the rays, called forth from primeval chaos by His Word."

Bacon, then proceeding with his demonstration, expounded to his hearer the texture of the coats, the dispersive and refractive powers of the humours, the functions of the retina.   Comparing the lens modelled by organic life, with the lens formed by art, and explaining how the visual angle conveys to the mind the idea of size, he described those inventions, by which, as he declared to his contemporaries, we may be enabled to read the smallest letter at an otherwise incredible distance, and to number the grains of sand: to behold the most minute object expanded into portentous magnitude, the moon and the planets brought down from heaven.

"And how," said Marco, "have you attained this wondrous knowledge which you possess?"

"Whatever I have learnt, unworthy as it may be of the name of knowledge, has been acquired by avoiding the causes of error, the idols by which man is so speciously deluded. Submission to undue authority is one commanding idol. We talk of the independence of the human mind; but man loves to grovel before any intellectual authority, except that which is grounded upon obedience to the Almighty will.

"Let any teacher arise; and listening multitudes will crowd around his chair, provided he does not appeal to Holy Writ. Announce positions utterly unintelligible to the human mind, and they are acknowledged implicitly, if propounded as the wisdom of science, the doctrines of human intellect, the results of human reason. It is true that man frequently resists one tyrant: but, if he releases himself, he only surrenders himself instantly to a new thraldom: it is only to place his neck again beneath another yoke. Every yoke is light to him excepting that of his Redeemer.

"Another great cause of error, and closely allied to the former, is a cowardly subscription to popular opinion. All writers, all philosophers, all reasoners, confess in theory, that the wise are few, the foolish infinite in number. But when it comes to the actual tug and warfare of daily life, their courage fails: the sage will shrink from the censure, still more from the ridicule of the united voices of those, whom, singly, he will contemn and despise.

"No less delusive are the inveterate restraints of usage, a slavish conformity to the customs, still more to the fashions of the world: the fear of doing or saying, nay, even of thinking, any one thing which the world dislikes, the pigmy bonds which tie down the giant to the earth, counteracting his energies, and subjugating his powers.

"Lastly, would I place the concealment of ignorance by the ostentation of false knowledge: symbols accepted for realities, words substituted for ideas, conventional fallacies honoured as self-evident truths. A mutual concession maintaining the system of mutual adulation. Each flattering and flattered in his turn. The deceived tacitly conniving with the deceiver, in order to avoid being roused to a sense of the real deficiency under which he labours, or to have his proud self-confidence dispelled."

"But you appeal to experiment," said Marco, "as the dispeller of falsehood and the test of truth."

"Certainly, so far as relates to all the varied phenomena of nature, the appearances, constant and unvarying to our senses, which in our present state of being have, as towards us and in our sensations, a substantive existence; but all the qualities of matter, as they are called, are merely relative. They are like the pattern of a tesselated pavement, they are formed only by the position of the pieces. If you alter that position, the pattern is lost. Therefore, in the only real and intrinsic meaning of the term, truth is not in anywise to be attained by experimental philosophy. Real philosophy radiates only from the knowledge of God. One science rules and governs all others, the knowledge of the Word of the Lord. There is only one road to salvation. Nor should the human intellect ever be exerted in the pursuit of science, unless on the full and entire conviction, that in all things, human reason is to succumb before that Revelation which has been vouchsafed to mankind."

"But," replied Marco, "are not you speaking most strangely in contradiction with yourself, annulling the very doctrines which you so recently proclaimed, when in that mouldering flesh you sought and saw proofs of eternal foreknowledge and boundless wisdom?"

"Unquestionably," answered Bacon, "those proofs are there to be found, because, His overruling and active Providence being previously acknowledged, the Holy Spirit speaking through the psalmist, teaches us how to derive instruction from the manifestations of God's design and power. So far is most right: we obey the light which descends to us. But if, discarding the knowledge given to us by the Holy Spirit, we endeavour, when contemplating these manifestations, to rise upwards by our strength, and to deduce by human arguments the existence of that design and power, we shall be forming for ourselves a system of physical or 'natural theology,' the most imperfect and deluding, nay, most mischievous creed which the will-worship of the human mind can possibly compose. We are holding up our dim and smoky torch to illuminate the sun.

"Could we view this globe as it came from the hands of the Creator, when everything which He made was very good, we should have everywhere around us not only the evidence, but also the effects of His unbounded beneficence. But the earth on which man is placed, is no longer as it was framed: it has been cursed for our sin. In every portion of our physical and mental creation, in the soil upon which we tread, the body in which we live, the thoughts and actions of the soul, we are pierced by the thorns and thistles, and taste the sorrows of the death which by our rebellion we have incurred. No human reasoning whatever can account for the presence of evil: no human argument whatever can reconcile the existence of evil to a system of beneficence. Nothing but the unqualified acceptance of the whole Word of God, the whole scheme of redemption, as declared in and by that Word, can give us any comfort or confidence in God's mercy, or account for such an inscrutable mystery.

"Be assured, that if, rejecting the Scriptures, or expunging any part of them, and endeavouring to supply the place of God's Holy Word by the arguments which human intellect suggests, you are ever seduced into the presumption of attempting to explain away the positive and certain existence of evil in this scene of being, you will find it quite impossible to give a consistent answer to the errors of the disciples of Manes. Read their history; it is full of awful warnings. Yielding to the legitimate deductions from 'science, falsely so called,' and once swerving from the truth, they were led onwards, until they adopted the miserable belief, that the universe was shaped out of eternal, self-existing matter, by a mighty and incomprehensible, yet limited and malevolent power."

"Such is the creed," said Marco, "of the heretics of the South, the Albigenses, so many thousands of whom have perished by the sword, or have withered in agony in the slow flames of the smoking pile, or are at this moment suffering the protracted torments of living death, immured between the four walls of the cell, where, when the spirit has departed, the body decays in its dungeon tomb."

"The same," replied Bacon; "ineffably wicked as this persecution may be; and though the heaviest load of guilt is incurred by their merciless persecutors, we must not allow the pity for their sufferings to induce us to defend their errors. The Albigenses hold that evil raging in this world in such infinitely varied forms, pain, famine, and disease, is totally inconsistent with the idea of an all-wise and beneficent Creator. How, for instance, would you, if tutored by the teacher of a natural theology, reply to one of their most popular arguments, drawn from the perpetual and cruel warfare of the various tribes of the brute creation, and of the miseries which they inflict upon each other, in what these

misguided men style the vast charnel-house of the world? Why,
ask they, is the innocent sheep surrendered to the jaws of the
ravening wolf? Why is the envenomed fang of the viper given as
the means of producing a painful death?"

Marco spoke out most readily. "Contrivance proves design,
and the predominant tendency of the contrivance indicates the
disposition. Evil no doubt exists, but it is never the direct object
of contrivance. Consider only how the earth teems with a superabundance of animal life. Perhaps there is no species of terrestrial
animal whatever which would not overrun the earth, if it were
permitted to multiply in perfect safety. At least, if any single
species were left to its natural increase without disturbance or
restraint, the food of other species would be exhausted by its
maintenance. Destruction must always follow superabundance."

"And your opponent," replied Bacon, "would destroy your
argument by your last word. He would ask you, How can you
reconcile the permission of superabundance with the dictates of
infinite wisdom? You speak entirely as man speaks concerning
the acts of man. You address your argument to human reason;
human reason will answer, that it would have been perfectly
practicable so to regulate the fruitfulness of the animal, and the
productiveness of the ground, that all might have fed and been
satisfied: and that the whole of the machinery of devastation
and destruction might have been avoided. Natural theology
descants upon the impress of wisdom and power exhibited in the
created world. But the natural theologian wholly refuses to read
the indelible characters in which the punishment inflicted for
disobedience against God is written on this mundane globe.
Idolizing human nature, the natural theologian blots out the
testimonies of our corruption.

"Argue with as much subtlety as you can, you will find that
you never can refute the objections of your adversary, excepting
by a simple appeal to the Bible, revealing to us that the earth was
cursed for man's sake. It is no longer good. It has like its inhabitants lost the full blessing first imparted by the Creator.
Natural theology teaches us nothing of the promise of salvation;
yet nothing except the mystery of redemption can countervail the
mystery of sin. Recollect the course of the argument which a
professor of 'natural theology' is compelled to take. His inductions must be entirely based upon matters cognizable by sense.
He seeks only to influence through the understanding. Let him
be compelled to dispute with an unbelieving opponent who contests

his premises, and in what position will he stand? If he finds one permitted evil, which could have been avoided: one difficulty connected with the existence of evil, which he cannot solve: one doubt suggested by the prevalence of evil, which he cannot remove: he will be driven to the pinch of acknowledging that 'creation might have been produced by a being whose views rested upon misery.' What can result from such dubious disputations, except the greatest danger to the soul? Why should we court the attacks of the enemy? Temptations enough will always rise within us. And the natural theologian, casting away the armour which would render him invulnerable, grasps the broken spear, and braces the pierced shield, and rushes upon his adversary. Consider the state of the man of the most cultivated intellect, nay, of the best intentions, who, in any degree, alloys his faith by a theology inevitably conducting to such baneful fallacies. Compare his anxious secret discomfort, with the perfect peace of him, who, 'becoming a fool that he may be wise,' strives not to create a religion based upon intellect, but simply answers, 'My thoughts are not your thoughts, neither are your ways my ways, saith the Lord.'"

Marco replied, "Yet I must recur again to your own precepts, when you exhorted me to view the fearful and wonderful conformation of the body as evidencing, according to Scripture, the power of the Almighty."

"True," said Bacon, "but the psalmist does not rest in vague contemplation of the Deity. He warns you to dread the vengeance of the Lord, and invites you to implore His mercy. He teaches you, that the God, who made the heart, is the God who knows the heart. He compels us to acknowledge that the body was shapen in iniquity and conceived in sin. Natural theology is a miserable compromise between faith and infidelity. Had I contemplated this mortal frame as a natural theologian, I could not have proceeded beyond the proof that the body was organized by a designing and disposing Intelligence, and what is gained by such a proof? Was there ever any human creature in his right senses by whom that position was denied? Natural theology spends its force in refuting tenets which no one holds, in assailing an enemy who does not exist, an absolute atheist: and evades, at the same time, every consideration which is distasteful to our natural conceit and pride.

"If you ask the natural theologian why the body was rendered accessible to pain and amenable to disease, he would be reduced

to such miserable inanities as to tell you that pain is a salutary
provision, inasmuch as it teaches vigilance and caution, and gives
notice of dangers; and that mortal diseases are intended to tire
us out, and thus reconcile us to death.   But why, may the sceptic
inquire, could not pleasure convey the same association to the
mind?   What reason can we give for the introduction of death
into the world?   Why has the mysterious relation between sin
and death so been carried out, that every medicine to which the
power has been imparted, of granting some alleviation to the ills
our flesh inherits, has been rendered unpleasant or disgusting,
exhibiting how mercy is implied in chastisement?   Unless we
acknowledge that our disobedience rendered us justly liable to
the condemnation of death, we shall only be taken in our craftiness,
and our contemplations will lead us, not to wisdom but to destruction."

   Marco would not yield.   "And what," said he, "if we ascend
beyond this earth, and seek our 'natural theology' in the radiant
spheres?   Surely the habit of God through the wonders of the
external world, and its adaptation to the wants of man, is not only
compatible with firm religious belief, but with the highest devotional feeling.   Are we not told by the psalmist 'that the Heavens
declare the glory of God, and the firmament showeth his handy-
work?'"

   "Dismiss me from your thoughts, Marco," replied Bacon.
"Instead of the friar in his study, discoursing with a friend,
suppose you have before you a preacher addressing a congregation, in an age when, by the permission of Providence, those
sciences which I now recommend, shall be pursued with intoxica-
ting vigour: when the handmaid, instead of waiting with humility
for the commands of her mistress, shall rudely endeavour to
usurp her authority.   Consider this preacher as one, who, self-
humiliated and yet triumphant in the prerogative derived from
his high and sacred commission as a member of the apostolical
hierarchy, is equally preserved from the delusions of spiritual
pride, and the chill of worldly wisdom, and he might answer
arguments like yours in the following words:

   "'The heavens do declare the glory of God, but not His will;
they are all-perfect, all-harmonious; but that brightness and excellence which they exhibit in their own creation, and the divine
benevolence therein seen, are of little moment to fallen man.
religion is something relative to us, a system of commands and
promises from God towards us.   But how will the sun, and moon,

and stars teach us our duty? How will they speak to sinners? They do not speak to sinners at all. They were created before Adam fell. We see nothing therein of God's wrath, of which the conscience of a sinner loudly speaks. So that there cannot be a more dangerous, though a common device of Satan, than to carry us off from our secret thoughts, to make us forget our own hearts, which tell us of a God of justice and holiness, and to fix our attention merely on the God who made the heavens; who is our God indeed, but not God manifested to us sinners, but as He shines forth to His angels, and to His elect hereafter. When a man has so far deceived himself as to trust his destiny to what the heavens tell him of it, instead of consulting and obeying his conscience, he misinterprets and perverts the whole tenor of Scripture.'"

"Yet," replied Marco, "one word more. Methinks your visionary teacher goes much too far. I am not convinced that the arguments which you ascribe to him, disprove the position that 'natural theology' is a wholesome exercise of the understanding: which, admitted it be incompetent to sustain the hopes of man, may advance him in piety, and remove obstacles to belief. Nay, I will not recede from the assertion, that the ready inductions of natural religion may bring convictions of the greatest moral worth, at moments too when proofs of a different nature would be denied all access to the mind."

"The dealings of Providence with the hearts of men are inscrutable," was the reply of Bacon. "But the least invidious mode of judging of the general tendency of any system is, to consider the fruits it has produced."

"Unquestionably," said Marco.

"Then," replied Bacon, "your test of the tendency of 'natural theology' may be found at once in the conduct of a Simon de Montfort, bathing in the blood of the slaughtered citizens of Béziers: or the legate exulting, whilst the inhabitants of Minerbe, consuming at the stake, are offered as a grateful holocaust."

Marco looked at the friar with strange perplexity. "What can you mean? Do I understand you rightly? or do you misunderstand me? You are portraying the savage persecutors, whilst the Albigenses whom they assail, exhibit patience, charity, and forbearance."

"You are judging by the first impression," replied the friar; "but, pause. Examine the characters of those so strongly contrasted parties. Search out the instigating cause of their errors. Opposed as they seem in conduct, they are both equally under the influence of the great source of deceit to the unstable, the unwary, and the lukewarm: for what is called 'natural theology' is no other than one of the phases assumed by the religion of the world: one of the disguises assumed by its prince for our destruction.   Let me continue my anticipation of the preacher, who may be heard when centuries shall have rolled away.   Contemplating the period in which we have lived: reviewing in the pages of history the acts of men by whom the cross of the Redeemer has been rendered the symbol, not of love, but of fell destruction; we may imagine him describing our sins and errors in the following guise: 'The adversary of mankind devised a new idol, to be adopted by the world as the new Christ, and it remained in the Temple of God for many a year.   The age was rude and fierce. Satan took the darker side of the Gospel, its awful mysteriousness, its fearful glory, its sovereign, inflexible justice, and here his picture of the truth ended.   God is a consuming fire; so declares the text, and we know it.   But we ought to know more, that God is love also, but Satan did not add this to his religion, which became one of fear.   The religion of the world was then a fearful religion.   Superstitions abounded and cruelties, the noble firmness, the graceful austerity of the true Christian, were superseded by forbidding spectres, harsh of eye, and haughty of brow, and these became the patterns or the tyrants of a beguiled people.'

"Such were our fathers and grandfathers, the leaders of the crusades.   Our world is one priding itself upon warlike spirit, upon courage and bravery, upon zealous adventure, upon profuse bounty and largesse.   Qualities which bear a delusive resemblance to Christian graces, are perhaps the most insidious of worldly sins; they take you unawares.   Without any open opposition to the Gospel, their supporters, slaves of the powers of the world, pick and cull so many of the doctrines of the Bible, as, when considered singly, can be wrested to afford a fancied support to ambition, cruelty, ferocity, and revenge; the crimes which Christianity condemns are joyfully perpetrated in the name of the Gospel.

"Another age may be characterized by tendencies, in which the lusts of the heart assume a totally different disguise.   Natural theology as a religion of the world will amalgamate with the cultivation of taste and the progress of refinement.   The prevailing character of human society will be a universal approbation of suavity and delicacy of thought.   Outward propriety is accepted in place of inward purity.   Profligacy, if deprived of half its grossness, will be represented as losing all its deformity. Our relative duties, the works which are the proofs and fruits of faith, will be enjoined, not because they are to be practised in obedience to the commands of God, from whose behests alone they derive their character of virtues, and by whose grace alone they can be efficiently performed, but as possessing an inherent merit. Morality will be inculcated, not as resulting from the direction and control of our inclinations, attesting our love towards a God of holiness and justice: but merely for its utility, as a habit conducive to the happiness of man, the good of the individual, and the welfare of human society; thus rendering each individual the arbiter of his own conscience, a judge in his own cause.

"Luxuriating in the pleasures of literature, stimulated by the wonders of science, the human mind, reducing all things to a human standard, will render the human intellect its idol. In such a state of things, the religion of the world will be metamorphosed into 'natural theology,' or a nominal Christianity, differing from natural theology only by its name. In this our age of fear, has the religion of the world arrayed its spurious zeal in the garb of knighthood, and invested it with the splendour of war and luxury. So in the future age of arts and sciences, the religion of the world assumes the chaste aspect of literature and philosophy. Every declaration of God is examined by the measure of our finite understanding. Rationalism is substituted for faith, and just so much of religious sentiment retained, as the mind of man can comprehend, and the natural heart approve.

"Whilst the gentle gale breathes sweetly, and the bright sun shines, none of the monsters of the deep will rise to view. So long as the shadows of Christian virtue continue the world's favourites, natural theology, as a phase of the religion of antichrist, will retain its specious character of decorum and amiability, but no longer. Let sensuality command profit or applause, the gifted poet becomes the willing pander to the lowest appetites of human nature. Is the established order of civil subjection condemned by the opinion of the world? The philosopher will serenely assist in delivering up to slaughter, those who refuse to join the ranks of anarchy. Is the cathedral or cloister stigmatized by the opinion of the world, as the stronghold of superstition? and the advocates of civilization deliver the priest and recluse to the sword, with as much exultation as the Inquisition now immolates the heretic. If any form of faith is deemed to impede the civilization of the human race, projected by the philosophical theorist, the crime of conscientiously adhering to religious belief, will be visited with all the enmity of the power of evil.

"These extreme consequences may not follow in every case. Some advocates of 'natural theology' may be unconsciously aided and exalted by a better spirit. Some will carelessly admit this system in words, but never allow it to influence their thoughts. Some will assent to its positions for the purpose of avoiding offence, mistakenly extending the duty of mutual charity, into the permission of conniving at incontestable error. Some, lastly, may instruct their disciples to search for the attributes of the Deity in the visible creation, fully declaring, at the same time, the absolute necessity of a better guide. Yet, in its best and most enlightened stage, natural theology will always tend downwards, and exert a bad influence. The guardians of truth will be cajoled to surrender the integrity of the sacred volume: and to accept the sophistries of earthly wisdom as an adequate compromise. Natural theology will prompt those who are the commissioned expounders of God's word to vie with one another in making the largest surrenders to sceptical infidelity. It will seduce the teachers of the Gospel to seek toleration for Christianity as a favour from enlightened unbelief. It will prompt them to prophesy smooth things, in order to purchase a hollow truce from those who despise the law of the Lord. Natural theology will never suggest any dependable principle of self-restraint, any enduring sense of good-will towards men, or any abiding determination to uphold the glory of God on high. It offers no example, denounces no threats, promises no rewards.

"A knowledge of God, derived from the light of nature, is an act of obedience to the divine power. Natural theology, on the contrary, is an artificial thing, entirely founded upon vain curiosity and profitless speculations concerning the intentions of God. Revelation commands us to submit implicitly to his will as an inscrutable mystery. The more the empire of man is extended, the more should we endeavour to diminish the temptations inducing him to live by sight and not by faith: thus withdrawing his dependence upon the Lord of spirits, and substituting his earthly idol for the Father of Heaven."

"But," said Marco, "do you not act with singular inconsistency in expatiating upon the evils resulting from science: and yet, by example and precept, advocating its cultivation?"

"It is you who are not attentive, and who give to my words a meaning wholly alien to their import. I am perfectly consistent," replied Bacon, "my mean endeavours seek only to place the human intellect in due subjection to Him from whom all good gifts and all perfect gifts are alone obtained. Man may pass the torch of science from hand to hand; but he must always recollect that the light is darted from above; he cannot steal the sacred fire; he can receive nothing except it be given from heaven.

"All true knowledge is, in its degree, revelation. I speak the word neither lightly nor unadvisedly; but with a careful hope that I shall not be misconstrued. All created things are equally beneath the appointment of God's overruling power. The living soul was breathed into us by the Lord of hosts: and He who gave us our intellectual being, directs its operations at His will, and in conformity to the wisdom which operates during all eternity. There is no medium whatever between submission to that particular Providence which constantly applies itself to every atom of matter and to every energy of spirit, and the total rebellion against the Divine supremacy, against the omnipotence of Him who was, is, and ever shall be."

"Carried to such an extent," said Marco, "does not this doctrine render man a mere machine, the passive instrument of unyielding destiny? If we thus deprive man of all power of judgment, does he not cease to be responsible?"

Bacon paused, and then spoke. "Could you suppose," said he, "that I was unprepared for this difficulty? It is one from which we never can escape. It seems imposed upon us as a perpetual trial of faith. It is utterly impossible for human intellect to comprehend how the uncontrolled free will of man, the power of judgment of right and wrong, the liberty of action whereby we are rendered responsible and accountable beings, can be coexistent with that foreknowledge which belongs inseparably to the Sovereign and Creator of the universe. Yet we all admit, without argument, a doctrine which no argument can embrace. It is a mystery of which we are sensible, in every moment of our lives. Every human being is coerced to feel, that, whilst he possesses the unfettered power of choosing his own path, he never does choose any path, excepting that by and through which God works the fulfilment of His immutable decrees; and that though man is bound to use all means appointed for good, whether physical or moral: nay, that it is tempting God to abstain from them, yet that none can or will succeed, except by the permission of the Almighty.

"With respect to the peculiar application of this doctrine to the subject upon which we are now conversing, the control and direction of human knowledge, I would ask you whether you admit such a dominion as that possessed by the Romans was otherwise raised up than by the Divine hand?"

"It were worse than heathenism to deny the truth, to which the conscience of the Gentile bore a willing, a joyful testimony. Never did pagan Rome refuse to confess, that the fortunes of the Republic were to be ascribed to the protection of the tutelary deity."

"Then, by what secondary and human means," said the Friar, "do you suppose that their conquests were accomplished?"

"Amongst the most prominent causes," said Marco, "I should place the excellence of their military discipline, their proficiency in the use of arms, the dexterous vigour with which the Roman soldier urged the thrust of his keenly-pointed glaive. If they invaded a foreign land, the Roman camp was surrounded by those ramparts which yet, even in this remote island, testify the science of an Agricola, and the unwearied diligence of his legions. Whether in attack or defence, how assiduous was the skill of the Romans, displayed in the mechanism of the machines employed by them in beleaguering town and tower. The ballista hurling the rock through the air; the catapult sending forth the mighty shaft! In all these arts of war, we see the elements of the power which enabled them to lord it over the subject world."

"Supposing the art of metallurgy had not been known, could the Romans have acquired their universal Empire?"

"Surely not. Man's unaided strength could never enable him to create the military power needed to sustain the sovereignty. Unclothed in armour, destitute of shield, sword, or spear, the individual strength of the naked savage might have qualified him to gain the mastery over his immediate adversary; but he never could have so learned to combine his strength as to produce the marshalled host, which is indispensable for maintaining an extensive dominion."

"And thus," said Bacon, "you must necessarily arrive at the conclusion, that the great fourth monarchy, foredoomed as the era leading to the consummation which awaits the destinies of human kind, was founded by the science of the first cunning worker in metals, to whom the knowledge of smelting the dull ore was revealed. Do you really give credence to the prophecies of Holy Writ? Are you really a believer, admitting the prescience, which, when the seven hills were covered with tangled forests, saw the nation of fierce countenance, beheld the eagle raised against the holy city's walls? You are: and how can you then at the same time deny that the same prescience operated with equal force, when the first artificer in brass and iron was taught the lesson through which alone the Romans were to subdue the vassal nations? The designs of God are not partial and successively developed, but perfect in all eternity. Like Himself they constitute a unity. You cannot strike out any one link of the golden chain connecting earth and heaven.

"Intellect advances in man as it pleases his Creator. Little can be hazarded by conjecture, even when we reason upon constantly recurring probabilities, respecting the capabilities of improvement in any branch of human knowledge or science. But in nowise can the march of intellect be directed or accelerated or retarded by the mere sovereignty of the human will. Accidents which no human being could foresee, opportunities which no human power could create, contingencies which no human ingenuity could arrange, have ever led, and will always lead, to the inventions and discoveries marking the progress of the generations of Adam. All the productions of literature and philosophy and science, all the inventions and conceptions destined to influence the whole frame and substance of human society, are merely a cloud of witnesses bearing the clearest testimony that the powers of the human mind are under the perpetual guidance of Him, who is about us in all our ways.

"Yet these truths do not in any manner check us in our attempts to obtain intellectual improvement; on the contrary, they stimulate and spur diligence. They afford the most lasting encouragement, because they teach us to rely upon everlasting strength. Employ to the utmost of thy ability the gifts which God bestows: use them in gladness and confidence. Tokens of His free grace, from Him they receive their efficacy and their power. Boldly sow thy seed with an unsparing hand, but humbly ask of Him the increase. Repine not if the harvest be delayed: it may not come to maturity until the bones of the husbandman are decaying in the grave; but, if the produce be granted, then bring before the Lord the fruits which, from His bounty, thou hast received.

"Labour in the cause of science, strive to diffuse learning, not as if our faculties were bestowed upon us merely for our own pleasure or pride, but with the humble and prayerful hope of being enabled to act as faithful stewards, in the due employment of the talents received by human kind for the service and glory of God. Failing to do so, our knowledge, however specious its pretensions, however noble its aspect, however graceful its form, will be defeated in all its objects; and draw down upon the unprofitable servants who have perverted the good gifts of the Almighty, the inevitable retribution of misery, destruction, and despair."

.   .   .   .

Every review of the progress of the human race, affords the most clear and cogent exposition of the truth, that "the history of inventions," can only be considered as exemplifying the particular providences and permissive dispensations by which the whole universe is ruled. Yet this acknowledgment of God's active power is not in accordance with the prevailing opinions of the world: and those who propound the doctrine are almost sure to be encountered by the trite Horatian maxim that the deity is not to intervene unless the knot be worthy of the deity.

It might not be unimportant in the study of ethics, to consider how much mischief has been done by popular adages and commonplaces: how much selfishness may have been strengthened by the proverb: how many a falsity, sanctioned by the current stamp of a familiar quotation, may have been received as unquestionable truth and sound wisdom. In this instance, however, the heathen at least is guiltless of the false lesson which his lines have been made to convey. And it is really difficult to understand how the instruction, not inappositely or unreasonably imparted to the dramatic poet, could ever be applied, by any believer in revelation, to the highest destinies of mankind. How can we utter such a thought? We repeat amongst the holiest truths, that God always intervenes, the sparrow falls not to the ground without the decree of the Almighty; and is there any *reality* in our words if we suppose that there can be a single incident in the immutable system of causation, independent of His eternal will?

It may appear strange, that, whilst few can be found sufficiently irreverent to deny openly before men that the temporal affairs of the world are under the direct guidance of God, and that empires rise and fall by His behest: still fewer are sufficiently bold to confess before men, that the empire of mind is equally under His control. But is it not the same "God whose name is blessed for ever and ever," who "removeth kings, and setteth up kings," and who "giveth wisdom unto the wise, and knowledge to them that know understanding"? Are those whom He permits to become the intellectual rulers of mankind independent of Him, who, from His throne, beholds all the dwellers upon earth? If we inculcate the pursuit of science and literature, upon the assumption that the powers of natural reason are independent of religious light, we virtually deny the supremacy of Providence.

This error, so injurious in its practical consequences, is occasioned, in great measure, by our constant habit of considering the religious teaching of the mind, as not merely separable, but in fact separated, from its intellectual instruction, whereas the means of inculcating faith, and imparting mental cultivation, have from the beginning been rendered identical. Consider the application and tendency of the art of writing, the only means of cultivating knowledge, whether precise or speculative. Writing is the corner-stone of the fabric upon which the whole structure of inductive science depends. I will not ask when or how this art was taught to man, nor propound as absolutely certain the suggestion, that all alphabetical characters, however apparently varied, result only from the modifications of one type. But, waiving these inquiries, we possess the most certain and indisputable evidence, that in the order prescribed by Providence with respect to fallen man, the means destined for the preservation of divine truth, or employed in furthering the progress of human knowledge, have been inseparably conjoined.

Had this art of speaking to the eye been concealed from man, had letters not been known, the Bible could not have existed. Had not the writing of God been graven by His finger upon the tables, His commandments, even under the theocracy of Israel, could only have been preserved authentically by a perpetual miracle. The absence of written characters would have necessitated a constant effusion of the Holy Spirit for the transmission of divine truths. Had not writing been imparted to us, then all doctrine must have depended upon oral tradition: and, writing being absent, how could religious knowledge have been defended against alteration and corruption? God's word could not have been entrusted to the natural and unaided memory of man; either our faculties must have been totally altered, for the preservation of the lessons of salvation, or it would have been indispensable that an unbroken succession of inspired preachers should have been raised up, from time to time, from generation to generation, from age to age. Prophet must have been the disciple of prophet; apostle the immediate forerunner of apostle. When tempted, we could not have answered, "It is written." When seeking comfort, we could not have been told, "It is written." Holy *Scripture* could not have been given for our instruction: the whole scheme of revelation must have been totally changed.

In the cultivation of the human intellect, the first lesson is thus sent forth from the Holy of Holies. The whole rich banquet of human knowledge is composed of the crumbs which have fallen from the table of the Lord. All the records and memorials of human literature and human science are secondary and derivative: and exist merely because it pleased God that we should continue to learn His will from the divine volume, after the bodily presence of the teachers who declared His truths had been withdrawn: and, pursuing the question onwards, we shall still find that the further improvement of intellect proceeds from a source above human control.

Consult the annals of human intellect in every branch and gradation, and they will afford the testimony, not of its own strength, but of its weakness, unless when raised up by influences wholly beyond the sphere of human power. Is it possible by any artificial treatment of the mind to make a true poet? Experience has fully convinced us that neither example nor education, neither the refinements of civilized life, nor the energetic rudeness of the nomade, can of themselves bestow the talent. Who ever doubted but that the poet must be born?

If we view the whole band of real poets who have existed since the beginning of the annals of mankind, how very small is the unfilled vessel in which, as they float down the stream of time, all those who deserve that name are embarked. The predicate of the true poet is equally true with respect to all the other creative talents imparted to the human intellect. Their possessors cannot be made, they must be born. Man cannot cause their development. Perhaps, even more rare than true poetical power is mathematical talent, in that its highest excellence resulted from the union of consummate subtlety of thought and patient labour. Still more rare, is the genius which divines the general laws of nature, the reasoner who, for the first time, seizes the principle which connects phenomena before unexplained, and thus adds another original truth to our knowledge of the universe.

Reckon the possessors of these talents as they appear in the whole history of our species, how scanty is their number. How remote are the periods in which those men have been raised up by whose influence any efficient advance in knowledge has been gained. Such an acquisition is reserved alone for those who have been gifted with a clearness of ideas, wholly withheld from the average scale of human intellect, and who have been enabled to apply these ideas vigorously and distinctly to ascertained facts and exact observations. Unless these men are called forth by providential destiny—for no normal process, no activity of thought, no school, no academy, no university, no education, no external circumstances, can form such characters—the process of intellect by which facts become science, is wholly unknown.

No preconceived study, no cultivation of the intellect, ever has forced the production of the qualities of the mind distinguishing the great discoverers of abstract truths. Equally independent also of study, or the coercion of human direction, are those peculiar external and internal incidents concurring in the formation of the practical inventor, unfolding to him the application of those powers of material nature which have produced such wondrous changes in the whole condition of human kind, discoveries altering the physical condition of man, and affording the instruments whereby his intellectual progress is effected, and the vehicles in and by which the mind proceeds. No mode of reasoning can point out the cause, why the Roman philosopher, viewing the insect magnified through the globular crystal and the landscape diminished in the concave gem, should have failed to discover the microscope and the telescope. The attractive virtue, and the polarity of the magnet, might have been equally revealed, or equally concealed. What restrained the contemporaries of Virgil from learning to multiply his verses by the stamps which impressed the name of the dealer upon his wares? Why were the types of the Mœso-Gothic bishop employed but upon one copy of the gospels? The whole theory of the steam-engine, every contrivance or machine, depending upon the elasticity of the air or the vaporization of the fluid, came within the grasp of the philosopher of Alexandria, and of those by whom his works were possessed in a later age.

Can the annals of technology afford satisfactory proofs that any one of the great physical inventions which really constitute eras in the history of intellectual or social "civilization," has been produced by the strict analogical inductions of reasoning? Once opened, the mine has been more and more worked, deeper shafts have been dug, easier methods discovered of raising the precious ore: yet, not by the skill of the scientific metallurgist, but by the chance footsteps of the herdsman, the first discovery of the hidden source of wealth was made. Much has been improved, facilities

have been gained, powers have been extended, further contrivances happily applied; but all great inventions have, in their
first impression, been independent either of volition or of study,
or of intellectual excellence. They have proceeded from sudden
conceptions, descending, fully formed, as from the empyrean world
of archetypal ideas, flashing upon the mind without previous
investigation. Strangely, unexpectedly, unbidden like a dream,
the irradiation excites surprise in the very individual to whom the
thought has been imparted, and who, when considering the invention, experiences, like Watt, not the pride of possession, but
the pleasurable sense of novelty, which arises from the first contemplation of the results of the discoveries of others. And the
inventors, unassisted by the results of practice, or by the lights of
education, display nought but the guidance of an unseen power.
Why will intellect refuse to learn humility from her own annals?
Davy promises with exulting confidence to apply his knowledge
for the benefit of the navigator, and to give him a new ocean
triumph. The vessel, covered with the combinations of zinc and
copper, whose galvanic action is to defeat the corrosive properties
by which the metal is consumed, sails gaily from the port; and
returns heavy as a drifting log, the keel a mass of zoophytes,
scarcely able to drag through the waves. Planned according to
the strictest deductions of science, the "safety-lamp" is held up as
the proud trophy of philosophy rendered subservient to practical
utility. It constitutes the theme of the eloquent essay, furnishes
an oration; and is flung aside by the workman, who finds he dare
not trust its uncertain aid. His chemical knowledge leads him
to suspect that it may be possible to delineate the outward world
by means of the sun-beams, that the light and the shade may be
detained and fixed in permanent imagery. He reasons, he tries,
he begins to succeed, and the vision fleets away from his grasp.
He records his attempt and his total failure, and leaves to his
successors to contest amongst themselves, his labours utterly
forgotten, the glory of the chance invention, perhaps the most
marvellous in our wonder-working age. Such are the results of
the reasoning powers, as applied for the purposes of discovery by
one who was amongst the most gifted of our generation; and who
finally earned no other meed from the world's friendship except
the cold sympathy of funereal praise, when, a disappointed, heart-
sickened, and forlorn wanderer, he wasted into the tomb. Contrast these total failures with the illumination which nightly per-
vades our metropolis. Ask who planned the tubes and the receivers,

feeding the cressets, from whence proceed the rays which, reflected from the aerial canopy, envelop the distant city in preternatural dawn. Seek the inventor: and you must decide between the claims of an obscure manufacturer, and a still more humble ad- venturer, whose name has no other record except the insolvent's register in the jail. From the simplest application of the mechanic arts to the most complicated, from the lever and the wedge, to the printing-press and the steam-engine, we have no choice if we attempt to reason upon their causation, between the chance atoms of Epicurus, and the confession, that all the crafts, all the con- trivances, all the endowments of man, are the free gifts of the Almighty: and, as it pleases His infinite wisdom, imparted or permitted, restrained or withheld.

It is, I believe, a popular doctrine, that the condition of mankind is, of necessity, progressive. Mind, it is assumed, will inevitably gain its victories over mind. Human intelligence com- mands, and we are advancing in the career of intellectual improve- ment with irrevocable force and accelerated rapidity. Such appear to be the collective and theoretical aspirations of European "civilization."

Are we consistent? The individual and practical expectations of mankind are much more calculating, cautious, and dubious. Adventurous as the merchant may be, the richest capitalist upon the crowded exchange does not feel certain that his prosperity will be continuous. He is fully aware that correspondents may break, prices fall, banks fail, and that the utmost diligence and integrity cannot infallibly protect him even from beggary. No student, however enthusiastic, is so arrogant as to predict for himself an indefeasible advance in his professional career. He looks around him, and views one companion whose bodily health has yielded to labour: another, whose mind has proved unequal to the task: many, who, with all physical and mental advantages, have never been able to launch in the flowing tide of fortune. Was a general ever so fool-hardy as to believe that he could chain the winged Victory to his standard? He knows too well that the treachery of the friend, the sagacity of the enemy, the heat of the summer's sun, the storm and tempest of the winter's sky, may defeat the best- arranged plans of strategy. No man of common sense rejects, in the anticipations of his individual futurity, those haps and hazards, those chances and changes, which, in the world's false language, we call accident or fortune.

On what reasonable ground can we refuse to admit the same

qualification of our hopes, the same damp upon our expectations, in our estimate of the prospects of science? Without disputing the assertion, that the resources of knowledge are inexhaustible, the history of technology itself incontestably proves the fact, that continued progress does not in any respect follow inevitably from the relations or nature of man. And how should it? Intellect is not an independent formation. Our intellect is not detached from ourselves. The exercise of intellect is in all respects directed and controlled by every other of the secondary causes involved in the physical and moral relations of the world. Man, mysteriously compounded by the alliance of body and soul, is himself only a part of the macrocosm, holding the specific place appointed for him: and the immaterial principle is always compelled to acknowledge the fetters of matter in and amongst which she moves.

An indispensable condition for the successful prosecution of science, is the well-being of the community to which the philosopher belongs. Prosperity does not necessarily promote the advance of science; but scientific advance is inexorably linked to mundane prosperity. Commercial opulence brings together the collections in which the naturalist alone finds the materials for his systematic knowledge. The munificence of the ruler enables him to endow the academy or the institute. Wealth employed in the foundation of the college, or expended in social luxury, imparts its powerful impulse, alluring the philosopher by the promise of its distinctions and enjoyments.

But, let the decree go forth, and the whole material foundation of science is destroyed. Poverty strikes the city of royal merchants, her pleasantness is laid waste. The treasure-house is empty. Plague and pestilence taint the gale in which the destroying angel waves his sword. The festive hall is desolate. War is let loose, rebellion triumphs. The cannon-shot beats down the museum, the murderous shell falls upon the observatory: the seats of learning are despoiled. In these darkening periods, when the ancient forms of society break up, men's minds are always equally affected by the change: nay, even the disquietudes which are the harbingers of political convulsions, produce the same effect. The blossoms are blighted whilst the clouds are gathering previous to the howling of the storm. Energy of thought is succeeded by servility: clearness of idea gives place to obscurity of conception. Steadiness of intellectual action vanishes before confused conceptions and rhetorical declamation; and, together with the state or empire in which science has been fostered and cultivated, the whole fabric of intellect, real civilization, declines and falls.

Periods are discernible in which some branches of the acquirements termed science and literature, for we cannot separate them, have received great advances: yet, in the sum total of the annals of the human race, in the aggregate history of human cultivation, eras of progression form only the smallest part. Without designating them as exceptions from a general rule, they nevertheless bear the character of sudden developments, offering facts in total opposition to what may be termed the mechanical theory of intellect.

The physical powers of man continue undiminished, the formations of the human body continue unaltered. Nerves do not lose their ancient powers of sensation: the fibres of the muscle always retain the same irritability. Our organs act as they have always done. But the very short and transient epochs during which, in the estimation of the philosopher, the knowledge which he worships as science has continued progressive, are divided from each other, and in the most overwhelming proportion, by periods, when science becomes wholly stationary, some of the most marked intellectual faculties seeming at the same time to be in abeyance, or wholly lost.

No psychological theory, grounded upon the assumption that intellect acts by mere human relations, can solve the phenomena thus exhibited. Nought but perplexity shall we encounter, until we prostrate our reason before the sovereignty of the Almighty. The same revelation which forbids us from vainly speculating upon the mysteries of divine Providence, has plainly pointed out the course pursued by the legislator of the universe. Races and nations receive their rewards and their judgments collectively: they are collectively favoured and punished: they are made collectively responsible, and are dealt with in their generations as though they had an individual existence. With man, there is no present time. Before we can think the thought, this moment is lost in the ocean of all precedent eternity. With us, all is either past or future. With God there is no succession, all is present.

So far as human knowledge is useful, every appearance justifies us in the supposition, that these apparent seasons of barrenness may be conducive, nay, necessary, for the real improvement of mankind. He, from whom the intellect emanates, who views at once the source and the termination, equally exercises His wisdom in determining the course of the stream, whether it flows through fertile pastures or through desert sands.   Alternations of quiescence and activity constitute the order of animated nature. Fallow foreruns the plough, sleep prepares for labour, night brings on the day.   And in the same manner it may be needful, that during given periods, particular faculties of the human mind should remain unexercised, in order that they may afterwards awaken with great impetus and vigour: and that other faculties may also in the meanwhile be employed in preparing the means for future exertion and utility.

Attempting to analyze the course of events, we may perhaps conjecture that there was a peculiar fitness in the restraint imposed upon the mental powers of the mediæval period, when considered as introductory to our own.   Stationary as the middle ages may have appeared to be with respect to some of the faculties of the intellect, others were exhibited in full and beneficial activity. There may have been a deficiency in originality of literary conception.   The voluminous writers who then flourished may have been mere servile imitators; but this servility disposed them to diligence, and the monk who dared not assert a truth, or entertain a doctrine unsanctioned by his predecessors, became the instrument of preserving the scanty relics which Providence has permitted us to possess of ancient literature, perhaps for the purpose of just enabling us to judge of the abominations which the gospel was intended to efface, and the false doctrines it was destined to supersede.   Had the learned men of the middle ages been more ambitious, had they disdained the task of the commentator and the copyist, sage and philosopher, poet and historian would have been wholly lost.

Judged by our modes, they reasoned vaguely and inaccurately. But what are the ample possessions of modern science but an inheritance derived from them and cultivated through the results of their practical observation and practical skill?   They were set to work for us, in order that we might think for ourselves.   Had not the alembic of the swart Adept produced the solvent, how could the voltaic pile have received its energy, and the highest generalizations of chemical science have been attained?   No mechanical principle, unknown to Archimedes, may have been displayed in the printing-press; but if the power of inventing the printing-press had not been granted to the obscure burghers of Leyden or Mayence, so must of necessity our modern knowledge have been deprived of its universality and diffusion; for to this discovery, is all the so-called "civilization" of the present day to be ascribed.

The intermission of the visible evolution of peculiar energies of mind in particular periods, is therefore entirely compatible with the general improvement of collective humanity. But, should it be proved, that at any period the human mind has been visited by a real degradation and torpidity, or by an unquestionable diminution of its more exalted faculties, may we not also reverently and humbly ask the question, whether any progress of our intellect, for good, can be expected, if, refusing to retain God in our knowledge, we resist His guidance, and strive against His will? Is it not accordant to His known dispensations, that if the power bestowed by Him upon us be abused, the gift should fail? Surely the employment of those mental endowments, so emphatically termed *talents*, involves as much responsibility as the disposition of the worldly possessions, constituting the elements of temporal prosperity.

The application of our intellectual faculties for the purpose of satisfying the mere natural curiosity of the mind, cannot in anywise be distinguished from the wanton expenditure of our riches for the gratification of the mere natural appetites of the body. We are bound to honour the Lord with our substance: can it be less imperative upon us to honour him with the infinitely more precious gifts of the soul? Undue indulgence in the more gross inclinations of our corporeal nature, tends to sink man beneath the earthly level providentially assigned to human kind. Undue indulgence in the more refined desires of the soul, not less corrupt, when unrenewed by God's Holy Spirit, than the fleshly heart, deludes man into the belief, that he already belongs to a higher sphere than that which is now his own. Placed by the will of his Creator, a little lower than the angels, he attempts to rush into the sanctuary, where the fiery seraphim cover their faces before the glory of the Most High.

What is then our duty? Sobriety and vigilance. Depreciate not the marvellous powers of the human intellect: they proceed from Him, to whom the fulness of the universe belongs. Worship them not; because they were lent to us for His service. Cultivate them diligently, for sloth is sin; yet let our moderation be known in all things.

In the present state of intellectual advancement, when new subjects of inquiry display such glittering and seductive variety and splendour, there is the greatest danger of our being tempted to

refuse that service which God demands, of not always thinking
our own thoughts, nor always speaking our own words, nor always
following our own ways.   He warns us to obey the obligation of
entering into His rest, constituting not the open and hebdomadal,
but the secret and daily sabbath of the soul.   If we fail to honour
Him in delight, may we not fear that He will be honoured in His
vengeance until the word of desolation be fulfilled?

THREE GENERATIONS

OF AN

IMAGINARY NORFOLK FAMILY

BY

SIR FRANCIS PALGRAVE, K.H.

[NOW PUBLISHED FOR THE FIRST TIME]

TABLE OF CONTENTS

CHAPTER I.

THE FOUNDER OF THE FAMILY.

(EDWARD I.)

TESTIMONY grounded upon opinion is rarely available otherwise than as a testimony of the opinion of the person who gives it. "As the fool thinks, so the bell clinks"; and in that point wise men and fools are much the same; and, letting alone graver matters, there are not many cases in which the discrepancies are more amusing than the manner in which the climate of our island has been characterized by foreigners and by ourselves. Count Castel Cicala, with visions of Naples floating before him, writes home that, in England, no fruit ripens naturally, except roasted apples; and that the difference between a fair day and a foul day, even on the Malvern Hills, is that of looking up a chimney or looking down it. But what sayeth John Bull? First, he goeth to his barometer, and duly marketh the concavity of the sinking mercury; next, he draweth on his waterproof boots; then he buttoneth up his mackintosh, tieth his comforter round his neck, taketh out his umbrella, and setteth out for his walk, repeating that, after all, there is no country in which a man can enjoy so great a proportion of his time pleasantly in the open air as in England. I dare not exercise my own private judgment upon this important national question; but, in describing the ancient state of English society, it is not unimportant to remark that the climate of England has certainly changed within the period of historical memory; and we are sufficiently warranted by incidental notices, so minute that they can be scarcely suspected of inaccuracy, and too simple to be the result of exaggeration or love of the marvellous, in supposing that, as late as the twelfth century, the general temperature of Britain was not exceedingly unlike that of Canada at the present day. Above one-third of the surface of the land was copse and forest ground; the marshes were also very extensive in the eastern parts of the island, whitherward I am conducting my reader. Norfolk and Suffolk were

[189]

almost separated from the Mercian Shires—a term still in use amongst the common people, as distinguishing their counties from the rest of England—by the Fen Country, then a bleak and dreary waste, but of which the greater portion has now been rendered productive by capital and labour.   In part this change has been effected by man; yet those providential workings which, to prevent irreverence, we may be permitted to designate as the operations of nature, have aided.   On the coasts, the driftings of sand have converted many an estuary into a valley, and filled up many a channel by which the Broads, as they are called, formerly communicated with the North Sea; and it is with difficulty that the testimony of the Rolls of Parliament, as well as of the historian, can convince us that Lake Lothing was once the wide and open haven of Kirkley Road, in which, in the reign of Richard II., the fleets of England assembled.   Such being the ancient state of the country, we may easily understand why twelve sticks of eels and pannage for a hundred and ninety-seven swine hold a prominent station in the Domesday survey of the value of the thorp or vill of West Walsham, a locality unaccountably omitted in Blomefield's accurate history, though North Walsham and South Walsham occupy all the space which their importance deserves.   Upon this land there were settled sixteen bordarii, ten cottarii, and four sokemen, who are stated to have had the privilege, which, in point of fact, belongs to no one human creature, to go where they would, whilst the whole township was held by Godric of the king. I cannot give any further explanation of the rights and duties of these different occupants, not wishing to seem wiser than my predecessors; and since the judges in the time of Edward II. said that there were a great number of words in Domesday which they could not explain, otherwise than as they sounded, I will not endeavour to define the state and condition of these several parties with more minuteness.   All I shall say is, that it is quite certain that the villein never appeared with a collar round his neck, engraven with the name of his master; and that, as secured by the charter of William the Conqueror, so long as he paid his rent, he continued upon the land.

I should, I fear, weary the reader unprofitably, and I must husband his patience, which wives rarely do, since I may make large demands upon it, if I were to attempt to collect, through the channels of the Pipe Rolls, now in my custody, the scanty evidences relating to West Walsham in the Anglo-Norman period; and I shall therefore fly down at once to the reign of Edward

Longshanks, when I find the domain in the possession of a family of "Clares." The earliest member of this family of whom I can find any mention is Alan de Clare, who, bearing the "three chevrons, within a bordure gules as a difference," appears, according to the last visitation for the county of Norfolk, held in 1637, recorded in the books of the College of Arms, as a cadet of the noble family of the same name; he, according to the same record, duly certified by Vincent, being lineally descended from the thirteenth son of Richard, Earl of Hertford, in the reign of Henry Plantagenet. It is true that we have no other accounts of this said thirteenth son in any other documents; but, without attending to such a trifling deficiency of evidence in starting, every subsequent link in the descent is duly deduced upon paper; and, so long as there were any representatives of the Clares of West Walsham, they constantly asserted their consanguinity accordingly. Wise men never make themselves disagreeable by questioning the authenticity either of pictures or pedigrees; therefore. were it in my power, I would fain emulate the prudence of a distinguished dealer, not a hundred miles from Charing Cross, who, when a friend happened incidentally to speak of an artist whom he found engaged in his studio, painting five Cuyps on five easels at once, replied, "Yes, and I know where they all are now; but I would not make the gentlemen uneasy by telling them so"; and if there were a single branch, sprig, or leaf of any of the families which once claimed under the "Clares of West Walsham" now extant, I might have shrunk from the painful duty, if I told all the world what I knew concerning their lineage. But the tree is quite dead; the last blossom of it, who married the cheesemonger at Yarmouth, died without children, and therefore I may now disclose, not only with a safe conscience, but with an easy mind, my firm belief that if our Alan had followed the calling of his father, and some say he did help in heating the goose, he would have been a tailor in the ancient town of Clare, from which place of local habitation he obtained his local name. Whatever may have been the custom on the continent, the *de*, in England, never had the aristocratic force ascribed to that much-valued syllable, or its brother, *von*, in France or Germany. It was originally as unaristocratic as any other particle; merely indicating the place of habitation or domicile. Alan was designated in the same manner as the proud baron, beneath the shade of whose lofty castle he was born, and it may be suspected that many a plebeian has been engrafted upon the stock of a noble family by the same help; the particle being merely descriptive, and telling nothing more; whereas, amongst our continental neighbours, it is, in opinion at least, the designation of nobility.

Alan was received at an early age into the household of his lord, and, like Giovanni Acuto, had none of the pacific tendency ascribed to his calling. Full-grown, stout, and strong, he more than once performed service, for half a fee, on behalf of Earl Richard; bearing the shield of his master on his arm, in order that he might be known as part of his master's retinue—much in the same way that a footman now wears his master's livery, and bears his crest upon his buttons; and when, afterwards, Alan became a landed gentleman, he adopted the cognizance as his own, adding, as a difference, the red border suggested by his saddler, under whose direction the painter decorated this kind of gear; for, at this period, the code of arms, afterwards so strict and stringent, had no existence. I have never been able to discover that, at this period of our English history, a coat of arms was considered as conclusive evidence either of gentility or of lineage. In the days of Alan's great-grandson it certainly was otherwise, but then times had changed. As for our Alan, he had risen rapidly in the world by the process which hath elevated so many a rosy-cheeked chaplain or swarthy ensign to ease and opulence—he gained the hand of the fair Alice, the lady of West Walsham, and thus became himself the lord of the domain.

Alice was of that mature and prudent age when, as wise men say, and experience shows, unmated dames or damsels, spinsters or widows—and she was included in the first category—are always most accessible to the wooer. She had fully attained her years of discretion and something more. For it usually happens with old ladies (let alone old gentlemen) that after the years of discretion have gone off, the years of indiscretion often begin. Her happy husband scarcely numbered half her years, and he had before him the prospect of outliving the fortune which matrimony with the ancient maiden had bestowed upon him, and reverting to his pristine penury and liberty.

In our calculating era, an affectionate husband like Alan, under similar circumstances, would have secured himself by "opening a policy" at the Equitable or the Amicable; but Alan managed so ably as to indemnify himself in another manner, and the birth of the stout bullet-headed baby, which event deprived the mother of her existence, confirmed the domain to the father by that peculiar usage in our Common Law denominated the "curtesy of England."

What did the "wisdom of our ancestors" decree? One-third of the husband's land shall be the dowry of the widow, and this without any condition or restraint. It followed the espousal before the altar; she acquired it by the delivery of the ring. In the wife's land the surviving husband acquired a larger estate, the usufruct of the whole, but dependent upon a contingency. There must be one child born alive to entitle him to the privilege. The right given to the lady was not always convenient to the gentleman, and hence, in modern times, the lawyers and the judges sanctioned various devices by which the dowry was most frequently frustrated in practice, though subsisting in law; but this sufficed not: a commission of right learned sages, with much discretion, reported on the expediency of abolishing this relic of barbarism and feudality; and hence, with great impartiality, it was finally enacted that dower should be extinguished and abolished in every case, whilst "tenancy by the curtesy" is not only retained, but extended to every case, without any contingency whatsoever. Alan was therefore not absolutely inconsolable when he was thus deprived of his consort, and the infant throve apace. I ought to have mentioned that, just after the birth of Gilbert, for so he was christened, a violent hail and thunderstorm crossed Norfolk—in the Chronicle of Bromholm it is recorded as an earthquake. Most of the windows of the south side of the priory were driven in, and the small statue of Herbert Losinga, or the Lickspittle, which still adorns the transept of Norwich Cathedral, was blown down, though immediately afterwards restored. Events like these have been, and are so often considered as omens of the character or destiny of the party, that the reader may well expect to find some effects connected with them in the future destiny of the urchin. However, if the kind reader has formed such expectations, he will be disappointed, for in the case of Gilbert de Clare they prognosticated nothing at all; but I must nevertheless be trusted upon my own responsibility for having introduced them into this portion of my story; and, leaving young Gilbert, for the present, under the management of his nurse, the stout wife of John the huntsman, re-enter the main path of my family history.

"When it is term time I am overdone, and I long for vacation; and when it is vacation time I am tired of doing nothing, and then I long for term time; and I can't help thinking that one's life is

made up of term time and vacation." This speech, uttered by a
learned judge not many years ago, which, to a certain extent, is
true of nine-tenths of mankind, describes to its fullest extent the
existence of Alan de Clare. During the winter season, when no
cattle could be depastured, the family fed principally on salt beef,
and then he longed for fresh mutton; and when mutton was in
season, he thought he relished his can better with salt beef. More
out of idleness than of industry, he used to attend a little to the
cultivation of his respectable demesne; but when the fields were
in tilth, he used to stand his horse upon the merebalk, and think
that it was troublesome work, and that it would look pleasanter
if the fields were in "shack"; and when autumn brought "shack,"
he longed for the season of tillage.

Thus did year follow after year in monotony, he becoming
somewhat stouter, and Gilbert a good deal taller, as the years
rolled on, when an event occurred affording a partial relief from
the dreariness of the waste of time. Objects of sight which we
have never seen are more easily raised up by the imagination
than objects of sound which we have never heard. We can
picture to ourselves Alan de Clare sitting at the head of his table
much more readily than we can suppose we heard him speaking
old English, let alone Anglo-Saxon. Yet for the nonce I can
convey a tolerably accurate notion of the strains which greeted
his ear from without, just as he was about to cut open the herring
pie which stood before him, the said pie being composed exactly
according to the recipe employed in preparing the same dainty
dish as it was wont to be rendered yearly by the city of Norwich
to the king. The music, then, which saluted him was the drone
of the hurdy-gurdy, the squeak of a flageolet, the twang of the
fiddle, and lastly, a deeper note of the same class as the last,
proceeding from that ancient instrument, now, I fear, entirely
disused, the "bladder and string," which, when skilfully managed,
as it was on this occasion, produces a strumming grunt, not very
much unlike that of a tenor. Young Gilbert scampered out with
great delight to invite the minstrels in; they advanced, and the
instruments being, as they expected, silenced by a largesse, they
sat down upon a little bench by Alan's side. Welcome as their
merry song might be to the young, it was their gossip and news
which possessed most interest for wiser heads and mature age,
and the intelligence which those professionals had to impart,
concerning the actings and doings of the great world, was infinitely
more attractive to Alan than the geste or the roundelay. Such

was the detailed account which Tappetankarde, the leader of the "noise," as such a band was usually termed, promulgated concerning the approaching Bohourdice or Jousts, about to be held upon the heath receiving its name from the great metropolis of the modern sporting world. There were to be fifty on each side—Lancashire against all England. The only point on which Tappetankarde was not fully informed was whether, as some said, the trial of skill and strength was to be for a bear, who might afterwards be baited for their amusement, or whether the bouts were to be merely for honour and glory.

"Your noble family of Clare," said Tappetankarde, speaking with the soft silver voice acquired by habitual dependence upon caprice and extorted bounty, and with as much of the manner of a well-licked spaniel as any tailless biped could assume, "hath always greatly shone in these martial exercises. Good Earl Richard, your uncle—good *Earl* Richard"—underlining the word to the ear by the stress he laid upon it—"how stalwart was he in the great tilting match at Hog's Norton, when, by his prowess alone, the adverse bachelors were chased like chaff before the wind."

The nature of the consanguinity between the Clares of West Walsham and *the* Clares was, of course, as well known to Tappetankarde as to every one in the room. But Alan, as most folks do upon such occasions, assimilated himself to the compliment, clumsy as it was, with the same readiness that the 'pothecary's assistant answers to "doctor," or the shop-boy speaks of "our house of business"; and he added, fully assenting by his tone, although his words neither affirmed nor denied the kindred— "Aye, indeed, we never shall see his like again."

It is quite unnecessary that I should inform the reader, who, without doubt, is fully aware of the fact, that to Earl Richard we owe the introduction into this country of the Austin Friars, the colony which he formed being located in the convent at Clare. A worthy friar belonging thereto, Brother Barnaby, cousin to Alan's father the botcher, had, in the course of his quest through the diocese, visited West Walsham, upon the strength of their common progenitor, and there he still was, his utmost importunity not having been able to extract the smallest donation from his otherwise not unhospitable entertainer. The sly mendicant, with all the tact of a collector soliciting subscriptions by the vivacious detail of the merits of a lying-in charity, instantly took his cue from the minstrel. "And, surely, your honour," said he, turning to Alan, "will wish to see your name inscribed on the roll of benefactors to the foundation of your noble uncle. How much, indeed, do we owe to your exalted family: in every branch have the Clares shown their munificence; and may you be preserved from the fate of your bold kinsman, Gilbert, the Earl Marshal, he who perished by treachery nigh Hertford, in that fatal tournament. Ye must be concerned, sir, ye must be warned, and not expose your lineage to the chance of the recurrence of such a loss." "Ah!" sighed Alan, who was now fully convinced that he was a genuine Clare, every inch of him, "I can hardly even now think of the earl without tears; yet he will always live in our recollections, and this boy of mine," grasping Gilbert affectionately by the hand, "was named after the earl"—an assertion of indisputable veracity, inasmuch as it was nigh upon forty years since this chieftain had been bruised to death, being flung from his steed, not without surmises that the breaking of the reins which caused the accident had been occasioned by their having been previously half cut through at the instigation of some secret enemy.

I cannot tell exactly to what extent the management of the friar succeeded. At the dissolution, the commissioners certified to the king that in the church they found one holy-water pot of latten, with the arms of Clare within a bordure, worth twopence, and one very old cope which appeared to have been made out of a kirtle, with the same bearing sewn thereon, worth a groat; and also that the said prior and convent were said to be seised, or otherwise well entitled to a yearly rent of half a mark, issuing out of lands in West Walsham, in the county of Norfolk, but of which the title-deeds were not to be discovered in the charter chest.

Further, therefore, I cannot pursue this interesting inquiry, leaving it entirely open to conjecture how far Alan was mollified by Barnaby's dexterity. All I shall add is the supposition that the absence of the instruments of donation prevented Jermyn, the senior commissioner, from discovering that, when old Harry afterwards granted the so-called rent of half a mark to him as a reward for his services, the manor and lands of West Walsham became Jermyn's property also. Good man, it cannot be conceived that he was to be charged with any fraud, but somehow or another the church property did not keep in the family, for the Commissioners of Concealment, in the reign of James the First, reclaimed the whole on behalf of the crown. Thus affording a pregnant example of the applicability of the Italian proverb, *Quel, che vien' di ninche nanche, se ne va di tinche tanche*; or, if you like the parallel apophthegm better in French than in Italian or English—I will not quote the latter—*Ce qui vient au son de la flûte, s'en va au son du tambour.*

If I cannot distinctly trace one consequence from this conversation with Brother Barnaby, I receive a full compensation by being able to deduce another: the determination which Alan formed of distinguishing himself, "like his ancestors," as he boldly said to his bailiff, in the approaching "fortune," as these military exercises were termed. His preparations were speedily made; but when he arrived at Swaffham, he was rendered somewhat vacillating in his purpose, partly by an attack of what we should term a lumbago, and partly from causes of graver import, the fear, in fact, of paying more for his frolic than it deserved.

Commend me to his worship the chamberlain of the city of London for a biographical parallel. When you receive the voted freedom (?), how much richer than the gold box is the address of the Plutarch of Guildhall!

How it flames upon the emblazoned vellum, which, if you are wise, you will be sure to frame and glaze! Now in these classical productions the wind-up is always in the similitude. There we have them—Peel and Numa, with Confucius and Justinian as supporters, besides Hortensius and Denman, Brougham and Cicero, side by side. This last parallel I grudge. I expect they will one day vote me the freedom for my services, and I wanted Cicero for myself, the great point of resemblance between us two being this: that people had no right to wonder at him if he produced his philosophical works so late in life, for he had, in truth, been employed most in these cogitations when least was seen of them: and so have I.

Amongst my lucubrations, there is none in which I have more delighted than the expansion of the philosophical Italian proverb which saith *Tutto il mondo è paese*—all the world is one country; in other words, that matters go on in the main pretty nearly the same all the world over. And out of the main points, in which such a uniformity has constantly prevailed, is the astounding discrepancy between the actions which men practise and the laws which they profess to obey. Open the statutes, and we find that the debt of the jobber or the gambler is not only void, but subjects the party to a heavy penalty. But go to the east, or go to the west, and you will find that these denunciations have no more force or influence amongst us than the decrees of Lycurgus or the slocas of the Dherma Rajah. The "Black-board" of the Stock Exchange will convince you that the minutes of the committee in "Capel Court" are more binding than the judgments of the tribunals of Westminster Hall; and the engagements in the *book* kept by the turf men at Tattersall's afford better securities than their sealed bonds. In the age of "lancet Gothic" and "Early English style" a tournament was to be ranked in the same category with a boxing-match, an illegal assembly, in the eye of the law, alike prohibited by religious doctrine and secular policy. But inasmuch as, like the prize-ring, the amusement was patronised by so many of the influential classes, who were called upon to execute the law, the eye of the law was easily persuaded to blink. It does not appear that the proclamation issued by the king in council, strictly prohibiting his lieges from resorting to the jousts advertised to be held at Newmarket, deterred many of the fancy from repairing with great glee to the trysting-place. And at least half-a-dozen conservators, or justices of the peace, might be seen exercising their barbed horses on the heath every day. One attempt, however, was made to avert the tumult and disorder. The rector of West Walsham faithfully performed his duty, by exhorting his hearers to abstain from the detestable "sports," anathematized by the council of Lateran. As to the majority of the congregation, his admonitions produced about as much impression as would ensue from a sermon against gambling or horse-racing delivered by his present successor in the same rectory. All the moral we can draw from the recollection is that the church then seemed to do her duty; what she does now—it is not for us to say.

Alan was not comfortable during the sermon; he indirectly felt a twinge, though whether in his conscience or in the small of his back it is rather difficult to ascertain, our manuscript materials not being so explicit upon this point as might be desired. "That anathema, pronounced in the presence of his Holiness," quoth Alan, as he came out of church, to his bailiff, who enacted esquire, "hangs much upon my mind; I have a kind of impression, which I cannot shake off, that we ought to consider the awful fate of Earl Richard as an evil foreboding to our family; and I have almost wondered to see that awkward bachelor, that whelp, my cousin, young John, repairing to the exercise. His mother, my aunt Joan, would have done better to have tied him to her apron-strings." The youth, the Earl's fourth son, thus irreverently described by Alan, had given a sound thrashing to Alan's groom, who intruded his master's cattle in the castle stable. Furthermore, John de Clare, when he heard that Alan would present himself on the Heath, had expressed a certain degree of expectation that he should see Alan heels upwards, before the sport was over, as a reward for his unhandsomeness in assuming the ancient baronial arms. For although at this period the noble code of heraldry had not established the principles which, in the course of the next century, rendered the bearing an absolute inheritance not to be invaded without the utmost jeopardy, still there was a kind of feeling about the matter. Alan, respectable as he certainly was, yet had the ill-luck to be considered by many of the neighbouring land-holders much as an apothecary is viewed in the ballroom at Bath, or a Jew broker at the Hackney assembly; in short, as one who, though you could not avowedly and openly quarrel with him for it, had yet clumsily intruded himself into the society of a class to which he did not belong. None of these hesitations concerning Alan's gentility, however, influenced his conduct, for when, some time afterwards, a "good-natured friend," Friar Barnaby, began to talk about these reports, Alan, before the sentence was finished, assured him that they had never even reached his ears; and indeed, whatever was the cause of his abstaining from the prosecution of the adventure, the matter ended by his stopping at home, and prudence at least was consulted in the course which he had pursued.

It does not always follow that "those may laugh who win." In courtship it is not always a necessary consequence; in electioneering it is not always a necessary consequence; neither was it so in the English tournament of the thirteenth century. Dust and sweat, whacks and thwacks, shoulders dislocated, and bones broken; knights and bachelors killed outright in the field, or lingering through a painful existence; a coarse and hardened exertion of animal strength, wasting and abusing the vigour bounteously bestowed. Those who escaped in person yet suffered in purse. The law, as is too often the case, was strong enough for punishment, though not for prevention. In addition to heavy amercements fixed upon those who had trespassed against the proclamations, their horses, arms, and accoutrements were seized. And Alan expressed a great deal of very proper sympathy when it was known that "my connection," the gentle bachelor John, had been compelled to pay nearly a year's income before,

having obtained his quietus at the exchequer, he was enabled
again to brace his triangular target, exhibiting the bearing
without the difference, the chevrons unbroken by the bordure.

Alan, without having any positive cause of anxiety, was
worried and uncomfortable; he was growing old, and did not
much like it. People who parade their disconnection with this
wretched world, and their happy hope of the future, are very
generally those who have least realised the certainty. They
seem to have a kind of notion that they can trick the grim tyrant,
and that, by constantly telling him they are ready to depart, he,
out of pure contradiction, will not take the trouble to come.

There was not very long since a garden in the county of
Surrey entirely filled with emblems of mortality. In one grove
you might behold an angel sounding the last trump, and in the
foreground a pyramid falling to pieces, displaying the corpse
casting aside the shroud, and rising through the fragments of
the tomb. Pass on through this gloomy avenue, and you would
meet the skeleton with his hour-glass, shaking his dart at the
unbeliever, who trembles with dismay. Go further, you enter a
Gothic fane, over whose portal is the funeral raven, bearing in
his beak the scroll of summons to the grave. Enter now the
fabric, and you hear the clear sharp sound of the clock bell. The
minute elapses, and it strikes again, and again, and again, each
stroke succeeding its predecessor just as the vibration is fading
into silence; and so it continues day and night, and night and
day, and you admire the dial-plate around which are inscribed
the texts and scrolls teaching you to redeem time, and telling
you that "the best portion of our existence might be employed
in the preparation for eternity." Trite as the visible objects in
this retirement may have been, they could hardly have been
contemplated with indifference; but the company of this incessant speaking monitor would, as it should seem, be more than
sufficient to subdue the strongest brain. And who was the
ascetic by whom the scene was planned and the machinery
framed? It was the celebrated Jonathan Tyers, Ned Shuter's
patron, and Nan Catley's protector, the original inventor and
first proprietor of Vauxhall Gardens, who, after managing his
concerts and cascades, his ridottos and coloured lamps, from
Monday till Saturday, retired regularly to his before-described
hermitage at Denbies every Sunday.

Alan, being, as I observed, in this state of mind, he occupied
himself accordingly. He talked a great deal about the necessity

of making his will, and had a great deal of conversation with
the parson. It did not, however, come to anything, and this
strengthens the presumption that all his devotional charity had
been exhausted by the donation, *inter vivos*, to Brother Barnaby,
on behalf of the Austin Friars, of part of the cast-off wardrobe
of the late Dame Alice. Alan, however, went to work more
earnestly upon his tomb, which still exists, though sorely dilapi-
dated, in West Walsham chancel.

People now alive, I have heard, can well recollect when this
monument, now exhibiting a mutilated effigy of a knight in full
armour, his shield exhibiting the bearings of the Clares of Swaffham, was half concealed by the pews—erections as unsuitable
to the character of the Christian temple as they are deformities
to its architecture. Two ragged hassocks, a trestle, the grate,
and part of the iron chimney of a stove, a broom worn to the
stump, and the broken frame, which whilom contained the
prohibited degrees, were heaped up beneath the arch, which was
used as a lumber-hole. The figure and all the sculpture were
completely covered by the repeated coats of whitewash, which
indeed almost obliterated their outline. This is now entirely
removed by the care and labour of a learned East Anglian
antiquary, who fully indemnified himself by carrying off from
the church every article of *virtu* in his line which could be
abstracted by means of his own dexterity and half-a-crown to
the sexton. The brazen fillets which had not yet been purloined
by the preceding officials he ripped up out of the stones. The
few quarries of stained glass which had escaped the staff of
[William] Dowsing, consisting of a crowned initial of the virgin
and the upper half of the tub containing the three clerks of
St. Nicholas, he did pick out of the leads, and having by means
of a crowbar slipped aside the slab of Alan's tomb, he did plunge
into the depth, and he groped and grubbed and grubbed about
amidst the earth and the dust and the rubbish, in full expectation that he should be well rewarded by the precious discovery
of a nouche or a sword-hilt; but, unlike his friend Gough, under
similar circumstances, he could not find even the joint of a
finger-bone to carry off as a trophy. At first he suspected that
the president, to whom he had confided the secret of his intended
exploration, had been there before him. Had the matter been
so, the retaliation would have been fair, for he had done the
like to the president. But they had good reasons for not falling
out (the initiated will understand me); and if they had known

as much about Alan's history as I do, they would have saved themselves the trouble, for the tomb was destined to become a cenotaph.

"Let me look at our stock of bacon," exclaimed Alan, early in the morning of the twentieth day of July in the year 1282. Fresh and clear was the air, the cocks were crowing, and Alan and his son Gilbert had not yet begun their accustomed substantial breakfast, therefore there was nothing in itself very singular in Alan's proceeding; yet there was an appearance of unusual solemnity about him, and when he had carefully examined the flitches, it was observed that he selected the smallest of the lot, which certainly did occasion some remarks; he then went into the stable, and walking gloomily up and down, he pointed to his very worst nag, a long-tailed pony, and told his groom that he wanted "Snail," for such was the beast's significant name, in the course of the day; lastly, he went up into his store loft and brought down a sack of leather, to which a broach or small spit was appended.

The reason of these preparations may be briefly told. Edward, whose plans for the subjugation of the last remnant of the ancient royalty of Britain were now fully matured, had declared war against the helpless Llewelyn, alleging, as the justifying reason for the invasion, the violations of the allegiance resulting from the feudal law by which the principality was held. When the declaration was promulgated, it excited much comment in one respect, because the term of "feudal law" had never yet been heard in England. It was perfectly strange, as indeed it always was in this country, never having found a place in any common-law document or in any English text-book whatever. But the concurrent summons which commanded all the king's lieges, owing any military tenure, to attend the muster at Chester with horses and arms and all their service, afforded a sufficiently intelligible commentary upon the terms employed. The fact is, that Edward was proceeding with a singular degree of policy, which may be called disingenuous, but which had yet a foundation in something like consistent principle—"Cæsar never did wrong but with just cause." Why did Shakespeare obliterate this verse, though so severely censured by the critics of his day?—it is as easy to be understood as it is difficult to be construed. The dependence of the sovereigns of the Scots and of the Cymry upon the imperial crown of the successors of Egbert was incontestably the same as that which

had bound the vassals of the Carlovingian sovereigns. But the
consistent form into which these relations had been moulded by
the skilful jurists of Lombardy had not been introduced into
England. And the claim which all Christendom would have
acknowledged as just, if preferred against a duke of Brunswick
or marquis of Moravia, might have been represented as in the
highest degree unjust if urged against a dependent of the English
crown. With these matters, however, our friend Alan did not
trouble himself; like most persons, he was perfectly well
acquainted with all the law which related to his own concerns,
which, of course, implies not merely the knowledge of the laws
he ought to obey, but also of knowing how to sail as near the
wind as possible in evading the law; and just as the banker
contrives to dispense with the mortgage stamp, and the maltster
to get on the blind side of the exciseman, even so did Alan, like
the other military tenants of the crown, understand, by good
practice, how they could reduce the amount of the aid claimed
by their sovereign to its scantiest amount, and yet without
coming within the grasp of the exchequer—a court which,
unlike most other human institutions, appears unaffected by old
age, and not to have lost the slightest degree of the strength of
its grip since the reign of the Norman conqueror. The military
sergeanty, then, by which the manor of West Walsham was
held, was, according to the *Testa de Nevill*, to be performed
upon a horse worth half a mark, with a "sack and broach, and
a flitch of bacon, for forty days, and until the tenant should
have eaten the bacon, when he was to be entitled to return."
All the duties he performed so nearly to the letter, that when
he appeared before the constable at the muster at Rhuddlan,
much as that great officer of war and state was displeased, and
not without reason, at the inadequacy of his equipments, he
found it impossible to fix the lord of West Walsham with any
positive default so as to establish an amercement. It was more
than doubtful whether "Snail" would have produced the sum
for which he was to be valued; but Alan contended that he
had been worth as much in Norfolk, and that if the king chose
to fight so far away beyond the shires, he (Alan) was not bound
to answer for the deterioration occasioned by the journey. With
respect to the bacon, no dimensions had been described; and
with respect to the "sack and broach," as the constable himself
was in perfect ignorance of what service was to be performed
with these implements, no cavil concerning them could be well

raised. Much discussion also arose as to whether the services
were accumulative—that is to say, whether the service of forty
days was to commence after the flitch had been devoured, or
whether the consumption of the food might not be performed
within the term; and the matter was compromised by Alan
assenting to the proposition of continuing in the king's pay and
wages during the remainder of the campaign.

Alan was no coward, and without doubt he would have
fairly earned his meed; but he was not destined to die by the
edge of the sword. Longshanks had thrown a great raft or
floating pontoon over the water at Conway, and Alan unfortunately slipped through the planks, like the personages in the
Vision of Mirza, that admirable specimen of allegory of the
golden age of English literature. This untoward accident was
the proximate cause of Alan's death. But John the Taverner,
who had been most unwillingly "elected," or, in plain English,
compelled, by the constable of the township to march as one of
the "six thousand able-bodied men, between the ages of sixteen
and sixty," directed to be raised for the county of Norfolk,
reported that it was all owing to Squire Alan's having apostatized
from real English drink. On the fatal day he had indulged in
such abundant draughts of sweet metheglin and potent cwrw,
that his centre of gravity had ascended from his rump to his
poll, and thus betrayed his footsteps into the rush of waters
below.

CHAPTER II.

FEUDALITY.

(Edward I.-II.)

It was the opinion of the erudite Matthew Bramble, as recorded in his literary correspondence, published by the once popular writer to whom the sobriquet of "Smellfungus" was not ill applied, "that the historical philosophers of his day had most unduly extended their speculations with respect to the feudal system, and, indeed," continues he, "I expect that even the fashion of wearing trunk-hose and fardingales will be ascribed to this potent and pervading cause."

Even now, perhaps, the notions generally prevailing respecting the institutions thus denominated are hardly more precise, amounting to a vague notion that, when combined with chivalry, it rendered human life a bright, gay transparency. Knights employed solely in true love and fighting, pages clad in silk, and damsels waving white handkerchiefs in their whiter hands: a realisation of poetry, and imparting a general tone of bravery and sentiment to the community. Others take the opposite extreme. Your radical considers the system as the origin of every institution which opposes the progress of liberal opinions. Every opinion which has been transmitted to us from the olden day is considered the offspring of this feudal monster, from whom the still more hideous portent of "church and state" has lineally descended. Ask the radical mayor, when presiding in the council of the borough, redolent of tobacco and reeking with municipal reform, how he has been released from the golden chain and denuded of the scarlet gown, and he will answer, with exceeding satisfaction, that the march of improvement has cast aside those rags and fetters of feudality.

The fair and philosophic priestess of democracy calls upon us to execrate the "feudality of Virginia"—bless the mark!— yet even these expressions may be excused when we recollect that, in a work considered as a great standard authority, we are taught that the perpetual rapine and anarchy, originally arising from the "feudal state," received its happy correction from the spirit of chivalry—chivalry, of which valour, humanity, courtesy, and justice were the characteristics—chivalry, the cheap defence of nations, from which arises the three chief circumstances which distinguish modern from ancient manners, "the point of honour," the refinements of gallantry, and the humanity which accompanies all the refinements of war.

As I wish to act tenderly towards my readers, I will spare them the greater portion of the dark ages, and content myself with remarking that, as far as relates to feudality itself, it had become rather an institution of peace than of war amongst the Barbarians who absorbed the great fourth monarchy, continuing its succession, now perhaps expiring unto our own age. It is almost disheartening to find how the prestige arising from the names of those ancient nations passes away as we approach them; and that, for instance, a contemporary of the Burgundians describes them as good, dull people, who principally got their living by hiring themselves out as carpenters, a trade in which they were well skilled.

Upon this point, and many others, why should I be thus modest? I could explain myself most clearly, if folks would not be scared by the abstruseness of which I am so unjustly accused. They say I use hard words—hard words, forsooth! Have we not the irrefragable authority of the very first page of Entick's New Spelling Dictionary, teaching to write and pronounce the English tongue with ease and propriety, price two shillings and sixpence, bound in sheepskin, that "abacus," "abaddon," "abba," "abduct," "abeb," and "abracadabra" are all integral elements of our vernacular language; and if so—and who can gainsay it?—am I to presume that any man, woman, or child, in this enlightened age of penny magazines and penny cyclopædias, can possibly require that the term *emphyteusis* should be explained? or who ought to be ignorant that, without attending to particularities, it implied, according to the civil law, a species of contract not unlike a lease, by which the one party, who possessed the land, granted to another the enjoyment thereof for a specific period, upon certain engagements and stipulations; a conditional property which ceased if the conditions were violated, or when the term for which the grant had been made expired. If I add, that from the term Emphyteusis, the well-known word "feud" is derived, all those who are skilled in the

mazes of etymology will admit that the road is at least somewhat
clearer than that described in the epigram by which Ménage
gained so much celebrity :—

> Alfana vient d'equus, sans doute,
> Mais il faut avouer aussi,
> Qu'en venant de là ici,
> Elle a bien changée sur la route.

In fact, the real aspect of feudality is lost to those who
consider it as a mere military institution, and who, whenever
they see a ruined dungeon or tower, consider it as the catholic
monument of the tenure by which the baron held his power.
Unquestionably the land itself may in the first instance have
been won by the sword and defended by the lance, but the main
characteristics lie deeper; and the most pervading influence
exercised by the system of tenures, at least in England, resulted
from the opposite working of two antagonistic principles, both of
which were, at one period, equally embodied in the practical
jurisprudence of the middle ages. It seems, indeed, as if the
progress of human society necessarily depended upon the opposing
influences of antagonistic principles, and unless this dualism
exists, the result is the total absence of all moral vitality.

The law of the "fief" or "feud"—I use the term as conveying an intelligible and definite idea—was, that whenever or
howsoever the period for which the feud had been granted was
vacated or expired, it fell back, or escheated, as the lawyers say,
to the overlord, from whom it had been obtained; and then,
if previously granted for the life of the tenant, it would lie in
the lord's lap until it was taken up again, leaving the kindred
of the deceased entirely in the power of the superior.

The feeling, on the contrary, which the people embodied in
every act and thought was diametrically opposed to the feudal
law. Popular opinion taught that there was no one thing which
belonged to any ancestor that could be justly taken away from
his kindred; not, indeed, imparting a right guided by any very
precise rule of inheritance, but that, having once been in the
blood, in the blood it must remain. Thus the great offices of
state became hereditary in families as naturally as the tree grows
in the soil. If there had been a House of Commons in those
days, the important office of whipper-in of the treasury bench
would have become as noble a grand seigniory as that of earl
marshal; and the silver-mounted instrument of flagellation,
recently presented by the grateful pack to the highly respectable

functionary who fulfilled the duty so much to their satisfaction, would have been as proud an heirloom in the family of Bill Holmes as the baton in that of the family of the Howards.

Whatever you held, station, duty, office, or land, entitling you to any honour or profit, was, according to the universal feeling, to appertain equally to your children. If, elucidating my positions by modern symbols, you wore either an epaulette or a shoulder-knot, every babe of yours would be born with the germ of the ornamental appendage, to be developed as occasion should arise. And it must be further observed that, as a consequence deduced from this principle of inheritance, it was so extensive that every usurpation or usage, custom or courtesy, necessarily grew into a right. Sir John Bumpsaddle's country would have become his "free warren," and the heirs of the Waterloo heroes would, until the latest generation, have become entitled to apply to the court of king's bench for a *mandamus* to compel every future Duke of Wellington and lord of Strathfieldsay to invite them to dinner at Apsley House, on the eighteenth day of June.

Now in the earlier stages of this feudal tenure, whilst it scarcely was doubted that, as a matter of law, the land reverted to the lord upon the death of the beneficiary, yet, in obedience to the general feeling, it scarcely ever happened that in practice a renewal of the grant was refused to the heir.

However precarious the estate of the tenant was, and it frequently received the denomination of *precaria*, because the heir was forced to pray for its renewal, yet, practically speaking, the renewal gradually became more and more certain. In some cases the refusal to admit the next heir would have been so discordant to the prevailing feeling, that the lord could not encounter the general odium; in others, a stranger would not dare to provoke the vengeance of those who deemed themselves unjustly denied their ancestral right; so that at a distant, though perhaps not entirely undefinable, era, the Teutonic feeling of inheritance gained in many cases the victory over the Roman law.

But, on the other hand, when the hereditary principle was fully recognized, the lord, in England at least, might virtually have often defeated it. When the son came to take up the barony, the king might ask any sum he thought most reasonable or unreasonable, and the relief demanded by the exchequer might be such as entirely to prevent the heir from redeeming the territory out of the powerful hand into which it had been seised. It is quite evident that by this process the sovereign, if he had been strong enough, might have annulled the right of inheritance, and dealt with the soil of the realm as his own, and, upon the death of each vassal, have transferred the land to the highest bidder in the market; and viewing him as a mere landlord, there is not much doubt but that he ultimately would have considered the land simply as a source of revenue and annual gain.

But the great landholders were too many for his majesty. And the clause in the great charter which provided that the king should exact no more than the accustomed sum gave the tenant an indefeasible inheritance, subject only to the chance of a little extra extortion, when any decent opportunity or pretext for squeezing should arise.

That military service was, at an early period, one of the prices paid for the land is unquestionable; and it was apportioned according to a rude estimation of value. As much as would maintain or keep a knight was called by the Anglo-Saxons his "living," and the Norman probably rendered the system nearly universal; but in what manner the service was imposed or the "fees" lotted out, we cannot pretend to decide, since, in the reign of Henry III., the treasurer of the exchequer informs us that scarcely any information was preserved. At a more recent period, nay, in the next following reign of Longshanks, when Alan de Clare saved or lost his bacon, military service, such as it was, became practically unavailing. It does not appear that the crown could compel the services of the lieges beyond the limits of the realm. "Sir earl, you shall either go or hang," might be the threat of Edward; but, "Sir king, I will neither go nor hang," was the ready reply; and so the dialogue ended. Taken at its utmost worth, the quarantine of service was quite inadequate to any efficient operations; the feudal muster, just adequate to a foray, could not be kept together for a campaign; and the whole scheme became simply a mode of raising a branch of the revenue which the sovereign and his officers transacted in partnership, though not entirely upon equal terms, he taking the largest share of the odium, and they the largest share of the gain.

During the absence of his father, Gilbert exercised the duties, and therefore claimed all the privileges, of the master of the family. As such, he had privately given a cordial invitation to Tappetankarde, the minstrel, who, as soon as the "governor" had departed to Wales, constantly reappeared in the hall, and became the constant companion of the bachelor, whose bounty he enjoyed.

That "all who live to please, must please to live" is a truth of perpetual endurance; and, indeed, in one guise or another, it may perhaps be asserted that the noble art of catching pennies constitutes the rationale of social existence. As for Tappetankarde, he would have ill sped if, when the tambourine was struck in vain, and a dull ear was turned to his squeaking viol, he had not found some other means of ensuring patronage. There was no game, whether of strength or dexterity, chance or combination, in which he was not a proficient.

Whether Gilbert chose quoits or nine men's morris, bumble-cap or shovel-board, the minstrel was equally ready to encounter him, with so much cleverness as would have ensured gaining the game, and so much tact as always enabled him to lose it, when a due attention to his young patron's brow informed him that it was expedient to cede the victory. In particular, Tappetankarde was a great proficient in the noble recreation invented, as it is weened, by Palamedes, at the siege of Troy, and in which, as wise men insisted in ancient days, so much state-craft was included.

Certainly, when we consider the proceedings of the shrewd and solemn statesmen of the old times, the white-headed, moustached men who sat in council, dressed in slashed velvet, around a tapestry-covered table, their caution and care, when they discussed and considered the possible consequences of every act of politics and policy, we do become impressed with the opinion, that so long as the *ragione di Stato* was taught as a science, they always felt they were playing a deep and responsible game; and so they were; for, if they failed, their heads might, and occasionally did, become the stakes which were forfeited by their want of skill. Yet with all my respect for antiquity, I cannot think they were truly wise. They acted on the principle that every man had his price, by which, when found, every human being could be moved as precisely as the pieces on the board. The politician admitted that he might err in his calculations, but he never doubted but that, could he discover the real data, entire certainty would ensue. Not thus could they succeed. The wisdom of man is perpetually defeated by the inscrutable order of human affairs, modifying or annulling schemes by contingencies which no foresight could anticipate, and by influences which no subtlety could analyse.

In our own days, statesmen go into the other extreme, prognosticate nothing beyond the next division, and provide for nothing excepting quarter-day. Their *ragione di Stato* is a game of hazard, trusting to merely the spin of the ball or the chance of the die.

The happy medium might be, perhaps, better learned from the ancient British game, so appropriately termed "Vachgammwn," or the miniature war, converted by a slight alteration into "backgammon"; and in which the whole course of the tables being directed by chance, the skill of the players is shown by the ability with which they avail themselves of the favourable cast or struggle against their adverse destiny.

Gilbert, being anxious to improve himself in chess, had, for nearly a whole week, kept Tappetankarde so steadily at the campaigns of the black and white armies, that Tappetankarde, acute as he was, began to feel himself somewhat in the condition of the Scotch courtier, who, when asked by King James to measure with him, could not make out whether His Majesty wanted to ascertain whether he was the taller or shorter of the two. On the Wednesday, therefore, Tappetankarde, having twice given checkmate to Gilbert, found himself placed at dinner below the salt. Tappetankarde was not proud, no, not he, and he would have cared but little for his position, had it not been accompanied by the more palpable inconvenience of a vast inferiority of cheer, neither claret nor hippocras ever circulating in the antarctic hemisphere. On Thursday, he endeavoured to remedy his blunder, by allowing his queen to be captured, when he had his five best pieces in command; but, tinker-like, in attempting to mend one hole he had made two, for Gilbert, exclaiming with much vexation, "Do you take me for a mawkin?" swept the whole array off the squares, and with so much ire, that Tappetankarde was in no small fear lest, like Ganelon, in the romance, his head might be broken by the fated board. If the truth must be told, Gilbert was out of sorts. He was in the worst of all possible humours, he was cross and could not tell why. All the whole time he was playing the last game, he felt that strong and inexplicable impression of the approach of a stranger, which might perhaps induce us to deduce the anticipation from the theory of animal magnetism, if we could be quite sure whether at least as many instances have not occurred to us in which the presentiment has been forgotten, by reason of its having proved insignificative, as remembered

14—2

in consequence of its having been fulfilled. In this instance the event was too important to be ever effaced from Gilbert's memory, for the foreboding was ever bright and vivid during the remainder of his life, inasmuch as a short and slender, grave, yet babbling personage, wearing the well-known—too well-known—furred robe, the livery of the legal officers of the Crown, —I use the term, of course, in its ancient sense of sergeanty, or official service,—entered the chamber, and without a "by your leave" or "with your leave," forthwith called in his myrmidons, and commanded them to take possession of the "capital tenement" of the lordship, which had escheated to the Crown by the decease of Alan de Clare.

"As for you, my fine bachelor, you, who are the only son and heir," continued he, turning to Gilbert, and attempting to suit his action to the word, "I seize you also as an infant, and thus falling within the royal prerogative of wardship and livery." I say "attempting," for although no resistance was offered by him who was the minor in the law, still it was irresistibly ludicrous to see the worthy escheator, with a visage of the size and colour of a turnip, and a body standing upon a pair of legs slender as those of a cock-sparrow, professing to seize the brawny, full-limbed "infant" glowing with health and vigour, beneath whose armpit he could have passed, walking bolt upright as under the portal of an arch.

"What is this?" exclaimed Gilbert, equally stunned by the intelligence of the loss of his parent and excited by the arrest thus attempted to be made of him; and to these must also be added, and enhancing them in no inconsiderable degree, the still subsisting vexation arising from his suspicion that Tappetankarde had treated him like a child in the chess game; for so strangely are our minds constituted that, even under the greatest sorrow, it will often happen that some miserable, petty, present trouble stands for the moment almost on the same level with the heaviest affliction.

"What is this—I an infant? Why, there is not a man in the township whom I cannot throw, a horse which I cannot ride, a corslet which I cannot wear, a battle-axe which I cannot wield!"

"Maugre all these proofs of manhood and discretion, your honour is yet an infant in the eye of the law. It is true that the heir of the burgess is esteemed of full age when he can tell twelve pence, measure an ell of cloth, beget a child, or do such and the like bits of business as shall prove he is fit for his calling;

but as for the heir of him that holdeth in chief, were you as stalwart as Guy of Warwick or Bevis of Hampton, you are still but an infant in the eye of the law, until you attain twenty-one years of age, all reckoned and told until the midnight of the last day."

"And so I am," roared Gilbert de Clare, "full twenty-one years, full and complete last Barnaby bright." "It is by the jury," replied the escheator, "that the fact will be declared." And speedily did he carry his threats into effect, for that great engine of justice and injustice, which has been equally the means of protecting and betraying the free-born Englishman, was now immediately called into full activity. The complete panel, the awful twelve, who had followed close upon the heels of the escheator, now trooped into the apartment, and the oath being administered, all strangers, under which denomination Gilbert was cruelly included, were desired to withdraw.

"John Reeve, John Reeve," exclaimed Gilbert, "do go haste fetch dear old Mabel, who nursed me; surely her testimony will defend me from this thraldom." And John was about to start, when one of the officials informed him that her testimony could not be admitted in this stage of the proceedings, the inquest-men were the witnesses for the king, and he the escheator had carefully chosen them, but that after "office found," he might then, when he thought it advisable, produce his testimony in the chancery to prove his majority.

Gilbert could not well understand the justice of this course, but it was unnecessary to continue the discussion, for out came the inquest, who had fully performed their duty, by declaring Gilbert de Clare, the only son and heir of the said Alan, deceased, was then of the age of seventeen years or thereabouts, by reason whereof the wardship of his body and the custody of his lands appertained to our sovereign lord the king. So short a time had elapsed between the enclosing the jury and the production of their inquisition, very fairly written in "court letters," upon stout parchment, that it might have appeared to a bystander as if the document had been brought ready engrossed from the chapel of the Master of the Rolls, and that the enthralment of Gilbert, and the seizure of his property, had been settled beforehand.

In ancient times, such compendious modes of proceeding were not uncommon; the pithy memorandum under the Tudors, "the abbot of Glastonbury to be tried and hanged," preceded the special commission; the instructions were carried into effect, and the operations performed. Under the Stuarts, the traitor was "begged" and the grant promised without much apprehension of an undutiful acquittal; and it required no vast share of prescience to foresee the fate of the "protestant joiner," if tried at Oxford, or of the Jesuit if tried in Guildhall. I must not advance into more recent eras, and retreating, as fast as I can, from the court-house in Kilkenny and the committee-room in Westminster, I shroud myself in mediæval darkness. With respect to our friends at West Walsham, it was soon afterwards known that John le Taverner, who had faithfully trudged all the way from Wales, for the purpose of conveying the intelligence to Holmby, having chanced to linger in the vicinity of Beeston, was kindly invited by Sir Hugh de Ingham to enter the castle, where he was instantly seized and cast into what he afterwards designated a horrible dungeon. Full fathom five below the surface of the soil it certainly was, but the short stone staircase by which you descended or ascended, and of which the door had fallen off the hinges, led through a rising range of chambers successively occupied as cellar, butlery, larder, and buttery, and the latter being tenanted for the nonce by a buxom "deystere," who came to look after the cheese, the confinement was not perhaps much more irksome to the prisoner than the cooping of a free and independent Norwich elector at the present day. The week of John le Taverner's detention enabled Sir Hugh de Ingham to be the first bearer to the exchequer of the intelligence that a wardship had fallen in.

Having thus taken Old Time by the forelock, Sir Hugh's diligence brought him home again in sufficient time to make such arrangements with the under-sheriff as enabled him to take the station of foreman of the jury; and before the close of the following day, Sir Hugh produced his letters patent, by which the wardship and minorage of the said Gilbert de Clare was duly granted to him for his advantage and benefit; and without rendering any account or reckoning for the same to any other person or persons whomsoever.

The law gave to the guardian so appointed the most unlimited right of using, or misusing, the property thus entrusted to his care, and in the place of the anodyne practice grounded upon an "amicable suit," and administered by the attorney—whereby it not unfrequently happens that a thousand pounds is expended, in a "reference to the master," in order to decide whether the allowance for the infant at school shall be one hundred and forty-seven pounds ten or one hundred and fifty— was substituted the more summary plan of jobbing both ward and estate, by what carpenters usually call "rule of thumb." A very good rule, however, and often better than an ocean of book learning.

Under these circumstances there was some degree of courtesy on the part of Sir Hugh de Ingham, who was sufficiently good-tempered in the main, permitting Gilbert to continue as tenant under his own roof, though of course not as his own master. It will hardly be considered, however, as an unfair requital for this indulgence, if Gilbert, as soon as he was left to his own devices, began very earnestly, with the assistance of John the Reeve, to endeavour to procure such evidence as might enable him to proffer his *probatio aetatis*, and thus redeem him from his thraldom. I do not know what Crabbe could have done, had he lived in the reign of Edward the First; but I do know what he could not: he could not have written his *Parish Register*, because there were no parish registers; and the only mode by which proof could be afforded was by a separate examination of the witnesses, who bore the fact in their memory, being the only case, be it observed, in which such a proceeding was allowed by the Common Law.

The synchronisms by which Gilbert intended to support the evidence of his witnesses were the calf with eight legs and the great storm. With respect to the first, Gilbert, to his great dismay, could not find that, though all the old men had heard of the monster, it had ever been seen by any one at all. This, I must confess, has been pointed out to me as a woeful impeachment of the veracity of my chroniclers, or at least as exhibiting such an example of credulity as would deprive them of all respect in this enlightened age. A good friend, therefore, advised me at all events to deal with the calf just as the British Association did with the four-eyed fish from Surinam, which they swallowed first and sunk afterwards, greatly to the edification of all who obtained cognizance of the affair. But I could not venture to imitate this example, and so the matter must stand. As to the storm, Gilbert was more successful. Losinga had been duly restored to his pristine honours; and, as the expenses occasioned by the damages had firmly impressed themselves upon the memory of the old prior, our youth had no difficulty in obtaining an assurance that his testimony would be given on that score;

but this was only half the battle, for it was needful to connect this event with Gilbert's appearance in the world, a fact not quite so notorious as its concomitants. Gilbert, therefore, forthwith directed his course to the cottage of his old wet-nurse, dear old Mabel, who still retained the greatest and in some respects most unfortunate fondness for him. She had always called him her boy, which was well enough as long as he was an urchin; but, in proportion as her intellect began to fail, she never could persuade herself that he had grown older. As he entered, she patted him on the cheek, kissed him, and inflicted other similar endearments, to which he submitted with entire resignation; but when she, with great affection, brought out a whipping-top and three apples, which she had carefully put in store for him, he found it useless to persevere with his interrogatory, and returned home in despair of avoiding his impending destiny.

According to our feelings, the most galling badge of servitude to which the villein had become liable was the law which restrained him from giving his daughter in marriage without the assent of his lord. The burden at least was equally imposed, for, as I have already intimated, the infant heir was liable to the same slavery. Magna Charta was no charter of liberties to him; the only provision it contained being that he or she should be married without disparagement—that is, to a person equal in station; but with that qualification, whether brown or fair, short or tall, the youth or the maiden, as the case might be, was compelled to rest entirely satisfied. With widows the case was still harder. Until the relict had attained the mature age of sixty years, no excuse would avail; and in one of our earliest Treasury records the dames and damsels of the noblest families of England are inventoried together with the cattle and other beasts, sheep and pigs of their respective domains. It is very remarkable that the advance of civilization, so far from producing any mitigation of this real relic of barbarism, rather enhanced it. Under the guidance of our eighth Henry, the plan of fiscal management was improved; and until the final abolition of military tenures after the Restoration, the "marriages" of the wards, "regularly made" before the Master, with the approbation of the Court, constituted an important branch of the revenue of the Crown. Manners, however, are not to be altered so speedily as laws, and for a long time afterwards matrimony continued according to the old form, as much a matter of money as before. Roger North details, with steady gravity and complacency, the several bargains in this line begun, broken, and concluded by his great hero, the lord keeper; and the "marriage brokage," or the percentage due to the worthy representative of Sir Pandarus of Troy, by whom, in an honest way, the matter was negotiated, continued still to be paid, though under the rose, perhaps almost to the period when the empire of damasks and curls, hoops and full-bottom wigs, declined and fell.

Gilbert therefore had no choice, and Magdalen, the only daughter of Sir Hugh de Ingham, being neither above nor below the ordinary average of person and personability, he e'en took her, according to the old song or formula, "for richer for poorer, for better for worse"; and, having duly endowed her at the church porch, he acquired in his turn, in due time, the possessions which descended to William de Clare, who will soon appear—at least in kit-cat—in this my portrait gallery.

CHAPTER III.

GRIEVANCES.

(Edward II.–III.)

I SHALL begin with one of mine own, which haunts me more than I choose to say. Amongst the innumerable reasons which put me out of humour with the modern applications of science, and cause an incessant yearning in my mind after the simplicity of past times, is the manner in which some of the most beautiful objects are thereby utterly marred, ruined, extirpated, and destroyed.

Compare the king's high-road with the shareholders' road —the *Eisenbahn*, as it has been emphatically termed by the Germans, who are longing to inoculate their fatherland with all the poisons engendered amongst us by the fatal system which has produced our so-called commercial prosperity. What has the community gained by sacrificing the budding verdure of the hedgerow—the bank starred with the faint primrose or fanned by the tall spires of the honeysuckle—the transition from the forest shade of the overhanging oak and elm to the wide prospect from the summit of the sunny hill? Why, that we should be imprisoned upon a track, whose nicely-adjusted gradients either sink us to the bottom of a ditch or whirl us on the giddy summit of a tottering causeway, with smoke and clatter as the inseparable companions of our Lenore-like career. Upon the river, the white swelling sail is replaced by the sooty chimney, and the rhythmical cadence of the oar is changed for the hiss of the boiler and the grunt and groan of the safety-valve.

Perhaps, after all, the most beautiful of the living features of the ancient landscape was the water-mill. How pleasant it was to enjoy the sound of the fresh, rushing, gushing stream, broken into beads and threads of snowy silver, through which you viewed the huge heavy revolving wheel.

And let us here sit and contemplate the broken floats, the bright orange tints of the iron bands, the dark glaucous tresses of the humid confervæ depending from the timbers, and all the beauties resulting unsought, but not unseen, from all the accidents of time and tide. Contrasted with this whirling turmoil is the smooth, placid, glassy pond above, disturbed only at the very edge, from whence the hoarded element begins to ripple in its hastening flow.

Not long ago I took a walk with the intention of visiting such a favourite haunt in the neighbourhood of an ancient city, which, by the increasing wealth and continuous exertions of its inhabitants and rulers, is losing daily every feature of its ancient historical glories. The corporation pull down the gates; the paving commissioners destroy the cross; the justices—ill-luck to their worships!—"improve" the castle; and—unkindest hit of all—the dean and chapter restore the cathedral. In a town confessedly a *parvenu* your novelties, both moral and architectural, are at least in keeping; but in the old metropolis of an old bishopric they strike one with a feeling of painful incongruity which renders the glaring novelties still more grating to my mind. Well, as I continued my stroll, I came to a quiet bend of the rivulet, where I saw a youngster, fishing-rod in hand. Izaak Walton may expatiate upon the tender mercies of impaling the worm upon the hook, and physiologists may prove to their own satisfaction that fishes have about as much feeling as themselves, yet, stand on the brink of the Alpine lake, swarming with the beings which the teeming waters brought forth on the third day of creation, view their arrowy forms circling and darting through the element, in the full and vigorous enjoyment of their existence, and can we then believe that the dominion given to man over the animal race—our constant companions, whom we touch, and feel, and handle, but whose nature is as mysterious as that of the angels of heaven or of darkness—is to be employed in converting into wanton sport their agony and destruction? The poor ill-taught boy, however, was to be considered only as an object of pity; besides, his amusement had failed. I never angle myself, except for fame. Sometimes I get a nibble—a glorious nibble—but no bite; and Tom was evidently in the same plight, for his basket was empty; so, having on that score also a species of sympathy with him, I asked the cause of his want of success. "There used to be fish enough," said he, "when I first went to school, but the gas-works have poisoned them all!" I looked, and loathed the contaminated waters; and the sky, though the sun shone brightly, did not appear as clear as usual, when a flight of odd-looking insects, as it were, settled upon the sweet opening flowers of a hawthorn before me. "Look at the blacks," said Tom, "how they shower down when the wind sets this way. It is not to be wondered at if the May does not thrive."

Never was I less grateful to the "*amis des noirs*," and all the anti-slavery societies, than at this moment, inasmuch as the apparition of the sable visitants powerfully prepared me for the disappointment which I was to experience. On the site of the old water-mill stood a hideous pile of red bricks, flanked by two obelisks of dingy scarlet, vomiting forth the murky clouds which sullied the atmosphere, and working that gigantic power by which the old hydraulic machinery is for ever superseded. Possibly Ringleford Mills may let a great deal higher to the company than they did to the dusty miller; but I shall always sorrow for the water-mill, and wish myself in the days when corn was ground by stream, and not by steam.

I do not intend, though I could, to devote this whole chapter exclusively to mills. I cannot dismiss the subject without adding that, whenever I see a mill, it brings Adam Smith and his followers to my mind; for it appears to me that by the argument which we pick out of the hopper some of their most important definitions become undefined, or instead of being general and universal, are true only according to the aspect in which they are viewed. I believe that if I define *rent* as "a yearly sum which I pay out of my pocket, and which I don't receive," this definition will be found to be as generally applicable as "rent of land is that portion of the produce of land which remains to the owner after all the outgoings belonging to the cultivation are paid, including the ordinary profits of the capital employed." Possibly, if I am encouraged, I may come to rent by and by. But my business at present is concerning that which concerns everybody, to wit, wealth; and whether the term be, according to the opinions of the greatest leaders in the science, considered as meaning "the material products which are necessary, agreeable, and useful to man, and are not furnished by nature in unlimited abundance," or "the material objects necessary, useful, or agreeable to man, which have required some portion of human labour to appropriate or produce, the latter part of the definition being intended to exclude such material objects as air, light, and rain," we shall find an equal want of catholicity.

Light and air are "no sources of wealth," quoth the great

antagonist of population. The pilot who weathered the storm brought his notions to a better market than the philosopher. Pitt's *Works*, vol. i, vol. ii, vol. iii, vol. iv, chalked by the Jacobin upon the range of darkened rectangles, may be read as volumes which, without being opened, contain sufficient evidence to refute him. Thanks to the acuteness of the financier, the impalpable elements and the vibrating æther became as much government wealth as the hemp and tallow in Portsmouth dockyard; and if he had empowered the authorities at Somerset House to farm the window-tax, light and air would have yielded a rent as assuredly as the fattest land which ever was tilled. Wealth, then, at least that which constitutes wealth in the theory of the political economist, is merely the creation of the law. All human jurisprudence respecting property is but an amplification of the commandment "Thou shalt not steal"; and wealth is constituted by the right of exclusive enjoyment which the code of property bestows. It is not the capital and the labour which render the field the source of wealth, but the law which forbids even the king from reaping the corn; but let the ground be planted with tobacco, and the forfeited crop becomes the property of the exciseman. Wherever the penalties of the law can secure an exclusive possession, we find economic wealth; and this brings me back to the station from whence my cogitations arose, and which I will exemplify by the history of a noble Flemish family.

The Count of Flanders, having bestowed away all his domains and exhausted his treasury, gratified a faithful dependent by conferring upon him all the air of the country, which the grantee forthwith turned to the most profitable account, by forbidding the waving of the "woven wing" unless upon payment of a stated sum. Not a windmill could be built in Flanders unless licensed by him. Thus the courtier was enabled to bequeath a noble seigniory to his descendants, the *Molinaers*, whose "canting coat," canting and allusive—"*de gueules trois moulins-à-vent or*"— denotes the name which the lineage assumed. The privileges of the Abbot of St. Alban's, from which no inconsiderable portion of the wealth of the convent was derived, were to the same effect. By virtue of divers ancient patents and charters, he was owner of a soke mill, where alone it was lawful to grind the corn of the tenants of the manor. Though the breeze might blow, yet no one could avail himself of it for any purposes of work, unless the abbot sanctioned the employment; and thus he became lord and proprietor not merely of the air, but of the abstract right of grinding. Neither windmill nor horse-mill could turn within his seigniory, so stringently was the right of mulcture enforced, a right not entirely obsolete even at the present day.

Although my friends, the reviewers, have chosen to compare me to the knight of La Mancha, I am not sufficiently his emulator to break a lance in defence of this monopoly, which had ceased to become beneficial either to the owner or to the community.

There are some species of rights of property which are tolerated, or rather not tolerated, by those who are affected by them, with the greatest impatience and ill-will. This is not always in exact proportion to their pecuniary importance, but quite as often in consequence of their opposing some slight obstacle to personal convenience, and still more, if importing any species of inferiority.

I am not anatomist enough to be able to recollect the name of the duct which, joining each Eustachian tube, enables all useful truisms to go in at one ear and come out of the other. Be this as it may, no one travels out of our heads with greater velocity than the maxim which teacheth that affronts rankle deeper than injuries. And whatever may be construed as an affront, the nod unreturned, the "not-at-home," however fancifully, is a painful reality to those who are subjected to its influence.

The toll taken by the abbot was moderate, the "golden thumb" of the miller was neither better nor worse than the average touch of the fraternity; but the thirlage was, nevertheless, most odious to the unkindly townsmen of St. Alban's, who constantly endeavoured to evade it, and frequently with more success than they deserved. Like the Copts, who make a point of honour never to pay taxes till they are bastinadoed, the townsmen never would render suit and service to the mill without a "suffering," and every householder of St. Alban's who wished to retain his standing in society started his own handmill in defiance; and maugre the abbot and his seneschal, it seemed as if, night and day, the quern was turning.

The town, like many others of the same class, had grown up under the protection of the venerable abbey, dedicated to the proto-martyr of Britain. Strictly speaking, or according to the letter of the law, the great mass of the inhabitants were villeins, but their subjection was little more than nominal, except as to those rights of their lord from which direct pecuniary benefits were derived. Many merchants, as they were styled, great dealers in corn and grain and cattle, then dwelt in St. Alban's; and many flourishing masters and workmen in all arts and crafts appertaining to building, who derived much gain not merely from the encouragement offered by the monks in the erection of sumptuous edifices, of which the renowned "Abbey Church" is now the only relic, but by their good repute, which frequently caused them to be invited to execute fabrics in various parts of the realm. Like the men of Como, who, from the age of the Lombard kings to the works now performing in the Duomo of Milan, have displayed their hereditary architectural skill, so did the men of St. Alban's, who were eagerly sought in every part of England when any building was to be raised.

Well earned was their opulence, but riches beget pride. The length of their purses enabled them to oppose a regulated resistance to their superior, and they more than once, in the early part of the reign of Edward the First, contested the right of the abbot in a court of law. The plea was often tried; but in whatever shape the facts were pleaded, the case was so clear, that no inquest could hesitate for a moment in declaring the rights of the abbot; and therefore the townsmen were compelled to submit, yet very grudgingly; and every now and then, sometimes oftener in the year and sometimes seldomer, the seneschal made a seizure of an upper millstone, the convenient and summary mode of dismantling the rebellious machinery.

The year 1324 opened ominously; for on the first day of the week did the month of old Janus begin. "As sure as I am alive," exclaimed Eleanor, wife of Henry Grindcobbe, one of the most opulent "merchants" in St. Alban's, as she reckoned on and on to the end, tracing the notches in that venerable relic of antiquity, the log almanac, "Childermass falls on a Friday," —a conjuncture, according to popular notion, which boded to all mortals during the year a more than ordinary share of troubles and misfortune,—and whilst she was groaning, the abbot's bailiff, John Hathercombe, yclept also Holofernes, walked in.

Grindcobbe may have been originally a mere sobriquet, but after it had become an hereditary surname, which certainly was the case in the then present owner thereof, it still continued particularly pertinent and applicable. No reasoning would induce Grindcobbe to abandon his violation of the abbot's franchise: he would grind his handmill and make his wife whirl it; and the offending instrument stood so offensively prominent in the timber porch, that it would have required much more than an ordinary degree of forbearance on the part of the seneschal if he had refrained from vindicating the rights of the seigniory.

"A murrain seize you all!" exclaimed Grindcobbe, as soon as the bailiff, accompanied by two stout yeomen, had declared his errand. "Henry Grindcobbe," replied John Hathercombe, the surly bailiff, "you and your father before you have been warned again and again—ay, and you have smarted for your warning; and is it not your goodwife from whom I shall earn a guerdon? Are you not ashamed, you stingy loon, who are as full of money as an egg is full of meat, to set her to slave like a Scottish limmer at the quern, as you did last week, when you and your maid Madge went a-milking, and you kicked down the pail and laid it on the cow? You are voted to be a nuisance by everybody in the town, and out of it too, from my lord the abbot on the high dais to the cow-boy on the common; and now you have made yourself disagreeable to your wife, you fool, you." It is hardly necessary to observe that, by the vituperations, the bailiff neither consulted his own dignity nor facilitated the execution of his office, but he was thoroughly foul-mouthed, and if even he had not any good cause to exercise his faculty of objurgation, he was sure to make one, and on this occasion it must be confessed that the first provocation proceeded from his adversary. Grindcobbe turned pale with anger, but speedily recovering his outward composure, and placing his arms akimbo, insulting them by his attitude, and sparing them with his tongue, he left the officers in the full enjoyment of the booty, which they seized. Hathercombe and his assistants duly took up the upper stone, which they set upon its edge, like a wheel, and the slow progress of the little procession, as the sweating captors trundled the trophy, afforded full opportunity to the whole town to witness their triumph. True as it may be that a rolling stone gathers no moss, yet now it certainly did collect a wonderful crowd, who viewed the operation with all the sympathy with which the honest population of Deal or Dover contemplate an anker of Schiedam progressing, for His Majesty's benefit, to the custom-house upon the shoulder of the officer.

The spoil was now safely deposited in the abbey, but the excitement continued unabated; and the townsfolk continued loitering about the highways, with that kind of obscure appetite for some further stimulus, either in word or deed, which is so often the forerunner and the cause of popular insurrection.

Though in a very limited degree, this was very speedily afforded. The townsmen had by degrees thickened round the market cross, whilst on the topmost step of the base was stationed a short, thick-set, sturdy man, aged, but bitterly vigorous, girt with a very white apron, and holding a trowel in his hand, who, having been engaged in deep converse with a companion, now addressed the multitude.

"Oh, friends and neighbours all," exclaimed he, "and particularly ye who are my brethren and fellows of the craft, was it for the intent of countenancing such oppressions and grievances as we now groan under that the worthy knight St. Alban became the patron of the foul shavelings who now rule and lord it over the freemen of Verulam? No, no, no! Saint Alban loved the working-man, as did the wise heathen Greek philosopher, Peter Gower, before him. Peter Gower, friends, was almost a neighbour of ours, for although I do not well know whether he came much into this our county of Hertford, yet he was much at Cambridge, where he taught school, and a capital school it was, and Peter Gower's school-house is yet standing. And when I was young, I myself, being only a plain Lodgeman, built a new window in the upper storey, according to the last new fashion of our craft, with right handsome dividing munnions in the middle, as straight as my leg." Possibly the speech of Johannes le Lathomere, had he thus continued, would have afforded us much valuable information as to the history of Gothic architecture in general, and of the alterations sustained by the very curious building, still standing, and bearing the name of Pythagoras, in particular; but inasmuch as John's supporters were crooked, exactly in the shape of a pair of callipers, the simile by which he described his performance drew forth a loud laugh from a bevy of ruddy wenches close by—an explosion of mirth which, putting him rather out of sorts, brought him back again to his substantive theme. "Ay, my friends and brethren," resumed he, "Saint Alban loved the working-man; and as for us free-masons, how did the good saint cherish us? He was steward of the pagan king's household, and when he built the walls from whence were taken the bricks which strengthen yonder tower, he settled one pay of right good standing throughout the realm, he gave us free and accepted masons two shillings a week for our travail, and threepence a day for our cheer. Before that time, through all the land, a mason had but a penny a day and his meat, until St. Alban amended it."

"Certes," cried out another wight, John Spichfat, the

carpenter, who had hitherto listened with an air of gratified approbation, "I nowise gainsay all that St. Alban did for your craft, but did not glorious King Offa do as much for ours?"

"Nay!" vociferated Robin the Hellyer, "did he not also do as much for us, who tile the roof-tree, or who hew the balk, as for those who square the stone? It was for all of us who live by hammer and hand that King Offa granted his charter."

"Oft and oft hath my grandfather," cried out Grindcobbe, "told me that his grandfather well knew one Tokey Wigodson, whose great-grandfather's uncle by the mother's side had seen the charter in the treasury of the abbey. It was written on purple parchment; the golden letters shone like the stars, and the seal showed you the portraiture of King Offa in his royal robe, with a garland upon his head, all done by geometry, just like an emperor of the old Romans, upon the Onion pennies that the plough turns up in the field."

I must here pause. I do not wish to offer inscrutable difficulties to my admirers, and, perhaps, if I do not here give an explanation, which I beg to borrow or steal from my crony, my Stukeley, future ages might fail to discover that the appellation "Onion pennies," from a certain King Onion (no other than the British Eynon), was, and perhaps still is, the name given to Roman medals by the country folks in the places where such relics are usually found.

With respect to glorious King Offa, I may abstain from vouching for the authenticity of this charter, which, to the last, was firmly believed by the villeins to have been purloined or destroyed by the monks. Yet there is much which is very remarkable in the existing vestiges of the reign of this monarch, and by which he is distinguished amongst his compeers; his coins, for example, exhibit a singular style of art, differing entirely from that of his predecessors and successors. Rude as they may be, they are distinct imitations of Roman types; whilst his seal, the only one ever used by an Anglo-Saxon until the days of the Normanised Confessor, and appended to the grant by which Offa endowed the monks of Saint Denis, equally displays his effigy as an imperial sovereign. Loud applauses followed the speech of Hellyer or Tiler. John Coppethorn, not long since a competitor for the comfortable appointment of warrener to the abbey, but who had been defeated in his expectations by the superior interest of the nephew of the seneschal of the establishment, now took up his speech with increasing vehemence. "The strand and land, the wood and wold, by Offa's grant are ours. The hind and the doe, the buck and the roe. To us he did yield the beasts of the field, ours are they by his grant, and not to these proud losels do they belong." "Nay, more," now spake a priest, whose threadbare cassock bespoke him unbeneficed, "was it ever intended the beasts of the field, whom man tends not, or the fowls of the air, whom he feeds not, should be usurped by any one from the rest of human kind? To all were they given, to all do they belong." "It is all along," retorted the mason, in a voice of thunder, "of our not sending our burgesses to Parliament, as we did in the days of King Offa, so that we have no one to speak out for us in the great council of the realm."

The Curfew bell now began to sound from the several steeples and towers of the town. Being in the merry month of May, it was just at the turn of the twilight, and in almost an imperceptible moment the albescent amber glow, which marked the region of the departed sun, suddenly faded into darkness. The polled priest, for reasons best known to himself, suddenly beckoned to the mason, who, coming down from the stone cross, joined him; and no other speaker following, the crowd, after waiting awhile longer, began to disperse, and in a short time the streets were wholly cleared. Night advanced; various sounds, however, still continued to be heard, which, though significant of peace and tranquillity, showed that the inhabitants had not all yet ended their weary day. Here, as you passed by, might be distinguished the plash and bustle, indicating the operations of the mash-tub and the brewery. There, the bright light radiating above and below the door, and the clinking of the iron, indicated that the smith was forging the shoe for the steed of the early traveller. Further on you might listen to the low wailing of the infant, mingled with the mother's cradle lullaby; but all these gradually died away, as the pointers of the Great Bear turned upwards, until the silence of the night was made hideous by the shrill cries of a female voice ejaculating "Murder! murder! murder!" As is usual in such cases, the uproar speedily produced the protrusion of about a dozen heads through half a dozen casements, the said heads respectively belonging to the pairs who had been raised thereby from their respective rests and nests, provoked to the investigation much more by curiosity than by fear. "Bah! it is nothing but neighbour Grindcobbe beating his wife," said John le Pestour the baker, in a tone of disappointment.

"And if she were lapped in Morell's skin," replied John le
Tannere, speaking for himself and helpmate, the shrieks rising
sharper than before, "she would get no worse than she deserves.
It is a scandal thus to terrify the whole street for such a thing."
"I do not think the woman will have a whole bone left in her
body," grunted out another voice. "Will ye go down and see
to it, Master Constable?" "Nay, nay," replied this worthy
official, "I must not: I know the law. Every Englishman's
house is his castle. I dare not enter, excepting for felony or
breach of the peace; and Master Grindcobbe is entitled by
Magna Charta to beat his wife, provided the stick be not thicker
than his thumb; but if so be as how he beats his wife so as to
disturb his neighbours, then he is guilty of a breach of our by-laws,
and I will assuredly do my duty in proper time, and I will duly
present him at our Court Leet next Midsummer-day." All the
other interlocutors and interlocutoresses had by this time
abandoned Eleanor Grindcobbe to the whacks and the thwacks
of her affectionate helpmate, and the hearers being fully satisfied
by the explanation of the law, as given by the constable, their
pates dodged down, and left Goodman Grindcobbe in full
enjoyment of his crabstick and his fair Eleanor.

Such matters were then far too common in Saint Alban's to
occasion much remark, yet the gossips were, of course, desirous to
know the cause of the fracas, of which the facts lie in the compass
of the smallest nutshell that ever grew upon a hazel twig since
the days of Cassibelawn. The quarrel arose, then, from the
absence of Goodman Grindcobbe at the time when, according to
his ordinary domestic arrangements, he ought to have returned
home, an absence protracted till almost the witching hour of
night; so that when his wife unbarred the door, he was exposed
to a summary interrogatory, not delivered in the most gentle
tones, and, as is usual on such occasions, the inquiry assumed
a character which makes it perfectly intelligible why, in French,
the word *question* is synonymous with torture. Had he been
mellow, his evident transgression against the rules of sobriety
would have brought with it its own excuse, as well as its own
punishment. But he was provokingly sober, and therefore very
cross. Instead of informing his spouse where he had been
loitering, he defended himself by becoming the assailant, taxing
her with having given such information to the bailiff as led to
the seizure of the mill. Nettled and provoked equally by the
concealment and the charge, Eleanor rebutted his not unfounded

suspicion by a direct accusation, connected with Madge and the milking-pail, which I shall not repeat. Grindcobbe replied, using an expression which I shall not record, and the result was the tussle before described. Whether Grindcobbe was or was not justified in proceeding to baculation, I will not attempt to decide; but yet, as far as such an excuse can extend, I must be permitted to observe that, if prudence had permitted him (for who would trust a woman with a dangerous secret), he might at once have satisfied his jealous, anxious consort that her suspicions were unfounded. But what was the secret by which Grindcobbe's lips were thus sealed? It has been a matter of great consideration and anxiety with me; it kept me awake all last night, tumbling and tossing, according to the Homeric simile, like a black pudding on the coals, whether I should or should not expound the cause of Grindcobbe's absence from Curfew toll to midnight, which occasioned the catastrophe herein-before described. On the one hand, the exclusion of any further particulars thereof, in this my narrative, would be the result of the old maxim, "le sécret d'ennuyer est celui de tout dire," so often repeated to me by my dear grandmother, who, though I must confess I do not think she quite knew the meaning of the words, could repeat them as glibly as if they had been taught her when she was *en pension* in the convent at Rouen. But, on the other hand, I do not like to subject my readers to the gnawing of the perpetually excited appetite resulting from an unfinished story. Is there any one who, like Diggory, would not almost give his ears to know what it really was which befell John Grouse in the gun-room? And I believe that we almost owe a grudge to the memory of him who left untold the Tale of Cambuscan bold, for depriving us of the pleasure which, as we cannot help persuading ourselves, the completion of the legend would have bestowed.

CHAPTER IV.

THE COURT LEET.

WE have been so much accustomed to consider history as
a splendid melodrama, set to the sound of kettledrums and
trumpets, that even now, when they say that a "better-directed
spirit of inquiry" is arising, there is extreme difficulty in persuading the "enlightened" public—possibly you, my reader, may
be an exception—that it is often in the uninteresting details of
law and policy.that the mainsprings of national character are to
be found; and perhaps no institution has been more influential
than this very ancient tribunal, which interposed between the
lord and his vassals, and effectually placed the whole correctional
police in the hands of his tenantry—bond and free, sokeman and
villein, being invested with equal power, acting by their jury,
who had replaced the more ancient rulers of their tribes.

It was the business of the Leet to present all offences which
came to their knowledge and jurisdiction, and which could in
anywise disturb the community. The substantial crime of the
thief, and the imaginary transgression of the forestaller, the
vendor of unwholesome victuals, and the disseminator of false
news, were alike subjected to the summary jurisdiction of this
tribunal, which was considered as the main authority by which
local tranquillity was to be preserved. With respect to the
principle of the court, it may be made easily intelligible.
Instead of rendering that useful member of society, the common
informer, an object of opprobrium and contumely, it imposed
upon the responsible members of the community the duty of
bringing to justice all offenders, by making them liable to a fine,
if any offence was wilfully concealed; and thus, when the inquest,
upon the suggestion of old Shaw, the constable, presented our
friend Grindcobbe for the trespass of belabouring his wife, all
the odium of making the accusation evaporated when cast on
the collective community. "Put a fine of three shillings and
fourpence upon his head," exclaimed John Tibcroft, the
seneschal.

Grindcobbe, with exceeding wrath, called out, "What new grievance is this? Why am I to be singled out for punishment? Is it because of my principles that I am to be thus prosecuted? I alone to be restrained of the natural rights of a married man? This is the very crabstick," continued he, "with which I did chastise her, moderately, and as befitteth a husband. Look at it, measure it, Master Seneschal, is it a hair's-breadth beyond the size allowed by the usage and custom of old England?" "It is really only a thought larger than the thickness of Gaffer Grindcobbe's thumb," said John Shaw, in a kind of supplicatory tone, examining the stick with much attention, in order to ascertain whether it exceeded the standard by which, according to the Common Law doctrine, the instrument of domestic castigation was to be measured, the speaker being the only one present who appeared to have any sympathy with the offender.

"Well, Master Grindcobbe," now observed the seneschal, "and doth any seek to restrain you of the liberty which, if exercised in discretion, is as needful for the welfare of the State as for the comfort of the Englishman's fireside?—

> A spaniel, a woman, a walnut-tree,
> The more they are thrashed, the better they be.

But there is a time for all things, and you know full well that you might have done the needful upon your wife to your heart's content, if ye had but observed our ancient ordinance. It hath an excellent precedent for its father, the by-law enacted by their wise masterships of London: 'No man shall, after the hour of nine of the night from Lady-day unto Michaelmas, or after the hour of eight of the night from Michaelmas until Lady-day, keep any rule, whereby any sudden outcry or noise shall arise or continue, such as singing or revelling in his house, beating his wife, or otherwise, to the disturbance of his neighbours.'" And such, in sooth, was the real state of our jurisprudence. The discipline which the *Baron*, as he was technically called, could inflict, *licite et rationabiliter ex causâ regiminis et castigationis uxoris suae*, might be carried to any extent short of actual danger to life or limb, and when, and as often as he thought expedient, without any limitation or restriction, excepting in certain cities and towns, where the operation of beating wives was prohibited during the then ordinary hours of rest, for the same considerations of tenderness and humanity which have induced modern legislators to prohibit (under a penalty of forty shillings) the beating of carpets before seven o'clock in the morning, the reason being assigned in the words which I have actually quoted from the law.

Vexed as Grindcobbe was by the enforcement of this wise police regulation, he had speedily the compensation of seeing a far more stringent proof of the power and impartiality of the court exerted upon his old enemy, the bailiff, who, for various reasons, was anything rather than popular amongst the majority of the community. After disposing of a known harbourer of rogues and thieves, inflicting a fine upon a wealthy yeoman who had surcharged the common, and taking such notice of William Richards, the sheep-stealer, that before the following morning he had decamped from the town, a fourth name was heard. "We present Thomas Withernam, my Lord Abbot's bailiff," said the foreman of the jury in a slow and solemn voice, "as a common scold, and as such he must be adjudged to the ducking-stool."

"A sorry joke," exclaimed Withernam—"a sorry joke," yet at the same time looking somewhat disturbed. "No joke at all to me, Master Withernam," said the seneschal, "but a most unpleasant and painful duty; but it is our duty, and we must submit to the great sorrow which we sustain in being compelled to administer even-handed justice"; and whilst he was yet speaking, the jury rushed upon the unfortunate functionary, for the purpose of pinning him in the ducking-stool, in which many an excellent mistress of a family had sat before him, and which, pendent to the end of a swipe or lever, was placed imminent over the brink of a horse-pond. It was whilom the laudable custom of the House of Commons, when, at the opening of the new parliament, the Speaker was elected, that he should not merely disqualify himself by proclaiming his insufficiency, but that he should resist with all his might and main—a struggle carried on with so much vehemence that, if my memory serves me truly, it required half-a-dozen able-bodied county members to fix Onslow in the dreaded chair; and influenced by a much more sincere desire of escaping the honour did Withernam endeavour to disengage himself from the tormentors by whom he was surrounded. A violent plunge enabled him to shake off two or three of the more puny; and turning as much as he could of his countenance to the seneschal, who continued sitting with apparent affliction and imperturbable gravity—"Are ye all crazed?" he screamed out; "why, this is flat against the law."

"Hold!" exclaimed the seneschal, "bring our friend Wither-nam back again before the court. Against the law, sirs! If we abuse our franchise it will be seised into the hands of the crown; and now, friend Withernam, what is the point you raise?"

Withernam, quite comforted with the persuasion that the rough play rather abetted by his fellow functionary, the seneschal, was now at an end, and yet somewhat affronted, as well he might be, by having been rendered the object of such a game, now addressed the court with a sour sweet smile, saying, "Why, Master Seneschal, if ye will have me finish this sport in due form, ye know full well that, when ye make your entry upon the roll, the scold must be styled *communis rixatrix*—the law confineth the offence to the feminine gender; and how can I, Thomas Withernam,"—stroking, as he spake, a beard of decent magnitude,—"a man, and a man of worship too, be amenable to the punishment wisely reserved to the weaker vessel alone?"

"Sirs," said the seneschal, "in the law as laid down by the defendant I fully coincide—none but women are duckable; but the fact that defendant is not a woman, if such be the case, should have been specially pleaded. It should appear upon the record: it is not a fact of which the court can take judicial notice."

"Not take notice!" said the astonished culprit. "Don't you know that I am a man by the very sound of my name? Am I not known as Tom Withernam all the world over?"

"Certes," said the seneschal; "but how can the court raise the presumption that 'Tom' is a name necessarily implying that the bearer thereof is a man. It is certainly male in some instances—*exempli gratiâ*, Tom-cat; but it is also as certainly female, Tom-boy; and lastly, epicene or neuter, Tom-fool; and therefore who can take judicial cognizance to which of the three genders you belong? Not that I should wish to imply anything derogatory by these observations, but it is as a matter of argument these cases are cited."

"And is not my beard to testify for me?" exclaimed Withernam, with exceeding anger. "Many a woman hath a beard," quoth the seneschal, "and very good women too. And, sirs," turning to the jury, "the defendant hath alleged nought by which his plea can be sustained." In less than a minute the splash and plunge, accompanied by shouts of laughter, proclaimed that Withernam was visiting the depths of the abyss; and instantly he rose again, dripping like a water-god, though fuming like a volcano. The erudite Dr. Platt, who, in his rare and amusing history of Shropshire, hath figured the *brank* or mouth-piece by which the virago was restrained, considers it a more eligible mode of castigation than the ducking-stool, which, as he truly observes, sets the unruly member at liberty twixt every dip; and the unfortunate sufferer availed himself of this licence, for, "I will appeal to the Court of King's Bench, yea, even to the High Court of Parliament," spluttered Withernam, as soon as his head peered above water.

"Well and good," said the seneschal, who had advanced to the edge of the pond—"well and good, but execution is not thereby stayed; and there will be nothing to prevent your moving the Court of King's Bench next term to reverse the judgment." And the immersions having been repeated until the unfortunate diver was nearly exhausted, he was safely placed on shore and permitted to return to his home.

I am told by a *ci-devant employé*, who not long since filled an office of considerable consequence and importance, being, in fact, the individual denominated the "Court Newsman," that it is considered as one of the *arcana imperii* never to be divulged, that the main art in navigating the vessel of the state during her tempestuous voyage consists in knowing how to throw out tubs to the whale. This operation requires not only much judgment as to the time when you cast out the object upon which the monster is to exercise its sport or visit its fury, but also as to its nature. Sometimes a royal marriage will answer the purpose, a rumour of war, or a report of invasion; but in cases of real cogent necessity it has been long found that by far the best tub you can cast overboard is a minister—an operation which in despotic governments is generally performed by the commanding officer; whilst under constitutional governments it is most usually effected by the rest of the crew, the colleagues of the victim who is sacrificed for the good of the administration, if not for the community.

I shall not expatiate further upon this delicate subject, simply observing that it is to an application of this general principle that we are to ascribe the conduct pursued by the seneschal towards his fellow-functionary, the bailiff, which, without doubt, has already excited the curiosity of the intelligent reader; but the fact is, that the increasing tokens of popular discontent in St. Alban's had excited no small degree of anxiety in the "secretum" of the abbey. As the most active officer, Withernam was the most obnoxious to the townsfolk, and the seneschal therefore, not without forethought, willingly surrendered him to the somewhat distorted equity of the popular tribunal, which, as I have before stated, held a position in the borough not without analogy to that of the parliament in the monarchy of England. It was trusted that by this dexterous manœuvre the antipathy excited by the privileges of the abbey would be spent upon the person of him who had been the means of calling them into action, but with what success remains to be told in the pages of this our trustworthy history.

Thus have I disposed, and I hope satisfactorily, of one difficulty which had arisen; but I know as well as possible that a critical reader may have an inclination to inquire how it came to pass that, at a period so near to the time when my friend John Trafford truly spoke the sentiments of the county court, in declining to exercise the elective franchise, the inhabitants of a peddling borough should be so anxious to claim a right which the suitors of the shiremoot had so recently scorned. The solution is simply to be found in the fact that even then the tide was turning. As in the river the small narrow thread forced up from the estuary by the ocean-wave gradually widens and widens, displacing the still downward-flowing current, until the whole course of the fluid mass is changed, so is it with human affairs; and whilst one course of opinions may yet appear to prevail in the largest and most influential portions of the community, another, totally opposite, may be irresistibly gaining strength in the stratum below, until they completely prevail.

Perhaps even in our present age of hope and fear, when the very foundation of every social institution appears to be undermined, the monarchy is not in a state of greater convulsion and uncertainty than it was in the period which intervenes between the reign of our Second Edward and the twilight of the Reformation—I say the twilight, and not the dawn, for just preceding that great convulsion the world was hushed in an ominous silence. I have been compelled to employ rather an awkward circumlocution to denote the period to which we allude. A consistent chronological nomenclature is essential to the right understanding of history, and when we are treating upon the progress of society in Latin Christendom, we want a common measure more pertinent than can be supplied by the reigns of kings. In the same manner as the artificial divisions of geography, the red and the blue lines upon the map, impede instead of advancing our knowledge, by concealing the physical features of the earth, so does the separation of the periods by regal accessions equally prevent us from observing the real chronology of the social eras of the people. For some purposes, at least, our chronology would be better distributed by considering events in relation to the great ecclesiastical councils, the States-General of Europe, at once the results and the organs of the feelings of the age; and if we individualize this era, we may do so by terming it the age of the Council of Constance, the most thoroughly reforming assembly, at least in intention, which the European commonwealth ever beheld.

As long as the original feelings of the barbarian races yet continued to prevail, kings were viewed rather as the leaders of the people than as the lords of the soil, claiming their descent from the primeval heroes of the race, or at least asserting that descent, and they were then placed by the habits of society in constant proximity to the people. Instead of being separated from the great mass of his subjects by an imperviable barrier, encircled by state and shrouded in the veil of majesty, the sovereign was constantly brought into immediate contact with every rank and order of the community. Hardly was the levee of the president of the United States so open to the "public" as the presence-chamber of a Plantagenet; and the white staff of the Lord Treasurer, broken upon the shoulders of the intruder, afforded the sufficiently efficacious means of preventing the royal presence from being profaned.

In our own country this social approximation was encouraged and facilitated by the constant progresses made by the old English king through every portion of his realm. East, west, north, and south was he constantly performing the journeys to which he was urged and compelled, by the most stern of all necessities—the need of filling his belly. Ignoble as the comparison may appear, the king moved about like a caterpillar on a cabbage-leaf. If he did not travel, he could not eat. Dispersed through his dominions, the most considerable portion of the king's property consisted of the produce of his demesne lands, which could only be rendered available in the reasonable proximity of the place where they were stocked or grown. If Henry, the son of John, had continued vibrating between Westminster and Windsor, slender indeed were the advantages which he could derive from his beeves beyond the Trent, or his barley crops on the borders of Wales. Did he wish to touch the proceeds, and therefore direct a sale? Each process was duly issued. Writ followed writ, and *distringas* was succeeded by *distringas*, *alias*, and *pluries*, and in proper time his majesty received a roll of parchment, and it must have been a good year when he did not find himself the debtor; for when the fat oxen had been coined into groats by the Yorkshire seneschal, the *compotus* always showed how happily the money had come in just at the very time when it was wanted, for the purpose of defraying the charges of the repairs of the roof of the hall, the battlements of the tower, and five bays of the barn. And, if he had directed the transportation to the metropolitan palace of the good ale brewed, even at Woodstock, the expense of conveying the casks entrusted to the thirsty carriers would have made a greater drain on the royal purse than if he had purchased the best vintage of Gascony. In short, if the king wished to feed upon his beef, he was compelled to repair to the pastures where the beeves themselves were fed, and, if the good liquor was not "drunk on the premises," the sovereign was completely spared from every temptation of acquiring that felicity in his own cellars. Such a mode of living created something like an inversion of universal suffrage. The representative of the ploughman did not approach the throne, but the king approached the cottage, and possibly these migrations added to the real strength of the monarchy. Instead of the king being a species of abstract idea, or at best a spectacle, he was surrounded with acquaintances, nay, more, with votaries, who saw in him the living master, from whom their obedience was claimed.

All this primeval simplicity, however, gradually gave way before increasing opulence. Arras decked the walls of the chamber, from whence the rushes were swept away. The luxuries of the fathers became the wants of the children. Women now constituted an integral portion of society. "Ladies love and druery" became the cause, or the pretence, for greater refinements or dissipations; etiquette expanded into a science, and a court, in the modern sense of the term, was created—a magic circle, in which the sovereign was placed, surrounded by the most imposing attributes of dignity and power, created by the fancy of the poet, the flattery of the minion, and the gloze of the lawyer, rendering the wearer of the crown equally independent of his duties and heedless of his moral responsibility....

CHAPTER V.

RESISTANCE.

(Edward II.-III.)

It would be a great point gained if in history we could somehow or another get rid of those conventional ideas which arise from the phrases, epithets and characters which custom attaches to peculiar individuals, and judge for ourselves. In this, as in many other points, I have had my wits much sharpened by disputing with my friend, Cabezudo. By the way, I am very happy to say that, upon the postulation of Don Carlos, he has lately been appointed to the archbishopric of Toledo; but, inasmuch as this fact is only known to myself and to "our correspondent in the north of Spain," I will not call him his Grace or give him his real title until the announcement has been duly made. Well, then, it was not long since, in conversation with Cabezudo, as we paced up and down the silent aisle of Canterbury cathedral, he suppressing his regret at the extinction of the ancient ritual, I loudly declaring mine at the munificent, yet, in my opinion, ill-judged alterations by which the historical character of the venerable edifice has been so much impaired— I trust I shall at last be able to persuade my friends of the truth of my favourite apophthegm, with which I will bore them till it reaches the very centre of their brains, that anything, once gone, can never be brought back again, and that a modern antique is the most glaring of all architectural innovations. And here, for instance, in this very choir, the mellow, massy oaken carving, the Corinthian pilasters and cherubs' heads, mitres and palm-branches of the school of Sir Christopher—a style redolent of high church and Dr. Sacheverell—possess a real, extrinsic, and historical beauty, which the most correct imitation of the style of the Gothic era, foreign as it is to our present habits and modes of thinking, can never attain—"I am not quite sure," said Cabezudo, "after all, if poor John Lackland"—I forget how it was that we came to talk about him—"has not been very hardly treated by

[238]

historians. Had we a full and fair account of the transactions of his reign, it would bear a very different aspect. All the subsisting annalists and historians are his determined, nay, virulent opponents. What would you think if the history of any administration were to be sought in the columns of the opposition newspapers, or in the speeches of the opposition members? Would you like to cull the merits of Peel from the 'Chronicle of the Morning,' or measure those of Melbourne by the 'Standard of the Evening'?

"With respect to the murder of John's nephew, nothing can be said, because nothing is known; but it is quite certain that the judgment which condemned him as a felon in the court of his feudal superior was contrary to every form of law. Surmise weighed against suspicion, I do not know whether an advocate might not fairly urge that Philip Augustus himself assisted in spreading the reports—for all the points of accusation brought against poor John resolve themselves into reports—which enabled him to effect the condemnation of a dangerous rival, whose dominions he coveted and thus obtained.

"With respect to John's alleged cruelties, I will not maintain that Aaron of York retained all his grinders, or that the archdeacon of Northampton was lodged with much comfort, even though he may not have worn a cope of lead—a legendary punishment, by the way, and as such employed by Dante in his rhymes—but when I recollect how tales of terror win upon the willing ear, and the dear delight which we all feel in supping upon horrors, you may at least allow me to indulge in the innocent luxury of paradoxical scepticism."

"People who reason like you," said I, "and there are many of you—act like Charles the Seventh, refusing all food, lest he should die of poison. Certainly he preserved himself from that mode of death, but at the expense of killing himself by starvation. You reject so much historical testimony upon the possibility of falsehood, that, having no facts left, you are reduced to a mere shadow of hypothesis and conjecture." "By no means," replied Cabezudo, "my error I feel too surely lies in the contrary direction; and I only wish you simply to accustom yourself to the habit of trying your witnesses, instead of implicitly adopting the current fictions of popular opinion and popular lies; but let that pass, and I will rest my vindication of your much-injured monarch upon a solemn instrument of unquestionable authenticity—one whose existence you cannot

challenge—and proving incontestably that John was willing to
sacrifice the dignity and rights of his crown for the purpose
of ensuring the tranquillity and comfort of his people, and the
protection and pacification of his realm."

"And this," cried I, "you parade as a discovery. 'Thank 'ee
for nothing,' says the gallypot, as the Spectator wrote in his
memorandum-paper. Magna Charta was unquestionably an
invaluable gift, yet I doubt if John himself would have claimed
much merit, when goaded into the right path of duty by the
point of the sword and spear."

"Magna Charta!" exclaimed Cabezudo, "by no manner of
means; that is the last thing which I should have thought of.
No, I mean the instrument whereby King John, of his own free
will, and of the Common Council of his barons, that is to say,
by assent of parliament, granted to St. Peter and St. Paul, and to
the Holy Roman Church, and to His Holiness Pope Innocent III.
and his successors, all those the kingdoms of England and of
Ireland, receiving them back again as the liegeman of the Holy
See, binding himself and his heirs as papal homagers, and
rendering for the same, in lieu of all other services, the sum of
one thousand marks sterling every year."

Accustomed as I had been to Cabezudo's mental vagaries,
I was not prepared for anything so astounding as this escapade.
I was struck all of a heap. "What!" exclaimed I, "do you
vindicate the character and conduct of King John, by appealing
to the act which has covered him with ignominy—an act justly
viewed as the very acme and climax of royal degradation and
hierarchal arrogance?"

"Well is it for mankind," quoth Cabezudo, "that while soft
words butter no parsnips, hard words break no bones; but,
restraining your indignation, pause and consider the great object
which John honestly endeavoured to obtain. The feudal ceremony was, in fact, an alliance, the tribute a subsidy; and at this
small price did your monarch propose to acquire a guarantee of
perpetual neutrality, or rather more, a protection, by which, at
so small an expense, the whole realm would have been placed under
the safeguard of public opinion, and secured against every hostile
invasion. How much you are the slave of words; consider how
much more truly independent you would have been could such
a consummation have been obtained," continued Cabezudo; "but
as you once truly said, kings have hard measure dealt to them
by historians, priests have worse."

I need not say that this laudatory quotation from one of my own works (which, by the way, I consider as one of the best of them) quite won my heart, and induced me to listen to his rhapsody with more attention than it would perhaps otherwise have earned.

"Well," exclaimed Cabezudo, "do you know the *Orbis Sensualium Pictus* of John Amos Comenius?"

"Sure I do," was my reply. "It was the delight of my boyish days. I never think of the book without pleasure; and in order to ensure the same agreeable recollection to my sons, I transferred my copy to each of them respectively, as they attained their spelling age. This pious and excellent minister of a sect—the Moravians—by whom so much has been effected for the cause of humanity, was the first who attempted to afford instruction in an attractive form, by the introduction of what, in the black-letter lay-book translation, sent forth in 1658 by worthy Charles Hoole, from his school in Lothbury, are termed 'brass cuts.' Whatever improvements have been made in nursery literature may be all traced to the first impulse given by Comenius. Translated into every European language, 'the world of things obvious to the senses' may yet be consulted as the most amusing encyclopædia of morals, men, and manners, as they existed and prevailed about the period of the English Commonwealth or the Thirty Years' War."

"And you recollect, of course, his illustrations?"

"Certainly, and their quaintness, as well as ingenuity; for who besides Comenius ever contrived to give a portrait of the human soul by the figure of a man without either outline or shading?"

"John's intentions were excellent," resumed Cabezudo, "but he was compelled, for the sake of economy of space, if not of money, to cram as much matter as possible in each of his said cuts; and hence, in his forty-sixth chapter, there is one unfortunate giant who is at once 'jolt-headed, bottle-nosed, blubber-lipped, blab-cheeked, goggle-eyed, wry-necked, great-throated, crump-backed, crump-footed, and steeple-crowned,' and which said giant only escaped being supplied with two heads and four arms in consequence of the fortunate accident of there being a small spare corner in which room could be found for the representation of a compound dwarf, who is equally doomed to become the individual exemplification of another entire set of deformities. Now it appears to me that the unlucky 'priest' is treated by most of your modern historians exactly in the same way, and that, whether he be invested with cape or cassock, ruff or band, whether he exhibit full-bottom wig or feather-top, scratch or shaven crown, the abstract historical 'priest' is usually represented as infected not only by the most varied, but the most incompatible vices and failings.   In the same breath we find the clergy accused of fanatic asceticism and unbridled profligacy, of factious resistance to royal authority and the most unprincipled support of tyranny.   Conduct which in every other portion of society ensures the highest praise, earns for us only vituperation and scorn.   Do you blame the senator for vindicating the rights of the legislature, the soldier if he sacrifices his life for glory, the freeman if he dies for liberty?   In us consistency is a crime, and every action which, if resulting from secular policy, in laymen earns the highest praise, invariably brings down the severest censures, when exerted by a churchman, as a portion of the duty of the order to which he belongs.   The 'cause for which Hampden bled on the field, and Russell on the scaffold,' is hailed with enthusiasm by those who could view Becket prostrate in this edifice before the altar, not merely without sympathy, but sounding a trumpet-voiced exultation that the proud prelate had received condign punishment for his 'fanaticism and arrogance'—for such are the terms into which the most ardent patriotism and the most undaunted courage of the priest are rendered, according to the current vocabulary of a calumnious world."

As is usually the case with my dear friend Cabezudo, he perhaps diminished the effect due to his arguments by the vehemence with which they were urged, but an impartial examination of the facts of history leaves no doubt of his correctness in the main.   Becket struggled to defend lawful rights by lawful means,—we speak of the liberties of the church.   Technically, it is proper that such language should be employed; for unquestionably it was under the aspect of ecclesiastical immunities that the franchises were claimed.   But the people, the commonalty, for whose benefit the battle was fought on holy ground, considered them as the liberties of the realm.   This was the prevailing feeling at the era of the Reformation, which Henry strove to counteract, partly by historical argument and partly by more efficient means.   As to Becket's martyrdom, Henry kindly informed the world, by proclamation under the sign-manual, that "Becket gave opprobrious words to the gentlemen which then counselled him to leave his stubbornness, and, taking Tracy by the bosom, violently shook and plucked him in such a manner as he had almost overthrown him to the pavement of the church, so that, upon the fray, one of the company perceiving the same, struck him, and so in the throng Becket was slain." It would have been rather perilous if any one had attempted to verify the royal narrative by a comparison with the original historians. Henry might command that Becket should be esteemed a rebel and a traitor; the shrine is plucked down, the tomb violated, and the ashes cast to the winds; but if there be any praise rendered to him who by lawful means resists an unlawful command, and willingly encounters death in defence of the cause of freedom, the civic crown is due to Becket, and his meed, the patriot's—of glory.

It has been said heretofore, I care not to recollect by whom, that every sovereign in Europe awakes with a crick in his neck on the morning of the 30th of January; but this sympathetic anniversary would be placed more correctly on the 22nd day of March, the day when Thomas, the noble Earl of Lancaster, expired before the gate of Pontefract castle, by the hands of the executioner. In the personal character of the earl there was little to excite respect, but he was of royal lineage. Had he been slain on the field of Boroughbridge, he might have been lamented; had he perished by the hand of the assassin, he would have sustained a royal fate; but a judicial sentence, followed by an ignominious execution, even as the meanest malefactor, opened a new and strange field of speculation, giving to men's minds a train of thought from which, but a little time before, they would have shrunk with fear and horror.

It must be confessed that Edward of Carnarvon was compelled to play a desperate game. The precise extent of the plans of the Earl of Lancaster cannot be exactly ascertained. "Look," whispered the traveller, as he espied the dark, strong tower, newly erected by the earl on his demesne, "it is there that he seeketh to immure the king, even as a wild beast, apart from all human converse or society." In a figurative sense the scheme was true, and, if Earl Thomas had been allowed to pursue his enterprises, Edward might nominally have been allowed to wear the crown; the restrictions partially imposed upon him at various periods of his reign, and by none more efficiently than by the earl, would, without doubt, have been renewed in such a guise as to reduce his authority to a nullity, or possibly to effect that catastrophe which was delayed, but not averted, by his fate.

It is a curious though a lamentable proof of the tendency of mankind to idolatry, that, in the middle ages, many who lost their lives, as the consequence of a political struggle, were honoured, not figuratively but literally, as martyrs, and became, as such, the objects of erring devotion and mistaken piety. Simon de Montfort was considered as the parallel of Becket, and the same benefits were ascribed to his intercession; and his votaries believed that as soon as the hateful dynasty of Plantagenet was expelled, the mailed opponent of tyranny would have stood in the sainted shrine like the soldier saints, Maurice or Gereon. Even more rapidly did the popular canonisation of Thomas, Earl of Lancaster, proceed. Lamps burnt before his effigy in the metropolitan cathedral. [Sequences] were composed and chanted in the services consecrated to his festival. The image was plucked down and the worship prohibited; but opinion cannot be suppressed by writs and parchments, and the belief that the House of Lancaster was marked by destiny as the future royal line continued to corrode and undermine the authority of the Plantagenet's sons and sons' sons, until the accomplished time was fulfilled.

Such, then, was the state of the public mind during the period to which my irregular annals have arrived, and such the sentiments which more or less imparted their influence to every rank of the community.

It is not for me to decide in what respect I most resemble famous King Midas; but this I do know, that I entirely sympathise with the servant of the Lydian monarch in his unbearable desire to reveal the mystery, and having resisted the temptation during two whole chapters, I must even declare the secret that Grindcobbe's unlicensed absence from his spouse, at the hour when he was bound to snore at her side, was the cause of the dire conflict which I have imperfectly described.

When the crowd had begun to separate, Grindcobbe and the freemason and the tiler still lingered in conversation, hovering near the stone cross. An ordinary hearer might have thought in good faith that they were discussing the great staple of country conversation, the weather, and the prospect of the coming harvest. A more experienced ear would have detected in the heaviness and languor of their discourse, the sentences following at slow intervals, the blank and vacant pauses, and the still more vacant replies, a confirmation of the apophthegm of the ex-Bishop of Autun, that speech is given to man for the purpose of enabling him to conceal his thoughts, and that the ostensible subject of the discourse had the smallest possible connection with the real sentiments of the parties in such discourse engaged.

At the approach of a stranger, who walked towards them, Grindcobbe suddenly started. There was no need for bidding them good e'en, he went on his way.

It became darker—murky darkness—no moon; you could scarce discern the countenance before you, when another approached, a friar, who, coming close up to Grindcobbe, seized him by the arm, and laying the index and other fingers on his wrist, whispered a word in his ear. "We are ready," was the prompt answer, and following their conductor, they proceeded in silence beyond the inhabited boundary of the town, until they reached the site of the deserted Verulam. Antiquarians owe little thanks to Abbot Ealdred, who battered down the ancient Roman structures, lest they should afford harbour to rogues and thieves. Considerable portions had, however, escaped the demolition. Gaping vaults, and tall dark fragments of walls and towers, still remained to mark the stern power of the Empire, and many a legend scared the wanderer from venturing within their precincts even in the brightness of day.

In the midst of the ruins rose a small chapel or oratory, whose door opened at the friar's touch and admitted them into the sanctuary, hot and crowded with steaming worshippers. Above the altar was suspended a rich curtain, which, rumbling upon its rod as it was drawn aside by the sacristan, disclosed the "painted table" representing the noble martyr, whose coronet declared his dignity, whilst the white scarf, which crossed his armour, shone as the portentous and fatal sign of civil war. And now was chanted the metrical hymn, commencing the service appropriated to his memory, and which, lurking in a single manuscript, testifies the veneration which the duke received:

> Gaude Thoma Ducum decus
> Lucerna Lancastriæ.

The office being completed, the friar, standing on the steps of the altar, began a discourse in which political reasoning was combined with that distortion of scripture doctrines concerning the equality of mankind which has so often been employed against the throne....

Loud applause followed. "And when," exclaimed the free-mason, "shall we have a true and righteous king to reign over us?"

"He should be of the true old English line," replied a leather-jerkined workman, speaking in a northern accent—"of the line of the Confessor, which liveth in the Scottish king."

"And what shall be done for the son of the carter, the foul changeling, who now usurps the royal power?" said the tiler.

"Tush," said Grindcobbe, who was considered as the most influential delegate of the burgesses, "bad and vile as foul Edward of Carnarvon may be, that is a story which I do not believe. I saw the poor fool who made the claim, being, as he asserted, the rightful heir, hanged upon the copped thorn, and a sad death he died; but it was at the full of the moon, and he was plainly beside himself."

"If so," replied the tiler, "even the same was the king, for he was fearfully terrified when the report was spread."

"Sirs," said the friar, "if there be a right heirship it is in the Earl Henry; for, as ye well know, the noble Edmund was the first-born, over whom Edward—a curse upon his straight longshanks—was most unjustly preferred. But who was the first king? Was he not, as the Frenchman telleth us in his rhyme, a great, strong, stalwart villein whom the people chose, and reigning by their power. Now, sirs, Edward of Carnarvon, who now reigneth, and who was chosen by the people, hath forfeited his seigniory. When the king departeth this life, the throne, as ye all know, becomes vacant; and was I not in the abbey choir when the archbishop presented this Edward to the people, and asked if they would accept him as their lord?"

"And was he not seated upon the throne," said the mason, "by reason of his being the heir?"

"Certainly not as heir," replied the friar, "not even was he yet permitted to place his foot upon the golden cloth covering the lowest of the steps by which the throne is ascended; and though richly clad, not one royal vestment did he assume."

"And what ensued?"

"The people chose him. 'We will have him,' was the shout which filled the lofty vault, and which was repeated by the countless crowds who surrounded the holy building. Thus chosen, Edward was conducted by the archbishop before the altar, and upon the Gospel book he swore to observe his covenant. In mercy, equity, and truth will he govern; and the laws which the people choose shall he protect and defend to the utmost of his power. The contract sealed on his part, the archbishop then anointeth him with the holy oil. The mystic sacerdotal garment is given to him—the symbol of the royal priesthood—the crown is placed upon his head, and the sceptre delivered into his hand. Then, and not till then, is he placed in the seat, and becomes entitled to the liegeman's homage and fidelity; and the oath was put into Latin, and entered upon record in the chancery, to the end that, if broken, the record may be brought into parliament, and judgment may be given according to law."

"A goodly ceremony," said Grindcobbe, "and how did the oath sound?"

"Jack will be a gentleman," said the friar, "if he can learn French; and if I repeat the very words, what will they profit you? The king swore that he would keep the laws which the people shall have approved—*lesquels la communauté del royaume aura esleu—quas vulgus elegerit*—as the oaths were recorded by the Master of the Rolls."

This was perfectly true; and ambiguous as the phrases may be, and, however construed, subversive of the royal prerogative, it is thus that they appear upon the roll.

"And now, sirs," resumed the friar, "hath not Edward of Carnarvon refused to amend abuses when thereunto required? Hath he not broken the laws and usage of the realm? Hath he not administered the laws with injustice and without mercy?"

A groan from the congregation filled up each pause, and rose still deeper when assent was given to the question whether he, Edward of Carnarvon, had not forfeited the crown.

"And now, sirs," said the friar, "soon as the morrow dawns, let each who from afar appeareth here as a brother depart to his home. You, William the Slater, tell our friends in the Guildhall of London that we shall be up and doing at their behest. John Attwood, bear our greeting to the freemen of Kent. Robert the Mason, ye have business at Bury. Guide your workmen as an honest craftsman in the service of the abbot, and do your duty in the secret chapter when the door is closed. And you, Walchere, let your countrymen know that the burghers of Ghent and Ypres have many a well-wisher in old England, who honour them for their steadiness in the righteous cause.". . .

CHAPTER VI.

THE MOVEMENT.

(EDWARD III.)

BLENDED with much that was woefully perverted, and with more that was innocently erroneous, there was a considerable portion of truth in the friar's speech; about as much, in fact, as usually enters into any speech made by a leader of a party; and, if my readers will permit me, it may not be entirely irrelevant to examine some few of the more important points which the levelling doctrines of the early Radicals involved.

It does not admit of any doubt but that the doctrine of strict, indefeasible lineal succession is of modern origin, and that the death of the individual monarch occasioned both in fact and in law a complete vacancy in the throne. Upon the death of the king of England all the royal tribunals had expired, and until the successor had been inaugurated: whatever deference might be paid to the rising sun, he had no authority as a sovereign.

Not that the monarchy was elective in the ordinary sense of the word. In the earlier ages the crown belonged alone to the right royal line, and to none save the members of that line. But though assured to the lineage, the right did not vest absolutely in any individual, and the sovereign was to hold his authority by the assent of the people over whom he ruled, and who selected him from his kindred, kinsmen, or brethren by their will. In extreme cases personal fitness would of necessity decide their choice. The king did not rule as an abstract idea, he was a king in action and a king in deed; he judged his people in peace, he led them forth in war. Would you appoint a magistrate who could not hear the voice of the pleader, or a general whose infirmities prevented him from mounting a horse?

Furthermore, nothing could be less determinate than the right of succession. By what rule of inheritance was the claim of the heir to be decided?

In the simplest case, that of parent and child, many a question would arise which no positive law had yet decided, and for which no exact precedent could be found. Was the son, whose nativity preceded the acquisition of the royal dignity, entitled to the throne? or was the infant Porphyrogenitus to exclude the first-born child? Did the adult uncle take precedence of the adolescent nephew? Was priority of descent to prevail over proximity of lineage? All these questions, which repeatedly arise in mediæval history, I will undertake to solve to the satisfaction of any inquirer who will begin by satisfying me as to the rules of succession in the empire of the Czars, and the comparative legality of the claims of Isabella or Carlos, of Maria or Miguel—cases which, perhaps, may induce us to doubt whether, in this respect, the age of civilization has advanced much beyond the barbaric age.

From the accession of the first Plantagenet, the principle of primogeniture had become practically established, but the theory of royal election yet prevailed, exemplified by those ancient ceremonies which have subsisted even until the present day.

From the most remote antiquity does our coronation ritual descend. Prayer and anthem, collect and psalm, even the same whose sweet and swelling harmony we in our times have heard in the vaulted quire, resounded at the inauguration of the Anglo-Saxon Basileus. The gorgeous train of prelates, earls, and barons had graced the enthronement of Edward of Carnarvon's ancestors. And of old each English king had sworn upon the Gospel book that he would honour holy church, exercise justice, abolish all bad laws and customs, and keep the good, in use and vigour.

But a further obligation was imposed upon Edward of Carnarvon; and where was its precedent to be found? In no antecedent muniment can we trace the forcible yet ambiguous clause which obliges him to assent to the enactments of the community. And when we recollect how strictly all established forms were retained by usage, can we doubt but that some most cogent reason and paramount authority had introduced the change?

Edward of Carnarvon ascended the throne under the condemnation of a father's curse. In such words of bitterness there is an ominous fatality; and if there be any prophecy to which the means are given of working its own accomplishment, it is when a parent imprecates evil upon his child. Disgraced, humiliated, he assumed the royal authority, and it is difficult to resist the supposition, that the opportunity was seized of imposing upon the young monarch some additional security for the concessions extorted with so much difficulty from his mighty sire. Be that as it may, that ancient oath was rendered the foundation of the proceeding, which, for the first time in England, exhibited the spectacle of the subject sitting in judgment upon the anointed sovereign....

...I have already noticed that, until the accession of the sovereign, there was, in early days, an interregnum involving a complete cessation of coercive justice. I will not assert that such was the doctrine at a later period, or that, in theory, no pleas of the crown could be held in the interval between the day when William Russell, the Speaker of the House of Commons, speaking in the name of the whole parliament, renounced allegiance to the grey uncrowned head, "and the joyous proclamation of the peace" was made in the name of the new king. But at all events the opinion still prevailed, and the period was one in which all classes made the most of their holiday. The good citizens of London were, as usual, the first in the field and, by fair means or by foul, compelled every prelate, peer, or other who entered the city to swear to the conservation of their liberties; and, throughout the whole kingdom, the towns and boroughs simultaneously prepared, at least, to obtain a higher stage of real or fancied independence....

...At St. Alban's proceedings commenced by a significant display. In the course of the eve of the Conversion of St. Paul, in the year 1327, there arose in the market-place the chopping-block, upon which appeared an axe, and it was soon understood that any opposition to the good of the commons would lead to a practical employment of the instrument so conveniently placed at hand....

...Amongst all the revolutions of England there is one singular characteristic. Wild or absurd or unjust as the demands of the Englishman may be, he assumes, at least in words, that his claims are according to law, and the insurgents had procured, in due form, a copy or extract of that passage in Domesday which relates to the tenures of the town[a].

It may appear singular that the villeins should accept the most signal monument of the Conquest as containing the charter of their liberties; and, if they had endeavoured to obtain a version of its language, the judges would have answered that they were unable to translate them, excepting as the words sounded, but it was law, and therefore harmonised with their

[a] Here should follow the extracts from Domesday.

general theory of liberty; and the twelve selected men proceeding to the abbot and convent, they preferred all the demands which had been the objects of popular aspiration—to hunt and to fish, and to send members to Parliament, and to turn their hand-mills at their free pleasure and will[a].

...The villeins had so much command of money, that they harassed the convent by every species of legal process, and adding thereto the expedient of blockading the monastery, and thus preventing the ingress of provisions, they compelled the unwilling abbot to affix the convent seal to the indenture of agreement, all the other members of the convent, nevertheless, protesting against the act and deed....

During five long years did the villeins hunt the hares in the field, snare the rabbits in the warren, exerting the privilege of turning the hand-mills, and returning the members, until a more auspicious period for the monastery arrived....

...The judges who now make their circuit, they are the justices of trailbaston, by whom all acts of violence are to be redressed. Was it bribery if the abbot, before they held their session, sent his cellarer to them with a tun of the very best claret wine, followed by Nicholas Hamstide at the head of a goodly train of provision-carts, well laden with beef and mutton for my lords, and hay and corn for their steeds? Was any clever management practised in the selection of the jury, by whom the verdict of illegal conspiracy was pronounced against the villeins for their successful dealings against their lord.... Whilst fear of the judgment was impending, the abbot, with a happy mixture of severity and kindness, invited the so-called burgesses to dinner, and partly working upon their fears, and partly upon their affections (for a kind and loving lord was he, though he asserted his ancient rights), they surrendered up their charters, their common seals, and their mill-stones. The first were burnt, the second hammered into an ornament for the shrine of the Protomartyr, and the last buried in the pavement of the cloister; but the quarrel was not buried with them; affronts sink deeper than injuries, and though the talliages imposed by the abbot were most moderate, and his treatment most kind, still, the round faces of the mill-stones in the pavement always seemed to the townsmen as the trophies of their disgrace, and the incitement to signal vengeance....

[a] Here the Parliamentary proceedings, etc.

CHAPTER VII.

CURRENCY.

(RICHARD II.)

...IF William de Clare did not find himself overburdened with coin, his eldest son Thomas, to whom I must now introduce my readers, was, in proportion to his views, even less furnished with the great symbol of worldly opulence. His rental was larger than that of his ancestors, but the money either would not go so far or ran away further than it ought to do, and my knight and squire seemed to feel himself in equal difficulty. In the meanwhile, the country at large was certainly not decreasing in opulence, though the general complaint throughout the commonwealth was that everything was becoming dear; more especially was the labour market evidently rising in every department—at least if the Rolls of Parliament are to be credited, "outrageous wages" being the constant burden of the doleful ballad of our supreme legislative assembly. These lamentations were, however, diversified indeed by earnest expostulations to the young sovereign—for Richard of Bordeaux was now upon the throne—to spare the means of the community; and, as may be easily understood, the public expenditure constituted the principal subject of conversation round the table of that old-established inn, the Woolpack, in Southwark, where we shall find a goodly company now assembled.

"I trust," said [Thomas] de Clare, "that our lord the king will be graciously pleased to permit the expenses of his household to be diminished. What will become of the realm if the inordinate costs which he sustaineth be not restrained?"

"Had he the cunning of his grandsire," replied a very yellow, dingy personage, with a cap fitting so very close to his head that you could not make out what had become of his ears, and who sat at the lower end of the board with an empty stoup before him, "he would be enabled to provide for himself, ay, and for his people, without tax or subsidy."

[252]

"Assuredly," replied William Lovekin, the Mercer, and who also filled the profitable office of Bridge warden; "yet, if my recollection serves me rightly, subsidies and benevolences were as thick as mustard during the whole of his glorious reign. Every victory which he gained over his enemies of France is to me a doleful remembrance. Cressy compelled me to part with my wife's best ambling nag; and as for Poitiers, it cost me a child's fortune."

"Ay," said the stranger, grinning like a skull, "that was merely the result of sound wisdom. All the taxes which you paid would not have been enow to furnish Dame Alice Perrers with gowns and kirtles for a single quarter."

"Fie upon her for a shameless baggage!" exclaimed the Mercer, with much indignation. "Truth, it mattered little to her how the King's subjects were spoiled and pillaged. Sir!" exclaimed he, his voice rising a full octave as he struck the table with his clenched fist, "she dealt continuously with me, from the time when she first became notorious, until she was impeached by the House of Commons in the Parliament which worked wonders. Oft and oft hath the harlot, in one bargain, bought of me Genoa velvet to the tune of an hundred pounds. My heart used to bleed when I touched the money which the King had wrung out of the very sweat and sinews of the poor."

"Pardon me, good master," replied the stranger, "sweat and sinews are nasty expressions; I don't like them. But did Dame Alice always pay you for her handsel?"

"For everything, by the Groom of her Chamber, and down upon the nail, and in good red gold, broad and shining bright from the Mint. One might easily see that the money came fresh out of the Teller's chest, hardly a piece that was soiled or tarnished. At all events, none cracked in the ring. It was a noble deed in King Edward thus to strike broad golden money, such as none of his ancestors ever did before!"

"It all goes to the Apostolic Court, to the Horseleech of Rome, by which we are sucked dry," remarked Nicholas Borser, one of the King's chaplains or clerks. "These foreigners get every piece of preferment that falls."

"And yet it is a marvel," observed the Haberdasher, "there should be still so much money in the country, sucked and plundered as we have been—aye, and always shall be, even to the world's end."

"Why," said Croumere, "some folks say that it is owing to

the wise regulation which compelleth every merchant stranger to bring in two marks of bullion for every sack."

"Not much comes from that," rejoined John Whitlemead. "I will not undervalue the wisdom of the High Court of Parliament, but they might as well e'en let the matter alone, for how are the Florentines and Flemings to buy our wools, unless they pay for them in money? Leicester and Cotteswold will not part with their fleeces for a song, and it is that which brings the ducat and the florin into the land. The *Geste* telleth of a valiant knight, one Jason, who, after many and sore perils, brought home a fleece of gold. It is my sign, good masters, and ye can have good cheer there; and when I opened shop, I took it for the honour of our mystery, for wise clerks say it signifieth the riches produced by the clothing of the silly sheep, and we drapers have full cause to honour him. And if ye will dine at our Hall on the Feast of Bishop Blaize, ye shall see Jason and the Dragon, true to the life, all made of marchpane, on the table."

"Master," said the sallow stranger, again interrupting the discourse, "ye may be a good warm citizen and a discreet ruler in your gild, but it is not for such as ye to prate about the symbols in which the wise disclose and yet reveal their lore. Is it not the *quinta essentia* which restoreth the feeble reason? the fire which vivifieth the red stone of the sages with the blue bird of Hermes and the Dragons of Demogorgon?"

A pause of solemn silence ensued: all stood aghast, and yet no one could tell why, when a new interlocutor took up the speech, whose Christian name I cannot exactly ascertain. I possess a large portion of the Rowley manuscripts, which I acquired against the bid of a collector equally eminent for his zeal and his irascibility, almost incurring the danger of being knocked down by him together with the lot. It was he who, having begun his career when a schoolboy by the acquisition of the celebrated set of the Islington turnpike tickets, complete from the first establishment of the Trust, has since been possessed with that insatiate appetite which increases exactly in proportion to the quantity which it devours. From these Rowley documents, invaluable as they are, I cannot exactly make out whether the person who now spoke was the celebrated founder of St. Mary Radcliffe or his brother; but it was one of them, either William or Thomas Canning, who, pausing a moment, did not entirely give that support to the Draper which the latter invited by a look of intelligence. Canning fully admitted the effect produced by the wool trade. "But then," continued he, "since the passing of the Statute of the Staple, we merchants can do our business with much less money. The introduction of the Bills of the Staple hath given new life to all our trade. By such a Bill, which bestows upon the creditor the right, should the debtor fail in payment, to seize all his lands, his goods, his chattels, we merchants with prudence and good management, deal with our stock ten times over. Is not a penny four times paid as good as a groat? Let me have the Staple Bill, and with one hundred nobles in my cash chest, I can do business to the same amount as if I had a thousand. It is a treasure which defies the thief, for to him the parchment is as useless as an old song. It only grieves me," continued Master Canning, "that the Crown inevitably loses thereby, for when a letter of credence issueth, by which the King condescends to ask us merchants for a small loan of money in proportion to our means, and we are called upon to declare our substance, it would be against sound principle were we to bring into the valuation a Staple Bill, *a chose in action*, which is not taxable by the law."

The round-headed personage, who answered to the name of Theophilus, continued speaking as if he were half in a dream. "Violence may not purchase the virtue of sapience. If King Edward had but performed the vow which he made to induce the clerk of Catalonia to continue to employ his science for the profit of the realm, grace, my masters, was ready at hand; talliages and taxes would have ceased in the land." All this was said, or sung, by Theophilus, his wan visage lighting up as if by the kindling of an internal fire.

"Our noble," resumed the Draper, "is of the finest touch in Christendom."

"It may well be so," said the stranger, "and the impress which it bears is the attestation of its origin."

"The name of the mint-master or of the mintage town?" said the Draper in a tone of inquiry.

"Pish!" said Theophilus, "look and see."

The Draper, the Haberdasher, and the Bristol Merchant had severally in their purses, or about their persons, a good store of specimens of every coin current by law or usage in the realm, whether in good red gold or sterling silver, not even excluding the baser varieties of gally halfpence, suskins, dodkins, and the varieties of Nuremberg tokens, which, although called in by proclamation, continued to circulate most extensively in England;

so that, at this present day, they usually constitute a portion
of the contents of every money-crock found in or near a ruin.
Often may they be seen in the hoard of the incipient or insipient
antiquary, who vainly endeavours to read the legend never
intended to be deciphered, or to blazon the heraldic insignia
never borne by any king or kaiser, sufficiently like the real
armories to induce him to suppose that he recognizes them, and
yet so unlike—thanks to the whim or fancy of the Swabian
artist—as to baffle any attempt to appropriate them into any
coeval dynasty.

But, however much coin may have abounded, not a single
piece, whether more or less valuable, was produced by the Draper
or the Bristol Merchant for the purpose of making the inspection
which Theophilus had demanded. Without any direct cause of
suspicion, the innate caution of men who have made money, and
know how to keep it too, restrained them from any unnecessary
exhibition of such tempting opulence before strangers; but the
Squire, with an equally characteristic absence of instinct, after
fumbling for some time, drew out his only specimen of King
Edward's precious currency, and, holding it carefully to the
light of the smoky lamp, he began to examine the impress which
it bore. "On this side we have our late gracious Sovereign as
the lord of the sea, France and England riding on the foam and
curling wave, with hempen saddle and horse of tree." The
effigy thus described by Thomas de Clare in the words of the
old prophecy does, in fact, exhibit our Edward triumphant in
the floating bark, a type upon which an argument has been
founded by the learned Selden, as to our natural dominion over
the waters by which our island is surrounded.

"Right," said Theophilus, "as far as thou canst spell; but
there is more mystery than thou weanest of in the text which
encircles the portraiture. But, tell me, what seest thou on the
reverse of the coin?"—a speech which he accompanied with a
delicate yet effectual seizure of the subject of his discourse,
which he held up before the eyes of the late owner, from whom
it had parted for ever.

"A cross placed upon the contour of a rose," replied the
Squire.

"Hermes hath marked it with his serpent," replied the
stranger, "and the red dragon brooded over the sullen Saturn,
until he fought and won the victory. And why did Raymond
transmute the dull lead and base copper into Sol, fine as the

ore of Ophir, and then multiply each particle an hundredfold?
What consideration moved the sage? Could lucre or gain tempt
him who in his chamber hath at his command more riches than
are buried in the Indian mines? No, but Edward promised—
what say I—nay, swore upon the Halidom, that all he obtained
should be employed in rescuing the Holy Land from Paynim
thraldom. But it was Christian blood which he sought to spill,
and it was his sword which pierced the Christian heart.

"No longer would holy Raymond further his worldly ambition
or nourish his sinful pride. Seven long years was he immured
in the Tower, until the secret way was opened for his release,
and he quitted the ungrateful shores of England to earn the
crown of martyrdom."

"And is the art clean lost out of our island?" inquired
Thomas de Clare.

"Never can it be lost," said Theophilus; "there hath ever
been a continued succession of philosophers in all ages, although
the foolish world taketh no heed of them. Every master before
he departeth is bound, if he findeth one worthy of the dignity,
to leave as heir to his science——"

"A son, perchance, if he hath one," said Thomas de Clare.

"Nay," replied Theophilus, "not always so. It is not for
nighness of blood or nearness of kin that the secret can be taught.
Virtue alone can win the art, and to one alone can the hallowed
possession be conveyed. No man, unless he be of excellent
virtue, can reach the great gift by which, if abused, the world
would be turned upside down."

"And did Raymond Lully succeed in finding a worthy heir
in this our country?"

"Alas, he did! a true man—one who hath suffered in the
flesh—one who, like his master, pined seven long years in the
pit, because, when seized by the officers of King Edward, and
brought before the Council with his gear, he refused stoutly to
waste the gift upon worldly wrath or carnal covetise—worm
that I am—even me."

That Theophilus, as he was styled among his brethren, though
whilom known as plain John Kyme in his own township of
Spotforth, in the county of York, had been thus incarcerated
is entirely true; but he forgot to add that, proffering his own
invaluable services, he came before the Council without summons,
to inform them or to give evidence how the King's profit could
be best served by his art; and, as is usual in such cases, not

without some undefined expectations that the "very intelligent and talented witness" would soon be called upon to act as practitioner.

The bait was swallowed in the first instance by my Lords. The sum of a hundred marks was accordingly disbursed to John Kyme by the High Treasurer to commence his experiments, but no proceeds were forthcoming. Sometimes Kyme laid the fault upon the water and sometimes upon the air, until it becoming apparent, even to the Chancellor of the Exchequer, that no profit was to be realized, the Ministry most unjustly accused him of imposture. He was elevated to a station from which he could look down upon the grinning multitude. An operation was performed which removed some superfluous projections from either side of his poll, and he was kept in confinement in the Wakefield Tower, until he so worked upon the pity of the King's Almoner, who chanced to visit him, as to obtain his discharge....

CHAPTER VIII.

THE VILLEIN AND THE LABOURER

(Edward III.)

...As in every history of a Court the King and his Prime Minister constitute the chief personages, so in the minor chronicles of the "fine old English gentleman," no less than in those of his degenerate successors, must the owner of the demesne and his steward constantly appear on the scene, and our attention must now be engaged by Thomas de Clare and his reeve. I must, however, here pause and premise that in 1349, the year at which we have now arrived, the word "Gentleman" or "Generosus" was not yet in use, and I have applied it to the landlord simply for the purpose of more easily distinguishing his station in society. Of Thomas, the son of William, beforementioned, I have little to say, excepting that he was not so prosperous as his grandfather Gilbert, whose arms were splendidly blazoned in his hall window. William Huxter, the reeve, might require a longer delineation, but it is sufficient here to observe that he was admirably qualified for the situation which he held. Entirely bent upon guiding his master in such a way as might best serve his own interest, he never appeared to direct or counsel him. A clever manager—and such was William Huxter in his sphere—is he who, all the while that he squeaks through the mouth of Punch and moves his wooden limbs, contrives to keep his head below the cloth; for should his desire of glory lead him to become visible, the prestige is gone for ever. I never heard of but one operator who openly showed to all the world that he pulled the puppets and held out his collecting-hat at the same time.

"How shall we possibly get in our harvest?" said Thomas de Clare to the reeve. "Only six of the twenty holdings, each of which, in the days of my honoured ancestor, Sir Gilbert, could provide an able bondsman, are now held by villeins of birth and blood. The pestilence has cleared off all the rest. And as to those that remain, there is no forcing them to work to any purpose, even by taking the law into our own hands."

"Your honour may put the recusant in the stocks," said the steward, "and keep the wretch there day and night, with the comfort of a gutter dripping on his head to keep him cool."

"Yes," said Thomas, "and so come in danger of the Judges, for those cankered lawyers arrest and wrest every plea to the advantage of the churl. One would think that they themselves were hereditary bondsmen; for, whenever they can, they turn the scale in favour of the villeinage. 'I may lick my own villein,' they tell me, 'as much as I choose, but I must thump him with my own fists'; nor would my commands avail you, Huxter, in an action of assault and battery. If I am rightly informed, [William] Huxter, they manage these things better in France."

"We have let and demised the vacant holdings," quoth [William] Huxter, "for good rents, payable in white money, at the four most usual quarter-days in the year, and money makes the mare go. But here are John Woodward and his two brothers—there were eleven of them before the great sickness—who have been told that your honour wants hands for the farm."

John Woodward advanced, "making his manners," according to the old English fashion, not yet entirely out of use, by clutching hold of a tuft of his shaggy black locks, which hung over his forehead, and giving the same a hard, downward tug or pull, an action which I believe may be best explained by consulting the article "Tappie Touzie" in Jamieson's *Scottish Dictionary*.

"Well, Woodward," said Thomas de Clare, "you and your brothers are the best reapers in the township." The clown grinned assent. "Ye shall have good wages as leaders of the meisney."

Woodward and his companions did not appear at all elated by the offer of work, or anxious to accept it, but continued in disrespectful silence.

"Ye shall have good wages," reiterated Thomas de Clare— "twopence a day."

Silence.

"Threepence," said the steward, increasing the bidding.

Silence as before.

Both master and steward now looked equally puzzled: self-interest restrained both from making any advance, for Thomas de Clare did not like spending more than he could well spare, and Huxter kindly considered all his employer's money as his own. Pride also had some share in stimulating them to oppose the audacious pretensions of the churl; but necessity was urgent, and the further proposal, "Ye shall have your meat also," was extorted by the passive resistance of the labourer.

"Two silver groats and our meat," said Woodward, at length condescending to reply.

As the vendors of labour were silent before, now equally so was the purchaser; for whilst, on the one hand, he was deterred by the certain prospect of the same exorbitant sum being demanded by every other hand whom he should be compelled to hire, so, on the other, he was urged to comply, by the equal certainty that, if he did not, his harvest would rot upon the ground. And whilst he was deliberating, the labourers had quietly turned their backs upon him and were walking away; a prompt determination, therefore, was needed, and with an exceeding ill-will and grudging he agreed to the terms, and the natural monopoly of strength obtained the victory....

...If we wish to recollect the reign of the third Edward by a significant characteristic, we shall find one perhaps more important to us than the title of King of France in his royal style, or the *fleur-de-lis* on the emblazoned shield. In his reign first arose the stocks on the parish green, and the whipping-post started out of the soil when the proud battlements of Windsor were rising in all the splendour of chivalry....

...Long previously to this era, the system of predial servitude in England had been gradually wearing away, and whilst the theory of the law was modified, the practice was evidently milder than the theory. I will say as little as possible of ancient times, and shall only observe, that in the calamitous and lawless period from which England was rescued by the Norman invasion, the merciful chastisement designed to preserve the English from the lowest stage of barbarism, the situation of the common people had evidently become much deteriorated, so that not only slavery, but the slave-trade, existed to a considerable extent, and so continued under the new dynasty. Bristol was particularly active in this branch of commerce, the thralls being thence shipped for the Irish market. Considering the impoverished condition in which the Emerald Isle then was, it might afford some matter of curious conjecture as to the articles obtained by the merchants in exchange. It is most probable, however, that these supplies were intended for the Danes, who were an opulent community.

Good Bishop Wilstan, working with patient zeal, came over to

Bristol from Worcester, for months at a time, preaching Sunday after Sunday against this traffic, stained as it was by the utmost profligacy and cruelty, and the traffic was completely abolished by the Canon of the Council of London under the primacy and direction of Anselm, Archbishop of Canterbury. Henceforward, all traces of personal servitude cease, and we now meet with the villein—low in the social scale and subjected to definite and prescribed services and labour. He was to harrow and plough the land in the spring, to reap the harvest in the autumn, and to carry the crop to the barn....

The land upon which the villein's cottage was erected was declared to be the property of the landlord; the villein's child could not be married without the lord's licence. His earnings were declared to be at the lord's mercy. If beaten by his master, the court of law could give him no redress. If he fled, he might be brought back in bonds and placed again beneath the yoke of domestic tyranny.

All this was law; but, by a happy consistency, the law was always at variance with itself. The land was the lord's; but so long as the villein rendered his services, he was maintained in the possession of his tenement, and not an hour's labour, a hen's egg, or a farthing, a bundle of furze, or a wisp of hay could be exacted beyond what had been sanctioned by the immemorial custom of the domain; and whilst the ermined justices of the royal tribunals strictly and sternly protected the rights of the superior, it was nevertheless the invariable maxim of the courts that the law was always, and in every case, to be construed in favour of liberty. The lord's right to the property of the serf resolved itself into the power of taxation, and if the villein rendered chevage to the lord, the law was interposed between him and the collectors of the subsidy. The power of chastisement could not be delegated. The master was compelled to act as executioner. If the lord sought to reclaim his villeins, he was compelled to bring his action against each individual; but if the villeins asserted their liberty, they joined in one process, thus diminishing their expenses and their pains. No evidence could avail against the villein to prove the servitude of his blood, excepting the production of kindred in a higher degree, and it had become the maxim of the cardinal law *that every presumption was to be raised in favour of liberty*....

...The emancipation of the villeinage was proceeding in England silently but rapidly, when the great pestilence was

sent from the far regions of Asia to desolate the realms of
Christendom. It was the common belief that the third part of
mankind perished by the Divine vengeance. Terror might
exaggerate and ignorance might enhance the exaggeration, but
the main fact of the depopulation occasioned by this scourge is
incontestably proved by the "pride," as the statute terms their
conduct, of the agricultural labourers, who, demanding "outrageous wages," and combining to obtain their own terms, were
placing their employers at their mercy. The landholders at once
determined to put down the labourers, so their determination
placed that statute upon the record which constitutes the great
era in the rural policy of the realm; and the regulations first
imposed, placed freedom but at a small distance from predial
servitude. The ploughman was free, but he was bound to serve
the master who required his work at the price which the law
imposed. If he refused, he was placed in the stocks, which the
villein had hitherto filled. He was not ascribed to the glebe of
the manor, but he was confined within the boundaries of the
township; and though he could not be seized by the seigniorial
officer, he was branded with the hot iron as a fugitive if he sought
to escape this predial servitude....

The services of the villein gave him a certain title to his land,
the hire of the labourer gave him none; and the landlord would
therefore probably regret the disappearance of the ancient
vassalage, and the rise of a new class from whom, if the law
could have been fully enforced, the same labour would have
been obtained. As it was, the first effects seem to have been
unmitigated oppression. Villein and free were goaded into one
confederacy, and brooded in sullenness on the contemplation of
revenge. Such were the results of the "Statute of Labourers,"
created by the masters....

CHAPTER IX.

THE MONEY MARKET.

(RICHARD II.)

...TRULY hath it been said of old, that you cannot get more from a cat than her skin; and the unfortunate tenants of West Walsham had been so racked and worried, that it was quite hopeless to attempt to exact any further supplies from them.

The few villeins who remained were better off; they stood out upon their rights, and sullenly rendering their ancient services, defied the power of the lord. But, if all the lands had been unoccupied, Thomas de Clare would scarcely have found an husbandman willing to venture upon a holding under one who, by his agents at least, had so often broken the custom of the country. The "rents seck" which would become due at the next Hoke Day, much as they had been raised, would not have paid one tithe of the debts which he owed; and the golden visions of the adept being dispelled, he was in sore perplexity. Added to this was the necessity of consulting with his sergeant upon the legal difficulties which environed him; and to obtain which opinion he, accompanied by his untrusty seneschal, was fain to repair to the great metropolitan mart or centre of business—the Cathedral of St. Paul's. Thick and driving as the throng may now be in a great city, the currents of population were in proportion greater during the middle ages in the narrow streets of Paris or of London. This pressure was partly occasioned by the smaller dimensions of the roadway, but more by the hosts of itinerant dealers and handicraftsmen pursuing their occupations *sub dio*; increased also by the hosts of mendicants, sound or diseased, seeking charitable aid. Modern police legislation removes the aspect of this mass of poverty and misery, but it may be doubted whether it is really diminished in extent, though somewhat changed in kind. It is like the house of a slut, made clean to the eye by sweeping the dust behind the door....

[264]

...Nothing is more puzzling than the difficulty, not unfrequently occurring in society, of deciding which is the leader and which is the bear. In the present case I must, having a due and decent respect for station, assume that Thomas de Clare was the principal, and his steward the follower, though, in fact, the latter, physically at least, was steersman through the living tide, as they slowly progressed towards the Metropolitan Cathedral; and when at length they were within the shadow of its spire, the crowd in front of the church was so dense that they could hardly make their way into the area of the "Parvis."

"A wondrous congregation hath the preacher at the Cross this morning," said Thomas de Clare. "In truth, I recollected not that the deposition of St. Alphage was a feast day of devotion. It is surely not so in our diocese?"

"And a pious man, without doubt, is the preacher," said the steward, "for he speaks so loud."

"Pious, indeed!—a heretic, a rank heretic—a foul Lollard!" replied Thomas de Clare, "attracting such idle crowds; none else could do so in these wicked times. If he were an orthodox, sober man, a prebendary or a minor canon, you would have sufficient elbow-room here."

It happened, strangely enough, that a stout serving-man, in the well-known livery of Ferrers of Groby, who was forced against Thomas de Clare by the throng, exclaimed at this juncture, it was as bad as going to church at Lutterworth; and the squire was about to put a question which would, as he anticipated, at once have fully confirmed his suspicions. Before he could speak the opportunity was lost; but this was of little consequence, for they could hear now sufficiently with their own ears. The coped wall, which more immediately surrounded the pulpit, whilst it still concealed from them the person who was holding forth, would hardly have intercepted the voice of the discourser if it had been as lofty as the steeple; for verily this personage, whatever his character might be, roared like a bull. Rendered husky by thirst, hoarse by exhaustion, the distich which he was vociferating—

> When once I begin, I'll break every bone,
> And pull from the skin the carcass, anon—

was followed by a volley of somewhat unseemly execrations, which were scarcely intelligible, in consequence of the fury with which they were exploded.

The licence allowed in those days to the eloquence of the pulpit

was such that the strange tenor of the discourse would excite
little surprise; but even the seneschal was rather puzzled by the
clapping of hands and plaudits which followed, interrupted with
piercing shrieks, even as when a pig bleeds and expires beneath
the butchering blade. Cries of "Harrow!" and "Murder!"
arose louder and louder. The shrieks were, as it seemed, those
of babes and children; and Thomas, with a look of unfeigned
horror, exclaimed, "It is all over with the faith! the heretics
have got the upper hand! the Vaudois have come over, and are
celebrating their hideous Sabbath in unhallowed triumph!" He
would have retreated if he could, but there was no flying from the
evil: he was forced round the corner by the stream, and then
found himself, to his extreme surprise and unmitigated delight,
not amongst a congregation listening to a sermon delivered by
a Wickliffe, but in the midst of the enraptured audience of a
mystery or stage-play.

The aspect of the structure in which Herod was raging in the
most orthodox mood will be fully understood without much
further description when the reader is told that it was nearly of
the same form and size as the proscenium or exterior of the booth
where the humble votaries of Thespis exhibit at famed Bartholomew Fair. The three soldiers, under the command of the King of
Jewry, had just completed the slaughter of all the Innocents, who
were lying in gory heaps,—an exhibition which, like other displays
of the horrific, had excited the strongest tokens of approbation
which could be notified by the shudders and cheers of the assembly,
—when Tivitevillus and Secundus Demon and Tertius Demon
now entered, emitting fire in every direction. They spit fire, they
belched fire, they bombarded the audience with fire. The chief
fiend, before he commenced his proper business, inveighed, in
rumbling, alliterative verse, against the vices of the times, and
particularly against the horned head-dresses of the women—a
fashion then recently introduced from Bohemia by good Queen
Anne—and by which, as he maintained, the good ladies had
grievously trespassed upon the infernal costume of himself and
his companions. Other sallies of wit followed, eliciting much
applause, which was redoubled when each hideous goblin pitch-
forked a soldier into "hell's mouth" gaping before them, and
which, snapping like a huge rat-trap, at once closed itself and
the scene. After a short pause, Simeon entered, intonating a
paraphrase of the *Nunc Dimittis*, in a voice which testified that
he had not yet recovered from his previous exertions in the

character of the Devil, and the presentation was enacted in all its particulars, exhibiting that singular union of solemn and profane allusions of pious sentiments and licentious ribaldry which form the particular characteristics of the dramatic performances of the middle ages.

"I suppose," said I to Cabezudo, "that we may exonerate our ancestors from any charge of direct impiety in these strange representations, abhorrent as they may be to all our notions of fitness and decorum? There is a period in the human intellect when the sublime is not degraded by the ridiculous, or, perhaps, when the sense of the ridiculous, not unfrequently the result of conventional ideas, exists only under an aspect totally different from that which it assumes in more civilized society. For all this allowance must be made; yet one main cause of the want of reverential feeling, still often exhibited so fearfully in your country, is to be traced at once in the proscription of the Word of Truth by the corrupt policy of your Church. Had the plain and unmutilated text of Scripture been presented to the people, how could even your priesthood have concealed from the people the fact that in these wretched farces the third of the Commandments was most sinfully and deliberately infringed. And how injurious, even to the coarsest mind, must these mysteries have proved! Presented without reverence, the most sacred truths must have been degraded to the level of a devised fable; the most sacred incidents of Holy Writ turned into a gainful spectacle; the holiest words, repeated as in mockery by the buffoon and the harlot, must have subverted every notion of decency and religion. Nay, the edifice itself must have been desecrated in the coarse feelings of the multitude."

Cabezudo put his hand into his waistcoat pocket and took out a red leather case, which he opened and produced a pair of spectacles. They were tortoiseshell spectacles. Then, after carefully wiping the glasses with his glove, he presented them to me.

"Well?" says I.

"Well!" says he, pointing to what is usually called a dead wall, but which, in the instance before us, was most satisfactorily enlivened by the placards, of various colours and sizes, with which it had been decorated by the industry of the bill-sticker, unmindful of the warning which bade him "beware," the monitor itself betraying its harmless impotence by the placards with which it was concealed. Strange was the miscellany thus displayed. The eloquence of the auctioneer exerted for his client and sounding

the praises of his lots, and the address of the candidate less
dexterously trumpeting his own. Carriages knocked up, and
horses to be knocked down. Machines and steamers. The goods
of the bankrupt, sold for the benefit of the attorneys; and the
announcement of the shop opened by the young tradesman,
destined to the same end. Brown stout and coffee; Madeiras
and magazines; food and poison. A mass of *provocations* to the
multitude, of which the pervading spirit seemed at first to be that
of business and activity—Puff! puff! puff! Quack! quack!
quack! resounding from every line—but which, as you studied
the matter more, and thought about it more, seemed to groan
forth deeper and deeper tones of folly and of vice and misery.

I supposed from the motion of Cabezudo that he intended
that I should collect his reply from the Sibylline leaves thus
spread before me, but as yet I could not exactly satisfy myself
as to his meaning. I turned with a humble, supplicating look to
my hierophant, who, taking the barnacles out of my hand and
adjusting them in their proper position on my nose, recommended
me to recommence my parietarian study.

"Oh!" said I, "I have it," pointing to a placard so fresh that
it had evidently been just affixed over another of the preceding,
whose place it partially usurped, and reading the large lettered
sentences in the announcement of—"Theatre Royal, under the
patronage of the officers of the Blues—the Stranger, by particular
desire—Character of Mrs. Haller—Jim Crow—Cachouca—Ballet
—Comic Song—Hokey Pokey Whankey Fun, King of the Cannibal
Islands." "Really, Cabezudo," exclaimed I, "this is abominably
unfair. How can any comparison be instituted between the
levity of the young gay soldiers who patronise the representations, and the idle silliness of those who resort to them, and the
deliberate profanation effected by the tonsured patrons of the
mediæval mystery. Possibly the vice of the old morality may
be more innocent than the false virtue of the drama; but at
least we never attempt to ally the daubed tinsel attractions of the
stage with the doctrines of religion. And do you think we could
by any possibility allow the vocalist who regales the audience
with Hokey Pokey Whankey Fun to be heard in the choir?"

"Certainly not," replied Cabezudo, "because he would make
but an awkward prima donna." But so saying, he stepped
forward, and cruelly peeling off the bill-sticker's scroll, I read,
somewhat obscured by the paste and shreds of its subsequent
compeer and rival:—"Grand Musical Festival—Performances at

the Cathedral—Selections from Don Giovanni—Messiah—Signor Albertazzi—Madame Puzzi—Mosé in Egitto—Figaro—Calvary—Last Judgment—Fancy Ball—Figlia del Regimento—Bazaar in the Palace Gardens for the benefit of the Missions in Patagonia."

I answered nothing, but Cabezudo continued with his usual pertinacity: "You will, I think, admit that at least the balance may be fairly poised between ancient burlesque and modern piety. Follow up the inquiry, and you will gain little by the parallel. Would it shock your feelings to be told that the metropolitan cathedral was a public market, filled with the stalls of the huckster and the stands of the vendors of petty wares? Well, they put the bazaar into the church, you put the church into the bazaar, and receive the gifts of the visitors of Vanity Fair as the offerings of the Gospel. You, perhaps, will maintain that the end purifies the means. But will that gift be accepted which costs you nothing? Will the charity be effectual which brings no blessing upon the hands by which it is bestowed? And do you not, by this miserable conformity to the spirit of the world, exchange a scanty and polluted rill for the perennial flow of benevolence, proceeding from the only unfailing source of goodwill toward mankind?"

But we must leave Cabezudo, and enter the structure to which he alludes. "Paul's Walk," in the reign of Richard the Second, did not present so rich a variety of humours as it afterwards exhibited under our virgin queen; yet the characters of the throngs who resorted thereto were sufficiently diversified. Devotion seemed to be the last object which they sought, excepting when the tinkling of the bell, announcing the completion of the eucharistic sacrifice, induced a transient pause, checking for a moment the converse which filled the building with its busy hum. A large proportion of the crowd consisted of mere idlers, amongst whom the most conspicuous were the sleek and ruddy chantry priests—a class of ecclesiastics who, by their exemption from parochial duties and their undisturbed possession of good endowments, were generally tempted to live in a manner little creditable to themselves or their calling. There was also a good store of citizens' wives, with here and there a Netherlandish vrow from the other bank of the Thames, such as the portly mistress of the very accommodating tavern of the Maid and the Mackerel, which she rented under Alderman Walworth, who built it on the Bishop of Winchester's grounds; but a large proportion consisted of persons brought together upon matters of urgent necessity.

Even as the Temple of Jerusalem was resolved into the [Den]

of Thieves, so had the nave of St. Paul's become the mart of
the practitioners of the law. Each sergeant, upon his call, had
his pillar assigned to him by the steward and comptroller of the
Inn where the feast had been kept, by whom the whole covey
of new-hatched coifs was on such occasions escorted in great
state to the cathedral. There the new sergeant took his stand,
and his clients resorted thither for all purposes of consultation
and advice, and for the general transaction of business, or at least
as much as could be managed in so public a situation. Another
usage also prevailed, which will further remind us of the desecra-
tion of the Temple of Jerusalem; for, in addition to buying and
selling actually practised there, against which good Bishop
Braybrook had just issued his fruitless monitions, it was the
spot fixed as the appointed place for the payment of moneys due
upon bond, obligation, pledge, or mortgage, according to a form
which is yet employed in all legal instruments of that description, in which the "North Gate of the Royal Exchange" is usually
selected—a condition which at the present moment it might be
difficult to perform. Our ancient jurisprudence, however, did not
allow of equity of redemption, and many a bond had become
forfeited to a Christian Shylock, and many a fair manor and
broad demesne passed irrevocably to the mercers and merchant
taylors of London, in consequence of the spendthrift knight or
entangled baron having failed to appear before the shrine of
Saint Erkenwold, whilom bishop of London, exactly within the
appointed day and hour.

Extensive as is the area of the present structure, it only
occupies a portion of the ground covered by the ancient cathedral,
which must have been the finest and most impressive in England.
The lofty concave at the time when our companions entered
seemed but partially filled with the chequered light of the slanting
sunbeams, which, as they darted through the windows of the
southern clerestory, imparted the tints of the stained glass to
the whirling motes, circling in ceaseless gyrations, whilst occasionally a wandering butterfly or a buzzing wasp or a humming bee,
flitting, soaring, and poising in the stream of transmitted light,
was steeped for the moment in phosphoric splendour. The space
above was cast into comparative darkness, and from the vaultings
you might hear the twittering of the birds, the sparrows and the
martins, who had built their nests not only on the exterior, but
within the edifice, as if they had sought it for a refuge. The
building, however, bore many tokens of decay, and some marks

of violence,—tracery broken and images mutilated, injuries ascribed to the rude games and pastimes carried on within the sacred precincts, but possibly inflicted by the heretics, whose scarcely concealed opinions led them to condemn the practices by which the faith was so deeply corrupted and stained.

A large group was assembled near the tomb of the Anglo-Saxon prelate. Considering the professional purposes to which Saint Erkenwold's memorial was applied, he ought to have been honoured as the patron of scriveners, and portrayed as fondling a shark. He appeared, however, in full pontificals; but the eager or anxious countenances of the bystanders sufficiently declared, without any further symbol, their expectancies or their fears.

Amongst the persons thus brought together, there were two or three who were watching with great earnestness a bright spot, produced by a particular beam, which, separated from the rest in consequence of its passing through the unglazed centre of a massy quatrefoil, was advancing with steady and uniform, and yet vibratory, movement along the pavement, marking the appointed course of the great luminary, at once the object most familiar to the senses and the most incomprehensible to the mind. It was commonly supposed and reported by popular tradition that this aperture had been constructed by the celebrated Johannes de Sacrobosco, the astronomer, for the purpose of forming a meridian line: and as the principles of the mundane sphere were so well understood by him, there was no improbability in admitting such an account of its origin. When the subject was mentioned, many people shook their heads mysteriously. Strange hints were given of a learned clerk at Padua who had so constructed the great Sala del Consiglio that the rays which shoot athwart from the roof of it should reveal the secrets of futurity as they passed along its stained walls. Others whispered that Richard of Bordeaux, young as he was, knew more of the wisdom of the Chaldees than was consonant with Catholic faith....

If Pietro di Abano, whom Dante had recognized in the regions below, was to be considered as an accomplice of King Richard, this could only have been the result of his magical foresight; and John Rouse, who, in the time of Henry, took the style of an antiquary, is said to have said (I have not seen the passage) that old John Hollywood, or Holywood, had nothing whatever to do with the matter, and that the chance situation of the line on the pavement and the portion of the quatrefoil had produced the appearance—an assertion which he might have supported by the natural dials which exist in some of the Alpine regions. But, be this as it may, and whether the result of accident or design, the solar spectrum did, in fact, mark the hour of noon whenever it traversed a particular range of tesselated tiles by which the nave was crossed. And the twilight surrounding the brighter disk was just quivering by the side of the gnomonic line, when the rumbling of the movements announced the approaching stroke, and the slow lengthened clangour of the horologe bell resounded through and along the vaulted roof of the building.

"It is a done thing, Master Notary," exclaimed a pale and crabbed-looking man, wearing the parti-coloured hood of white and yellow, which constituted the livery of the Grocers' Company. "It is a done thing; and the manors of Great and Little Massingham, with all the demesnes thereof, and all the woods, underwoods, messuages, tenements, houses, and outhouses thereunto belonging," continued he, reading from a parchment deed, "now belong to me, William Walworth, my heirs and assigns, for ever."

"Squire Rookesby hath failed to tender to me, at the shrine of Saint Erkenwold, in the cathedral church of St. Paul, between the hours of eleven and twelve of the clock, the hundred marks which he borrowed from me, and bear witness, all of ye, that the hour is passed."

But their attention was diverted by loud cries of "Hoy! Hoy!" and a gaily-clad bachelor was seen running full speed from the transept door. It was Rookesby himself, scouring along for life or death, he having been unexpectedly retarded on his way by causes which, as a warning, may be slightly detailed.

The fashionable shoon of the age, the "pykys," as they were called, of which the toe-termination was about a yard in length, were fastened to the knees of the mediæval exquisite by silver chains, constituting a most inconvenient equipment for rapid progression. Even to walk easily in them required almost as much practice as the feat of dancing a hornpipe in fetters.

Thus embarrassed, we need not wonder that Rookesby, who, landing at Coleharbour bridge, had imagined, in his ignorance of civic topography, that the feat of progressing to the cathedral could be accomplished in a space which would have brought him to the appointed spot a full quarter before the due time, and who, besides, had never calculated upon the impediments which he was destined to encounter in the porch and parvis, should be so belated on reaching the fatal tomb. Darting forward with all the strength of despair, he rushed up to the shrine, exclaiming, "Take! Take! Take!" and he emptied the coin upon the slab of marble stone, certainly before the undulating resonance of the twelfth stroke had ceased, whilst the definite limb of the lucid circle had not even touched the fatal boundary.

Walworth, however, good man, had now assuredly put by all thoughts of lucre and pelf, for with that ferine quickness of eye which belongs both to lender and borrower—who, opposite as they appear in their transactions, ought, physiologically speaking, to be considered as one genus—he had discovered the breathless spendthrift as soon as the point of his shoon had crossed the portal. Thereupon had Walworth instantly plumped upon his knees, his face turned towards an effigy against the wall of the chapel, and so deeply engaged in his orisons, that he seemed as if the falling of the steeple would hardly have awakened him to a sensation of the existence of any mundane affairs.

"Take your money, Master William," said Rookesby, pressing his broad hand with crushing strenuousness on the shoulder of the devotee, who continued as immovable as the statue before him. Such, however, was the vehemence with which Rookesby addressed Walworth, that the worthy alderman—all aldermen are worthy—began internally to apprehend that although Saint Apollonia, before whom he was worshipping, might have the power of curing the toothache, it might be better not to have to trouble her, out of her proper department in the profession, for the purpose of mending broken bones; and therefore, turning his head over his shoulder, he blandly whispered, "Friend—I pray thee, friend—friend, hast thou no conscience thus to disturb a poor penitent sinner?"

"Conscience!" exclaimed Rookesby, "to be sure I have, enough and to spare; and is it not a proof of it that I am here at the very moment to pay the debt which I owe?"

"I charge thee not with a falsehood, friend," replied Walworth, "I defy the temptation of judging my neighbour; but, alas, that a Christian man should so deceive himself, as if the time of redemption were not past and forever!"

"By no manner of means," exclaimed Rookesby; "what can be truer than the sun? Was I not here, and did I not make the payment of the debt, as the light of heaven testifies, before the expiration of the hour within the time which the proviso required for making void the mortgage-deed?"

"Would that thou hadst," replied the worthy alderman, with

a great appearance of sorrow. "Had the manor been redeemed at the appointed time," continued he, fetching a deep groan, "I should have been saved a world of trouble. A lowly merchant like myself to become the owner of the capital messuage of an ancient barony, liable, if in an evil hour the king should choose, to be summoned as a peer; and this is the burthen which thy negligence hath cast upon me. Much wilt thou have to answer for, Master Rookesby!"

"Wretch! usurer!" cried out Rookesby, grasping the hilt of his sword and advancing towards Walworth, who did not look as if he were at all daunted by the attitude of his opponent, "thus to insult me! You lie, and you know it. The money was paid down before noontide was passed."

Such squabbles were unfortunately by no means of uncommon occurrence in the sacred edifice; but this dispute being rather above the usual average in interest, it had drawn together a crowd of spectators, some sympathising, others laughing, and others commenting upon the scene. But, besides these idle spectators, there were not wanting a due proportion of those industrious gentry who, in various ways, when any fight, whether fight-fistic or fight-forensic, takes place, usually contrive to transfer a portion of the superfluous wealth of either of the combatants or the by-standers into their own good keeping and safeguard. In a locality, however, so thronged with retainers of the law, it may easily be supposed that the more vulgar class of conveyancers would have comparatively a diminished chance of profiting by their vocation, and the professional, regular, and legal mode of diving into pouch, poke, and pocket would be the sleight carried on with far the greatest success and impunity.

"Pardon me, good sir," said a thin, clean-looking youth, with ink-bespattered sleeves, and a penner at his girdle, quickly and adroitly seizing Rookesby by the arm and drawing him away from his grim opponent, "but you are in danger of the Arches if you brawl in the church."

"Endanger the arches by brawling in *this* church," said Rookesby, looking instinctively at the solid ribs of the massy Norman structure, calculated to defy an earthquake, but in a tone of mixed anger and perplexity, the latter feeling, however, preponderating, for the first and most obvious idea, as suggested by the sense in which he had caught the words—namely, that the stranger mocked him—was rather counteracted by the supposition that it was a reproof for his profanation of the edifice. The scrivener's clerk—for such he was—proceeded to set Rookesby right, by explaining to him that the Court of Arches was the ecclesiastical tribunal, taking cognizance of such and other violations of propriety.

"Like our Consistory Court," answered Rookesby, not without alarm, the vision of a white sheet and stool of repentance (the sad sequel of an All-Hallows E'en invocation, performed by bouncing Margery to raise her future sweetheart), presenting itself to his imagination.

"Exactly so," replied Stephen Sharpenpen, "and this place abounds with its emissaries."

Thanks were heartily returned for this warning, of which Rookesby fully felt the value. This opening introduced further conversation, and Sharpenpen, who, amongst other honest modes of turning a penny, acted as touter or barker to Sergeant Clopton, easily effected his purpose of inducing Rookesby to advise with this legal oracle, who having first received his fee, an angel, gave it as his decided opinion, that in all cases where a certain place was appointed for the performance of a condition, which certain place happened to be within sound of a clock, the law would nevertheless intend that the sun was to regulate the time, and not the clock; and that if Walworth entered upon the land, not only would he be ousted by due process, but heavy damages recovered against him for the disseisin.

Rookesby made his reverence, and was preparing to depart, when Sharpenpen, intimating that something more was required to retain the assistance of the sergeant in the common pleas, Rookesby, after a brief pang, delivered up as much more as made up the needful dose, which sadly diminished his golden store.

A small proportion of Latin had been ferruled, cuffed, punched, and whipped into Rookesby; for at this period of our history the schoolmaster began to creep abroad, and education had made some progress amongst the higher classes; and so, turning to Sharpenpen, he said—

"Truly, I am nearly in the happy condition so well described by that learned clerk Orace, for thus quoth he—

Cantabit vacuus coram latrone viator";

a quotation which, however, was not literally true, for his purse still continued by a brace of broad pieces of good red gold, not destined, however, to continue much longer in their then nestling-place.

"Well may you spend, and better may you feed, good Master Sempronius," said a personage, who, turning out of a small door in the north wall, which led directly into Paternoster Row, the Doctors' Commons of those days, walked, or rather swung, up to the nearly despoiled Rookesby, with a most disagreeable and confident swagger. His countenance was as unprepossessing as his manner—narrow eyes, twinkling beneath the black scalled brows which shadowed them, shed an ominous light upon a copper-coloured and distempered visage, terminated by a straggling beard. His whole appearance betokened a drunken debauchee. But before I proceed, it may perhaps be necessary to explain that Titius and Sempronius have, ever since the age of Bartholus and Baldus, performed the same good service to the civilians which those worthy brothers-in-law, John Doe and Richard Roe, render to the modern practitioner—to wit, that of keeping a place in the blanks of precedents and forms of process until a real sufferer can be inserted in their room.

"Sempronius!" exclaimed Rookesby, thrown off his guard, as he generally was, by his irascibility. "My name is not Sempronius, sir; I am not a Lombard or a Roman—I am Giles Rookesby, of Rookesby Hall, in the county of Essex."

"Gramercy, Master Giles Rookesby, of Rookesby Hall," exclaimed the crafty sompner, or apparitor, the worthy purveyor of prey for the ecclesiastical court, taking out his pen and inserting the name as he wrote out the citation, grinning horribly all the while with delight at having so easily obtained the information which he sought; "and this is to require you to appear before the official, at St. Mary-le-Bow, to answer to the libel which shall be propounded against you in a matter of indecently brawling in the church, and submit to such correction *pro salute animae* as shall be then and there imposed."

Excusable as Rookesby might deem himself in his own opinion for having been provoked into the disturbance in which he had been engaged with Walworth, his conscience smote him sufficiently as to the fact; and destitute as he might be of any theoretical knowledge of the proper extent of the jurisdiction of the ecclesiastical tribunals, he had obtained a sufficiently experimental knowledge of the "penance" which they could impose. The service of the monition, therefore, which was thus performed, might well create in him no small degree of disquietude. He showed it by his looks; his countenance fell, and he cast an anxious glance to Sharpenpen as his friend and comforter. The nod of the scrivener was easily understood by the sompner; and the trio retiring to a side chapel, a negotiation was begun, Sharpenpen acting as the kind friend of both parties, which received a speedy termination. Rookesby, after turning aside and conferring with Sharpenpen, handed to him the two broad pieces together with the awful citation, and Sharpenpen, carefully folding the coin therein, re-delivered the now well-weighted parchment to the sompner, who, dropping it into the proper receptacle, walked away in great radiance.

Rookesby, sad, yet congratulating himself upon his escape, walked as quickly as he could out of the cathedral. Sharpenpen, keeping as close to him as possible, now followed behind like a shadow, now shuffled before him like a spaniel, and with much the same humble look of solicitation, though it must be confessed that it is almost wronging the faithful brute to compare him with such vermin as the scrivener. At first Rookesby did not understand the cause of this close attention; secondly, he understood it, but determined he would not understand it; thirdly and lastly, conquered by Sharpenpen's quiet perseverance, he could stand it no longer. But his purse had now been drained of all its contents, with the exception of about three shillings' worth of the before described base coin called "pollards and crockards," which he offered to Sharpenpen as a guerdon for his kind assistance. The scrivener declined to receive this foreign coin, intimating that it had been cried down by proclamation, and that he should be liable to a penalty if he received the same. Rookesby, really of a kind disposition, was vexed at not being able to reward an individual who, as he deemed, had rendered him an important and unpaid service—an uneasiness which would have been somewhat diminished if he had known the secrets of the alliance between the sompner and the man of indentures. Whilst he was considering how he could satisfy the claim thus made upon his gratitude, or at least his generosity, a small swarthy personage, who had been following the couple, came up and offered to exchange the "black money" for sterling coin, deducting one-half of the nominal value; which proposal being gladly accepted by Rookesby, the proceeds were handed over to Sharpenpen, who making his *congé*, disappeared, leaving Rookesby to return to a home which, however, he was not destined to enjoy....

We must now return to Thomas de Clare, who had made his way through the crowd just after the *démêlé* between Rookesby and Walworth began. His primary intention was, as I before mentioned, to have consulted with Sergeant Holt, a plan by no means agreeable to his trusty seneschal, who rather preferred that his master should be initiated in the mysteries of the money-market before he came in the lawyer's way.

I wish some philosopher, some metaphysician, such as there used to be, would write a good treatise upon the various modes of directing, nay, coercing (without any pretensions to mesmeric agency) the choice or determination of those with whom we have to deal, and who consider themselves as free agents all the while.

"What can you let us have for dinner to-day?" said my fellow-traveller to the mistress of the inn—I beg her pardon, the lady of the proprietor of the hotel at Scarborough—as we came in, wet and tired, towards the close of the day.

"Anything you please, gentlemen," was the prompt reply. "Mock turtle, gravy, ox tail; turbot, salmon, soles, haddocks, ducks, turkey polts, chickens," overwhelming us with the nomenclature of good cheer. Whilst labouring under this *embarras des richesses*, consulting and discussing what we should choose, our hostess, just at the right moment of our dubitation, without the slightest appearance of suggestion or persuasion, and in the most accidental and careless manner imaginable, dropped a word or two about "excellent mutton." She had us. She cast in the feather which turned the scale. It was impossible to resist; she had made up our mind for us; the "excellent mutton" was ordered, and the credit of the larder was saved.

It is by the same knack that the skilful professor of legerdemain is enabled, when presenting the open pack, to lead your fingers to the protruded card. Exactly similar, also, is the tact with which the practised attorney avails himself of the precise moment when he can give the turn-about to the much-bothered Justice, his worship quite believing that he has pronounced the decision of his own sagacity and volition, whereas he has simply been the mouthpiece of the clever man of law. But no one possesses this faculty to a greater extent than your well-practised toad-eater. And when Thomas de Clare was discoursing about his perplexities, and half-deploring the expenses of legal proceedings, and regretting the expedient of making sale of Fold-acre mead, an apparently incidental remark, that loans could now be obtained upon very easy terms by any landed gentleman, at once determined the dubious squire.

...At an early period the rueful borrower repaired to the Jewry, where the pale usurer dealt out his coin. The ruthless decree of Edward expelled the children of Israel, and when Thomas de Clare, in his character, joyfully exclaimed, "I am at least quit of the debt,—thirty marks, with lucre at the rate of a groat a week for each and every pound which Vives lent to me to pay my relief in obtaining livery of my lands——"

"Do not halloo till you are out of the wood, Sir Knight," was Father Barnaby's reply; "for if, as I ween, the bonds and obligations which you gave to Vives have all been duly seized into the treasury, there are they deposited under the three keys; and be assured that the debt which the Jew allowed to run into arrear will be levied to the uttermost farthing by the king, who succeedeth, if not to the vocation, yet to the gains of the race whom he hath banished from his realm."

The business of money-lending itself, however, was too profitable, and, it may be truly added, so necessary, that it continued to flourish quite as much as before. Supply was excited by demand, and the keen and industrious natives of Italy, generally known as ".Lombards," but of whom, in point of fact, the greater portion belonged to the communities now absorbed in the papal dominions, Sardinia and Tuscany, filled the place in the money-market which had previously been occupied by the Jews, upon whom they had been long intruding. Uniting, however, the characters of real and *bona fide* merchants with those of the banker, they occupied a much more advantageous position; for the union of the two callings enabled them, by various devices not entirely forgotten, to obtain a very decent gain for the use of the cash which they advanced, without making the direct charges for interest which had rendered their predecessors so odious; and though they were equally peccant, yet in some respects appearances were saved.

In the reign of Richard II., however, the prosperity of the "Lombards" had begun to decline. Fierce conflicts at home exhausted their wealth, new channels were opened for trade, but the greatest injury they sustained resulted from the unmanageable extent of the transactions in which the chief houses engaged, and whereby they were tempted onwards and onwards to speculations which were as sure to lead to ruin in the days of the Guelfs and Ghibellines as in the present day. Whoever may have been the individuals, it was therefore still from the orientals that the precious ore was to be obtained, and therefore Thomas de Clare and his seneschal naturally directed their course from St. Paul's towards Lombard Street, leaving the deserted Jewry on their way.

"Good-morrow, Master Frisky-ball," said Huxter, for such was the manner in which the name of the Frescobaldi was anglicised, addressing the apparent owner of one of those mansions, occupant in one sense, though, as we shall soon learn, his occupation was gone.

Amongst the many pictures of fallen greatness, I hardly recollect anything more pathetic than that presented by Queen Obereah, when our circumnavigators paid their second visit to Otaheite's favoured isle. No longer resplendent in the charms of mahogany cheeks, tattooed buttocks, and cocoa-nut oil, which rendered her the compeer of the goddess of Cythera, but old, haggard, deserted by all former admirers, and wailing, "Toottee is dead, and you can't get any more hogs." Almost as much compassion might have been inspired by the Florentine merchant addressing his visitors with, "King Edward is dead, and we can't get any of our money"—an exclamation of which the sad import was very speedily explained.

"We had lent," said Messer Taddeo, "to King Edward upwards of a hundred thousand pounds sterling, partly from our capital, and partly from the moneys which we had borrowed from others, when our correspondents, and particularly those who had deposited money in our hands, nobles, prelates, doctors of the law, alarmed at the extent of our dealings with his majesty, began, as soon as he exchanged a worldly crown for a crown of glory, to call all their moneys in. Bills of exchange dropped upon us in flights, like crows, indicating the approaching slaughter, until every ducat of balance was withdrawn. Complaint would have been instant destruction. We kept our own counsel; but though discretion might protract the crisis, it could not avert our ruin. We had accepted a lease from the king of his mines in the west, which we reckoned would have given us a decent profit. But the Cornishman was too strong for us, and ten thousand marks were wasted into dross by the assay of copper and tin. It were a long story to recount, but the end of it was that King Edward gave us a security upon the Irish revenue;—and what kind of a country Ireland is, all the world can tell!" continued he, with the significant gesture of placing his thumb against his nose. "Our Messer Lapo, who crossed over to Dublin, got his head broken at the treasury, and our bank is broken too, and my heart also."

Thus speaking, Messer Taddeo began to weep, and so affecting was his grief, that Thomas de Clare cried outright, and Huxter the seneschal took out his handkerchief, but did not wipe his eyes. Their sorrow might have been alleviated could they have looked into futurity. Failures, in mercantile matters at least, are frequently the precursors of success. The *banco rotto* was soon mended again. The Frescobaldi recovered all their former credit, and acquired such stability that, after the lapse of more than a century, they were still a house of great business in England, and as a factor or agent in their service did Thomas Cromwell make the first step in his career of varied and chequered fortune.

Foiled in the attempt to raise the supplies, Thomas de Clare and his companion proceeded a little further to the accounting-house of Stefano degl' Imperiali, the Genoese, whom they found at his desk, the maple-wood shining by long attrition, and seated upon a high chair or throne, from which he courteously descended. Few words passed, time was precious to all parties, and Thomas de Clare having explained his business, the Genoese, with perfect civility, and yet in the most take-it-or-leave-it manner imaginable, informed the squire it was the regular business of the firm to do good bills of the Staple, and that if he would be pleased to accept the money which he required, according to the usual chevisance of merchants, it was entirely at his command.

Overjoyed at this ready compliance, Thomas de Clare prepared his mind to begin to touch cash, when it suddenly struck him that it might be as well to know the meaning of the term *"Chevisance,"* which the merchant had employed. "It is a custom," said Imperiali, "amongst us dealers that the borrower do return the money to the lender, with an increase, at and after the rate of £10 for every £100 by the year for the usance." Spendthrift as Thomas de Clare assuredly was, he had all that morbid fear of being overreached and cheated equally characteristic of wanton waste and of dishonesty of mind.

There was nothing exceedingly exorbitant in the terms asked, or rather mentioned, by the Genoese, still less was there anything affronting in the proposition; but the squire chose to ascribe the characters both of extortion and insult to the proposition. "Usance!" he exclaimed, laying as much stress as he possibly could upon the last syllable. "Usury, foul usury, such as befits only a Jew or a Saracen. It is not that I care for the money, but I will not give countenance to the sin, nor encourage these foreigners in flaying us Englishmen. If I am to be plucked, it shall be at least for the benefit of my own countrymen"; and so, under the guidance of Huxter, who had a perfect knowledge of

the chorography of the district, they proceeded to Alderman
Philpot, "of that ilk," in the adjoining lane, opening like a darker
gorge into the dark defile.

About this time Philpot, Brember, and Walworth, all historical
personages in this eventful period, together with one or two other
citizens, good warm men, without doubt, but who were exempted
from celebrity, had become the joint contractors, as we should
now say, for several loans to the crown.

To this important individual, then, Thomas de Clare proceeded, and the squire approached his door with something like
apprehension, for Alderman Philpot lived in the highest circle of
city fashion. His *manoir*, for thus the great dwellings were
called, had lately been rebuilt in a style of which some few specimens yet survive in the city, having been often mistaken for the
remains of ecclesiastical buildings. The lower storey, employed,
as in Italy, as a warehouse, consisted of a large hall, supported
by clustered pillars supporting a fairly-groined vaulting. Chests
and bales of goods, stacks of bars of steel, and pigs of lead were
piled around, and Huxter made a kind of awkward bow as he
passed by the horse-block, the chopping-block, and the frieze of
leathern water-buckets, domestic ensigns of shrieval honour, all
of which, until a very recent period, were presented at the expense
of the corporation to those who were called to an office whilom of
so much respectability and dignity.

"It is a shame," said the worthy alderman, "that those
strangers are thus allowed to spoil and pillage the land, living
not by fair and honest dealing, but by brokage and every species
of fraud.

"Oft and oft have we petitioned parliament against them, but
redress cannot be obtained. But we citizens of London," continued Philpot, "have done our duty gloriously. We have begun
by reforming ourselves; determined to extirpate all abuses, we
never spare our individual interests, sacrificing all private advantages for the common weal and the ordinance newly made in our
common council, John Northampton, mayor. It is not for me
to name the alderman who brought in that ordinance. But the
consequence has been that, by its stringency upon us London
merchants, much as we lose in the way of business, all usance is
entirely extirpated and put down. Sir," continued Philpot with
solemn energy, "as I am an honest man, there is not a citizen who
would dare to show his face in Cheap if he were even suspected of
such a misdeed. We take usance! We who are taught from our

cradles that the love of money is the root of all evil!—we leave such abominations to the pope and the Jews."

Those who, from without, have contemplated the rapid progress of reform in the city of London may perhaps (as I once did) entertain the apprehension that, in their zeal for virtuous economy, they might perhaps go too far, and by their stoical disregard of their own feelings, perhaps place their body politic in such a stripjack naked starvation system as to endanger its very existence; nay, that even their own interests in purse, pudding, and patronage might all be sacrificed on the altar of patriotism; but I have been rather comforted of late by seeing how much wise discretion they have learned from the far-famed follower of the knight of the sorrowful countenance. Sancho, as is well known, first began to apply the lash on his own hide, but as after a stroke or two he found the operation not entirely pleasant, he continued the discipline upon the trees around him, uttering such groans as melted the very heart of his compassionate master, whilst his dear back and buttocks were wholly unharmed.

And thus, gentle reader, may we rest in the comfortable assurance that whilst the civic legislation resounds with professions of salutary reform, the lord mayor, sheriffs, aldermen, and common council all take good heed never to cut so deep as to establish a raw.

"A right Christian act," replied Thomas de Clare, convinced of the alderman's sincerity, "thus to renounce your own profits; but without doubt you will be amply rewarded hereafter."

"Far be it from me so to praise a body of which I am such an unworthy member in my humble capacity. As for my gains, dear friend," continued Philpot, "may I realize them in heaven; very thankful am I to be permitted to co-operate in any good deed or work; yet I hope I may be allowed to rejoice at the gospel forbearance which we are enabled to exercise towards our debtors, as truly it is our bounden duty to do."

"A true and loyal English merchant," said Thomas de Clare to the reeve when Philpot had quitted the chamber for the purpose of bringing the money which he had agreed to advance; for Philpot, after a short explanation, had speedily agreed to assist the squire with even more than he required, for the merchant, hearing that one hundred and fifty pounds were required to clear off the more pressing and immediate encumbrances upon the West Walsham estate, intimated that, by doubling the amount, Thomas de Clare might save the expense and trouble of another journey to London. The seneschal was about to reply, when Jenkyn, the merchant's servant, as he was then termed, but who would now be denominated his head clerk, and who had been left behind in the adjoining apartment—half for the purpose of attending upon the visitors, for Master Philpot was a civil man; and half, perhaps three-quarters, for the purpose of watching them, for a cautious man was Philpot as well as 'cute, and there were writings lying upon the tables—entered the room. The "servant" was quickly followed by a serving-man, a personage who, addressing his superior in the establishment, informed him that a baston of the Fleet was waiting without to speak to the alderman.

"It is wonderful," quoth Thomas de Clare to the reeve, "how the worthy alderman gains in public character and confidence. I know well that he had been appointed one of the treasurers of the subsidy granted to the king for carrying on the war, but I had not heard that the affairs of the navy came within his commission; yet, to be sure, forces by sea, forces by land, are all one." Thomas began to speculate upon the rank of the maritime officer thus announced, and perhaps my readers have begun to do the same, when the door opened and the baston and its bearer came in.

"Master Nicholas," said the serving-man to the miserable wretch who tottered into the apartment, the pallid hue of whose countenance could scarce be discovered through grime and hair, "please do not come between us and that window,"—through which, being open, a pleasant gale was blowing fresh from the water-side. "It is not so much on account of your smell, but there has been so much sickness in your prison that it is hardly safe"; and thus speaking, Jenkyn went to a cupboard, and taking out some fine dried Seville oranges, their rich brown coats studded closely with cloves, articles then and long afterwards considered as a powerful prophylactic against infectious diseases, he gave two to Thomas de Clare and the reeve, the third he kept for himself, and placing the fourth before the chair of the alderman, he returned again to the calculations upon which he had been employed.

The unfortunate creature thus exhaling the fetid atmosphere produced by the *squalor carceris*, the duresse of imprisonment, so emphatically defined by the civilians as one of the tortures compelling satisfaction from the debtor, had obtained his temporary enlargement by means of a custom then equivalent to a day rule. Under the protection of the baston or staff, delivered to him by the warden, he was enabled to come from the dreary walls either to seek relief from his friends or to crave pity from the creditor. Twenty years' incarceration sustained by Nicholas Carminow had blotted him out of the memory of the few who had known him at the period when, besides being the agent and accountant of Philpot, he was also a merchant, nearly as opulent as his principal. His present appearance was for the purpose of suing for that mercy which, during the long period of detention, he had so often craved in vain. It must be, however, remarked that this mode of giving temporary relaxation to the prisoner had been restrained by a recent statute, to which, nevertheless, it does not appear that much attention was paid, as appears from the examples upon the Parliament rolls. When Philpot returned, the unfortunate visitor threw himself upon his knees, exclaiming, "Mercy, good master, mercy! if not for my sake, yet for hers, the willing companion of the horrors of the noisome dungeon!"

"You have but to produce the thousand crowns due upon the balance of an account," replied Philpot, "and you may bound away like the roe."

"Doth it not suffice," groaned Nicholas Carminow, "that, maimed and wounded as I was, in vainly attempting to defend the good ship, the *Katherine of Plymouth*, against the Breton pirates, I should have lost ten times that sum, at the same time that I was despoiled of the proceeds, which I had, according to the best of my judgment, invested for you as your share of the adventure? Great as your loss was, how much heavier was mine, good Master Philpot, generous patron!"

"I must be just before I am generous," quoth Philpot, with much calm dignity; "and you had better keep out of the way of old Touzer, lest he should fly at you. It is wonderful how naturally these mastiffs do hate a beggar."

A loud growl from the brute—the four-legged one, I mean—announced that this danger was not imaginary. Touzer's white snout began to protrude from beneath the table, and Carminow began to creep out of the chamber in an agony of despair. So doing, he touched, by accident, the arm of Mistress Agnes, the only child and heiress of that lordly mansion, as she was entering to speak to the alderman. The maiden shrunk back with disgust. Philpot, incensed beyond bearing with what he supposed to be an intentional insult—perhaps more than an insult, a revengeful desire to communicate infection—set the mastiff at the offender. The ferocious animal leaped upon Carminow, seizing him by the throat, and his life and his sufferings were on the point of coming to an end. The alderman, however, was now somewhat alarmed, for he recollected that the death of the debtor would extinguish his claim, so he called off the dog, and the victim was left bleeding upon the ground.

During these transactions, Thomas de Clare and Huxter had retired into the comptoir on the ground floor.

"I like the alderman all the better for his honest, plain-spoken energy," said Thomas de Clare, who, rendered uncomfortable by this glimpse of character, was endeavouring to talk himself into boldness, so as to quell, if possible, the apprehensions excited thereby. "This is the true way to be generous—first, be just: a wise and loyal merchant, aye, and a royal one—I like him all the better!"

How much longer this eulogium upon Alderman Philpot might have continued, it is impossible to say. At all events, he heard part of it; for whilst the knight was yet speaking, he came in, apparently in great glee, actually rubbing his hands with joy.

"What a source of happiness it is," said Thomas de Clare to his companion, "to have an approving conscience. Why is the alderman so blithe? It is because he feels that he has been fulfilling the obligations which his station imposes upon him!"

"Aye, my dear young friend," said Philpot to Thomas de Clare, who was about a year his senior. "In refusing to listen to the dictates of compassion, I have been performing a disagreeable and irksome duty; but it *is* a duty, and in that the best comfort is found here and hereafter. And then, Jenkyn," continued he, turning to his clerk, "how nicely we shall fix the warden with debt and costs. This little book will squeeze the money out of him more effectually than if he were lying on his back, enduring *peine forte et dure* in Newgate Pressyard."

The volume which the alderman had opened was of a size common enough amongst manuscripts, but not easily definable by the technical phrases of the printer or the binder, and placing the catalogue-maker in sad perplexity whether to describe it as small octavo or large duodecimo. But, at all events, the weight of the tome was not more than that of the pocket Bible grandmamma is wont to carry. And in this small space and narrow verge could the "writer of court letter," in the reign of Richard II., easily comprehend the Statutes at large.

"Now, here is the Act, Jenkyn," continued the alderman, "passed in the first year of the king.

"'It is ordained and appointed that from henceforth no

warden of the Fleet shall suffer any prisoner there, being by judgment at the suit of the party, to go at large, by baston or otherwise, unless he shall previously have satisfied him at whose suit he is confined, and the plaintiff shall have his recovery against the said warden.'

"Now, the warden hath plainly infringed the statute, and rendered himself fully liable; so that whether old Carminow lives or dies in Saint Bartholomew's hospital, it is all one to us. Is it not so, Jenkyn? And now, Master Thomas, I am at your service, if you please."

If the truth must be told, Thomas de Clare had been in a state of increasing discomfort during these exhibitions of sharp practice; but there was no help for it. The money was handed to him in the purse, but before he had time to open it, Jenkyn, at the nod of his master, presented the bill, neatly written upon a slip of fair vellum, in order that the knight might affix his seal thereto. Thomas de Clare was not in a hurry, and having perused the writing, he paused. "But is there not a mistake?" said he, addressing the alderman. "Your good mastership intimated that you would be quite contented to advance the money to me for the term of one year; and in this script the debt is payable forthwith, and without delay."

"Right, right, my young friend," said the alderman; "but this is our mode of transacting business in the city. When we do such bills we never appoint any particular time for payment. Good for to-morrow—good for twenty years, if it suits you to let the matter stand over. Furthermore, understand me, as I have before said, it would be a crying sin to exact usury, and it would be dishonourable if I, an alderman, a father of the city, were to demand any profit for giving you the help of my money. But I am always ready to perform my Christian duty, to show forbearance to my debtor, to give him time."

"Thank you," said Thomas de Clare, heartily.

"Well, then," continued Philpot, "although I could certainly sue you upon this obligation, yet these are but words. I have a heart within my breast. I will forbear to give you any trouble whatever about the money. I won't think about it until full twelve calendar months shall have expired, and so on, as often as it may suit your convenience." The countenance of Thomas de Clare became still brighter. "But," continued the alderman, "you will excuse my observing, that it is customary upon such occasions for the borrower, when he first receives the money, to compliment the lender by returning him ten pounds out of each hundred. It is for your security that I do so, not for mine. Life is uncertain, death is sure. We are all mortal—here to-day, gone to-morrow. If I were to die without having made a memorandum of the transaction in my book, for the guidance of the consciences of my executors, only think how entirely you would be at their mercy. Before you could look round you, your lands might be extended and your goods swept away."

Sad work—but there was no resisting. Thomas de Clare, opening the bag, turned out its contents upon the table, and counting out the required douceur, he slid the pieces to the alderman, and slowly began to tell over the balance which remained. "Why," said he, dreadfully agitated, partly with fear and partly with anger, "I have given you back thirty pounds. There ought to be two hundred and seventy remaining; and I can only make out one hundred and fifty. What a strange mistake."

"None at all, my excellent young friend," said Alderman Philpot; "but the fact is that cash is exceedingly scarce in this city just now. It was my haste to oblige you which made me give my promise rather inadvertently, as I was coming down here, for when I went out to talk the matter over with Jenkyn, I really began to be afraid that I should be compelled to break my word, for I have a heavy payment to make at the exchequer. But Jenkyn said, 'Sir, excuse me, this will not do; your character is at stake. Sir, give me leave most respectfully— (Jenkyn never forgets what is due to his superiors)—most respectfully to urge that this must not be. Sir, your word should be your bond, and, whatever may be the inconvenience to yourself, you must fulfil your engagements with Master Thomas, and however much you may lose by the business, you must make up the full amount to him in commodities.' Jenkyn's honest unsophisticated advice quite overcame me, and so, however much I may be pinched by the transaction, I have arranged to make up the whole amount for which you have sealed the bill, in Spanish figs, Cotteswold wool, and Suffolk cheese, all ready to be delivered to your carrier, or, if you prefer it, at Coleharbour wharf."

"Suffolk cheese!" exclaimed Thomas de Clare, "how am I to get the cheese to West Walsham? and if I could, it would be sending pardons to Rome. My bailiff took a load of my own cheese to last Norwich fair, and though it was as full of eyes as a peacock's tail, we could not sell a single weigh."

"My good friend," said the alderman, "it is your interest, not mine, that I am forwarding.   Cheese is looking up in our market, and figs are running so low at Grocers' Hall, that if you will be a holder till next Martinmas, I am sure you will clear cent. per cent. by your bargain.   But if you prefer realizing at once, I am sure that my excellent friend Alderman Walworth will give you the utmost value."...

CHAPTER X.

THE LIBRARY.

(RICHARD II.)

COMPARISONS, we are told, are odious. This unpleasant quality arises, I suppose, from the circumstance that the process of forming such parallels often leads us to a clear conviction of some disagreeable truth which we would fain have concealed sometimes from others, but oftener still from ourselves. But whether we like them or not, comparisons will always present themselves instinctively to the mind in every species of moral reasoning.

This is most peculiarly the case with respect to distant countries or distant times. We cannot obtain any very clear idea of their habits and customs, opinions or modes of thought, unless we measure them by their similitude or dissimilitude to our own; and there are perhaps few sublunary matters contrasting more forcibly with each other than the principles respectively embodied in the ancient library and the modern library. What a train of ideas is raised up in our minds by the term of the "dark ages!" and in the present age of gay and exuberant literature it is certain that our first feeling upon entering the Bibliotheca of the Holy Trinity, nigh Aldgate, would be that of triumphant exultation at the progress made by the human mind since the era when Duns Scotus was a luminary, and Aquinas reverenced as the great teacher of mankind.

The general arrangement of the building was fashioned according to the plan yet preserved in some few of our ancient buildings which still retain the architecture of the Gothic age. Between each pier, the pairs of brown oak presses with the desk at foot formed as many studies as there were windows in the apartment, at once effecting the greatest economy of space and the greatest opportunity of seclusion. The arrangement, in fact, was entirely domestic, and it was evidently seen that learning, instead of expanding her portals to the "public," was sought only by a select and tranquil community.

The most striking feature, however, to us modern observers, would have been what we should consider the paucity of volumes, as well as their general size and solidity. Acquainted as we are with the term "boards," nothing but an examination of a genuine and unaltered specimen of the ancient "bibliopegistic art," as it is familiarly termed by the worthy president of the bibliomaniac fraternity, can enable us to appreciate the weight and strength of the cover, composed of oaken plank, tough bull's hide, and hammered brass, by which they were literally shielded. There could be no light reading in those days; and still more strange to our practice was the manner in which each massy tome was secured by a bright chain of iron, the last ring of which, strung upon a rod of the same metal, enabled the Schoolman or the Father at the other end to traverse athwart the table, much in the same manner as the prisoner in the ancient Scottish gaol shuffled from side to side in his cell.

We, who are all, more or less, accustomed to test the value of a book by the "sensation" which it creates upon its first appearance, and by the rapidity with which the copies are dispersed, can scarcely tolerate the possibility of such barbarities. Yet it is not certain whether this mode of diffusing information had not some advantages, and whether the links thus attaching the volume did not tend to a much sounder concatenation of ideas than is now effected by the rapid gyrations of the book-club, or the orb within orb of the circulating library.

My friend Cabezudo, who, by the by, has, upon the postulation of Don Carlos, been lately appointed by the pope to the arch-bishopric of Toledo, often says: "We are on the verge of an era when all the higher powers of the mind will be palsied, perhaps to a degree never known before. Plans at present so rife in the social world, from whatever sect or party they proceed, whether in practice or in theory, are radically wrong. Your knowledge, such as it is, is not chemically united, but mechanically diffused; and as soon as the agitation ceases in the public mind, it falls to the bottom, leaving the fluid as vapid as before; and in every compendium, every abridgment, every encyclopædia, I find what experience has long since shown to be the surest test of intellectual debility."

Cabezudo—I must not call him his Grace until his promotion shall have been duly announced by "our correspondent in the north of Spain"—certainly carries his notions in this, and in many other respects, much too far. I don't go with him; no,

not I.   Still, it must be acknowledged that the forced and feverish
anxiety for the extension of knowledge which now prevails is
fearfully prejudicial to the cause of literature, and still more to
the only true object and end of literature—the discipline of the
human mind.   The "publications of the day" are never intended
to live till the morrow, and the inordinate appetite for the "last
new work" will be the most efficient means of checking the
composition of the works which never grow old, retaining their
freshness through all time and ages.   It is by this overflow that
our habits of discursive reading are fostered and encouraged.
The one book bought at the stall with the price of the dinner,
thumbed at the edges, and dog's-eared in the corners, cracked in
the back, annotated in the fly-leaf and scratched in the margin,
the inmate of the pocket and the companion of the fireside, and
thoroughly mastered from cover to cover, has always produced
more real cultivation, and afforded more real delight, than a
thousand "consulted for reference," fluttered over as the amusement of the idle hour.   More injurious than absolute idleness is
this semblance of occupation, which satisfies the vanity of the
intellect without inculcating one useful precept or repressing one
noxious thought.

We must suspend, however, these discussions, and join the
prior, who, followed by two strangers,—the one, a canon, as we
ascertain from the amice which he wears,—appears engaged in
assisting his companions to become acquainted with the contents
of the collection, which they are subjecting to a methodical and
diligent examination.   The canon had inquired for histories, and
the first volume placed in his hands was the celebrated work of
Petrus Comestor, so surnamed from the learning which he had
devoured, and which contains a popular version, not indeed
entirely free from apocryphal legends, of the narratives of the
scriptures.   The canon glanced at its contents, and returned it
to its place, intimating that he wished for books more immediately
relating to the enterprises of the king's noble progenitors and the
fortunes of the realm.   Whilst speaking, he darted at a gigantic
folio, which he seized.   "Surely," exclaimed he, "here is one
whom I know full well—Matthew Paris, the monk of St. Alban's!
Demure and sanctified as he seems in this his portraiture, as
desperate a rebel, saving your presence, as ever suffered or
escaped the punishment of treason.   He was made for his craft.
A quick wit and a biting tongue, diligence which enables him to
collect every tale debasing the royal authority, and the skill

which teaches him to appear as if he wept, when inwardly he rejoiced at every disaster which befalls the sovereign."

"Matthew," answered the prior, "like most of the annalists belonging to his order, fully perpetuates the traditional feelings of the Anglo-Saxon race. From the bounty of our primeval monarchs they derive their wide possessions. The old English speech is yet studied in their schools; they can yet point out the cell in which the atheling sought shelter from the scorn of the Norman Conqueror; they yet hear the expiring voice of our ancient freedom. Admitting, as I am willing to do, that Matthew gives, perhaps occasionally, a darker colour than was strictly needed, yet I believe his outline is true, and am sure his diligence is unparalleled. You will none of you be enabled to complete your annals, unless by the aid of the monk of St. Alban's monastery."

"How so?" said the canon.

"Why," replied the prior, "do ye honour the rights of the twelve peers of France?"

"Should I not honour them?" said the canon. "Is not the Count of Flanders their premier? Doth not his rank grace him almost as much as a royal crown? It is a service more proud than sovereignty."

"Well, then, canon, it is in our English Matthew Paris that you find the first distinct recognition of the college of the Douze Pairs and their privileges; and whoever may attempt their history hereafter must, bating so much as is recorded by good Archbishop Turpin, be content to adduce our Matthew as their warranty."

A most exciting sounding of tinkling brass interrupted the colloquy, and attracted Froissart—for none other than Froissart was the canon—to the adjoining window; and as he approached, he saw through the quarrels that every casement in the street was opened, and decked with eager spectators in every length of protrusion, from the tip of the cap of the hindmost in the rank of window-gazers to the whole body, bending forward from the hip and thigh, all gazing with intense curiosity.

"I suppose," said Froissart to the friar, "it is a rare thing to see a swarming of bees in London, and indeed I should hardly have expected it in the streets of this great town; but I think Thomas Cantipatensis hath given us some like example."

"I apprehend," said the third of the party, who was no other than Sergeant, afterwards celebrated Judge Belknap, "that the

hive in this case will be the convenient edifice, called the 'Tonel,'"
—a term which, not being very intelligible to the chronicler, the
lawyer readily explained as the place of confinement for minor
offenders.   A wooden cell, intended for minor offenders, nearly
in the shape of a tub, and not much larger, and which, long after
it had been demolished, became the origin of the generic appellation of the "round house," sufficiently familiar to every reader
of our old plays.

The procession which occasioned the din was now close before
them.   First appeared a motley group of men and boys, each
bearing a brazen basin, upon which he beat with all his might
and main.   Next followed the persecutors of the vagrant and the
night-walker, the sergeant at mace of either counter; and lastly,
the rumbling cart in which stood the wistful hero of this inglorious
triumph—a grave, grey-bearded, respectable, knavish-looking
personage, round whose neck was suspended the symbol of his
offence against good morals and society, an enormous whetstone.

It will be recollected that when a once celebrated reformer of
abuses propounded his educational schemes, he proposed to
substitute for cane and rattan, supple-jack and birch, the more
bitter pangs of scorn and ridicule.   In the middle ages the system
of inflicting ludicrous punishments was a recognition of the same
philosophical principle, and the spreader of false intelligence or
scandalous reports was, according to the custom of London,
exhibited for the edification of the public in the manner which
I have just described; but why the sharpener of steel and iron was
thus rendered an emblem of lying or spreading false or scandalous
reports, instead of the more intelligible "red tongue," as practised
in every dame school from time immemorial, is more than I can
explain.

"A pestilent varlet," continued the sergeant in his explanation, "who says that he has secret but sure intelligence that my
Lord Duke, the rightful heir of the sainted house of Lancaster,
prepares ere long to reassert his rights to the crown."

"Claimeth he thus the crown?" quoth Froissart, affecting the
surprise of one who hears a novelty.

"There is full evidence, these wretches say," continued the
lawyer, "in an ancient chronicle that Edmund Crouchback, the
real first-born of King Henry, whose rights my Lord Duke
inheriteth, was cruelly and unrighteously postponed to his younger
brother Edward, whose fair form and straight length of limb
rendered him a more seemly heir-apparent, and through whom

Richard of Bordeaux, as they contemptuously call our king, derives his descent; if indeed, as they shamelessly say, he has any royal blood at all in his veins. If they had their deserts for such treasonable reports, we should see their heads on the bridge gate, their bowels torn out, and their quarters distributed to the good cities and towns of the realm."

Froissart did not at all relish this discourse. A twinge of conscience came across him that, if his papers were examined, he might be at least adjudged to a ride in the cart by the side of the unlucky quacksalver who was now parading before them, let alone his possible chance of undergoing the other ceremonies; besides which, the sergeant spoke so obscurely or so confusedly, that Froissart could hardly tell whether he was repeating the words spread by the culprit or adopting them as his own. And equally fearing lest silence should be construed into assent, or speech betray him into dangerous discussions, the prudent foreigner replied, "Such matters place us, who labour to chronicle the deeds of high emprise, and the fates and fortunes of kingdoms, in strange perplexity. Without the means of searching out the truth, we must of necessity be often compelled to adopt the idle rumours and the wanton, if not the malignant fiction, happy indeed if our own feelings and wishes do not add further per-versions to the narrative and provide enduring delusions for posterity!"...

CPSIA information can be obtained at www.ICGtesting.com
Printed in the USA
LVOW05s0939231113

362460LV00004B/74/P